third custom edition for the University of Alberta

Assessment of
student
achievement

with material taken from:

Assessment of student achievement, seventh edition
by Norman e. gronlund

Cover Art: *ID Site,* by Ted Cantrell.

Excerpts taken from:
Assessment of Student Achievement, Seventh Edition
by Norman E. Gronlund
Copyright © 2003, 1998, 1993, 1988, 1982, 1977, 1968 by Pearson Education, Inc.
Published by Allyn and Bacon
Boston, Massachusetts 02116

Printed in Canada

10 9 8 7 6 5 4 3 2

ISBN 0-536-97977-4

2005220101

AG/KS

Please visit our web site at *www.pearsoncustom.com*

PEARSON CUSTOM PUBLISHING
75 Arlington Street, Suite 300, Boston, MA 02116
A Pearson Education Company

To
Marie Ann Gronlund
and
Dave, Derek, and Erik

Contents

8   *Expanded Performance Assessments*   139

9   *Portfolio Assessment*   157

10   *Grading and Reporting*   169

Preface

The seventh edition of *Assessment of Student Achievement* is a practical guide that focuses on how to assess all of the intended learning outcomes of instruction, from simple to complex. It describes assessment as an umbrella term that includes both testing and performance assessment, each to be used where it is most appropriate. The premise throughout the book is that valid assessment is necessary for effective instruction and that the goal of both is improved student learning.

The chapters on the preparation and use of classroom tests and performance assessments are followed by a chapter on grading and reporting. The last two chapters on how to interpret standardized test scores and validity and reliability present the more technical aspects of assessment, but the concepts and procedures can be easily grasped without any previous knowledge in the area. They were placed last so that they could be used wherever they best fit the course schedule. Brief descriptions of validity and reliability and a list of ways to build in validity and reliability during the preparation of assessment instruments is included in Chapter 2, for those who want to use the more technical chapter later in the course.

This new edition includes a number of changes:

1. A new chapter on expanded performance assessment (Chapter 8) was added that focuses on the assessment of comprehensive and complex performance outcomes.
2. A new chapter on portfolio assessment (Chapter 9) was added that describes how to prepare, use, and evaluate classroom portfolios.
3. Chapter 3 was broadened to planning for assessment, and the section on preparing an achievement test was expanded to include all aspects of the test preparation. The chapter on assembling, administering, and evaluating the test was eliminated because much of the material was now covered in Chapter 3.
4. The earlier chapter on performance assessment was revised with a more limited focus on traditional performance assessments of skills and products.
5. The chapter on assigning grades was expanded to include reporting to students and parents.

6. Numerous new boxed material was added to chapters listing steps for preparing, using, and scoring performance assessments.
7. New references were added to the "Additional Reading" lists of all chapters.

The book now presents a well-balanced treatment of testing and performance assessment and its important role in instruction. The material is presented in a simple, direct, and understandable manner without slighting basic concepts or sacrificing technical accuracy. Numerous practical examples are provided, and checklists, boxed material, and summaries of main points are used to aid in learning the content. No prior knowledge of measurement or statistics is required to understand the material in the book. In short, it is a practical guide for beginners.

I would like to thank reviewers James Tate, Southwestern Oklahoma State University, and Jane Abraham, Virginia Tech, for their time and feedback.

My appreciation is also expressed to the authors and publishers referred to in the book, to the Allyn and Bacon editorial staff, to Irene Palmer for her excellent typing, and to my wife Marie for her patience and understanding during work on this revision.

N. E. G.

1

Achievement Assessment and Instruction

Studying this chapter should enable you to[1]

1. Explain why both testing and performance assessment are important in achievement assessment.
2. Write a definition of achievement assessment.
3. Describe the relation between instruction and assessment.
4. Distinguish among the various roles of assessment in the instructional process.
5. List the ways that assessments can directly aid learning.

All of us have taken various types of paper-and-pencil tests during our many years of schooling. Some of these were teacher-made tests requiring us to select an answer (e.g., true-false, multiple choice, or matching) or to supply an answer (e.g., short answer or essay). Others were standardized tests of aptitude or achievement, primarily using multiple-choice items. The widespread use of paper-and-pencil testing in the schools was due, at least in part, to the efficiency with which they could measure a large number of learning outcomes and the ease of scoring and recording the results.

---

[1]Space does not permit using the preferred two-step method of stating intended learning outcomes described in Chapter 3. These statements, however, should provide a focus for your study and for application of the content in each chapter.

In recent years there has been a reaction to the heavy emphasis on paper-and-pencil testing. Some critics have contended that there should be more emphasis on the assessment of **authentic,** "real-life" tasks (e.g., solving problems that exist in the real world). Others have contended that paper-and-pencil testing should be replaced, at least in part, by **alternative** types of assessment. Some reactions have been extreme but they highlight the importance of focusing more attention on the actual performance of students (see Box 1.1). If you want to determine if students can write, have them write something. If you want to determine if students can operate a machine, have them operate the machine. If you want to determine if students can conduct an experiment, have them conduct an experiment. In short, if you want to determine if they can perform a task, have them perform the task. There is little doubt that more emphasis on performance assessment in the schools would improve the assessment of our intended learning outcomes. However, paper-and-pencil testing still has an important role to play, even as we focus more directly on performance-based tasks.

Most types of performance have a knowledge component that is important to the performance. Good writing includes such factors as knowledge of vocabulary, grammar, and spelling. These are not well sampled by a writing task because we tend to use only the words we know, use sentence structures that we can punctuate easily, and substitute words we can spell for those we can't spell. Thus, in writing, we can structure it to conceal our weaknesses. A separate test of vocabulary, grammar, and spelling can identify these weaknesses and be used to improve writing skill. Just don't interpret the test results as measures of "writing ability." The tests measure

---

BOX 1.1 • *Commonly Used Assessment Terms*

Performance Assessments	Assessments requiring students to demonstrate their achievement of understandings and skills by actually performing a task or set of tasks (e.g., writing a story, giving a speech, conducting an experiment, operating a machine).
Alternative Assessments	A title for performance assessments that emphasizes that these assessment methods provide an alternative to traditional paper-and-pencil testing.
Authentic Assessments	A title for performance assessments that stresses the importance of focusing on the application of understandings and skills to real problems in "real-world" contextual settings.

knowledge useful in writing but writing ability is determined by assessing the actual writing (**performance assessment**). Similarly, in operating machinery, the actual operation of the machine is the ultimate goal, but tests measuring knowledge of how to operate the machine and the safety precautions to follow may be needed before the hands-on performance assessment. Likewise, before conducting an experiment, tests can be used to determine how well students know the information needed for a well controlled experiment.

Throughout this book, the emphasis will be on achievement assessment that includes both paper-and-pencil testing and performance assessment. Tests can provide direct measures of many important learning outcomes, ranging from simple to complex, and they can provide needed information for assessing and improving actual performance tasks. Thus, although we should strive for as authentic assessment as we can obtain, within the constraints of the school setting, both tests and performance-based tasks are needed for a complete assessment of student achievement.

As used in this book, **achievement assessment** is a broad category that includes all of the various methods for determining the extent to which students are achieving the intended learning outcomes of instruction. Because we are limiting our concern to achievement assessment, the single term *assessment* is used throughout the book as a matter of convenience.

Relation Between Instruction and Assessment

In preparing for any type of instructional program our main concern is "How can we most effectively bring about student learning?" As we ponder this question, our attention is naturally directed toward the methods and materials of instruction. However, at the same time we should also consider the role of assessment in the instructional process. When properly designed and appropriately used, assessment procedures can contribute to more effective instruction and greater student learning.

The close relation between instruction and assessment can be seen in Table 1.1. Both require that we clearly specify the learning outcomes to be achieved by students, and the provisions of well-designed assessments closely parallel the characteristics of effective instruction. This relation highlights the importance of broadening instructional planning to include assessment planning. The typical procedure of limiting instructional planning to the teaching-learning process is inadequate. Effective instruction requires that we expand our concern to a teaching-learning-assessment process, with assessment as a basic part of the instructional program. As with all instructional activities, the main function of assessment is to improve learning and it can contribute to this end in a number of ways.

TABLE 1.1 *Relation between Instruction and Assessment*

Instruction	Assessment
Instruction is most effective when	*Assessment is most effective when*
1. Directed toward a clearly defined set of intended learning outcomes.	1. Designed to assess a clearly defined set of intended learning outcomes.
2. The methods and materials of instruction are congruent with the outcomes to be achieved.	2. The nature and function of the assessments are congruent with the outcomes to be assessed.
3. The instruction is designed to fit the characteristics and needs of the students.	3. The assessments are designed to fit the relevant student characteristics and are fair to everyone.
4. Instructional decisions are based on information that is meaningful, dependable, and relevant.	4. Assessments provide information that is meaningful, dependable, and relevant.
5. Students are periodically informed concerning their learning progress.	5. Provision is made for giving the students early feedback of assessment results.
6. Remediation is provided for students not achieving the intended learning.	6. Specific learning weaknesses are revealed by the assessment results.
7. Instructional effectiveness is periodically reviewed and the intended learning outcomes and instruction modified as needed.	7. Assessment results provide information useful for evaluating the appropriateness of the objectives, the methods, and the materials of instruction.

Assessment in the Instructional Process

To be fully integrated with instruction, plans for assessment should be made during the planning for instruction. From the beginning of instruction to the end there are numerous decisions that teachers need to make. Carefully planned assessment procedures can improve the effectiveness of many of these decisions by providing more objective information on which to base judgments. Let us consider some of the decisions teachers need to make at (1) the beginning of instruction, (2) during instruction, and (3) at the end of instruction.

Beginning of Instruction (Placement Assessment)

There are two major questions that teachers need to answer before proceeding with the instruction:

1. To what extent do the students possess the skills and abilities that are needed to begin instruction?
2. To what extent have the students already achieved the intended learning outcomes of the planned instruction?

Information concerning the first question is frequently obtained from *readiness* pretests. These are tests given at the beginning of a course or unit of instruction that cover those prerequisite skills necessary for success in the planned instruction. For example, a test of computational skill might be given at the beginning of an algebra course, or a test of English grammar might be given at the beginning of a German course. Students lacking in prerequisite skills could be given remedial work, or they could be placed in a special section that had lower prerequisites.

The second question is frequently answered by a *placement* pretest covering the intended learning outcomes of the planned instruction. This might very well be the same test that is given at the end of the instruction; preferably it should be another form of it. Here we are interested in determining whether students have already mastered some of the material we plan to include in our instruction. If they have, we might need to modify our teaching plans, encourage some students to skip particular units, and place other students at a more advanced level of instruction. The function of placement assessment is summarized in Figure 1.1.

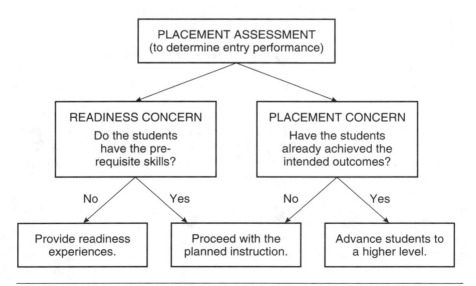

FIGURE 1.1 Simplified model for the instructional role of placement assessment.

In addition to the use of pretests, performance-based tasks may also be useful for determining entry skills. In the area of writing, for example, obtaining writing samples at the beginning of instruction can establish a base for later assessments of progress. This type of preassessment would be especially valuable if portfolios of student work were to be maintained during the instruction.

The contribution that preassessment can make to instruction depends on the nature of the instruction, how well we know students, and how the results are to be used. A pretest in arithmetic may be quite useful at the beginning of an algebra course, whereas a pretest in a course that lacks a clearly defined set of prerequisite skills (e.g., social studies) may be of little value. Similarly, the results of a test of basic skills may be of great value to a new teacher unfamiliar with the students and of less value to an experienced teacher familiar with the students' backgrounds. In addition, preassessment will contribute little to the instructional program unless plans are made to remedy deficiencies, place students in the most beneficial position in the instructional sequence, or use the results as a base for assessing future progress. To be most effective, the use of preassessment should be considered during the instructional planning stage.

During Instruction (Formative and Diagnostic Assessment)

During the instructional program our main concern is with the learning progress being made by students. Questions such as the following must be answered.

1. On which learning tasks are the students progressing satisfactorily? On which ones do they need help?
2. Which students are having such severe learning problems that they need remedial work?

Tests used to monitor student progress during instruction are called *formative* tests. Formative tests are typically designed to measure the extent to which students have mastered the learning outcomes of a rather limited segment of instruction, such as a unit or a textbook chapter. These tests are similar to the quizzes and unit tests that teachers have traditionally used, but they place greater emphasis on (1) measuring all of the intended outcomes of the unit of instruction, and (2) using the results to improve learning (rather than to assign grades). The purpose is to identify the students' learning, successes, and failures so that adjustments in instruction and learning can be made. When the majority of students fail a test item, or set of items, the material is typically retaught in a group setting. When a minority of students experience learning failures, alternate methods of study are usually prescribed for each student (for example, reading assignments in a second book, computer instruction, and visual aids). These corrective prescriptions are frequently keyed to each item, or to each set of items designed to measure a separate learning task, so that students can begin immediately after testing to correct their individual learning errors.

Formative assessment using performance-based tasks may involve periodic assessments of a product (e.g., writing sample, drawing) or of a process (e.g., giving a speech, operating a machine) with feedback to students concerning strengths and weaknesses. The aim here, as with formative testing, is to monitor learning progress and to provide corrective prescriptions to improve learning.

When a student's learning problems are so persistent that they cannot be resolved by the corrective prescriptions of formative assessment, a more intensive study of the student's learning difficulties is called for. It is here that *diagnostic* assessment is useful. Diagnostic assessment attempts to answer such questions as the following: Are the students having difficulty in addition because they don't know certain number combinations or because they don't know how to carry? Are the students' difficulties in reading German due to their inadequate knowledge of vocabulary or to their poor grasp of certain elements of grammar? Are the students unable to apply scientific principles to new situations because they don't understand the principles, because their knowledge of particular concepts is weak, or because the new situations are too unfamiliar to them? Thus, diagnostic assessment focuses on the common sources of error encountered by students, so that the learning difficulties can be pinpointed and remedied.

Diagnostic assessment can frequently be aided by the use of diagnostic tests. These tests typically include a relatively large number of test items in each specific area with slight variations from one set of items to the next so that the cause of specific learning errors can be identified. In detecting errors in the addition of whole numbers, for example, we might construct a test that includes a set of items requiring no carrying, a set that requires simple carrying, and one that requires repeated carrying to determine if carrying is the source of the difficulty. Unfortunately, diagnostic tests are difficult to construct in most areas of instruction. Therefore, we must depend more heavily on observation and judgment.

Diagnosing learning problems is a matter of degree. Formative assessment determines whether a student has mastered the learning tasks being taught and, if not, prescribes how to remedy the learning failures. Diagnostic assessment is designed to probe deeper into the causes of learning deficiencies that are left unresolved by formative assessment. Of course, this is not to imply that all learning problems can be overcome by formative and diagnostic assessment. These are simply methods to aid in the identification and diagnosis of specific learning difficulties so that appropriate remedial steps can be taken. Diagnosing and remedying severe learning problems

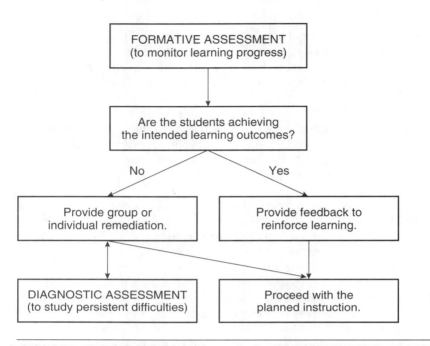

FIGURE 1.2   Simplified model for the instructional role of formative assessment.

frequently require a wide array of assessment procedures and the services of specially trained personnel. All we are attempting to do here is to show how formative and diagnostic assessment can contribute to improved student learning during instruction. The model presented in Figure 1.2 summarizes the process.

End of Instruction (Summative Assessment)

At the end of a course or unit of instruction we are concerned primarily with the extent to which the students have achieved the intended outcomes of the instruction. Questions such as the following must be answered:

1. Which students have mastered the learning tasks to such a degree that they should proceed to the next course or unit of instruction?
2. What grade should be assigned to each student?

Achievement assessment at the end of instruction for the purpose of certifying mastery or assigning grades is called *summative* assessment. This assessment is typically comprehensive in coverage and includes both tests and performance assessments. Although the results are used primarily for

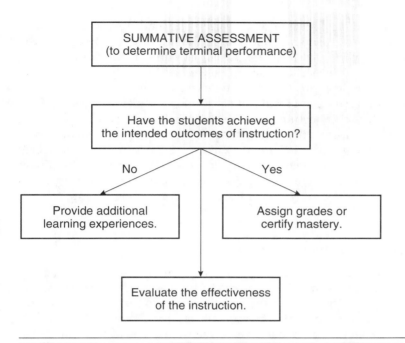

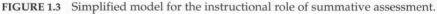

FIGURE 1.3   Simplified model for the instructional role of summative assessment.

grading, there should be some feedback to students and the results should be used for evaluating the effectiveness of the instruction. See Figure 1.3 for the summative assessment model.

Other Ways Assessments Can Aid Learning

As noted in the previous section, assessments can aid the teacher in making various instructional decisions having a direct influence on student learning. In addition, assessments can aid student learning in a number of other ways.

Student Motivation

A carefully planned assessment program can have a direct influence on student learning by (1) providing students with short-term goals, (2) clarifying the types of tasks to be learned, and (3) providing feedback concerning their learning progress. Short-term goals are more motivating than telling students "Some day you will find this knowledge or skill useful." An expected assessment stimulates learning activity and directs it toward the learning tasks to be assessed. Its contribution to learning depends to a large extent on how faithfully our assessments reflect all of the important outcomes of the instruction and how we use the results. For example, if the application of principles is stressed in our assessment as well as in our teaching, we can expect students to direct greater efforts toward learning how to apply principles. Also, if the assessment results are reported to students as soon as possible, this feedback concerning their strengths and weaknesses in the application of principles will further clarify the nature of the task and indicate what changes are needed for effective performance. Thus, properly used assessments can motivate students to work toward the instructional objectives of a course by arousing greater learning activity, by directing it toward the intended learning outcomes, and by providing prompt knowledge of results.

Retention and Transfer of Learning

Because assessments tend to direct students' learning efforts toward the intended outcomes of instruction, they can be used as tools for increasing the retention and transfer of learning. In general, learning outcomes at the understanding, application, and interpretation levels are likely to be retained longer and to have greater transfer value than outcomes at the knowledge level. By including assessments of these more complex learning outcomes, we can direct attention to their importance and provide reinforcing practice in the skills, applications, and interpretations we are attempting to develop. Thus, assessments can be used to supplement and complement our teaching efforts in these areas and thereby increase the likelihood that the learning will be of greater permanent value to the students.

Student Self-Assessment

All instruction should be directed toward helping individuals better understand themselves so that they can make more intelligent decisions. Periodic assessment and feedback of the results can help students gain insight into what they can do well, the misconceptions that need correction, and the degree of skill they have in various areas. Such information provides the students with a more objective basis for assessing their own strengths and weaknesses. Properly used assessments tend to provide evidence of learning progress in such an objective and impartial way that the results can be accepted with little resistance or distortion. This assumes, of course, that the assessments are properly prepared and are being used to improve learning rather than to threaten or label students. In the latter instance, self-assessment is apt to be distorted by the psychological defense mechanisms an individual uses to maintain a positive self-image.

Evaluating Instructional Effectiveness

Assessment results can be used to evaluate the effectiveness of various aspects of the instructional process. For example, they can help determine the extent to which the instructional objectives were realistic, whether the methods and materials of instruction were appropriate, and how well the learning experiences were sequenced. When the majority of the students do poorly on an assessment, it may be the fault of the students but the difficulty is more likely to be found in the instruction. The teacher may be striving for learning outcomes that are unattainable by the students, using inappropriate materials, or using ineffective methods for bringing about the desired changes. An analysis of the students' responses and a class discussion of the results should provide clues to the source of the instructional difficulty so that corrective steps can be taken.

Teachers' Standards for Student Assessment

It is generally agreed that student assessment plays an important role in effective teaching. A committee made up of representatives of the American Federation of Teachers, the National Council on Measurement in Education, and the National Education Association considered it so important that they came out with a report entitled *Standards for Teacher Competence in Educational Assessment of Students* (1990). In the report, they review the teacher's responsibilities for student assessment and summarize them by listing seven standards for teacher competence in student assessment. The following list, with abbreviated description of each standard, is taken from the report.

1. *Teachers should be skilled in choosing assessment methods appropriate for instructional decisions.* Skill in choosing appropriate, useful, administratively convenient, technically adequate, and fair assessment methods are prerequisite to good use of information to support instructional decisions.
2. *Teachers should be skilled in developing assessment methods appropriate for instructional decisions.* While teachers often use published or other external assessment tools, the bulk of the assessment information they use for decision making comes from approaches they create and implement.
3. *The teacher should be skilled in administering, scoring, and interpreting the results of both externally produced and teacher-produced assessment methods.* It is not enough that teachers are able to select and develop good assessment methods; they must also be able to apply them properly.

4. *Teachers should be skilled in using assessment results when making decisions about individual students, planning teaching, developing curriculum, and school improvement.* Assessment results are used to make educational decisions at several levels: in the classroom about students, in the community about a school and a school district, and in society, generally, about the purposes and outcomes of the educational enterprise. Teachers play a vital role when participating in decision making at each of these levels and must be able to use assessment results effectively.

5. *Teachers should be skilled in developing valid pupil grading procedures that use pupil assessments.* Grading students is an important part of professional practice for teachers. Grading is defined as indicating both a student's level of performance and a teacher's valuing of that performance. The principles for using assessments to obtain valid grades are known and teachers should employ them.

6. *Teachers should be skilled in communicating assessment results to students, parents, other lay audiences, and other educators.* Teachers must routinely report assessment results to students and to parents or guardians. In addition, they are frequently asked to report or to discuss assessment results with other educators and with diverse lay audiences. If the results are not communicated effectively, they may be misused or not used. To communicate effectively with others on matters of student assessment, teachers must be able to use assessment terminology appropriately and must be able to articulate the meaning, limitations, and implications of assessment results.

7. *Teachers should be skilled in recognizing unethical, illegal, and otherwise inappropriate assessment methods and uses of assessment information.* Fairness, the rights of all concerned, and professional ethical behavior must undergird all student assessment activities, from the initial planning for and gathering of information to the interpretation, use, and communication of the results.

The complete report of *Standards for Teacher Competence in Educational Assessment of Students* is presented in the Appendix of Linn and Gronlund (2000). The report is not copyrighted and reproduction and distribution of it are encouraged.

Summary of Points

1. In recent years there has been a reaction to the heavy emphasis on paper-and-pencil testing with a plea for more realistic and meaningful performance assessment.

2. A well-balanced assessment program should include both testing and performance assessment, with each used where most appropriate.

3. *Achievement assessment* is a general category that includes a broad range of methods for determining the extent to which students are achieving the intended learning outcomes of instruction.

4. Instruction is more effective when well-designed assessments are an integral part of the instructional process.

5. Assessment procedures can be used for measuring entry performance (placement assessment), monitoring learning progress (formative and diagnostic assessment), or measuring end of instruction achievement (summative assessments).

6. Achievement assessments can contribute to student motivation, the retention and transfer of learning, student self-evaluation skills, and an evaluation of instructional effectiveness.

7. Teachers' standards for student assessment focus on their competence in selecting assessment methods, developing assessment methods, administering and scoring them, interpreting and using assessment results, preparing valid grades, communicating assessment results, and recognizing inappropriate assessment methods and uses of assessment information.

References and Additional Reading

Airasian, P.W., *Classroom Assessment*, 3rd ed. (New York: McGraw-Hill, 1997).

Bloom, B. S., Madaus, G. T., and Hastings, J. T., *Evaluation to Improve Learning* (New York: McGraw-Hill, 1981).

Linn, R. L., and Gronlund, N. E., *Measurement and Assessment in Teaching*, 8th ed. (Upper Saddle River, NJ: Merrill/Prentice-Hall, 2000).

McMillan, J. H., *Classroom Assessment: Principles and Practices for Effective Instruc-tion*, 2nd ed. (Boston: Allyn and Bacon, 2001).

Popham, W. J., *Classroom Assessment: What Teachers Need to Know*, 3rd ed. (Boston: Allyn and Bacon, 2002).

Stiggins, R. J., *Student-Involved Classroom Assessment*, 3rd ed. (Upper Saddle River, NJ: Merrill/Prentice-Hall, 2001).

2

Nature of Student Assessment

Studying this chapter should enable you to

1. Describe a situation where both testing and performance assessment are needed and indicate why.
2. Describe the major types of assessment methods and give an example of each.
3. Distinguish between tests and performance assessments in terms of realism of tasks, complexity of tasks, assessment time needed, and judgment in scoring.
4. List the guidelines for effective student assessment.
5. Describe the meaning of validity and reliability and the role they play in preparing assessment procedures.
6. Distinguish between norm-referenced and criterion-referenced assessments.

As noted in the first chapter, *assessment* is used as a broad category that includes all of the various methods used to determine the extent to which students are achieving the intended learning outcomes of instruction. This includes both testing and performance assessments. To assess a student's driving ability, for example, an **objective test** is used to measure knowledge of how to drive and follow the rules of the road, and driving over a prescribed course (performance assessment) is used to determine skill in driving the automobile. The test on rules of the road covers a much larger sample of driving rules than are likely to be encountered in the driving performance, but skill in driving can only be determined by sitting behind the wheel and driving. Both are important. The knowledge test tells how well the student knows what to do and the performance assessment tells how skillfully the student can do it.

Teachers have tended to favor selection-type tests (i.e., multiple choice, true-false, matching) because many questions can be asked in a relatively short time, they are easy to administer and score, and the results can be expressed in numbers that are easily recorded, compared, and reported to others. Unfortunately, teachers have also limited selection-type tests almost entirely to knowledge of facts and terms. Various studies have shown that between 80 and 90 percent of teacher-made tests focus on knowledge outcomes. There is little doubt that this overemphasis on selection-type tests and simple knowledge outcomes has led to the movement toward assessment techniques that measure more complex learning outcomes in realistic settings. The fact that paper-and-pencil tests can be designed to measure a wide array of complex learning outcomes has frequently been overlooked in the movement toward performance assessment. It is our contention that education is best served by using both paper-and-pencil testing and the assessment of actual performance, with both focusing on more complex learning tasks than typically has been the case in the past.

Major Types of Assessment Methods

Assessment methods vary widely but they can be summarized in four major categories as shown in Table 2.1. Selected-response tests require the student to choose the correct or best answer, as in multiple-choice, true-false, and matching tests. Supply-response tests require students to respond with a word, short phrase, or complete essay answer. Restricted performance assessments are concerned with the performance of a limited task that is highly structured, such as writing a brief paragraph on a given topic, selecting laboratory equipment, measuring humidity, or locating information with a computer. Extended performance assessments involve more comprehensive and less structured performance tasks, such as writing a short story, conducting a laboratory experiment, predicting weather, or using a computer to solve a problem. Besides requiring more extended performances, the assessment typically requires students to integrate and apply knowledge and skills to performance tasks in a realistic setting. If there is a product involved (e.g., a short story), students may also be expected to review and revise the product before submitting it, to add greater realism to the task.

These major types of assessment can be further clarified by reviewing some of the characteristics that are typical of each. These have been summarized in Table 2.1.

TABLE 2.1 *Summary Comparison of Assessment Methods*

Testing		Performance Assessment	
Selected Response	*Supply Response*	*Restricted Performance*	*Extended Performance*
LOW ⬅ REALISM OF TASKS ➡ HIGH			
LOW ⬅ COMPLEXITY OF TASKS ➡ HIGH			
LOW ⬅ ASSESSMENT TIME NEEDED ➡ HIGH			
LOW ⬅ JUDGMENT IN SCORING ➡ HIGH			

Realism of Tasks

By realism of assessment tasks, we mean the extent to which they simulate performance in the real world. Traditional selection-type tests are low in realism because they involve selecting a response from a given set of possible answers. The response is limited to the listed alternatives and such highly structured problems seldom occur in the real world. The extended performance assessment is high in realism because it attempts to simulate performance in the real world. Assessing how well a student can drive an automobile, operate a machine, give a speech, or apply knowledge and understanding to a real-life problem (e.g., how to protect the environment) requires comprehensive sets of responses that approximate those occurring in the real world. In between these extremes are the supply-type tests (e.g., short answer and essay) and the restricted response performance assessments that provide a moderate amount of structure but greater freedom of response and thus more realistic type problems than the selection-type tests.

In addition to the movement to increase realism in assessment by moving toward extended performance assessment, there has also been a trend toward making traditional paper-and-pencil tests more authentic (i.e., have greater realism). This has resulted in the designing of tests to measure more complex learning outcomes and in the use of problems and procedures more like those in the real world. In a math problem, for example, students may be given more facts than are needed to solve the problem to see if they can select the facts needed to solve it. In solving a science problem, students might be given the freedom to select the procedure for solving the problem and be asked to justify the procedure used. In some cases this involves a shift from selection-type items to supply-type items but in others it may be a combination of the two items types (e.g., explain why the selected answer was chosen).

Complexity of Tasks

Selected-response items tend to be low in the complexity of the problem presented and in the nature of the expected response. Although items can be designed to measure understanding and thinking skills, they typically present a single, limited problem and require choice of the correct or best answer. Extended performance problems, on the other hand, typically involve multiple learning outcome, the integration of ideas and skills from a variety of sources, the availability of various possible solutions and the need for multiple criteria for evaluating the results (e.g., preparing a plan for reducing drug traffic in the United States). Similarly, performance of a hands-on nature involves complex movement patterns that are guided by the integration of information and specific skills from various learning experiences (e.g., playing a musical instrument, operating a machine, repairing electronic equipment). As with the realism category, supply-type tests fall in between the two extremes. Essay tests, for example, can be designed to measure the ability to select, integrate, and express ideas, but the tasks are usually more limited and structured than in performance assessments.

Assessment Time Needed

A large number of selected-response items can be administered to a group of students in a relatively short time and the results can be quickly scored by hand or by machine. This efficiency has no doubt been a major factor in their widespread use. Performance assessments tend to be extremely time consuming. Some tasks may require days or even weeks to complete (e.g., conduct an experimental study) and others may require assessing students one at a time (e.g., giving a speech, operating a machine). In most cases, evaluating the process or product of the performance is also difficult and time consuming. Supply-response tests, like the essay test, require more time to score than selected-response tests but less than that of performance assessments.

The greater amount of time needed for performance assessment may result in loss of content coverage because of the limited number of assessment problems that can be included in the instructional program. This raises a question concerning the extent to which the assessment results are generalizable to other comparable tasks. We can present "real-world" problems to students, but problems are frequently unique to a particular contextual setting and the real-world changes. Thus, transfer of learning is a key consideration in performance assessment. We can justify the greater time needed only if the assessment is an integral part of instruction and transferable learning outcomes are emphasized (e.g., reasoning, critical thinking, psychomotor skills).

Judgment in Scoring

The amount of judgment involved in scoring varies widely. Each selected-response item is marked right or wrong so the scoring is completely objective (i.e., different scorers will arrive at the same score). The essay test provides more freedom of response, and this introduces greater subjectivity into the scoring. Different scorers can and do arrive at different scores as they weight elements of the answer differently (e.g., completeness, organization, clarity of writing, and the like) and introduce other personal biases into their judgments. As the tasks become more comprehensive and complex, as in performance assessment, the demands on teacher judgment become even greater. Complex performance tasks that involve the integration of various types of information and skill and may have multiple solutions make it difficult, and in many cases undesirable, to have model answers as might be used with essay testing. With performance assessment we are most likely to have to depend on identification of the **criteria** of a quality performance and then apply the criteria by means of a **rating scale** or set of **scoring rubrics**. Each of these steps is based on subjective judgment.

A review of these categories makes clear that each assessment method has its strengths and weaknesses. When we use selected-response tests, we can obtain a comprehensive coverage of a content domain, and can administer, score, and interpret it easily, but we sacrifice realism and some types of complexity. When we use extended performance assessment, we can obtain a high degree of realism and increase the complexity of the tasks we can assess, but the time needed for assessment is frequently excessive and the evaluation of the performance is highly judgmental. A useful rule would be to use the most efficient method as long as it is appropriate for assessing the intended learning outcomes, but don't neglect complex learning outcomes just because the assessment methods are time consuming and the results are difficult to score or judge.

Guidelines for Effective Student Assessment

The main purpose of a classroom assessment program is to improve student learning. This is most likely to result if assessment is closely integrated with instruction and is guided by a basic set of conditions. The following guidelines provide a general framework for using student assessment effectively.

   1. *Effective assessment requires a clear conception of all intended learning outcomes.* During both instructional and assessment planning, we need to ask

ourselves—What are the intended learning outcomes of the instruction? What types of knowledge, understanding, application, and performance skills are we willing to accept as evidence that the instruction has been successful? Here, there is always the danger of focusing too narrowly on knowledge outcomes because they are easy to identify, state, and measure. Unless we include the more complex learning outcomes at this stage, they are likely to be neglected during assessment. We need to specify all intended learning outcomes in terms of student performance and make plans to assess them all.

2. *Effective assessment requires that a variety of assessment procedures be used.* The vast array of possible learning outcomes in any particular area of instruction means that various types of assessment procedures must be considered when planning for assessment. Selected-response tests may be used for some learning outcomes and essay tests for others, where ability to express ideas is important. In assessing performance skills, where we must depend largely on judgment, rating scales or checklists may be needed.

In assessing the more complex learning outcomes, a combination of methods may be most suitable. Solving a complex problem, for example, may involve gathering information from diverse sources, analyzing it, integrating it, writing out a suggested solution, and making an oral presentation to a group. Similarly, locating and correcting a malfunction in a machine may involve reading a technical manual, identifying machine sounds, selecting proper tools, testing machine parts, and making the needed repairs. In addition to correcting the malfunction, speed of performance, following the proper sequence of steps, and similar factors may be an important part of the assessment. In evaluating performance skills, multiple assessment is likely to be the rule rather than the exception.

3. *Effective assessment requires that the instructional relevance of the procedures be considered.* Instructionally relevant assessment means that the intended outcomes of instruction, the domain of learning tasks, and the assessment procedures will all be in close agreement, as shown in Figure 2.1. It also means that plans for using the assessment results in the instructional program must be considered. Will the classroom test be sufficiently diagnostic to provide for remedial action? Can the assessment of a complex performance skill be designed as an ongoing activity so that it can contribute directly to the instruction? These and similar questions are needed to obtain maximum integration of instruction and assessment. Remember, the main purpose of both instruction and assessment is to improve student learning. With a well-designed assessment program, assessment activities may become barely distinguishable from instructional activities.

4. *Effective assessment requires an adequate sample of student performance.* Assessment is always a matter of sampling. Our instruction typically covers numerous knowledge and skill outcomes, but because of the

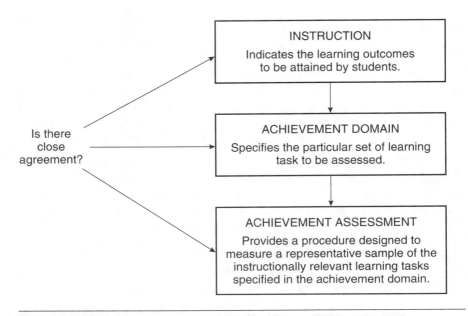

FIGURE 2.1 Sequence in preparing instructionally relevant assessment.

limited time available for assessment and other constraints, we can only measure or judge a limited sample of student performance in any particular area. In preparing a classroom test, for example, there may be 100 terms that the students should know but we only have room for 20 terms in our test. Thus, we must select a representative sample from the 100 words because we want to be able to generalize from performance on the 20 terms as to how well students know the 100 terms. If our sample is adequate, we can estimate that 18 correct answers on the 20 terms indicates that a student knows about 90 percent of the 100 terms (with allowance for a margin of error, of course).

Sampling is also a problem in performance assessment. In assessing driving skill, for example, it would be impossible to include all possible driving problems in a brief driving test so we must settle for a representative sample of them. It is interesting to note that, for licensing purposes, some states are now including driving on the expressway to obtain a more adequate sample of driving skill.

In the assessment of performance skills in the classroom there are typically two problems of sampling. In a writing project, for example, we might ask (1) does the project include a representative sample of the writing skills we are stressing in our teaching? and (2) does performance on this project represent what writing performance would be like on other similar projects? Because extended performance assessment (e.g., giving a speech, conducting an experiment, applying math to a real world problem) is so time consuming and context bound, the adequacy of sampling is always an important concern in planning the assessment.

5. *Effective assessment requires that the procedures be fair to everyone.* An assessment program that makes the intended learning outcomes clear to students, that uses assessment procedures that are instructionally relevant and adequately sample student performance, and uses assessment results to improve learning goes a long way toward creating an atmosphere of fairness. In addition, however, special efforts must be made to eliminate irrelevant sources of difficulty and bias of various types. Student performance may be inadequate because the directions were ambiguous, the reading level was inappropriate, or the performance called for knowledge or skills that were not intended as parts of the assessment task. Similarly, including racial or gender stereotypes in the assessment material may distort the results and create a feeling of unfairness. Fairness requires care in preparing and using assessment procedures, clearly communicating our intentions to students, and using the results to improve learning.

6. *Effective assessment requires the specifications of criteria for judging successful performance.* In the past, success was typically determined by comparing a student's performance to that of others (norm-referenced interpretation). If performance surpassed that of others it was considered excellent performance. If performance was lower than that of others it was considered poor performance. Although this method of judging success has its merits and is useful in certain situations, it is not satisfactory as a measure of how well students are learning the intended outcomes of instruction. For this purpose we need *criteria* that describe what students can do when they perform successfully (e.g., type 40 words per minute with no more than two errors).

Establishing performance criteria is difficult in many areas but, if the intended learning outcomes are clearly stated in performance terms, the criteria for success can be more easily established. In assessing vocabulary, for example, we can describe success in terms of how well students can define each term and use it in a sentence, how well they can distinguish between similar terms, and how well they can use the terms in a writing project. Effective laboratory performance can be described in terms of the selection and manipulation of equipment, the accuracy of measurements, the procedures followed, and the written description and interpretation of results. By specifying success in performance terms, we can describe what students are achieving and how well. The degree of success can be expressed by separate scores, scoring rubrics that describe degrees of effectiveness, rating scales, or whatever means is most useful for describing student performance.

Students should have a clear notion of what is expected of them and clearly specified criteria of successful performance can be used to clarify the learning tasks. In some cases, students may participate in defining the desired performance. In planning for oral reports, for example, a discussion of criteria and listing them on the board will cause students to focus on the criteria of a good oral report and help them improve their performance. This is one way that instruction and assessment can be blended together to the benefit of students.

7. *Effective assessment requires feedback to students that emphasizes strengths of performance and weaknesses to be corrected.* Feedback of assessment results to students is an essential factor in any assessment program. To be most effective, feedback must meet the following criteria:

- **A.** Should be given immediately following or during the assessment.
- **B.** Should be detailed and understandable to students.
- **C.** Should focus on successful elements of the performance and the errors to be corrected.
- **D.** Should provide remedial suggestions for correcting errors.
- **E.** Should be positive and provide a guide for improving both performance and self-assessment.

In performance assessment, our immediate goal is to improve performance. But if we are to develop self-learners, who will continue to improve performance on their own, then we need to also help them develop self-assessment skills. Thus, feedback must focus on both performance skills and self-assessment skills. For example, we not only suggest how to modify performance but also how to check on the effect of the modifications on performance and ways to determine future improvement. A final question concerning feedback might be, Will this feedback to students make them more dependent on the teacher or will it contribute to more independent learning? The most desirable choice is obvious and is illustrated in Figure 2.2.

8. *Effective assessment must be supported by a comprehensive grading and reporting system.* All too frequently teachers have used various types of assessment procedures and then assigned grades on the basis of scores on an objective test. Instead, we need to have the grading and reporting system reflect the emphasis in our assessments. If half of our learning outcomes are assessed by tests and half by performance assessments, and a single grade is used, the two types of assessment should receive equal weight in the grade. With the recent emphasis on performance assessment, more elaborate grading and reporting systems are needed to describe student performance adequately. Reports based on the intended learning outcomes and portfolios of student work are becoming increasingly important for reporting learning progress to students, parents, and others. These more elaborate reports are in harmony with the more elaborate assessment procedures being used.

Because letter grades are still required for some purposes (e.g., college admission), it may be necessary to use both letter grades and a more elabo-

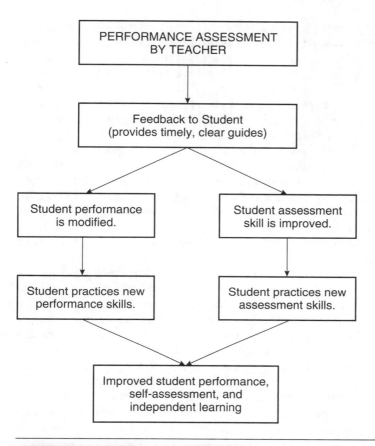

FIGURE 2.2 Role of assessment feedback.

rate report. In any event, the grading and reporting procedures should reflect and support the assessment procedures, be made clear to students at the beginning of instruction, and provide for periodic feedback to students concerning their learning progress.

Validity and Reliability in Assessment Planning

Two of the most important characteristics of a well-designed assessment procedure are **validity** and **reliability.** These characteristics are of primary concern during assessment planning and most of the suggestions in this book are directed toward preparing assessments that provide for valid and reliable interpretation of results.

Validity refers to the appropriateness and meaningfulness of the inferences we make from assessment results for some intended use. For example, if we give a vocabulary test, we would like to be able to interpret the scores as a representative sample of the terms we have been teaching. If we do a good job of (1) clearly defining the domain of vocabulary items to be measured, (2) carefully preparing the test specifications, and (3) constructiing a representative sample of relevant test items, our interpretations from the results are likely to be valid. We are now able to infer that high scores represent good knowledge of the vocabulary that has been taught. Note that it is the inference that is important. If we infer that high scores indicate good writing ability or good verbal ability, we are generalizing beyond the limited assessment domain being tested and the validity of our inference is in doubt, without further evidence. Thus, it is not the test scores that are valid or invalid but the inferences we make from them.

Performance assessments are typically viewed as providing more valid inferences concerning learning than traditional paper-and-pencil tests because they focus more directly on the types of performance tasks we are teaching. If we want to determine if students can read, we have them read something. If we want to determine if students can give a speech, we have them give a speech. If we want to determine if students can operate a computer, we have them operate a computer. In each case the task has the appearance of being valid (i.e., we have good *face* validity). However, it is not as simple as it seems. In performance assessment, the problem of defining the assessment domain, of specifying how the performance will be judged, and of obtaining a representative sample of performance tasks poses special problems. For example, there are many different types of reading, many different types of speeches, and many different types of problems to be solved on the computer. Each requires its own specifications and scoring rubrics, and because of the time-consuming nature of performance assessment, the sampling tends to be limited. This restricts the extent to which we can infer that performance on one assessment task is generalizable to performance on other assessment tasks in the same area.

With both tests and performance assessments we need to make plans and follow procedures that are most likely to yield valid inferences concerning learning. This involves selecting appropriate procedures, preparing them carefully, applying them effectively, and then interpreting the results within the limits of the particular achievement domain being assessed. In using the results we are also, of course, concerned about the consequences of the assessment. Did its use contribute to increased student learning, as intended? This is a legitimate validity-related question because our main purpose in assessing student achievement is to improve learning.

Reliability refers to the *consistency* of assessment results. For example, if a student earns a score of 60 on a test, we would like to be able to say that

60 accurately represents the student's test performance. Thus, if we tested the student at a different time or with a different sample of equivalent items, we would expect to obtain a similar score. Similarly, if a student receives a high rating on a writing project, we would like to say that it represents the student's writing skill and that if others rated the project the results would be similar. This consistency of results would indicate that they are relatively free from errors and thus we can rely on them (i.e., they have "rely-ability").

We cannot, of course, expect assessment results to be perfectly consistent over different occasions or over different samples of the same achievement domain. Such factors as ambiguities, variations in samples, fluctuations in motivation and attention, and luck can introduce errors that cause assessment results to vary. Likewise, in judging performance tasks, the personal biases of the rater can introduce error into the results. An important goal in assessment is to keep these various types of errors to a minimum so that our results are as reliable as possible.

In addition to being important in its own right, reliability is necessary to obtain valid inferences from assessment results. After all, if an individual's test score fluctuated widely on a given sample of items, we could not expect to draw valid inferences concerning the student's achievement. Similarly, if ratings varied widely on a student's writing project, valid inferences could not be made concerning writing skill. Thus, *reliability provides the consistency of results that makes valid inferences possible.* Of course, the consistency of results is just one important requirement for valid inferences. We could be consistently assessing the wrong thing, using inappropriate procedures, or generalizing beyond the achievement domain being assessed. Thus, reliability is a necessary, but not a sufficient, condition for making valid inferences.

Both the validity and reliability of assessment results can be provided for during the preparation of assessment procedures. When we clearly specify the intended learning outcomes, define the achievement domain to be assessed, and select a relevant and representative set of assessment tasks, we are providing for valid inferences concerning learning. When we include an adequate number of tasks in our assessment and we use procedures that are free from ambiguity, irrelevant sources of difficulty, unintended clues, and other factors that might distort the results, we are providing for both reliability and validity. In fact, most of the suggestions for constructing achievement tests and preparing performance assessments are directed toward improving the reliability of the assessment results and the validity of the interpretations we make from them.

A more elaborate discussion of validity and reliability and methods for determining them is presented in Chapter 12. Although high quality assessments can be made without a detailed study of validity and reliability, understanding the basic concepts involved can contribute to improved skill in preparing assessment procedures, making appropriate interpretations of the results, and using the results effectively.

Some of the most important features that enhance the validity and reliability of assessment results are presented in Table 2.2. This table makes clear that concern about validity and reliability takes place in the early stages of assessment planning and preparation, not after the assessment results have been obtained. The procedures listed in Table 2.2 will be described in more detail in the chapters on preparing tests and performance-based assessments. Here, we are simply emphasizing their importance in obtaining valid and reliable interpretations of assessment results and the need for early assessment planning to "build in" the desired features.

TABLE 2.2   *Desirable Features for Enhancing the Validity and Reliability of Assessment Results*

Desired Features	*Procedures to Follow*
1. Clearly specified set of learning outcomes.	1. State intended learning outcomes in performance terms.
2. Representative sample of a clearly defined domain of learning tasks.	2. Prepare a description of the achievement domain to be assessed and the sample of tasks to be used.
3. Tasks that are relevant to the learning outcomes to be measured.	3. Match assessment tasks to the specified performance stated in the learning outcomes.
4. Tasks that are at the proper level of difficulty.	4. Match assessment task difficulty to the learning task, the students' abilities, and the use to be made of the results.
5. Tasks that function effectively in distinguishing between achievers and nonachievers.	5. Follow general guidelines and specific rules for preparing assessment procedures and be alert for factors that distort the results.
6. Sufficient number of tasks to measure an adequate sample of achievement, provide dependable results, and allow for a meaningful interpretation of the results.	6. Where the students' age or available assessment time limit the number of tasks, make tentative interpretations, assess more frequently, and verify the results with other evidence.
7. Procedures that contribute to efficient preparation and use.	7. Write clear directions and arrange procedures for ease of administration, scoring or judging, and interpretation.

Norm-Referenced and Criterion-Referenced Assessment

An achievement assessment can be used to provide (1) a relative ranking of students or (2) a description of the learning tasks a student can and cannot perform. Results of the first type are interpreted in terms of each student's relative standing among other students (for example, "He is third highest in a class of 35 students"). This method of interpreting student performance is called **norm-referenced interpretation.** Results of the second type are expressed in terms of the specific knowledge and skills each student can demonstrate (e.g., "She can identify the parts of a microscope and demonstrate its use"). This method of interpreting assessment results is called **criterion-referenced interpretation** (see Box 2.1). Both methods of describing assessment results are useful. The first tells how an individual's performance compares with that of others. The second tells in specific performance terms what an individual can do without reference to the performance of others.

Strictly speaking, the terms *norm-referenced* and *criterion-referenced* refer only to the method of interpreting the results. Thus, both types of interpretation could be applied to the same assessment. For example, we might say, "Joan surpassed 90 percent of the students (norm-referenced interpretation) by

---

BOX 2.1 • *Terms Similar to Criterion-Referenced Interpretation*

Domain-Referenced Interpretation	Assessment results are interpreted in terms of a relevant and clearly defined set related tasks (called a *domain*). Meaning is similar to criterion-referenced interpretation but the term is less used, even though it is a more descriptive term.
Content-Referenced Interpretation	Essentially the same meaning as domain-referenced interpretation when the content domain is broadly defined to include tasks representing both content and process (i.e., reactions to the content). This term s declining in use and being replaced by criterion-referenced interpretation.
Objective-Referenced Interpretation	Assessment results are interpreted in terms of each specific objective that a set of test items represents. This is frequently called *criterion-referenced interpretation* but the more limited designation is preferable where interpretation is limited to each separate objective.

correctly completing 20 of the 25 chemical equations" (criterion-referenced interpretation). The two types of interpretation are likely to be most meaningful, however, when the assessment is designed specifically for the type of interpretation to be made. In general, norm-referenced interpretation is facilitated by a wide spread of scores so that reliable discriminations can be made among students at various levels of achievement. Criterion-referenced interpretation is facilitated by assessment tasks that provide a detailed description of student performance. In testing, this means a larger number of test items per task. In performance assessment, this means performance tasks that make clear what parts of the task a person can and cannot do.

Although norm-referenced and criterion-referenced interpretations apply to all types of achievement assessments, the differences can be most clearly indicated when applied to testing. A summary of some common characteristics of tests specifically designed for each type of interpretation is presented in Table 2.3. It must be kept in mind, however, that these are primarily matters of emphasis. For example, norm-referenced tests are typi-

TABLE 2.3   *Summary Comparison of Two Basic Approaches to Achievement Testing*

	Norm-Referenced Testing	*Criterion-Referenced Testing*
Principal Use	Survey testing.	Mastery testing.
Major Emphasis	Measures individual differences in achievement.	Describes tasks students can perform.
Interpretation of Results	Compares performance to that of other individuals.	Compares performance to a clearly specified achievement domain.
Content Coverage	Typically covers a broad area of achievement.	Typically focuses on a limited set of learning tasks.
Nature of Test Plan	Table of specifications is commonly used.	Detailed domain specifications are favored.
Item Selection Procedures	Items are selected that provide maximum discrimination among individuals (to obtain a reliable ranking). Easy items are typically eliminated from the test.	Includes all items needed to adequately describe performance. No attempt is made to alter item difficulty or to eliminate easy items to increase the spread of scores.
Performance Standards	Level of performance is determined by *relative* position in some known group (e.g., ranks fifth in a group of 20).	Level of performance is commonly determined by *absolute* standards (e.g., demonstrates mastery by defining 90 percent of the technical terms).

cally, but not exclusively, used for surveying achievement over a broad range of learning outcomes. By the same token, criterion-referenced tests are typically, but not exclusively, used for **mastery testing.** A review of the characteristics of each testing approach in Table 2.3 will reveal the differences that exist when each test is constructed to serve its principal use. It is not uncommon, however, to view the two test types as the ends of a continuum rather than as discrete categories, and to combine the best features of each in constructing achievement tests.

For most instructional purposes, criterion-referenced assessments are to be favored. We can best help students improve learning by determining what tasks they can and cannot perform. Thus, the classroom assessment program should be based on instruments and procedures that provide for this type of interpretation. Norm-referenced interpretation is most useful when we are concerned about the relative ranking of students, as in the selection and classification of students (e.g., advance placement, grouping, giving awards, and relative grading).

Most of the discussions of procedures for constructing tests and making performance assessment will apply to all types of tests and assessments. Where there are significant differences due to the type of interpretation to be made, these will be noted.

Summary of Points

1. Student assessment needs to be expanded to include the assessment of more complex learning outcomes than has been the case in the past.
2. Assessment methods vary widely but they can be classified as selected-response tests, supply-response tests, restricted-response performance assessments, or extended-response performance assessments.
3. Selected-response tests (e.g., multiple-choice tests) are lowest in realism and complexity of the tasks assessed, but require little time to administer and can be scored quickly and objectively.
4. Supply-response tests (e.g., essay tests) are higher in realism and the complexity of tasks they can measure (e.g., ability to originate, integrate, and express ideas) than selected-response tests, but they are more time consuming to use and more difficult to score.
5. Performance assessments, both restricted response and extended response, can be designed with high degrees of realism (i.e., like real-world problems) that focus on highly complex learning tasks, but they require large amounts of time to use and the scoring is judgmental and highly subjective.
6. A sound assessment policy would be to use the most efficient method available for assessing each intended learning outcome as long as it is appropriate, but don't neglect complex learning outcomes just because

the assessment methods are more time consuming to use and more difficult to score or judge.

7. Effective assessment requires a clear conception of all intended learning outcomes, a variety of assessment procedures that are relevant to the instruction, an adequate sample of tasks, procedures that are fair to everyone, criteria for judging success, timely and detailed feedback to students, and a grading and reporting system that is in harmony with the assessment program.

8. Validity and reliability are the two most important characteristics of any assessment method and must be considered during the planning and preparation of assessment procedures.

9. Valid and reliable interpretations of assessment results require clearly defined intended learning outcomes, a representative sample of instructionally relevant tasks, a sound scoring system, and freedom from irrelevant factors that introduce error.

10. Assessment results can be interpreted by comparing a student's performance to that of others (norm-referenced) or by describing the student's performance on a clearly defined set of tasks (criterion-referenced).

11. Criterion-referenced interpretation is especially important for instructional uses of assessment results but norm-referenced interpretation may be needed for selection and classification decisions.

12. In some cases both criterion-referenced and norm-referenced interpretation may be used with the same assessment.

References and Additional Reading

Linn, R. L., and Gronlund, N. E., *Measurement and Assessment in Teaching*, 8th ed. (Upper Saddle River, NJ: Merrill/Prentice-Hall, 2000).

McMillan, J. H., *Classroom Assessment: Principles and Practices for Effective Instruction*, 2nd ed. (Boston: Allyn and Bacon, 2001).

Oosterhoff, A. C., *Developing and Using Classroom Assessments*, 2nd ed. (Upper Saddle River, NJ: Prentice-Hall, 1999).

Smith, J. K., Smith, L. F., and DeLisi, R., *Natural Classroom Assessment*. (Thousand Oaks, CA: Corwin Press, 2001).

Stiggins, R. J., *Student-Involved Classroom Assessment*, 3rd ed. (Upper Saddle River, NJ: Merrill/Prentice-Hall, 2001).

Wiggins, G. P., *Educative Assessment: Designing Assessments to Inform and Improve Student Performance* (San Francisco, CA: Jossey-Bass, 1998).

3

Planning for Assessment

Studying this chapter should enable you to

1. List the types of learning outcomes to consider in planning for the assessment of student achievement.
2. State instructional objectives as intended learning outcomes and define them in performance terms.
3. Prepare a set of specifications for a test.
4. Describe the relative merits of selection and supply type test items.
5. Match test items to the specific learning outcomes they measure.
6. Describe the factors to consider when preparing items for a test.
7. Describe how to arrange items in a test.
8. Write clear directions for a test.
9. Review and evaluate an assembled test.
10. Administer a test properly.
11. Make a simple item analysis.

Planning for the assessment of student achievement involves a consideration of the following questions:

1. What do we expect students to learn?
2. What *types* of student performance are we willing to accept as evidence of learning?
3. What assessment instruments will best evaluate the students' performance?

The first question focuses on the goals of the curriculum as set by the school and influenced by the district and state. In recent years, states have developed **content standards** that provide guidelines for determining what students should know and be able to do. This has influenced districts and schools to modify curriculums and put greater emphasis on the more complex learning outcomes.

The second question focuses on the importance of specifying instructional objectives in performance terms and including all types of desired learning outcomes. These objectives must, of course, be in harmony with the goals of the curriculum and will reflect the state content standards to the same degree as the school curriculum. In final analysis, the assessment of student achievement is determined by what the students are expected to learn, and this is determined by the goals of the school curriculum. The instructional objectives are simply a means of stating the curriculum goals in more specific terms so that they are useful in both instruction and assessment.

The third question focuses on the match between the instructional objectives and the procedures of assessment. The objectives specify the intended learning outcomes in performance terms and the assessment method is used to determine the extent to which students' performance is satisfactory. For some performance outcomes a test will provide adequate evidence. In other cases, some type of observational technique will be needed to evaluate the ongoing nature of the performance (e.g., giving a speech) or to evaluate a resulting product (e.g., a written report). The key to effective assessment is to use the most direct and relevant method available.

Types of Intended Learning Outcomes

In planning for the assessment of student achievement, there are a number of types of learning outcomes that might be considered. Although the goals of the school and the nature of the instructional content will determine what specific types of learning outcomes are to be assessed, a review of the various types of outcomes shown in Table 3.1 will prevent any serious omissions. The list is not exhaustive, but it makes clear the range of outcomes to consider beyond that of knowledge, when preparing objectives for instruction and assessment.

Well-designed classroom tests can be used to measure many of the outcomes in the cognitive areas, but skills and products require the use of observational techniques such as checklists, rating scales, or holistic scoring rubrics.

TABLE 3.1 *Some Types of Intended Learning Outcomes*

Types	Sample Categories
Knowledge of	Facts
	Concepts
Comprehension of	Principles
	Methods
Application of	Process
	Analyzing
Reasoning	Comparing
Ability	Inferring
	Generalizing
	Evaluating
	Speaking
Observable	Oral reading
Skills	Laboratory skills
	Psychomotor skills
	Work-study skills
	Writing
	Drawing
Products	Designing
	Constructing
	Problem-solving

Role of Instructional Objectives

Well-stated instructional objectives provide a description of the intended learning outcomes in performance terms—that is, in terms of the types of performance students can demonstrate to show that they have achieved the knowledge, understanding, or skill described by the objective. By describing the performance that we are willing to accept as evidence of learning, we provide a focus for instruction, student learning, and assessment. Objectives help keep all three in close harmony. For example, for an objective emphasizing problem-solving strategies, we teach students how to apply problem-solving strategies, they practice applying the strategies, and we assess their skill in applying problem-solving strategies with new problems. Thus, the instructional targets, the learning targets, and the assessment targets are all the same. If the students are made aware of the objectives at the beginning of instruction, both teacher and students are working toward common goals and instruction and assessment are both part of the same process.

Stating Instructional Objectives

In stating instructional objectives, it is helpful to keep in mind that we are not describing the teaching procedures or the learning process. We are simply describing the student performance to be demonstrated at the end of the learning experience as evidence of learning. This permits us to use a variety of procedures, materials, and learning activities to achieve the desired outcomes.

A useful procedure is to first state the general objectives that focus on the broader learning outcomes and then define each general objective in more specific terms, as follows.

1. Understands Scientific Concepts
   1.1 Describes the concept in his or her own words.
   1.2 Describes the role of the concept in science.
   1.3 Distinguishes the concept from similar scientific concepts.
   1.4 Uses the concept in writing about science.
   1.5 Applies the concept in solving problems.

The specific learning outcomes listed under the general objective are not meant to be exhaustive, but they should provide a representative sample of the types of performance that we are willing to accept as evidence that the objective has been achieved. The general procedure for stating instructional objectives is presented in Box 3.1. The specific application of these steps is described and illustrated later for a unit on test planning.

Sources of Help in Locating Sample Objectives

In getting started with the identification and selection of instructional objectives, it helps to review various sources for ideas. Illustrative categories of intended learning outcomes and sample objectives can be found in the following sources.

1. *Taxonomy of Educational Objectives.* This is an older guide but it provides a classification of objectives in the cognitive, psychomotor, and affective domains. Each domain includes categories and subcategories that are designed to identify and classify all possible educational outcomes. For example, the cognitive domain includes the following major categories (Bloom, 1956):
   a. Knowledge (remembering previous learning material).
   b. Comprehension (grasping the meaning of material).
   c. Application (using information in concrete situation).

BOX 3.1 • *Stating Instructional Objectives*

The following steps provide guidelines for stating instructional objectives that are useful in instruction and assessment.

1. State the general objectives as follows:
   - **1.1** Write each as an intended learning outcome.
   - **1.2** State each in performance terms.
   - **1.3** Start each with a verb (e.g., "knows," "comprehends").
   - **1.4** Write each so it is general enough to identify a domain of specific learning outcomes.
2. List and state the specific learning outcomes as follows:
   - **2.1** Clarify each general objective with a representative sample of specific learning outcomes.
   - **2.2** Begin each with an action verb indicating observable student performance (e.g., "selects," "describes").
   - **2.3** Include a sufficient number to indicate attainment of the general objective.
   - **2.4** Check to be sure the specific learning outcomes are relevant to the general objectives and that the general objectives are in harmony with the school goals.

---

   d. Analysis (breaking down material into its parts).
   e. Synthesis (putting parts together into a whole).
   f. Evaluation (judging the value of a thing using criteria).

     These categories are listed in the order of increasing complexity and are clarified in the taxonomy by subdivisions that further describe the types of educational outcomes included. For detailed descriptions of all three domains of the taxonomy with illustrative objectives for each category see Gronlund (2000) at the end of this chapter.

2. *Instructors' guides accompanying student textbooks.* These guides typically contain objectives but they tend to focus on lower level outcomes, may be poorly stated, and are likely to lack close harmony with the goals of the curriculum. However, they are worth a review for ideas on possible learning outcomes to consider. It may be possible to modify some to put them in more usable form.
3. *Publications of educational organizations.* There are organizations in each of the main teaching areas that publish useful material on instruction that contains suggested objectives. For example, the National Science Teachers Association, the National Council of Teachers of

Mathematics, the National Council of Teachers of English, and the National Council for the Social Studies periodically issue yearbooks and other publications on instruction in their content area. The more recent publications will focus on learning outcomes that are in harmony with the newer curriculum emphasis on reasoning and problem-solving skills.

4. *State content standards.* The majority of states have developed content standards that provide guidelines for determining what students should know and be able to do in subject areas. These standards typically emphasize complex learning outcomes that focus on understanding of concepts and problem-solving skills. Thus, they may not represent a total curriculum in the content areas but serve as a framework for shaping the goals of the districts and schools. The intent is to move the school curriculum more toward a thinking curriculum and thereby improving both instruction and assessment.

Two illustrative content standards, developed by the California Department of Education, are shown in Figure 3.1. The standards are followed by examples of how students will show that they have met the standards. Although the standards are described as exemplary and compliance with them is not mandatory, schools and districts are encouraged to use them in curriculum development.

State content standards are typically reflected to some degree in the school curriculum and thus provide a valuable focus on the more complex learning outcomes. Although they are usually too general for direct use in instruction and assessment, a review of these will provide useful ideas for preparing instructional objectives. In those schools that emphasize standard-based instruction and standard-based assessment, it will be necessary to pay special attention to the content standards prepared by the state when writing instructional objectives.

Preparing and Using an Achievement Test

The preparation and use of an achievement test that measures the intended learning outcomes in a balanced manner involves the following steps:

1. Specifying the instructional objectives.
2. Preparing the test specifications.
3. Constructing relevant test items.
4. Arranging the items in the test.
5. Preparing clear directions.

Focus on Life Science

Cell Biology

1. All living organisms are composed of cells, from just one to many trillions, whose details usually are visible only through a microscope. As a basis for understanding this concept:

   a. *Students know* cells function similarly in all living organisms.

   b. *Students know* the characteristics that distinguish plant cells from animal cells, including chloroplasts and cell walls.

   c. *Students know* the nucleus is the repository for genetic information in plant and animal cells.

   d. *Students know* that mitochrondria liberate energy for the work that cells do and that chloroplasts capture sunlight energy for photosynthesis.

   e. *Students know* cells divide to increase their numbers through a process of mitosis, which results in two daughter cells with identical sets of chromosomes.

   f. *Students know* that as multicellular organisms develop, their cells differentiate.

Investigation and Experimentation

7. Scientific progress is made by asking meaningful questions and conducting careful investigations. As a basis for understanding this concept and addressing the content in the other three strands, students should develop their own questions and perform investigations. Students will:

   a. Select and use appropriate tools and technology (including calculators, computers, balances, spring scales, microscopes, and binoculars) to perform tests, collect data, and display data.

   b. Use a variety of print and electronic resources (including the World Wide Web) to collect information and evidence as part of a research project.

   c. Communicate the logical connection hypotheses, science concepts, tests conducted, data collected, and conclusions drawn from the scientific evidence.

   d. Construct scale models, maps, and appropriately labeled diagrams to communicate scientific knowledge (e.g., motion of Earth's plates and cell structure).

   e. Communicate the steps and results from an investigation in written reports and oral presentations.

FIGURE 3.1 *Sample California Science Content Standards—Grade 7.*

From *Science Content Standards for California Public Schools*, Copyright 2000, California Department of Education. Used by permission.

6. Reviewing and evaluating the assembled test.
7. Administering the test and making an item analysis.

Each of these steps will be described in turn. Performance assessment will be described in Chapters 7, 8, and 9.

Specifying the Instructional Objectives

As noted earlier, the first step in preparing instructional objectives it to list the general objectives as intended learning outcomes. The following list illustrates the procedure for a unit on planning an achievement test.

At the end of this unit in achievement test planning the student will demonstrate that he or she:

1. Knows the meaning of common terms.
2. Knows specific facts about test planning.
3. Knows the basic procedures for planning an achievement test.
4. Comprehends the relevant principles of testing.
5. Applies the principles in test planning.

These statements of general learning outcomes have been deliberately kept free of specific course content so that with only slight modification they can be used with various units of study. As we shall see later, the test specifications provide a means of relating intended outcomes to specific subject matter topics.

This list of general outcomes could, of course, be expanded by making the statements more specific, and in some cases it may be desirable to do so. The number of general learning outcomes to use is somewhat arbitrary, but somewhere between 5 and 15 items provide a list that is both useful and manageable. Typically, a shorter list is satisfactory for a unit of study, while a more comprehensive list is needed for summative testing at the end of a course.

Defining the General Outcomes in Specific Terms

When a satisfactory list of general learning outcomes has been identified and clearly stated, the next step is to list the specific types of student performance that are to be accepted as evidence that the outcomes have been achieved. For example, what specific types of performance will show that a student "knows the meaning of common terms" or "comprehends the relevant principles of testing"? For these two areas the specific learning outcomes may be listed as follows:

1. Knows the meaning of common terms.
   1.1 Identifies the correct definitions of terms.
   1.2 Identifies the meaning of terms when used in context.
   1.3 Distinguishes between terms on basis of meaning.
   1.4 Selects the most appropriate terms when describing testing procedures.
4. Comprehends the relevant principles of testing.
   4.1 Describes each principle in his or her own words.
   4.2 Matches a specific example to each principle.
   4.3 Explains the relevance of each principle to the major steps in test planning.
   4.4 Predicts the most probable effect of violating each of the principles.
   4.5 Formulates a test plan that is in harmony with the principles.

Note that the terms used to describe the specific learning outcomes indicate student performance that can be demonstrated to an outside observer. That is, they are *observable* responses that can be called forth by test items. The key terms are listed below to emphasize what is meant by defining learning outcomes in *specific performance terms.*

Identifies	Matches
Distinguishes between	Explains
Selects	Predicts
Describes	Formulates

Action verbs such as these indicate precisely what the student is able to do to demonstrate achievement. Such vague and indefinite terms as "learns," "sees," "realizes," and "is familiar with" should be avoided, since they do not clearly indicate the terminal performance to be measured.

Sample action verbs for stating specific learning outcomes at each level of the cognitive domain of the taxonomy are presented in Table 3.2. Although certain action verbs may be used at several different levels (e.g., "identifies"), the table provides a useful guide for defining intended outcomes in performance terms. For more comprehensive lists of action verbs, see Gronlund (2000) listed at the end of this chapter.

In defining the general learning outcomes in specific performance terms, it is typically impossible to list all of the relevant types of performance. The proportion that need be listed depends to a large extent on the nature of the test. In planning a test that is to be used to describe which learning tasks a student has mastered (criterion-referenced test), we should like as comprehensive a list as possible. For a test that is used to rank students in order of achievement (norm-referenced test), however, it is usually satisfactory to include a sufficient number of specific types of performance

TABLE 3.2 *Illustrative Action Verbs for Defining Objectives in the Cognitive Domain of the Taxonomy*

Taxonomy Categories	Sample Verbs for Stating Specific Learning Outcomes
Knowledge	Identifies, names, defines, describes, lists, matches, selects, outlines
Comprehension	Classifies, explains, summarizes, converts, predicts, distinguishes between
Application	Demonstrates, computes, solves, modifies, arranges, operates, relates
Analysis	Differentiates, diagrams, estimates, separates, infers, orders, subdivides
Synthesis	Combines, creates, formulates, designs, composes, constructs, rearranges, revises
Evaluation	Judges, criticizes, compares, justifies, concludes, discriminates, supports

to clarify what the typical student is like who has achieved the intended outcomes.

Preparing the Test Specifications

The writing of test items should be guided by a carefully prepared set of test specifications. The function of the specifications is to describe the achievement domain being measured and to provide guidelines for obtaining a representative sample of test tasks. Although the nature and detail of test specifications can be expected to vary considerably, here we shall describe one of the more commonly recommended procedures. In the construction of an **achievement test**, one of the most widely used devices has been a two-way chart called a *table of specifications.*

Building a Table of Specifications

Preparing a table of specifications involves (1) selecting the learning outcomes to be tested, (2) outlining the subject matter, and (3) making a two-way chart. The two-way chart describes the sample of items to be included in the test.

Selecting the Learning Outcomes to Be Tested.   The learning outcomes for a particular course will depend on the specific nature of the course, the objectives attained in previous courses, the philosophy of the school, the special needs of the students, and a host of other local factors that have a bearing on the instructional program. Despite the variation from course to course, most lists of instructional objectives will include learning outcomes in the following areas: (1) knowledge, (2) intellectual abilities and skills, (3) general skills (laboratory, performance, communication, work-study), and (4) attitudes, interests, and appreciations. It is in the first two areas covered by the cognitive domain of the taxonomy that achievement testing is most useful. Learning outcomes in the other areas are typically evaluated by rating scales, checklists, anecdotal records, inventories, and similar nontest evaluation procedures. Thus, the first step is to separate from the list of learning outcomes those that are testable by paper-and-pencil tests. The selected list of learning outcomes should, of course, be defined in specific terms, as described in the previous section. Clarifying the specific types of performance to be called forth by the test will aid in constructing test terms that are most relevant to the intended learning outcomes.

Outlining the Subject Matter. The stated learning outcomes specify how students are expected to react to the subject matter of a course. Although it is possible to include both the student performance and the specific subject matter the student is to react toward in the same statement, it is usually desirable to list them separately. The reason for this is that the student can react in the same way to many different areas of subject matter, and he can react in many different ways to the same area of subject matter. For example, when we state that a student can "define a term in her own words," "recall a specific fact," or "identify an example of a principle," these types of performance can be applied to almost any area of subject matter. Since particular types of student performance can overlap a variety of subject matter areas, and vice versa, it is more convenient to list each aspect of performance and subject matter separately and then to relate them in the table of specifications.

The content of a course may be outlined in detail for teaching purposes, but for test planning only the major categories need be listed. The following outline of subject matter topics based on a unit on achievement testing illustrates sufficient detail for the test plan.

A. Role of testing in the instructional process
   1. Instructional decisions and test types
   2. Influence of tests on learning and instruction
B. Principles of achievement testing
   1. Relation to instructional objectives
   2. Representative sampling
   3. Relevance of items to outcomes
   4. Relevance of test to use of results
   5. Reliability of results
   6. Improvement of learning

C. Norm-referenced versus criterion-referenced testing
D. Planning the test
   1. Determining the purpose of the test
   2. Identifying the intended learning outcomes
   3. Preparing the test specifications
   4. Constructing relevant test items

Making the Two-Way Chart.   When the learning outcomes have been selected and clearly defined and the course content outlined, the two-way chart should be prepared. This is called a **table of specifications**. It relates outcomes to content and indicates the relative weight to be given to each of the various areas. As noted earlier, the purpose of the table is to provide assurance that the test will measure a representative sample of the learning outcomes and the subject matter topics to be measured.

An example of a table of specifications for a summative test on a unit on achievement testing is given in Table 3.3. Note that only the general learning outcomes and the major subject matter categories have been included. A more detailed table may be desirable for test purposes, but this is sufficient for illustration.

TABLE 3.3   *Table of Specifications for a Summative Test on a Unit for Achievement Testing*

Outcomes / *Content*	*Knows*			*Comprehends Principles*	*Applies Principles*	*Total Number of Items*
	Terms	*Facts*	*Procedures*			
Role of Tests in Instruction	4	4		2		10
Principles of Testing	4	3	2	6	5	20
Norm-Referenced versus Criterion-Referenced	4	3	3			10
Planning the Test	3	5	5	2	5	20
Total Number of Items	15	15	10	10	10	60

The numbers in each cell of the table indicate the number of test items to be devoted to that area. For example, 15 items in the test will measure knowledge of terms; 4 of them pertain to the "role of tests" in instruction," 4 to "principles of testing," 4 to "norm-referenced versus criterion-referenced," and 3 to "planning the test." The number of items assigned to each cell is determined by the weight given to each learning outcome and each subject matter area.

A number of factors will enter into assigning relative weights to each learning outcome and each content area. How important is each area in the total learning experience? How much time was devoted to each area during instruction? Which outcomes have the greater retention and transfer value? What relative importance do curriculum specialists assign to each area? These and similar criteria must be considered. In the final analysis, however, the weights assigned in the table should faithfully reflect the emphasis given during instruction. In Table 3.3, for example, it is assumed that twice as much emphasis was given to "planning the test" (20 items) as was given to "norm-referenced versus criterion-referenced" (10 items). Similarly, it is assumed that knowledge outcomes were given approximately two-thirds of the emphasis during instruction (40 items) and that comprehension and application outcomes were each given approximately one-sixth of the total emphasis (10 items each).

In summary, preparing a table of specifications includes the following steps:

1. Identify the learning outcomes and content areas to be measured by the test.
2. Weight the learning outcomes and content areas in terms of their relative importance.
3. Build the table in accordance with these relative weights by distributing the test items proportionately among the relevant cells of the table.

The resulting two-way table indicates the type of test needed to measure the learning outcomes and course content in a balanced manner. Thus, the table of specifications serves the test maker like a blueprint. It specifies the number and the nature of the items in the test, and it thereby provides a guide for item writing.

Considerations in Constructing Relevant Test Items

The construction of a set of relevant test items is greatly simplified if the intended learning outcomes have been clearly defined and the test specifications carefully prepared. The quality of the test will then depend on how closely the test maker can match the specifications. Here we shall confine our discussion to some of the general specifications in preparing test items. More detailed procedures and rules for item writing will be described in the chapters that follow.

Selecting the Types of Test Items to Use

The items used in achievement tests can be classified as either *selection-type* items or *supply-type* items. The selection-type item presents students with a set of possible responses from which they are to select the most appropriate answer. The supply-type item requires students to create and supply their own answers. These two major categories can be used to classify the most widely used item types as follows.

Selection-Type Items
1. Multiple choice
2. True-false
3. Matching
4. Interpretive exercise

Supply-Type Items
1. Short answer
2. Essay (restricted response)
3. Essay (extended response)

These categories are sometimes referred to as *recognition* and *recall* items. This is a case of mislabeling that confuses the method of responding with the mental reaction needed to make the response. When measuring knowledge of facts, test responses might be limited to either the recognition or recall of the answer. However, when measuring complex learning outcomes with selection-type items, the answer is not achieved through mere recognition of a previously learned answer. It typically involves some use of higher mental processes to arrive at a solution (e.g., verbal or mathematical reasoning) before the correct answer can be selected. Similarly, a short-answer item may require reasoning or problem solving rather than simply recalling and supplying factual information. Essay answers, of course, typically require analysis, synthesis, and evaluation skills in addition to recall. Using the *selection* and *supply* labels makes clear how the responses are made but it does not imply limits on the types of learning outcomes that can be measured with each.

In deciding which item types to use in a test, a guiding principle should be: *Use the item types that provide the most direct measures of student performance specified by the intended learning outcome.* Thus, if you want to determine if students can spell, have them spell from dictation. If you want to determine if students can solve mathematics problems, have them solve problems and supply the answers. If you want to determine if students can write, have them write something. Use selection-type items for supply-type outcomes only if there is a compelling reason for doing so (e.g., electronic scoring) and then take into account, during interpretation of the results, that a less direct measure has been used. In some cases, of course, both types of items are useful in the same area. For example, a writing project may provide the best evidence of writing skill but a selection-type test would provide the most systematic coverage of the elements of grammar needed for effective writing.

There are a number of achievement areas where either selection-type items or supply-type items would measure equally well. In these cases, our choice between them must be based on other item characteristics. The preparation of good selection-type items is difficult and students can get a proportion of answers correct by guessing. However, these disadvantages are offset by the fact that (1) they can be scored quickly and objectively (i.e., scorers agree on the answers), (2) they eliminate bluffing, (3) they eliminate the influence of writing skill, (4) they provide an extensive sample of student performance (because of the large number of items used), and (5) they provide for the identification of specific learning errors. In comparison, supply-type items are easier to construct (although harder than commonly believed) but more difficult to score. The scoring of short-answer items is contaminated by answers of varying degrees of correctness and by adjustments needed for misspellings. The scoring of essay tests is tedious, time consuming, and influenced by bluffing, writing skill, and the shifting of standards during scoring. Another major shortcoming of supply-type items is the limited sample of learning tasks that can be measured. The short-answer item is restricted primarily to measuring knowledge outcomes. Although the essay test is especially suited to measuring complex learning outcomes, its sampling is limited by the relatively few questions that can be included in a test.

A summary comparison of the relative merits of selection-type and supply-type items is presented in Table 3.4. Although this should serve as a guide in selecting the types of items to use in a given test, as noted earlier, the most important question to ask is: *Does this item type provide the most direct measure of the intended learning outcome?* If the various item types are equal in this regard, the selection-type items would be favored because of the broad sampling, the objective scoring, and the pinpointing of specific learning errors.

Matching Items to Specific Learning Outcomes

Effective achievement testing requires that a set of test items be constructed that calls forth the performance described in the intended learning out-

TABLE 3.4 *Summary of the Relative Merits of Selection-Type Items and Supply-Type Items*

Characteristic	Selection-Type Items	Supply-Type Items	
		Short Answer	*Essay*
Measures factual information	Yes	Yes	Yes(*)
Measures understanding	Yes	No(**)	Yes
Measures synthesis	No(**)	No(**)	Yes
Easy to construct	No	Yes	Yes
Samples broadly	Yes	Yes	No
Eliminates bluffing	Yes	No	No
Eliminates writing skill	Yes	No	No
Eliminates blind guessing	No	Yes	Yes
Easy to score	Yes	No	No
Scoring is objective	Yes	No	No
Pinpoints learning errors	Yes	Yes	No
Encourages originality	No	No	Yes

(*)The essay test can measure knowledge of facts, but because of scoring and sampling problems it probably should not be used for this purpose.

(**)These items can be designed to measure limited aspects of these characteristics.

comes. While we can never be certain of a perfect correspondence between outcome and item, the following examples illustrate how items should be written to measure the specific type of performance stated in the specific learning outcome.

EXAMPLES

Specific Learning Outcome: Defines terms in student's own words.
    Directions: Define each of the following terms in a sentence or two.
1. Taxonomy
2. Cognitive
3. Measurement
4. Evaluation

Specific Learning Outcome: Identifies procedural steps in planning for a test.
1. Which one of the following steps should be completed first in planning for an achievement test?[1]
    A. Select the types of test items to use.
    B. Decide on the length of the test.

---

[1]The correct answer is indicated throughout this book by an asterisk.

    *C. Define the intended learning outcomes.

    D. Prepare the test specifications.

Specific Learning Outcome: Identifies the hierarchical order of the categories in the cognitive domain of the taxonomy.

  1. Which one of the following categories in the taxonomy indicates the highest level of learning?

    A. Analysis

    B. Application

    C. Comprehension

   *D. Synthesis

Specific Learning Outcome: Distinguishes between sound and unsound principles of achievement testing.

    Directions: Read each of the following statements. If the statement indicates a sound principle of achievement testing, circle the S; if it indicates an unsound principle, circle the U.

*S   U   **1.** The specific learning outcomes to be tested should be stated in terms of student performance.

S   *U   **2.** Achievement testing should be limited to outcomes that can be measured objectively.

*S   U   **3.** Each achievement test item should measure a clearly defined type of student performance.

Specific Learning Outcome: Identifies examples of properly stated learning outcomes.

  1. Which one of the following learning outcomes is properly stated in performance terms?

    A. Student realizes the importance of tests in teaching.

    B. Student has acquired the basic principles of achievement testing.

    C. Student demonstrates a desire for more experience in test construction.

   *D. Student predicts the most probable effect of violating a test construction principle.

It should be noted in these examples that each specific learning outcome provides a precise definition of the student performance to be measured, and the test item simply provides a task that makes measurement of the specified performance possible.

Improving the Functioning Content of Items

If test items are to call forth the performance described in the intended learning outcomes, great care must be taken in phrasing the items. We need to eliminate all barriers that might prevent a knowledgeable person from responding and all clues that might lead the uninformed to the correct answer. Only those who have achieved the outcome being measured should get the item right. All others (no matter how intelligent) should miss it.

Some of the common *barriers* to be avoided during test preparation are:

Vocabulary that is unnecessarily difficult.
Sentence structure that is unnecessarily complex.
Statements containing ambiguity.
Unclear pictorial materials.
Directions that are vague.
Material reflecting race, ethnic, or sex bias.

Awareness of such barriers during the planning and preparation of the test is the first step in their elimination. Essentially, we can avoid these barriers by (1) writing each test item so that it presents a clearly formulated task, (2) stating the items in simple, clear language, (3) keeping the items free from biased and nonfunctional material, and (4) using a test format and directions that contribute to effective test taking. Much of the material presented later in this book is directed toward constructing tests that prevent extraneous factors from distorting the test results.

Some of the common *clues* to be avoided during test preparation are:

Verbal associations that give away the answer.

Grammatical inconsistencies that eliminate wrong answers.

Specific determiners that make certain answers probable (e.g., sometimes) and others improbable (e.g., always).

Stereotyped or textbook phrasing of correct answers.

Length or location of correct answers.

Material in an item that aids in answering another item.

Just as in controlling extraneous factors that provide barriers to the correct answer, clues such as these can be eliminated by being aware of them and by following sound principles of test construction. Many of the rules for item writing and test preparation in the chapters that follow provide guidelines for this purpose.

Determining the Number of Test Items to Use

The number of items to use should be indicated in the test specifications, as noted earlier, and is modified by a number of practical constraints, such as the following:

1. Age of the students tested
2. Time available for testing
3. Type of test items used
4. Type of interpretation to be made

In the testing of elementary school students, the testing time typically should be no more than 20 or 30 minutes so that proper motivation is maintained. At the high school and college levels, students can be given tests lasting several hours (for example, a final examination), but most tests are limited to a testing time of 40 to 50 minutes because of the length of the typical class period.

In matching the number of items to available testing time, we are faced with the problem of estimating how many items students can complete per minute. Unfortunately, there are no simple answers. The size of the final product depends on the type of test item, the complexity of the learning outcome measured, and the age of the students. As a guideline, high school and college students should be able to answer one multiple-choice item, three short-answer items, or three true-false items per minute when the items are measuring knowledge outcomes. For measuring more complex learning outcomes such as comprehension and application, and for testing younger age groups, more time per item is needed. In estimating the number of items to be used, keep in mind the slower students in the group, for it is desirable to give all students an opportunity to complete the test. Experience in testing a given group of students is frequently the only dependable guide for determining proper test length.

In addition to our concern with total test length, consideration must be given to the number of test items needed for each type of interpretation to be made. This issue is especially crucial in criterion-referenced interpretation, where we want to describe student performance in terms of each intended learning outcome. For this purpose we should use at least 10 items per outcome. Where practical constraints make it necessary to use fewer than 10 items for an intended outcome, only tentative judgments should be made and these should be verified by other means. In some cases it is possible to combine items into larger item clusters for a more meaningful interpretation. See Box 3.2 for a summary checklist for evaluating the test plan.

General Guidelines for Item Writing

There are a number of general suggestions that apply to the writing of all item types. These provide a general framework for writing items that function as intended and that contribute to more valid and reliable results.

1. *Select the type of test item that measures the intended learning outcome most directly.* Use a supply-type item if supplying the answer is an important element of the task (e.g., writing). Use a selection-type item if appropriate (e.g., identification) or if both types are equally appropriate.

2. *Write the test item so that the performance it elicits matches the performance in the learning task.* The intended learning outcome specifies the

BOX 3.2 • *Checklist for Evaluating the Test Plan*

1. Is the purpose of the test clear?
2. Have the intended learning outcomes been identified and defined?
3. Are the intended learning outcomes stated in performance (measurable) terms?
4. Have test specifications been prepared that indicate the nature and distribution of items to be included in the test?
5. Does the specified set of items provide a representative sample of the tasks contained in the achievement domain?
6. Are the types of items appropriate for the learning outcomes to be measured?
7. Is the difficulty of the items appropriate for the students to be tested and the nature of the measurement (e.g., mastery or survey)?
8. Is the number of items appropriate for the students to be tested, the time available for testing, and the interpretations to be made?
9. Does the test plan include built-in features that contribute to valid and reliable scores?
10. Have plans been made for arranging the items in the test, writing directions, scoring, and using the results?

learning task in performance terms and the test task should call forth the same performance.

3. *Write the test item so that the test task is clear and definite.* Keep the reading level low, use simple and direct language, and follow the rules for correct punctuation and grammar.

4. *Write the test item so that it is free from nonfunctional material.* Material not directly relevant to the problem being presented increases the reading load and may detract from the intent of the item. Use extraneous material only where its detection is part of the task (e.g., in math problems).

5. *Write the test item so that irrelevant factors do not prevent an informed student from responding correctly.* Avoid trick questions that might cause a knowledgeable student to focus on the wrong aspect of the task. Use clear, unambiguous statements that maximize the performance to be measured and minimize all other influences. For example, word problems measuring mathematical reasoning should keep reading level and computational demands simple if an uncontaminated measure of reasoning ability is desired.

6. *Write the test item so that irrelevant clues do not enable the uninformed student to respond correctly.* Removing unwanted clues from test items requires alertness during item writing and reviewing the items after setting them aside for a while. The most common clues for each item type will be considered in the following chapters. It is also important to prevent the information given in one item from providing an answer to another item in the test.

7. *Write the test item so that the difficulty level matches the intent of the learning outcome, the age group to be tested, and the use to be made of the results.* When difficulty is being evaluated, check to be certain that it is relevant to the intended learning outcome and that the item is free from sources of irrelevant difficulty (e.g., obscure materials, overly fine discriminations).

8. *Write the test item so that there is no disagreement concerning the answer.* Typically the answer should be one that experts would agree is the correct or best answer. Most problems arise here when students are to provide the best answer (best procedure, best explanation). This involves a matter of judgment and to be defensible the answer must be clearly best and identified as such by experts in the area. Where experts disagree, it may be desirable to ask what a particular authority would consider to be the best method, the best reason, and the like. When attributed to a source, the answer can be judged as correct or incorrect.

9. *Write the test items far enough in advance that they can be later reviewed and modified as needed.* A good time to write test items is shortly after the material has been taught, while the questions and context are still clearly in mind. In any event, reviewing and editing items after they have been set aside for a while can detect flaws that were inadvertently introduced during the original item writing.

10. *Write more test items than called for by the test plan.* This will enable you to discard weak or inappropriate items during item review and make it easier to match the final set of items to the test specifications.

Arranging the Items in the Test

After the final selection of the items to be included in a test, a decision must be made concerning the best arrangement of items. This arrangement will vary with the type of test being prepared, but the following guidelines should be helpful.

1. *For instructional purposes it is usually desirable to group together items that measure the same outcome.* Each group of items can then be identified by an appropriate heading (e.g., knowledge, comprehension, application). The inclusion of the headings helps to identify the areas where students are having difficulty and to plan for remedial action.

2. *Where possible, all items of the same type should be grouped together.* This arrangement makes it possible to provide only one set of directions for each item type. It also simplifies the scoring and the analysis of the results.
3. *The items should be arranged in terms of increasing difficulty.* This arrangement has motivational effect on students and will prevent them from getting "bogged down" by difficult items early in the test.

Because most classroom tests include only a few item types, it is usually possible to honor all three of these guidelines. When this is not feasible, the item arrangement that best fits the nature of the test and use to be made of the results should be used.

Preparing Directions

The directions for an achievement test should be simple and concise and yet contain information concerning each of the following: (1) purpose of the test, (2) time allowed to complete the test, (3) how to record the answers, and (4) whether to guess when in doubt about an answer. The following sample directions for a multiple-choice test cover these four points.

> **EXAMPLE**
>
> *Directions:* This is a test of what you have learned during the first five weeks of the course. The results of this test will be used to clarify any points of difficulty and thus help you complete the course successfully.
>
> There are 60 multiple-choice items, and you have one hour to complete the test.
>
> For each item, select the answer that *best* completes the statement, or answers the question, and circle the letter of that answer.
>
> Since your score will be the number of items answered correctly, *be sure to answer every item.*

When two or more item types are included in the same test, it is usually desirable to provide general directions for the test as a whole and specific directions for each part. When this is done, the general directions should contain the information about purpose, time allowed, and what to do about guessing, and the specific directions should describe how to record the answers for that particular part. Also, some items, such as keytype exercises, require special directions for each item.

The use of separate answer sheets requires some elaboration of the instructions for recording the answers. If students are not familiar with the use of separate answer sheets, it might also be desirable to present a sample item with the correct answer properly marked. There is a variety of separate

BOX 3.3 • *Correcting for Guessing*

Use the correction for guessing formula only when students have insufficient time to consider all of the items in the test (e.g., speed test). Then, warn the students that there will be a correction for guessing. Use the following formula to correct the scores.

> Score = Right – Wrong/n-1

In this formula, n equals the number of alternatives in each time, and thus:

True-false items	$S = R - W$
Multiple-choice items	$S = R - W/2$ (3 alternatives)
	$S = R - W/3$ (4 alternatives)
	$S = R - W/4$ (5 alternatives)

answer sheets, and the specific instructions will have to be adapted to the particular type used. Unless machine scoring is to be used, however, a teacher-made answer sheet that simply lists the letters of the alternatives for each item is usually satisfactory.

The Problem of Guessing

In our set of sample directions, the students were told, "Since your score will be the number of items answered correctly, be sure to answer every item." This is an attempt to equalize the variation among students in their tendency to guess when in doubt about the answer. The directions make it unnecessary to correct for guessing. Although a correction for guessing may be appropriate for standardized tests, they are not needed for classroom tests where the students have an opportunity to respond to all items. It is only where students are unable to complete the test (e.g., speed test) that the correction for guessing might be appropriate for classroom tests. Here, the purpose is to prevent students from rapidly and randomly marking the remaining items just before time is up in an attempt to improve their score (see Box 3.3 for correction formula).

Reviewing and Evaluating the Assembled Test

After assembling the items into a test, it is desirable to review the test as a whole to be sure it meets the criteria of a good test. The types of questions to consider are listed in Box 3.4.

BOX 3.4 • *Checklist for Evaluating the Assembled Test*

1. *Balance*	Do the items measure a representative sample of the learning tasks in the achievement domain?
2. *Relevance*	Do the test items present relevant tasks?
3. *Conciseness*	Are the test tasks stated in simple, clear language?
4. *Soundness*	Are the items of proper difficulty, free of defects, and do they have answers that are defensible?
5. *Independence*	Are the items free from overlapping, so that one item does not aid in answering another?
6. *Arrangement*	Are items measuring the same outcome grouped together?
	Are items of the same type grouped together?
	Are items in order of increasing difficulty?
7. *Numbering*	Are the items numbered in order throughout the test?
8. *Directions*	Are there directions for the whole test and each part?
	Are the directions concise and at the proper reading level?
	Do the directions include time limits and how to record answers?
	Do the directions tell what to do about guessing?
9. *Spacing*	Does the spacing on the page contribute to ease of reading and responding?
10. *Typing*	Is the final copy free of typographical errors?

Administering and Scoring the Test

The administration of a carefully prepared informal achievement test is largely a matter of providing proper working conditions, keeping interruptions to a minimum, and arranging enough space between students to prevent cheating. The written directions should be clear enough to make the test self-administering, but in some situations it may be desirable to give the directions orally as well. With young students a blackboard illustration may also be useful. Above all, make certain that all the students know exactly what to do, and then provide them with the most favorable conditions in which to do it.

Scoring is facilitated if all answers are recorded on the left side of each test page, as we suggested earlier. Under this arrangement, scoring is simply a matter of marking the correct answers on a copy of the test and placing it next to the column of answers on each student's paper. If a separate answer sheet is used, it is usually better to punch out the letters of the correct answers on a copy of the answer sheet and use this as a scoring stencil. The stencil is laid over each answer sheet and the correctly marked answers appear through the holes. Where no mark appears, a red line can be drawn across the hole. This indicates to the student the correct answer for each item missed. If machine scoring is to be used, simply scan the students' papers to make certain that only one answer was marked for each item.

Unless corrected for guessing, a student's score on an objective test is typically the number of answers marked correctly. Thus, each test item is counted as one point. Although teachers frequently desire to count some items more heavily than others because of their importance or difficulty, such weighting of scores complicates the scoring task and seldom results in an improved measure of achievement. A better way to increase the relative weight of an area is to construct more items in that area.

Analyzing the Effectiveness of Test Items

After a test has been administered, the items should be analyzed for their effectiveness. One method of evaluating the test is to review the test item-by-item when it is handed back to students for a discussion of the results. Significant comments made during the discussion can be recorded on a blank copy of the test. The flexibility of this procedure makes it possible to pursue comments about particular items, to ask students why they selected the response they did (both correct and incorrect selections), and to spend as much time on each item as seems warranted. This procedure may bring forth some unjustified criticisms of the test, but it will also help identify defective items in need of revision. The extra time used in discussing the test results will not be wasted because students will be obtaining a review of the course material covered by the test.

Simple Item Analysis Procedure

The discussion of test results and review of the items can be much more effective if a simple tally of student responses is made on the master copy of the test. By recording the results of the 10 highest scoring students (H) and 10 lowest scoring students (L), like that in Figure 3.2, make the results easily interpretable. The answer is circled and the numbers to the left of each alternative indicate how many students in each group selected that alternative.

The result in Figure 3.2 provides all the information we need to estimate the following types of item analysis information.

1. The difficulty of the item (percentage of students answering the item correctly).
2. The discriminating power of the item (how well the item discriminates between high and low scorers).
3. The effectiveness of each alternative (all should be chosen and each one more frequently by the low scoring group).

UNIT TEST

Name _____ Date _____

Directions:

This test measures the knowledge, understandings, and applications you have acquired during the first four weeks.

There are 65 objective items, and you will have the full class period to complete the test.

Select the best answer for each item and circle the letter of that answer.

Your score will be the number of items answered correctly, so *be sure to answer every item.*

KNOWLEDGE OF TERMS

H	L	
		1. An assessment instrument is properly classified as *objective* when
1	3	A. the instrument uses objective-type questions.
1	2	B. the responses called forth by the instrument are free of opinion.
0	1	C. those preparing the instrument used standard procedures of construction.
8	4	Ⓓ there is agreement among scorers concerning the correctness of the answers.

FIGURE 3.2 Test copy with item analysis data to left of items (H = 10 highest scorers, L = 10 lowest scorers).

By simply looking at the answer sheet in Figure 3.2, we can see that 8 students in the high-scoring group and 4 students in the low-scoring group selected the correct answer. Also, more students in the low-scoring group selected each wrong alternative than in the high-scoring group, indicating that the distracters seem to be distracting those students who haven't learned the meaning of the term.

Because we are using 10 students in the high-scoring group and 10 students in the low-scoring group, we can mentally calculate the usual indexes of difficulty and discriminating power by using the following simple steps.

1. Determine the percentage of high scorers and low scorers passing the item by adding a zero.

   H = 8 out of 10 = 80
   L = 4 out of 10 = 40

2. Obtain *item difficulty* by adding the percentage correct in the high and low groups and dividing by 2. Add a percent sign to the answer.

$$\frac{80 + 40}{2} = 60\%$$

3. Obtain *discriminating power* by subtracting the percentage correct in the low group from the percentage correct in the high group. Add a decimal point to the answer.

$80 - 40 = .40$

The description of the procedure makes it sound more complicated than it is, but making a few mental calculations like this will reveal its simplicity. Item difficulty typically uses the percent sign and, of course, can range from 0% to 100%. Our **difficulty index** is based on the high- and low-scoring groups only, but this provides a satisfactory approximation of item difficulty. The **discrimination index** typically uses the decimal point and thus ranges from 0 to 1.00.

This simple method of analyzing the test results can be used as an aid in discussing the items when reviewing the test. Items that most students answer correctly can be skipped over or treated lightly, items missed by most students can be discussed in more detail, and defective items can be pointed out to students rather than defended as fair. Also, the frequency with which each incorrect answer is chosen may reveal common errors and misconceptions that can be corrected on the spot or serve as a basis for remedial work. In discussing the reasons students have selected the right or wrong answer for an item can sometimes be revealing. We assume that if they selected the correct answer they had learned the material. Not necessarily so, when using selection-type items (see Box 3.5 for common reasons for selecting alternatives). Having students discuss the reasons for their choices

BOX 3.5 • *Common Reasons for Selecting Multiple-Choice Alternatives*

Bases for Correct Choice
1. Possesses required information or skill.
2. Uses partial information that favors answer.
3. Uses clues given in the item.
4. Uses information from other items in the test.
5. Makes a blind, lucky guess.

Bases for Incorrect Choice
1. Lacks the information or skill required by the item.
2. Uses partial information that favors a distracter.
3. Uses misinformation that favors a distracter.
4. Makes a blind, unlucky guess.
5. Marks wrong answer through carelessness.

provides insights into student thinking that may contribute to both improved teaching and improved test construction skills.

Although the method of **item analysis** presented here is a crude one, it is probably satisfactory for most classroom tests. We are using it primarily as a basis for reviewing the items with students and for any insights the results might give us for improving test items in the future. A more detailed description of item analysis and cautions in interpreting item-analysis data can be found in Linn and Gronlund (2000).

Because of the small number of students involved in classroom testing, item-analysis information must be interpreted with great caution. If a test item is reused with a new group, the results may be quite different, due to changes in the instruction, the study habits of students, or some other factor. The tentative nature of the item-analysis data is not of great concern, however, when used to review tests with students for the purpose of improving learning.

Summary of Points

1. Assessment planning should be guided by what the students are expected to learn as specified by the school goals and the more specific instructional objectives.
2. Assessment planning requires a consideration of all possible types of learning outcomes in a given content area, not just those that can be measured by a test.
3. Assessment of performance skills and products typically requires some type of observation procedure, such as a checklist, rating scale, or holistic scoring rubric (see Chapter 7).
4. Preparing and using an achievement test includes specifying the instructional objectives in performance terms, preparing a table of specifications, constructing relevant test items, arranging the items in the test, preparing clear directions, reviewing and evaluating the assembled test, administering the test, and making an item analysis.
5. Test specifications typically consist of a twofold table of specifications that indicates the sample of performance tasks to be measured.
6. The types of test items used in a test should be determined by how directly they measure the intended learning outcomes and how effective they are as measuring instruments.
7. Each test item should provide a task that matches the student performance described in a specific learning outcome.
8. The functioning content of test items can be improved by eliminating irrelevant barriers and unintended clues during item writing.

9. The difficulty of a test item should match the difficulty of the learning task to be measured. Beware of irrelevant sources of difficulty (e.g., obscure material).
10. An achievement test should be short enough to permit all students to attempt all items during the testing time available.
11. A test should contain a sufficient number of test items for each type of interpretation to be made. Interpretations based on fewer than 10 items should be considered highly tentative.
12. Following a general set of guidelines during item writing will result in higher quality items that contribute to the validity and reliability of the test results.
13. Item arrangement within the test will vary with the type of test used. Where possible, items should be grouped by major learning outcome (e.g., knowledge, comprehension, application); similar items should be grouped together and should be arranged in order of increasing difficulty.
14. Test directions should clearly indicate the purpose of the test, the time allowed, how to record the answers, and to answer every item.
15. A correction for guessing should be used for speed tests only.
16. Review and evaluate the assembled test before using.
17. Administer the test under controlled conditions.
18. Item analysis provides a means of evaluating the items and is useful in reviewing the test with students.

References and Additional Reading

Bloom, B. S., et al. (ed.). *Taxonomy of Educational Objectives: Cognitive Domain* (New York: David McKay Co., 1956).

Carey, L. M., *Measuring and Evaluating School Learning*, 3rd ed. (Boston: Allyn and Bacon, 2001).

Gronlund, N. E., *How to Write and Use Instructional Objectives*, 6th ed. (Upper Saddle River, NJ: Merrill/Prentice Hall, 2000).

Linn, R. L., and Gronlund, N. E. *Measurement and Assessment in Teaching*, 8th ed. (Upper Saddle River, NJ: Merrill/Prentice-Hall, 2000).

Oosterhoff, A. C., *Classroom Application of Educational Measurement*, 3rd ed. (Upper Saddle River, NJ: Merrill/Prentice-Hall, 2001).

Stiggins, R. J., *Student-Involved Classroom Assessment*, 3rd ed. (Upper Saddle River, NJ: Merrill/Prentice-Hall, 2001).

4

Writing Selection Items
Multiple Choice

Studying this chapter should enable you to

1. Describe the characteristics of multiple-choice items.
2. Describe the strengths and limitations of multiple-choice items.
3. Distinguish between well-stated and poorly stated multiple-choice items.
4. Identify and correct faults in poorly stated multiple-choice items.
5. Match multiple-choice items to intended learning outcomes.
6. Construct multiple-choice items that are well stated, relevant to important learning outcomes, and free of defects.

Multiple-choice items are the most widely used and highly regarded of the selection-type items. They can be designed to measure a variety of learning outcomes, from simple to complex, and can provide the highest quality items. Because they play such an important role in achievement testing, they will be treated in this chapter in considerable detail. Other selection-type items (true-false, matching, and interpretive exercise) will be described in the following chapter.

Nature of Multiple-Choice Items

The multiple-choice item consists of a *stem*, which presents a problem situation, and several *alternatives* (*options* or *choices*), which provide possible solutions to the problem. The stem may be a question or an incomplete statement. The alternatives include the correct answer and several plausible wrong answers called *distracters*. The function of the latter is to distract those students who are uncertain of the answer.

The following items illustrate the question form and the incomplete-statement form of a multiple-choice item.

EXAMPLE

Which one of the following item types is an example of a supply-type test item?
    A. Multiple-choice item.
    B. True-false item.
    C. Matching item.
    *D. Short-answer item.

An example of a supply-type test item is the:
    A. multiple-choice item.
    B. true-false item.
    C. matching item.
    *D. short-answer item.

Although stated differently, both stems pose the same problem. Note, however, that the incomplete statement is more concise. This is typically the case. The question form is easier to write and forces the test maker to pose a clear problem but tends to result in a longer stem. An effective procedure for the beginner is to start with a question and shift to the incomplete statement whenever greater conciseness can be obtained.

The alternatives in the preceding examples contain only one correct answer, and the distracters are clearly incorrect. Another type of multiple-choice item is the *best-answer* form in which the alternatives are all partially correct but one is clearly better than the others. This type is used for more complex achievement, as when the student must select the best reason for an action, the best method for doing something, or the best application of a principle. Thus, whether the correct-answer or best-answer form is used depends on the learning outcomes to be measured.

EXAMPLE

Which item is *best* for measuring computational skill?
    A. Multiple-choice item.
    B. True-false item.
    C. Matching item.
    *D. Short-answer item.

The examples given illustrate the use of four alternatives. Multiple-choice items typically include either three, four, or five choices. The larger number will, of course, reduce the student's chances of obtaining the correct answer by guessing. Theoretically, with five alternatives there is only one chance in five of guessing the answer, whereas with four alternatives there is one chance in four. It is frequently difficult to obtain five plausible choices, however, and items are not improved by adding obviously wrong answers merely to have five alternatives. There is no reason why the items in a given test should all have the same number of alternatives. Some might contain three, some four, and some five, depending on the availability of plausible distracters. This would pose a problem only if the test were to be corrected for guessing—a practice that is not recommended for informal achievement tests.

Uses of Multiple-Choice Items

The multiple-choice item can be used to measure knowledge outcomes and various types of complex learning outcomes. The single-item format is probably most widely used for measuring knowledge, comprehension, and application outcomes. The interpretive exercise consisting of a series of multiple-choice items based on introductory material (e.g., paragraph, picture, or graph) is especially useful for measuring analysis, interpretation, and other complex learning outcomes. The interpretive exercise will be described in the following chapter. Here, we confine the discussion to the use of single, independent, multiple-choice items.

Knowledge Items

Knowledge items typically measure the degree to which previously learned material has been remembered. The items focus on the simple recall of information and can be concerned with the measurement of terms, facts, or other specific aspects of knowledge.

> **EXAMPLES**
>
> *Outcome:* Identifies the meaning of a term.
> > Reliability means the same as:
> > > *A. consistency.
> > > B. relevancy.
> > > C. representativeness.
> > > D. usefulness.
>
> *Outcome:* Identifies the order of events.
> > What is the first step in constructing an achievement test?
> > > A. Decide on test length.
> > > *B. Identify the intended learning outcomes.
> > > C. Prepare a table of specifications.
> > > D. Select the item types to use.

The wide variety of knowledge outcomes that can be measured with multiple-choice items is best shown by illustrating some of the types of questions that can be asked in various knowledge categories. Sample questions stated as incomplete multiple-choice stems are presented in the Box 4.1.

BOX 4.1 • *Illustrative Knowledge Questions**

1.11 *Knowledge of Terminology*
       What word means the same as _____?
       Which statement best defines the term _____?
       In this sentence, what is the meaning of the word _____?

1.12 *Knowledge of Specific Facts*
       Where would you find _____?
       Who first discovered _____?
       What is the name of _____?

1.21 *Knowledge of Conventions*
       What is the correct form for _____?
       Which statement indicates correct usage of _____?
       Which of the following rules applies to _____?

1.22 *Knowledge of Trends and Sequences*
       Which of the following best describes the trend of _____?
       What is the most important cause of _____?
       Which of the following indicates the proper order of _____?

1.23 *Knowledge of Classifications and Categories*
       What are the main types of _____?
       What are the major classifications of _____?
       What are the characteristics of _____?

1.24 *Knowledge of Criteria*
       Which of the following is a criterion for judging _____?
       What is the most important criterion for selecting _____?
       What criteria are used to classify _____?

1.25 *Knowledge of Methodology*
       What method is used for _____?
       What is the best way to _____?
       What would be the first step in making _____?

1.31 *Knowledge of Principles and Generalizations*
       Which statement best expresses the principle of _____?
       Which statement best summarizes the belief that _____?
       Which of the following principles best explains _____?

1.32 *Knowledge of Theories and Structures*
       Which statement is most consistent with the theory of _____?
       Which of the following best describes the structure of _____?
       What evidence best supports the theory of _____?

*Based on Bloom (1956), *Taxonomy of Educational Objectives* (see reference list in Chapter 3).

The series of questions shown in Box 4.1, of course, provides only a sample of the many possible questions that could be asked. Also, the questions are stated in rather general terms. The stems for multiple-choice items need to be more closely related to the specific learning outcome being measured.

Comprehension Items

Comprehension items typically measure at the lowest level of understanding. They determine whether the students have grasped the meaning of the material without requiring them to apply it. Comprehension can be measured by requiring students to respond in various ways, but it is important that the items contain some *novelty*. The following test items illustrate the measurement of common types of learning outcomes at the comprehension level.

EXAMPLES

Outcome: Identifies an example of a term.
  Which one of the following statements contains a *specific determiner?*
    A. America is a continent.
    B. America was discovered in 1492.
    *****C.** America has some big industries.
    D. America's population is increasing.

Outcome: Interprets the meaning of an idea.
  The statement that "test reliability is a necessary but not a sufficient condition of test validity" means that:
    A. a reliable test will have a certain degree of validity.
    *****B.** a valid test will have a certain degree of reliability.
    C. a reliable test may be completely invalid and a valid test completely unreliable.

Outcome: Identifies an example of a concept or principle.
  Which of the following is an example of a criterion-referenced interpretation?
    A. Jorge earned the highest score in science.
    B. Erik completed his experiment faster than his classmates.
    C. Edna's test score was higher than 50 percent of the class.
    *****D.** Tricia set up her laboratory equipment in five minutes.

Outcome: Predicts the most probable effect of an action.
  What is most likely to happen to the reliability of the scores for a multiple-choice test when the number of alternatives for each item is changed from three to four?
    A. It will decrease.
    *****B.** It will increase.

C. It will stay the same.
D. There is no basis for making a prediction.

In this last example, the student must recognize that increasing the number of alternatives in the items produces the same effect as lengthening the test.

These examples would, of course, represent measurement at the comprehension level only where the situations were new to the students. If the solutions to these particular problems were encountered during instruction, the items would need to be classified as knowledge outcomes.

Some of the many learning outcomes at the comprehension level that can be measured by multiple-choice items are illustrated by the incomplete questions in Box 4.2.

BOX 4.2 • *Illustrative Comprehension and Application Questions*

Comprehension Questions

Which of the following is an example of _____?
What is the main thought expressed by _____?
What are the main differences between _____?
What are the common characteristics of _____?
Which of the following is another form of _____?
Which of the following best explains _____?
Which of the following best summarizes _____?
Which of the following best illustrates _____?
What do you predict would happen if _____?
What trend do you predict in _____?

Application Questions

Which of the following methods is best for _____?
What steps should be followed in applying _____?
Which situation would require the use of _____?
Which principle would be best for solving _____?
What procedure is best for improving _____?
What procedure is best for constructing _____?
What procedure is best for correcting _____?
Which of the following is the best plan for _____?
Which of the following provides the proper sequence for _____?
What is the most probable effect of _____?

Application Items

Application items also measure understanding, but typically at a higher level than that of comprehension. Here, the students must demonstrate that they not only grasp the meaning of information but can also apply it to concrete situations that are new to them. Thus, application items determine the extent to which students can transfer their learning and use it effectively in solving new problems. Such items may call for the application of various aspects of knowledge, such as facts, concepts, principles, rules, methods, and theories. Both comprehension and application items are adaptable to practically all areas of subject matter, and they provide the basic means of measuring understanding.

The following examples illustrate the use of multiple-choice items for measuring learning outcomes at the application level.

EXAMPLES

Outcome: Distinguishes between properly and improperly stated outcomes.
   Which one of the following learning outcomes is properly stated in terms of student performance?
     A. Develops an appreciation of the importance of testing.
    *B. Explains the purpose of test specifications.
     C. Learns how to write good test items.
     D. Realizes the importance of validity.

Outcome: Improves defective test items.
   Directions: Read the following test item and then indicate the best change to make to improve the item.
   Which one of the following types of learning outcomes is most difficult to evaluate objectively?
     1. A concept.
     2. An application.
     3. An appreciation.
     4. None of the above.

The best change to make in the previous item would be to:
     A. change the stem to incomplete-statement form.
     B. use letters instead of numbers for each alternative.
     C. remove the indefinite articles "a" and "an" from the alternatives.
    *D. replace "none of the above" with "an interpretation."

When writing application items, care must be taken to select problems that the students have not encountered previously and therefore cannot solve on the basis of general knowledge alone. Each item should be so designed that it calls for application of the particular fact, concept, principle, or procedure indicated in the intended learning outcome. See Box 4.2 for

BOX 4.3 • *Multiple-Choice Items*

Strengths
1. Learning outcomes from simple to complex can be measured.
2. Highly structured and clear tasks are provided.
3. A broad sample of achievement can be measured.
4. Incorrect alternatives provide diagnostic information.
5. Scores are less influenced by guessing than true-false items.
6. Scoring is easy, objective, and reliable.

Limitations
1. Constructing good items is time consuming.
2. It is frequently difficult to find plausible distractors.
3. This item is ineffective for measuring some types of problem solving and the ability to organize and express ideas.
4. Score can be influenced by reading ability.

some of the many questions that might be asked at the application level and Box 4.3 for strengths and limitations of multiple-choice items.

Rules for Writing Multiple-Choice Items

An effective multiple-choice item presents students with a task that is both important and clearly understood, and one that can be answered correctly by anyone who has achieved the intended learning outcome. Nothing in the content or structure of the item should prevent an informed student from responding correctly. Similarly, nothing in the content or structure of the item should enable an uninformed student to select the correct answer. The following rules for item writing are intended as guides for the preparation of multiple-choice items that function as intended.

1. *Design each item to measure an important learning outcome.* The problem situation around which an item is to be built should be important and should be related to the intended learning outcome to be measured. The items in the previous section illustrate how to match items to intended outcomes. When writing the item, focus on the functioning content of the item and resist the temptation to include irrelevant material or more obscure and less significant content to increase item difficulty. Remember that the purpose of each item is to call forth the type of performance that will help determine the extent to which the intended learning outcomes have been achieved.

Items designed to measure complex achievement must contain some novelty. For example, where a knowledge item might require the identification of a textbook definition of a term, a comprehension item may require the identification of a modified form of it, and an application item may require the identification of an example of its proper use. Both the comprehension and application items would function as intended, however, only if the material was new to the students. Thus, items measuring complex achievement should require students to demonstrate that they have grasped the meaning of the material and can use it in situations that are new to them.

2. *Present a single clearly formulated problem in the stem of the item.* The task set forth in the stem of the item should be so clear that a student can understand it without reading the alternatives. In fact, a good check on the clarity and completeness of a multiple-choice stem is to cover the alternatives and determine whether it could be answered without the choices. Try this on the two sample items that follow.

EXAMPLE

Poor: A table of specifications:
   A. indicates how a test will be used to improve learning.
   *B. provides a more balanced sampling of content.
   C. arranges the instructional objectives in order of their importance.
   D. specifies the method of scoring to be used on a test.

Better: What is the main advantage of using a table of specifications when preparing an achievement test?
   A. It reduces the amount of time required.
   *B. It improves the sampling of content.
   C. It makes the construction of test items easier.
   D. It increases the objectivity of the test.

The first of these examples is no more than a collection of true-false statements with a common stem. The problem presented in the stem of the improved version is clear enough to serve as a supply-type short-answer item. The alternatives simply provide a series of possible answers from which to choose.

Note also in the second version that a *single* problem is presented in the stem. Including more than one problem usually adds to the complexity of the wording and reduces the diagnostic value of the item. When students *fail* such an item, there is no way to determine which of the problems prevented them from responding correctly.

3. *State the stem of the item in simple, clear language.* The problem in the stem of a multiple-choice item should be stated as precisely as possible and should be free of unnecessarily complex wording and sentence structure.

Anyone who possesses the knowledge measured by a test item should be able to select the correct answer. Poorly stated item stems frequently introduce sufficient ambiguity to prevent a knowledgeable student from responding correctly. Also, complex sentence structure may make the item a measure more of reading comprehension than of the intended outcome. The first of the two examples that follow is an extreme instance of this problem.

EXAMPLE

Poor: The paucity of plausible, but incorrect, statements that can be related to a central idea poses a problem when constructing which one of the following types of test items?
    A. Short answer.
    B. True-false.
    *****C.** Multiple choice.
    D. Essay.

Better: The lack of plausible, but incorrect, alternatives will cause the greatest difficulty when constructing:
    A. short-answer items.
    B. true-false items.
    *****C.** multiple-choice items.
    D. essay items.

Another common fault in stating multiple-choice items is to load the stem with irrelevant and, thus, nonfunctioning material. This is probably caused by the instructor's desire to continue to teach the students—even while testing them. The following example illustrates the use of an item stem as "another chance to inform students."

EXAMPLE

Poor: Testing can contribute to the instructional program of the school in many important ways. However, the main function of testing in teaching is:

Better: The main function of testing in teaching is:

The first version increases reading time and makes no contribution to the measurement of the specific outcome. Time spent in reading such irrelevant material could be spent more profitably in thinking about the problem presented. But if the purpose of an item is to measure a student's ability to distinguish between relevant and irrelevant material, this rule must, of course, be disregarded.

    4. *Put as much of the wording as possible in the stem of the item.* Avoid repeating the same material in each of the alternatives. By moving all of the common content to the stem, it is usually possible to clarify the problem further and to reduce the time the student needs to read the alternatives. Note the improvement in the following item when this rule is followed.

EXAMPLE

Poor: In *objective* testing, the term *objective:*
        A. refers to the method of identifying the learning outcomes.
        B. refers to the method of selecting the test content.
        C. refers to the method of presenting the problem.
      *D. refers to the method of scoring the answers.

Better: In *objective* testing, the term *objective* refers to the method of:
        A. identifying the learning outcomes.
        B. selecting the test content.
        C. presenting the problem.
      *D. scoring the answers.

In many cases the problem is not simply to move the common words to the stem but to reword the entire item. The following examples illustrate how an item can be improved by revising the stem and shortening the alternatives.

EXAMPLE

Poor: Instructional objectives are most apt to be useful for test-construction purposes when they are stated in such a way that they show:
        A. the course content to be covered during the instructional period.
      *B. the kinds of performance students should demonstrate upon reaching the goal.
        C. the things the teacher will do to obtain maximum student learning.
        D. the types of learning activities to be participated in during the course.

Better: Instructional objectives are most useful for test-construction purposes when they are stated in terms of:
        A. course content.
      *B. student performance.
        C. teacher behavior.
        D. learning activities.

It is, of course, impossible to streamline all items in this manner, but economy of wording and clarity of expression are important goals to strive for in test construction. Items function better when slim and trim.

   5. *State the stem of the item in positive form, wherever possible.* A positively phrased test item tends to measure more important learning outcomes than a negatively stated item. This is because knowing such things as the *best* method or the *most relevant* argument typically has greater educational significance than knowing the *poorest* method or the *least relevant* argument. The use of negatively stated items stems results all too frequently from the ease with which such items can be constructed rather than from the importance of the learning outcomes measured. The test maker who becomes frustrated by the inability to think of a sufficient number of plausible distracters for an item, as in the first following example, suddenly realizes how simple it would be to construct the second version.

EXAMPLE

Item one: Which one of the following is a category in the taxonomy of the cognitive domain?
   *A. Comprehension
   B. *(distracter needed)*
   C. *(distracter needed)*
   D. *(distracter needed)*

Item two: Which one of the following is *not* a category in the taxonomy of the cognitive domain?
   A. Comprehension
   B. Application
   C. Analysis
   *D. *(answer needed)*

Note in the second version that the categories of the taxonomy serve as distracters and that all that is needed to complete the item is a correct answer. This could be any term that appears plausible but is *not* one of the categories listed in the taxonomy. Although such items are easily constructed, they are apt to have a low level of difficulty and are likely to measure relatively unimportant learning outcomes. Being able to identify answers that do *not* apply provides no assurance that the student possesses the desired knowledge.

This solution to the lack of sufficient distracters is most likely to occur when the test maker is committed to the use of multiple-choice items only. A more desirable procedure for measuring the "ability to recognize the categories in the taxonomy of the cognitive domain" is to switch to a modified true-false form, as in the following example.

EXAMPLE

Directions: Indicate which of the following are categories in the taxonomy of the cognitive domain, by circling Y for *yes* and N for *no*.

   *Y N   Comprehension
   Y N* Critical Thinking
   Y N* Reasoning
   *Y N   Synthesis

In responding to this item, the student must make a separate judgment for each statement—the statement either is or is not one of the categories. Thus, the item calls for the type of performance stated in the learning outcome, yet it avoids the problems of an insufficient number of distracters and of negative phrasing.

6. *Emphasize negative wording whenever it is used in the stem of an item.* In some instances the use of negative wording is basic to the measurement of an important learning outcome. Knowing that you should *not* cross the street against a red light or should *not* mix certain chemicals, for example, is so important that these precepts might be directly taught and directly tested. Any potentially dangerous situation may require a negative emphasis. There are also, of course, less dire circumstances where negative phrasing is useful. Almost any set of rules or procedures places some emphasis on practices to be avoided.

When negative wording is used in the stem of an item, it should be emphasized by being underlined or capitalized and by being placed near the end of the statement.

EXAMPLE

Poor: Which one of the following is not a desirable practice when preparing multiple-choice items?
    A. Stating the stem in positive form.
    B. Using a stem that could function as a short-answer item.
    C. Underlining certain words in the stem for emphasis.
    *D. Shortening the stem by lengthening the alternatives.

Better: All of the following are desirable practices when preparing multiple-choice items EXCEPT:
    A. stating the stem in positive form.
    B. using a stem that could function as a short-answer item.
    C. underlining certain words in the stem for emphasis.
    *D. shortening the stem by lengthening the alternatives.

The improved version of this item assures that the item's negative aspect will not be overlooked, and it furnishes the student with the proper mind-set just before reading the alternatives.

7. *Make certain that the intended answer is correct or clearly best.* When the correct-answer form of a multiple-choice item is used, there should be only one correct answer and it should be unquestionably correct. With the best-answer form, the intended answer should be one that competent authorities would agree is clearly the best. In the latter case it may also be necessary to include "of the following" in the stem of the item to allow for equally satisfactory answers that have not been included in the item.

EXAMPLE

Poor: What is the best method of selecting course content for test items?

Better: Which one of the following is the best method of selecting course content for test items?

The proper phrasing of the stem of an item can also help avoid equivocal answers when the correct-answer form is used. In fact, an inadequately stated problem frequently makes the intended answer only partially correct or makes more than one alternative suitable.

EXAMPLE

Poor: What is the purpose of classroom testing?

Better: One purpose of classroom testing is:
                 (or)
            The main purpose of classroom testing is:

It is, of course, also necessary to check each of the distracters in the item to make certain that none of them could be defended as the correct answer. This will not only improve the quality of the item but will also prevent a disruptive argument during the discussion of the test results.

8. *Make all alternatives grammatically consistent with the stem of the item and parallel in form.* The correct answer is usually carefully phrased so that it is grammatically consistent with the stem. Where the test maker is apt to slip is in stating the distracters. Unless care is taken to check them against the wording in the stem and in the correct answer, they may be inconsistent in tense, article, or grammatical form. This, of course, could provide a clue to the correct answer, or at least make some of the distracters ineffective.

A general step that can be taken to prevent grammatical inconsistency is to avoid using the articles "a" or "an" at the end of the stem of the item.

EXAMPLE

Poor: The recall of factual information can be measured best with a:
        A. matching item.
        B. multiple-choice item.
      *C. short-answer item.
        D. essay question.

Better: The recall of factual information can be measured best with:
        A. matching items.
        B. multiple-choice items.
      *C. short-answer items.
        D. essay questions.

The indefinite article "a" in the first version makes the last distracter obviously wrong. By simply changing the alternatives from singular to plural, it is possible to omit the article. In other cases, it may be necessary to add an article ("a," "an," or as appropriate) to each alternative or to rephrase the entire item.

Stating all of the alternatives in parallel form also tends to prevent unnecessary clues from being given to the students. When the grammatical structure of one alternative differs from that of the others, some students may more readily detect that alternative as a correct or an incorrect response.

> **EXAMPLE**
>
> *Poor:*   Why should negative terms be avoided in the stem of a multiple-choice item?
> >   *A. They may be overlooked.
> >   B. The stem tends to be longer.
> >   C. The construction of alternatives is more difficult.
> >   D. The scoring is more difficult.
>
> *Better:*   Why should negative terms be avoided in the stem of a multiple-choice item?
> >   *A. They may be overlooked.
> >   B. They tend to increase the length of the stem.
> >   C. They make the construction of alternatives more difficult.
> >   D. They may increase the difficulty of the scoring.

In the first version some students who lack the knowledge called for are apt to select the correct answer because of the way it is stated. The parallel grammatical structure in the second version removes this clue.

9. *Avoid verbal clues that might enable students to select the correct answer or to eliminate an incorrect alternative.* One of the most common sources of extraneous clues in multiple-choice items is the wording of the item. Some such clues are rather obvious and are easily avoided. Others require the constant attention of the test maker to prevent them from slipping in unnoticed. Let's review some of the verbal clues commonly found in multiple-choice items.

(a) *Similarity of wording in both the stem and the correct answer* is one of the most obvious clues. Key words in the stem may unintentionally be repeated verbatim in the correct answer, a synonym may be used, or the words may simply sound or look alike.

> **EXAMPLE**
>
> *Poor:*   Which one of the following would you consult first to locate research articles on achievement testing?

A. *Journal of Educational Psychology*
B. *Journal of Educational Measurement*
C. *Journal of Consulting Psychology*
*D. *Review of Educational Research*

The word "research" in both the stem and the correct answer is apt to provide a clue to the correct answer to the uninformed but testwise student. Such obvious clues might better be used in both the stem and an *incorrect* answer, in order to lead the uninformed *away* from the correct answer.

(b) *Stating the correct answer in textbook language or stereotyped phraseology* may cause students to select it because it looks better than the other alternatives, or because they vaguely recall having seen it before.

EXAMPLE

Poor: Learning outcomes are most useful in preparing tests when they are:
    *A. clearly stated in performance terms.
    B. developed cooperatively by teachers and students.
    C. prepared after the instruction has ended.
    D. stated in general terms.

The pat phrasing of the correct answer is likely to give it away. Even the most poorly prepared student is apt to recognize the often repeated phrase "clearly stated in performance terms," without having the foggiest notion of what it means.

(c) *Stating the correct answer in greater detail* may provide a clue. Also, when the answer is qualified by modifiers that are typically associated with true statements (for example, "sometimes," "may," "usually"), it is more likely to be chosen.

EXAMPLE

Poor: Lack of attention to learning outcomes during test preparation:
    A. will lower the technical quality of the items.
    B. will make the construction of test items more difficult.
    C. will result in the greater use of essay questions.
    *D. may result in a test that is less relevant to the instructional program.

The term "may" is rather obvious in this example, but this type of error is common and appears frequently in a subtler form.

(d) *Including absolute terms in the distracters* enables students to eliminate them as possible answers because such terms ("always," "never," "all," "none," "only,") are commonly associated with false statements. This makes the correct answer obvious, or at least increases the chances that the students who do not know the answer will guess it.

EXAMPLE

Poor: Achievement tests help students improve their learning by:
   A. encouraging them all to study hard.
   ***B.** informing them of their progress.
   C. giving them all a feeling of success.
   D. preventing any of them from neglecting their assignments.

Such absolutes tend to be used by the inexperienced test maker to assure that the incorrect alternatives are clearly wrong. Unfortunately, they are easily recognized by the student as unlikely answers, making them ineffective as distracters.

(e) *Including two responses that are all inclusive* makes it possible to eliminate the other alternatives, since one of the two must obviously be the correct answer.

EXAMPLE

Poor: Which one of the following types of test items measures learning outcomes at the recall level?
   ***A.** Supply-type items.
   B. Selection-type items.
   C. Matching items.
   D. Multiple-choice items.

Since the first two alternatives include the only two major types of test items, even poorly prepared students are likely to limit their choices to these two. This, of course, gives them a fifty-fifty chance of guessing the correct answer.

(f) *Including two responses that have the same meaning* makes it possible to eliminate them as potential answers. If two alternatives have the same meaning and only one answer is to be selected, it is fairly obvious that both alternatives must be incorrect.

EXAMPLE

Poor: Which one of the following is the most important characteristic achievement-test results?
   A. Consistency
   B. Reliability
   ***C.** Relevance
   D. Objectivity

In this item both "consistency" and "reliability" can be eliminated because they mean essentially the same thing.

Extraneous clues to the correct answer must be excluded from test items if the items are to function as intended. It is frequently good practice, however, to use such clues to lead the uninformed away from the correct answer. If not overdone, this can contribute to the plausibility of the incorrect alternatives.

10. *Make the distracters plausible and attractive to the uninformed.* The distracters in a multiple-choice item should be so appealing to the students who lack the knowledge called for by the item that they select one of the distracters in preference to the correct answer. This is the ideal, of course, but one toward which the test maker must work continually. The art of constructing good multiple-choice items depends heavily on the development of effective distracters.

You can do a number of things to increase the plausibility and attractiveness of distracters:

a. Use the common misconceptions or errors of students as distracters.
b. State the alternatives in the language of the student.
c. Use "good-sounding" words ("accurate," "important,") in the distracters as well as in the correct answer.
d. Make the distracters similar to the correct answer in both length and complexity of wording.
e. Use extraneous clues in the distracters, such as stereotyped phrasing, scientific-sounding answers, and verbal associations with the stem of the item. But don't overuse these clues to the point where they become ineffective.
f. Make the alternatives homogeneous, but in doing so beware of fine discriminations that are educationally insignificant.

The greater plausibility resulting from the use of more homogenous alternatives can be seen in the improved version of the following item.

EXAMPLE

Poor: Obtaining a dependable ranking of students is of major concern when using:
   *A. norm-referenced summative tests.
   B. behavior descriptions.
   C. checklists.
   D. questionnaires.

Better: Obtaining a dependable ranking of students is of major concern when using:
   *A. norm-referenced summative tests.
   B. teacher-made diagnostic tests.
   C. mastery achievement tests.
   D. criterion-referenced formative tests.

The improved version not only increases the plausibility of the distracters but it also calls for a type of discrimination that is more educationally significant.

11. *Vary the relative length of the correct answer to eliminate length as a clue.* There is a tendency for the correct answer to be longer than the alternatives because of the need to qualify statements to make them unequivocally correct. This, of course, provides a clue to the testwise student. Learning this fact, the inexperienced test maker frequently makes a special effort to avoid ever having the correct answer longer than the other alternatives. This, of course, also provides a clue, and the alert student soon learns to dismiss the longest alternative as a possible answer.

The relative length of the correct answer can be removed as a clue by varying it in such a manner that no apparent pattern is provided. That is, it should sometimes be longer, sometimes shorter, and sometimes of equal length—but never consistently or predominantly of one relative length. In some cases it is more desirable to make the alternatives approximately equal length by adjusting the distracters rather than the correct answer.

> **EXAMPLE**
>
> *Poor:*   One advantage of multiple-choice items over essay questions is that they:
> - **A.** measure more complex outcomes.
> - **B.** depend more on recall.
> - **C.** require less time to score.
> - ***D.** provide for a more extensive sampling of course content.
>
> *Better:*   One advantage of multiple-choice items over essay questions is that they:
> - **A.** provide for the measurement of more complex learning outcomes.
> - **B.** place greater emphasis on the recall of factual information.
> - **C.** require less time for test preparation and scoring.
> - ***D.** provide for a more extensive sampling of course content.

Lengthening the distracters, as was done in the improved version, removes length as a clue and increases the plausibility of the distracters, which are now more similar to the correct answer in complexity of wording.

12. *Avoid using the alternative "all of the above," and use "none of the above" with extreme caution.* When test makers are having difficulty in locating a sufficient number of distracters, they frequently resort to the use of "all of the above" or "none of the above" as the final option. These special alternatives are seldom used appropriately and almost always render the item less effective than it would be without them.

The inclusion of "all of the above" as an option makes it possible to answer the item on the basis of partial information. Since students are to select only one answer, they can detect "all of the above" as the correct choice simply by noting that two of the alternatives are correct. They can also detect it as a wrong answer by recognizing that at least one of the alternatives is incorrect; of course, their chance of guessing the correct answer from the remaining choices then increases proportionately. Another difficulty with this option is that some students, recognizing that the first choice is correct, will select it without reading the remaining alternatives.

Obviously, the use of "none of the above" is not possible with the best-answer type of multiple-choice item, since the alternatives vary in appropriateness and the criterion of absolute correctness is not applicable. When used as the right answer in a correct-answer type of item, this option may be measuring nothing more than the ability to detect incorrect answers. Recognizing that certain answers are wrong is no guarantee that the student knows what is correct. For example, a student may be able to answer the following item correctly without being able to name the categories in the taxonomy.

EXAMPLE

Poor: Which of the following is a category in the taxonomy of the cognitive domain?
   A. Critical Thinking
   B. Scientific Thinking
   C. Reasoning Ability
   *__D.__ None of the above

All students need to know to answer this item correctly is that the taxonomy categories are new and different from those that they have commonly associated with intellectual skills. Items such as this provide rather poor evidence for judging a student's achievement.

The alternative "none of the above" is probably used more widely with computational problems that are presented in multiple-choice form. The publishers of standardized achievement tests have resorted to multiple-choice items for such problems in order to make machine scoring possible, and they have resorted to the alternative "none of the above" in order to reduce the likelihood of the student estimating the answer without performing the entire computation. Although this use of "none of the above" may be defensible, there is seldom a need to use multiple-choice items for computational problems in classroom tests. The supply-type item that requires the student to solve the problems and record the answers provides the most direct and useful measure of computational skill. This is another case in which it is desirable to switch from multiple-choice items to another item type in order to obtain more effective measurement.

13. *Vary the position of the correct answer in a random manner.* The correct answer should appear in each alternative position about the same number of times, but its placement should not follow a pattern that may be apparent to the person taking the test. Students who detect that the correct answer never appears in the same position more than twice in a row, or that A is the correct answer on every fourth item, are likely to obtain a higher score than their knowledge would warrant. Such clues can be avoided by random placement of the correct answer.

The easiest way to randomly assign the position of the correct answer in a multiple-choice item is to develop a code with the aid of a book: simply open any book at a random place, look at the right-hand page, and let the last digit of the page number determine the placement of the correct answer. Since the right-hand page always ends in an odd number, the code might be as follows: the digit 1 indicates that the correct answer will be placed in position A, 3 = B, 5 = C, 7 = D, and 9 = E.

Sufficient variation without a discernible pattern might also be obtained by simply placing the responses in alphabetical order, based on the first letter in each, and letting the correct answer fall where it will.

When the alternative responses are numbers, they should always be listed in order of size, preferably in ascending order. This will eliminate the possibility of a clue, such as the correct answer being the only one that is not in numerical order.

14. *Control the difficulty of the item either by varying the problem in the stem or by changing the alternatives.* It is usually preferable to increase item difficulty by increasing the level of knowledge called for by making the problem more complex. However, it is also possible to increase difficulty by making the alternatives more homogeneous. When this is done, care must be taken that the finer discriminations called for are educationally significant and are in harmony with the learning outcomes to be measured.

15. *Make certain each item is independent of the other items in the test.* Occasionally information given in the stem of one item will help the students answer another item. This can be remedied easily by a careful review of the items before they are assembled into a test.

A different type of problem occurs when the correct answer to an item depends on knowing the correct answer to the item preceding it. The student who is unable to answer the first item, of course, has no basis for responding to the second. Such chains of interlocking items should be avoided. Each item should be an independently scorable unit.

16. *Use an efficient item format.* The alternatives should be listed on separate lines, under one another, like the examples in this chapter. This makes the alternatives easy to read and compare. It also contributes to ease of scoring since the letters of the alternatives all appear on the left side of the paper. A copy of the test can be used as a scoring stencil: Simply circle the letters of the correct answers on the copy, then place the copy next to the student's paper so that the columns of letters correspond.

The use of letters in front of the alternatives is preferable to the use of numbers, since numerical answers in numbered items may be confusing to the students.

17. *Follow the normal rules of grammar.* If the stem is in question form, begin each alternative with a capital letter and end with a period or other appropriate punctuation mark. Omit the period with numerical answers, however, to avoid confusion with decimal points. When the stem is an incomplete statement, start each alternative with a lower-case letter and end with whatever terminal punctuation mark is appropriate.

18. *Break (or bend) any of these rules if it will improve the effectiveness of the item.* These rules for constructing multiple-choice items are stated rather dogmatically as an aid to the beginner. As experience in item writing is obtained, situations are likely to occur where ignoring or modifying a rule may be desirable. In a problem-solving item, for example, it may be useful to include extraneous information in the stem to see if students can select what is needed to solve the problem. Until sufficient experience in item writing is gained, however, following the rules in this chapter will yield test items of fairly good quality. See Box 4.4 for summary checklist.

BOX 4.4 • *Checklist for Evaluating Multiple-Choice Items*

1. Is this type of item appropriate for measuring the intended learning outcome?
2. Does the item task match the learning task to be measured?
3. Does the stem of the item present a single, clearly formulated problem?
4. Is the stem stated in simple, clear language?
5. Is the stem worded so that there is no repetition of material in the alternatives?
6. Is the stem stated in positive form wherever possible?
7. If negative wording is used in the stem, is it emphasized (by underlining or caps)?
8. Is the intended answer correct or clearly best?
9. Are all alternatives grammatically consistent with the stem and parallel in form?
10. Are the alternatives free from verbal clues to the correct answer?
11. Are the distracters plausible and attractive to the uninformed?
12. To eliminate length as a clue, is the relative length of the correct answer varied?
13. Has the alternative "all of the above" been avoided and "none of the above" used only when appropriate?
14. Is the position of the correct answer varied so that there is no detectable pattern?
15. Does the item format and grammar usage provide for efficient test taking?

Summary of Points

1. The multiple-choice item is the most highly regarded and useful selection-type item.
2. The multiple-choice item consists of a stem and a set of alternative answers (options or choices).
3. The multiple-choice item can be designed to measure various intended learning outcomes, ranging from simple to complex.
4. Knowledge items typically measure the simple remembering of material.
5. Comprehension items measure the extent to which students have grasped the meaning of material.
6. Application items measure whether students can use information in concrete situations.
7. Items designed to measure achievement beyond the knowledge level must contain some novelty.
8. The stem of a multiple-choice item should present a single, clearly formulated problem that is related to an important learning outcome.
9. The intended answer should be correct or clearly best, as agreed upon by authorities.
10. The distracters (incorrect alternatives) should be plausible enough to lead the uninformed away from the correct answer.
11. The items should be written in simple, clear language that is free of non-functioning content.
12. The items should be free of irrelevant sources of difficulty (e.g., ambiguity) that might prevent an informed examinee from answering correctly.
13. The items should be free of irrelevant clues (e.g., verbal associations) that might enable an uninformed examinee to answer correctly.
14. The item format should provide for efficient responding and follow the normal rules of grammar.
15. The rules of item writing provide a framework for preparing effective multiple-choice items, but experience in item writing may result in modifications to fit particular situations.

References and Additional Reading

Carey, L. M., *Measuring and Evaluating School Learning*, 3rd ed. (Boston: Allyn and Bacon, 2001).

Haladyna, T. M., *Writing Test Items to Evaluate Higher Order Thinking* (Boston: Allyn and Bacon, 1997).

Linn, R. L., and Gronlund, N. E., *Measurement and Assessment in Teaching*, 8th ed. (Upper Saddle River, NJ: Merrill/ Prentice-Hall, 2000).

Oosterhoff, A. C., *Classroom Applications of Educational Measurement*, 3rd ed. (Upper Saddle River, NJ: Merrill/ Prentice-Hall, 2001).

5

Writing Selection Items

True-False, Matching, and Interpretive Exercise

Studying this chapter should enable you to

1. Describe the characteristics of each item type.
2. Describe the strengths and limitations of each item type.
3. Distinguish between well-stated and poorly stated items of each type.
4. Identify and correct faults in poorly stated items of each type.
5. Match each item type to intended learning outcomes.
6. Construct items of each type that are well-stated, relevant to important learning outcomes, and free of defects.

The multiple-choice item provides the most generally useful format for measuring achievement at various levels of learning. Thus, when selection-type items are to be used, an effective procedure is to start each item as a multiple-choice item and switch to another item type only when the learning outcome and content make it desirable to do so. For example, (1) when there are only two possible alternatives, a shift can be made to a true-false item; (2) when there are a number of similar factors to be related, a shift can be made to a matching item; and (3) when the items are to measure analysis, interpretation, and other complex outcomes, a shift can be made to the interpretive exercise. This procedure makes it possible to use the special strengths of the multiple-choice item and to use the other selection-type items more appropriately.

True-False Items

True-false items are typically used to measure the ability to identify whether statements of fact are correct. The basic format is simply a declarative statement that the student must judge as true or false. There are modifications of this basic form in which the student must respond "yes" or "no," "agree" or "disagree," "right" or "wrong," "fact" or "opinion," and the like. Such variations are usually given the more general name of *alternative-response* items. In any event, this item type is characterized by the fact that only two responses are possible.

EXAMPLE

T   *F   True-false items are classified as a supply-type item.

In some cases the student is asked to judge each statement as true or false, and then to change the false statements so that they are true. When this is done, a portion of each statement is underlined to indicate the part that can be changed. In the example given, for instance, the words "supply-type" would be underlined. The key parts of true statements, of course, must also be underlined.

Another variation is the cluster-type true-false format. In this case, a series of items is based on a common stem.

EXAMPLE

Which of the following terms indicate observable student performance? Circle Y for yes and N for no.
*Y   N   **1.** Explains
*Y   N   **2.** Identifies
 Y   *N   **3.** Learns
*Y   N   **4.** Predicts
 Y   *N   **5.** Realizes

This item format is especially useful for replacing multiple-choice items that have more than one correct answer. Such items are impossible to score satisfactorily. This is avoided with the cluster-type item because it makes each alternative a separate scoring unit of one point. In our example, the student must record whether each term does or does not indicate observable student performance. Thus, this set of items provides an even better measure of the "ability to distinguish between performance and nonperformance terms" than would the single answer multiple-choice item. This is a good illustration of the procedure discussed earlier—that is, starting with multiple-choice items and switching to other item types when more effective measurement will result.

Despite the limitations of the true-false item, there are situations where it should be used. Whenever there are only two possible responses, the true-false item, or some adaptation of it, is likely to provide the most effective measure. Situations of this type include a simple "yes" or "no" response in classifying objects, determining whether a rule does or does not apply, distinguishing fact from opinion, and indicating whether arguments are relevant or irrelevant. As we indicated earlier, the best procedure is to use the true-false, or alternative-response, item only when this item type is more appropriate than the multiple-choice form. See Box 5.1 for a summary of strengths and limitations.

Rules for Writing True-False Items

The purpose of a true-false item, as with all item types, is to distinguish between those who have and those who have not achieved the intended learning outcome. Achievers should be able to select the correct alternative without difficulty, while nonachievers should find the incorrect alternative at least as attractive as the correct one. The rules for writing true-false items are directed toward this end.

BOX 5.1 • *True-False Items*

Strengths
1. The item is useful for outcomes where there are only two possible alternatives (e.g., fact or opinion, valid or invalid).
2. Less demand is placed on reading ability than in multiple-choice items.
3. A relatively large number of items can be answered in a typical testing period.
4. Complex outcomes can be measured when used with interpretive exercises.
5. Scoring is easy, objective, and reliable.

Limitations
1. It is difficult to write items beyond the knowledge level that are free from ambiguity.
2. Making an item false provides no evidence that the student knows what is correct.
3. No diagnostic information is provided by the incorrect answers.
4. Scores are more influenced by guessing than with any other item type.

1. *Include only one central idea in each statement.* The main point of the item should be in a prominent position in the statement. The true-false decision should not depend on some subordinate point or trivial detail. The use of several ideas in each statement should generally be avoided because these tend to be confusing and the answer is more apt to be influenced by reading ability than the intended outcome.

EXAMPLE

Poor: T   *F   The true-false item, which is favored by test experts, is also called an alternative-response item.

Better: *T   F   The true-false item is also called an alternative-response item.

The "poor" example must be marked false because test experts do not favor the true-false item. Such subordinate points are easily overlooked when reading the item. If the point is important, it should be included as the main idea in a separate item.

2. *Keep the statement short and use simple vocabulary and sentence structure.* A short, simple statement will increase the likelihood that the point of the item is clear. All students should be able to grasp what the statement is saying. Passing or failing the item should depend solely on whether a student has achieved the necessary knowledge.

EXAMPLE

Poor: *T   F   The true-false item is more subject to guessing but it should be used in place of a multiple-choice item, if well constructed, when there is a dearth of distracters that are plausible.

Better: *T   F   The true-false item should be used in place of a multiple-choice item when only two alternatives are possible.

Long, involved statements like the "poor" version tend to contaminate the achievement measure with a measure of reading comprehension. A basic rule of item writing is to focus on the intended function of the item and remove all irrelevant influences.

3. *Word the statement so precisely that it can unequivocally be judged true or false.* True statements should be true under all circumstances and yet free of qualifiers ("may," "possible," and so on), which might provide clues. This requires the use of precise words and the avoidance of such vague terms as "seldom," "frequently," and "often." The same care, of course, must also be given to false statements so that their falsity is not too readily apparent from differences in wording. At first glance, this seems like a simple rule to follow but it causes frequent problems.

EXAMPLE

Poor: T   *F   Lengthening a test will increase its reliability.

Better: *T   F   Lengthening a test by adding items like those in the test will increase its reliability.

The "poor" version of this item must be marked false because it is not true under all conditions. For example, if items are added to the test that all students fail, reliability would not be changed. However, the "poor" version would not be a good item to use in a test because it requires students to mark a very important principle of measurement false. We could say "usually will increase" but the qualifier would encourage those who are uninformed to mark it true and they would receive an unearned point. The "better" version has no such "giveaway" to the answer. In fact, an uninformed student might think that adding similar items to a test of low reliability could not possibly increase reliability—but it does. This example illustrates the great care needed in phrasing statements so that they are unequivocally true but do not contain "giveaways" to the answer.

4. *Use negative statements sparingly and avoid double negatives.* The "no" and/or "not" in negative statements are frequently overlooked and they are read as positive statements. Thus, negative statements should be used only when the learning outcome requires it (e.g., in avoiding a harmful practice), and then the negative words should be emphasized by underlining or by use of capital letters. Statements including double negatives tend to be so confusing that they should be restated in positive form.

EXAMPLE

Poor: *T   F   Correction-for-guessing is *not* a practice that should *never* be used in testing.

Better: *T   F   Correction-for-guessing is a practice that should sometimes be used in testing.

The double negatives in the "poor" version introduce sufficient ambiguity to cause the item to be a measure of reading comprehension. The "better" version clearly states the same idea in positive form.

5. *Statements of opinion should be attributed to some source unless used to distinguish facts from opinion.* A statement of opinion is not true or false by itself, and it is poor instructional practice to have students respond to it as if it were a factual statement. Obviously, the only way students could mark such an item correctly would be to agree with the opinion of the item writer. It is much more defensible to attribute the item to some source, such as an individual or organization. It then becomes a measure of how well the student knows the beliefs or values of that individual or organization.

EXAMPLE

Poor: T   F   Testing should play a major role in the teaching-learning process.

Better: *T   F   Gronlund believes that testing should play a major role in the teaching-learning process.

In some cases, it is useful to use a series of opinion statements that pertain to the same individual or organization. This permits a more comprehensive measure of how well the student understands a belief or value system.

EXAMPLE

Would the author of your textbook agree or disagree with the following statements? Circle A for agree, D for disagree.

*A   D   **1.** The first step in achievement testing is to state the intended learning outcomes in performance terms.

A   *D   **2.** True-false tests are superior to multiple-choice tests for measuring achievement.

Using about 10 items like those listed here would provide a fairly good indication of the students' grasp of the author's point of view. Items like this are useful for measuring how well students understand a textbook without requiring them to agree with the opinions expressed. It is desirable, of course, to select opinion statements that are shared by many experts in the area.

Another valuable use of opinion statements is to ask students to distinguish between statements of fact and statements of opinion. This is an important outcome in its own right and is a basic part of critical thinking.

EXAMPLE

Read each of the following statements and circle F if it is a *fact* and circle O if it is an *opinion*.

*F   O   **1.** The true-false item is a selection-type item.
F   *O   **2.** The true-false item is difficult to construct.
F   *O   **3.** The true-false item encourages student guessing.
*F   O   **4.** The true-false item can be scored objectively.

In addition to illustrating the use of opinion statements in test items, the last two examples illustrate variations from the typical true-false format. These are more logically called *alternative-response* items.

6. When cause-effect relationships are being measured, use only true propositions. The true-false item can be used to measure the "ability to identify cause-effect relationships" and this is an important aspect of understanding. When used for this purpose, both propositions should be true and only the relationship judged true or false.

EXAMPLE

Poor:	T	*F	True-false items are classified as objective items	*because*	students must supply the answer.
Better:	T	*F	True-false items are classified as objective items	*because*	there are only two possible answers.

The "poor" version is false because of the second part of the statement. With true-false items, students must *select* the answer rather than *supply* it. However, some students may mark this item false because they think the first part of the statement is incorrect. Thus, they receive one point because they *do not know* that true-false items are classified as objective items. Obviously, an item does not function as intended if misinformation can result in the correct answer. The problem with the "poor" version is that all three elements are permitted to vary (part one, part two, and the relationship between them) and it is impossible to tell what part the student is responding to when the item is marked false. In the "better" version both parts of the statement are true and the students must simply decide if the second part explains why the first part is true. In this case it does not, so it is marked false. Typically, a series of items like this is preceded by directions that make clear that only the relationship between the two parts of each statement is to be judged true or false.

7. *Avoid extraneous clues to the answer.* There are a number of *specific determiners* that provide verbal clues to the truth or falsity of an item. Statements that include such absolutes as "always," "never," "all," "none," and "only" tend to be false; statements with qualifiers such as "usually," "may," and "sometimes" tend to be true. Either these verbal clues must be eliminated from the statements, or their use must be balanced between true items and false items.

EXAMPLE

Poor:	T	*F	A statement of opinion should never be used in a true-false item.
Poor:	*T	F	A statement of opinion may be used in a true-false item.
Better:	*T	F	A statement of opinion, by itself, cannot be marked true or false.

BOX 5.2 • *Checklist for Evaluating True-False Items*

1. Is this type of item appropriate for measuring the intended learning outcome?
2. Does the item task match the learning task to be measured?
3. Does each statement contain one central idea?
4. Can each statement be unequivocally judged true or false?
5. Are the statements brief and stated in simple, clear language?
6. Are negative statements used sparingly and double negatives avoided?
7. Are statements of opinion attributed to some source?
8. Are the statements free of clues to the answer (e.g., verbal clues, length)?
9. Is there approximately an even number of true and false statements?
10. When arranged in the test, are the true and false items put in random order?

The length and complexity of the statement might also provide a clue. True statements tend to be longer and more complex than false ones because of their need for qualifiers. Thus, a special effort should be made to equalize true and false statements in these respects.

A tendency to use a disproportionate number of true statements, or false statements, might also be detected and used as a clue. Having approximately, but not exactly, an equal number of each seems to be the best solution. When assembling the test, it is, of course, also necessary to avoid placing the correct answers in some discernible pattern (for instance, T, F, T, F). Random placement will eliminate this possible clue.

8. *Base items on introductory material to measure more complex learning outcomes.* True-false or alternative-response items are frequently used in interpreting written materials, tables, graphs, maps, or pictures. The use of introductory material makes it possible to measure various types of complex learning outcomes. These item types will be illustrated in the section on interpretive exercises later in this chapter. See Box 5.2 for summary checklist for evaluation of true-false items.

Matching Items

The matching item is simply a variation of the multiple-choice form. A good practice is to switch to the matching format only when it becomes apparent that the same alternatives are being repeated in several multiple-choice items. See Box 5.3 for the strengths and limitations of matching items.

EXAMPLE

Which test item is *least* useful for educational diagnosis?
    A. Multiple-choice item.
  *B.** True-false item.
    C. Short-answer item.

BOX 5.3 • *Matching Items*

Strengths
1. A compact and efficient form is provided where the same set of responses fit a series of item stems (i.e., premises).
2. Reading and response time is short.
3. This item type is easily constructed if converted from multiple-choice items having a common set of alternatives.
4. Scoring is easy, objective, and reliable.

Limitations
1. This item type is largely restricted to simple knowledge outcomes based on association.
2. It is difficult to construct items that contain a sufficient number of homogeneous responses.
3. Susceptibility to irrelevant clues is greater than in other item types.

Which test item measures the greatest variety of learning outcomes?
   *A. Multiple-choice item.
   B. True-false item.
   C. Short-answer item.

Which test item is difficult to score objectively?
   A. Multiple-choice item.
   B. True-false item.
   *C. Short-answer item.

Which test item provides the highest score by guessing?
   A. Multiple-choice item.
   *B. True-false item.
   C. Short-answer item.

By switching to a matching format, we can eliminate the repetition of the alternative answers and present the same items in a more compact form. The matching format consists of a series of stems, called *premises,* and a series of alternative answers, called *responses.* These are arranged in columns with directions that set the rules for matching. The following example illustrates how our multiple-choice items can be converted to matching form.

EXAMPLE

Directions: Column A contains a list of characteristics of test items. On the line to the left of each statement, write the letter of the test item in Column B that best fits the statement. Each response in Column B may be used once, more than once, or not at all.

Column A		Column B
(B)	**1.** Least useful for educational diagnosis.	**A.** Multiple-choice item.
(A)	**2.** Measures greatest variety of learning outcomes.	**B.** True-false item.
(C)	**3.** Most difficult to score objectively.	**C.** Short-answer item.
(B)	**4.** Provides the highest score by guessing.	

The conversion to matching item illustrated here is probably the most defensible use of this item type. All too frequently, matching items consist of a disparate collection of premises, each of which has only one or two plausible answers. This can be avoided by starting with multiple-choice items and switching to the matching format only when it provides a more compact and efficient means of measuring the same achievement. In our example, we could have also expanded the item by adding other similar premises and responses.

Rules for Writing Matching Items

A good matching item should function the same as a series of multiple-choice items. As each premise is considered, all of the responses should serve as plausible alternatives. The rules for item writing are directed toward this end.

1. *Include only homogeneous material in each matching item.* In our earlier example of a matching item, we included *only* types of test items and their characteristics. Similarly, an item might include *only* authors and their works, inventors and their inventions, scientists and their discoveries, or historical events and their dates. This homogeneity is necessary if all responses are to serve as plausible alternatives (see earlier example).

2. *Keep the lists of items short and place the brief responses on the right.* A short list of items (say less than 10) will save reading time, make it easier for the student to locate the answer, and increase the likelihood that the responses will be homogeneous and plausible. Placing the brief responses on the right also saves reading time.

3. *Use a larger, or smaller, number of responses than premises, and permit the responses to be used more than once.* Both an uneven match and the possibility of using each response more than once reduces the guessing factor. As we noted earlier, proper use of the matching form requires that *all responses be plausible alternatives for each premise.* This, of course, dictates that each response be eligible for use more than once.

4. *Place the responses in alphabetical or numerical order.* This will make selection of the responses easier and avoid possible clues due to placement.

BOX 5.4 • *Checklist for Evaluating Matching Items*

---

1. Is this type of item appropriate for measuring the intended learning outcome?
2. Does the item task match the learning task to be measured?
3. Does each matching item contain only homogeneous material?
4. Are the lists of items short with the brief responses on the right?
5. Is an uneven match provided by making the list of responses longer or shorter than the list of premises?
6. Are the responses in alphabetical or numerical order?
7. Do the directions clearly state the basis for matching and that each response can be used once, more than once, or not at all?
8. Does the complete matching item appear on the same page?

---

5. *Specify in the directions the basis for matching and indicate that each response may be used once, more than once, or not at all.* This will clarify the task for all students and prevent any misunderstanding. Take care, however, not to make the directions too long and involved. The previous example illustrates adequate detail for directions.

6. *Put all of the matching item on the same page.* This will prevent the distraction of flipping pages back and forth and prevent students from overlooking responses on another page. See Box 5.4 for a summary checklist for evaluating matching items.

The Interpretive Exercise

Complex learning outcomes can frequently be more effectively measured by basing a series of test items on a common selection of introductory material. This may be a paragraph, a table, a chart, a graph, a map, or a picture. The test items that follow the introductory material may be designed to call forth any type of intellectual ability or skill that can be measured objectively. This type of exercise is commonly called an *interpretive exercise* and both multiple-choice items and alternative-response items are widely used to measure interpretation of the introductory material.

The following example illustrates the use of multiple-choice items. Note that this item type makes it possible to measure a variety of learning outcomes with the same selection of introductory material. In this particular case, item 1 measures the *ability to recognize unstated assumptions,* item 2 the *ability to identify the meaning of a term,* and item 3 the *ability to identify relationships.*

EXAMPLE

Directions: Read the following comments a teacher made about testing. Then answer the questions that follow by circling the letter of the best answer.

"Students go to school to learn, not to take tests. In addition, tests cannot be used to indicate a student's absolute level of learning. All tests can do is rank students in order of achievement, and this relative ranking is influenced by guessing, bluffing, and the subjective opinions of the teacher doing the scoring. The teacher-learning process would benefit if we did away with tests and depended on student self-evaluation."

1. Which one of the following unstated assumptions is this teacher making?
    A. Students go to school to learn.
    B. Teachers use essay tests primarily.
    *C. Tests make no contribution to learning.
    D. Tests do not indicate a student's absolute level of learning.

2. Which one of the following types of tests is this teacher primarily talking about?
    A. Diagnostic test.
    B. Formative test.
    C. Pretest.
    *D. Summative test.

3. Which one of the following propositions is most essential to the final conclusion?
    *A. Effective self-evaluation does not require the use of tests.
    B. Tests place students in rank order only.
    C. Tests scores are influenced by factors other than achievement.
    D. Students do not go to school to take tests.

The next example uses a modified version of the alternative-response form. This is frequently called a *key-type* item because a common set of alternatives is used in responding to each question. Note that the key-type item is devoted entirely to the measurement of one learning outcome. In this example the item measures the *ability to recognize warranted and unwarranted inferences.*

EXAMPLE

Directions: Paragraph A contains a description of the testing practices of Mr. Smith, a high school teacher. Read the description and each of the statements that follow it. Mark each statement to indicate the type of INFERENCE that can be drawn about it from the material in the paragraph. Place the appropriate letter in front of each statement using the following KEY:

    T—if the statement may be INFERRED as TRUE.
    F—if the statement may be INFERRED as UNTRUE.
    N—if NO INFERENCE may be drawn about it from the paragraph.

Paragraph A

Approximately one week before a test is to be given, Mr. Smith carefully goes through the textbook and constructs multiple-choice items based on the material in the book. He always uses the exact wording of the textbook for the correct answer so that there will be no question concerning its correctness. He is careful to include some test items from each chapter. After the test is given, he lists the scores from high to low on the blackboard and tells each student his or her score. He does not return the test papers to the students, but he offers to answer any questions they might have about the test. He puts the items from each test into a test file, which he is building for future use.

Statements on Paragraph A

(T) **1.** Mr. Smith's tests measure a limited range of learning outcomes.
(F) **2.** Some of Mr. Smith's test items measure at the understanding level.
(N) **3.** Mr. Smith's tests measure a balanced sample of subject matter.
(N) **4.** Mr. Smith uses the type of test item that is best for his purpose.
(T) **5.** Students can determine where they rank in the distribution of scores on Mr. Smith's tests.
(F) **6.** Mr. Smith's testing practices are likely to motivate students to overcome their weaknesses.

Key-type items are fairly easy to develop and can be directly related to specific learning outcomes. The key categories can, of course, be reused by simply changing the introductory material and the statements. Thus, they provide a standard framework for test preparation. Other common key categories include the following: (1) the argument is relevant, irrelevant, or neither; (2) the statement is supported by the evidence, refuted by the evidence, or neither; (3) the assumption is necessary or unnecessary; and (4) the conclusion is valid, invalid, or its validity cannot be determined. Although such standard key categories should not be applied in a perfunctory manner, they can provide guidelines to simplify the construction of the interpretive exercise. See Box 5.5 for strengths and limitations.

Rules for Constructing Interpretive Exercises

The effectiveness of interpretive exercises, such as those illustrated earlier, depends on the care with which the introductory material is selected and the skill with which the dependent items are prepared. The following rules provide guidelines for preparing high quality exercises of this type.

1. *Select introductory material that is relevant to the learning outcomes to be measured.* The introductory material may take many forms: written material, table, chart, graph, map, picture, or cartoon. In some cases the interpretation of the introductory material is an important learning outcome in its own right, as in the "interpretation of a weather map" or "the interpretation of a line graph." Here the nature of the introductory material is clearly

BOX 5.5 • *Intrepretative Exercises*

Strengths
1. An efficient means of measuring the interpretation of printed information in various forms (e.g., written, charts, graphs, maps, pictures) is provided.
2. More meaningful complex learning outcomes can be measured than with the single-item format.
3. The use of introductory material provides a common basis for responding.
4. Scoring is easy, objective, and reliable.

Limitations
1. It is difficult to construct effective items.
2. Written material is highly dependent on reading skill.
3. This item type is highly subject to extraneous clues.
4. It is ineffective in measuring the ability to originate, organize, and express ideas.

---

prescribed by the intended outcome. In other cases, however, the introductory material simply provides the means for measuring other important outcomes. The "ability to distinguish between valid and invalid conclusions," for example, may be measured with different types of introductory material. In this instance we should select the type of material that provides the most direct measure of the learning outcome, is familiar to the examinees, and places the least demand on reading ability. For young children this means pictorial materials should typically be favored.

  2. *Select introductory material that is new to the examinees.* Although the form of the material should be familiar to the examinees, the specific content used in an exercise should be new to them. Thus, if they are asked to identify relationships shown in a graph, the type of graph should be familiar but the specific data in the graph must be new. If the data were the same as that presented in the classroom or described in the textbook, the exercise would measure nothing more than the simple recall of information. To measure complex outcomes, some novelty is necessary. How much depends on the specific nature of the intended outcome.

  In some cases it is possible to locate introductory material that is new to the examinees by reviewing sources that are not readily available to them. Then it is simply a matter of adapting the material for testing purposes. In other cases it is necessary to prepare completely new material (i.e., write a paragraph, construct a graph, make a map, or draw a picture). In either case further revision will probably be needed when the dependent test items are being prepared. The process is essentially a circular one, with the writing of items requiring some changes in the introductory material and changes there providing ideas for new items. In carrying out this process of adapting and revising the material, be careful not to introduce so much novelty that the exercise no longer provides a valid measure of the intended learning outcome.

3. *Keep the introductory material brief and readable.* It is inefficient for both the test maker and the test taker to use extended introductory material and only one or two test items. If the introductory material is in written form, excessively long selections will also create problems for individuals with inadequate reading skills. Ideally, it should be a brief, concise selection that contains enough ideas for several relevant test items. Material of this type can frequently be obtained from summaries, digests, and other condensed forms of written material. In some cases pictures or diagrams may provide the most concise summary of the material. As noted earlier we should always favor the type of material that places the least demand on reading ability.

4. *Construct test items that call forth the type of performance specified in the learning outcome.* To adequately measure the intended interpretation of the introductory material requires careful phrasing of the questions and special attention to two important cautions. First, *the answer to an item should not be given directly in the material* since some mental process beyond "recognition of a stated fact" is required in measures of intellectual skills. Second, *it should not be possible to answer the question without the introductory material.* If an item can be answered on the basis of general knowledge, it is not measuring the ability to interpret the material in the exercise. A good check on this type of error is to cover the introductory material and attempt to answer the questions without it.

5. *Follow the rules of effective item writing that pertain to the type of objective item used.* All of the rules for constructing the various types of objective test items discussed in the last two chapters are applicable to the construction of items used in interpretive exercises. Even greater care must be taken to avoid extraneous clues, however, since items in interpretive exercises seem especially prone to such clues and they tend to be more difficult to detect in these items. If the introductory material includes illustrations, for example, special attention should be directed to such things as the size, shape, and position of objects as possible extraneous clues. These are frequently overlooked by the test maker who is concentrating on the intricacies of the mental response required, but not by the unprepared student who is frantically searching for any solution to the problem.

The greatest help in constructing interpretive exercises is to review a wide range of sample exercises that use different types of introductory material and different forms of dependent test items. For locating illustrative exercises, see the list of references at the end of the chapter. See Box 5.6 for a summary checklist for evaluating interpretive exercises.

BOX 5.6 • *Checklist for Evaluating Intrepretative Exercises*

1. Is this type of exercise appropriate for measuring the intended learning outcome?
2. Is the introductory material relevant to the learning outcomes?
3. Is the introductory material familiar but new to the examinees?
4. Is the introductory material brief and at the appropriate reading level?
5. Do the test items call forth the performance specified in the learning outcomes?
6. Do the test items call for interpretation (rather than recognition or recall)?
7. Do the test items meet the criteria of effective item writing that apply to the item type used?
8. Is the interpretive exercise free of extraneous clues?

Summary of Points

1. A good practice is to start with multiple-choice items and switch to other selection-type items when more appropriate.
2. The true-false or alternative-response item is appropriate when there are only two possible alternatives.
3. The true-false item is used primarily to measure knowledge of specific facts, although there are some notable exceptions.
4. Each true-false statement should contain only one central idea, be concisely stated, be free of clues and irrelevant sources of difficulty, and have an answer on which experts would agree.
5. Modifications of the true-false item are especially useful for measuring the ability to "distinguish between fact and opinion" and "identify cause-effect relations."
6. Modifications of the true-false item can be used in interpretive exercises to measure various types of complex learning outcomes.
7. The matching item is a variation of the multiple-choice form and is appropriate when it provides a more compact and efficient means of measuring the same achievement.
8. The matching item consists of a list of *premises* and a list of the *responses* to be related to the premises.
9. A good matching item is based on homogeneous material, contains a brief list of premises and an uneven number of responses (more or less) that can be used more than once, and has the brief responses in the right-hand column.
10. The directions for a matching item should indicate the basis for matching and that each response can be used more than once.

11. The interpretive exercise consists of a series of selection-type items based on some type of introductory material (e.g., paragraph, table, chart, graph, map, or picture).
12. The interpretive exercise uses both multiple-choice and alternative-response items to measure a variety of complex learning outcomes.
13. The introductory material used in an interpretive exercise must be relevant to the outcomes to be measured, new to examinees, at the proper reading level, and as brief as possible.
14. The test items used in an interpretive exercise should call for the intended type of interpretation, and the answers to the items should be dependent on the introductory material.
15. The test items used in an interpretive exercise should be in harmony with the rules for constructing that item type.

References and Additional Reading

Carey, L. M., *Measuring and Evaluating School Learning*, 3rd ed. (Boston: Allyn and Bacon, 2001).

Linn, R. L., and Gronlund, N. E., *Measurement and Assessment in Teaching*, 8th ed. (Upper Saddle River, NJ: Merrill/Prentice-Hall, 2000).

Mehrens, W. A., and Lehmann, I. J., *Measurement and Evaluation in Education and Psychology*, 4th ed. (New York: Holt, Rinehart and Winston, 1991).

Oosterhoff, A. C., *Developing and Using Classroom Assessments*, 2nd ed. (Upper Saddle River, NJ: Prentice-Hall, 1999).

6

Writing Supply Items

Short Answer and Essay

Studying this chapter should enable you to

1. Describe the strengths and limitations of short-answer items.
2. Distinguish between well-stated and poorly stated short-answer items.
3. Identify and correct faults in poorly stated short-answer items.
4. Match short-answer items to intended learning outcomes.
5. Construct short-answer items that are well stated, relevant to important learning outcomes, and free of defects.
6. Describe the strengths and limitations of essay questions.
7. Distinguish between restricted-response and extended-response essay questions.
8. Describe the strengths and limitations of essay questions.
9. Write essay questions that present a clear task, are relevant to important learning outcomes, and provide guidelines for scoring.
10. Score essay answers more effectively.

As noted in the last two chapters, selection-type items can be designed to measure a variety of learning outcomes, ranging from simple to complex. They tend to be favored in achievement tests because they provide (1) greater control of the type of response students can make, (2) broader sampling of achievement, and (3) quicker and more objective scoring. Despite these advantages, supply-type items can also play an important role in measuring achievement.

Supply-type items require students to produce the answer. This may be a single-word or a several-page response. Although the length of response

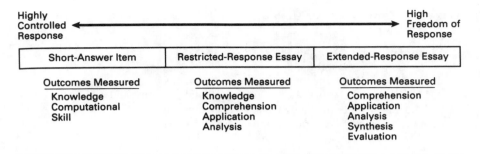

FIGURE 6.1 Supply-type items arranged along a "control of response" continuum and a list of learning outcomes typically measured by each item type.

ranges along a continuum, supply-type items are typically divided into (1) short-answer items, (2) restricted-response essay, and (3) extended-response essay (see Figure 6.1).

Short-Answer Items

The short-answer (or completion) item requires the examinee to supply the appropriate words, numbers, or symbols to answer a question or complete a statement.

EXAMPLE

What are the incorrect responses in a multiple-choice item called? *(distracters)*
The incorrect responses in a multiple-choice item are called *(distracters)*

This item type also includes computational problems and any other simple item form that requires supplying the answer rather than selecting it. Except for its use in computational problems, the short-answer item is used primarily to measure simple knowledge outcomes.

The short-answer item appears to be easy to write and use but there are two major problems in constructing short-answer items. First, it is extremely difficult to phrase the question or incomplete statement so that only one answer is correct. In the example we have noted, for instance, a student might respond with any one of a number of answers that could be defended as appropriate. The student might write "incorrect alternatives," "wrong answers," "inappropriate options," "decoys," "foils," or some other equally descriptive response. Second, there is the problem of spelling. If credit is given only when the answer is spelled correctly, the poor spellers will be prevented from showing their true level of achievement and the test scores will become an uninterpretable mixture of knowledge and spelling skill. On

BOX 6.1 • *Short-Answer Items*

Strengths
1. It is easy to write test items.
2. Guessing is less likely than in selection-type items.
3. This item type is well-suited to computational problems and other learning outcomes where supplying the answer is important.
4. A broad range of knowledge outcomes can be measured.

Limitations
1. It is difficult to phrase statements so that only one answer is correct.
2. Scoring is contaminated by spelling ability when responses are verbal.
3. Scoring is tedious and time consuming.
4. This item type is not very adaptable to measuring complex learning outcomes.

---

the other hand, if attempts are made to ignore spelling during the scoring process, there is still the problem of deciding whether a badly spelled word represents the intended answer. This, of course, introduces an element of subjectivity that tends to make the scores less dependable as measures of achievement. See Box 6.1 for strengths and limitations.

Due to these weaknesses, the short-answer item should be reserved for those special situations where supplying the answer is a necessary part of the learning outcome to be measured; for example, where the intent is to have students *recall* the information, where computational problems are used, or where a selection-type item would make the answer obvious. In these situations, the use of the short-answer item can be defended despite its shortcomings.

Rules for Writing Short-Answer Items

1. *State the item so that only a single, brief answer is possible.* This requires great skill in phrasing and the use of precise terms. What appears to be a simple, clear question to the test maker can frequently be answered in many different ways, as we noted with the previous sample item. It helps to review the item with this rule in mind and revise as needed.

2. *Start with a direct question and switch to an incomplete statement only when greater conciseness is possible by doing so.* The use of a direct question increases the likelihood that the problem will be stated clearly and that only one answer will be appropriate. Also, incomplete statements tend to be less

ambiguous when they are based on problems that were first stated in question form.

EXAMPLE

What is another name for true-false items? *(alternative-response items)*
True-false items are also called *(alternative-response items)*.

In some cases, it is best to leave it in question form. This may make the item clearer, especially to younger students.

3. *It is best to leave only one blank and it should relate to the main point of the statement.* Leaving several blanks to be filled in is often confusing and the answer to one blank may depend on the answer in another.

EXAMPLE

Poor: In terms of type of response, the *(matching)* item is most like the *(multiple-choice)* item.

Better: In terms of type of responses, which item is most like the matching item? *(multiple-choice)*.

In the "poor" version, a number of different responses would have to be given credit, such as "short answer" and "essay," and "true-false" and "multiple-choice." Obviously, the item would not function as originally intended.

It is also important to avoid asking students to respond to unimportant or minor aspects of a statement. Focus on the main idea of the item and leave a blank only for the key response.

4. *Place the blanks at the end of the statement.* This permits the student to read the complete problem before coming to the blank to be filled. With this procedure, confusion and rereading of the item is avoided and scoring is simplified. Constructing incomplete statements with blanks at the end is more easily accomplished when the item is first stated as a direct question, as suggested earlier. In some cases, it may be a matter of rewording the item and changing the response to be made.

EXAMPLE

Poor: *(Reliability)* is likely to increase when a test is lengthened.

Better: When a test is lengthened, reliability is likely to *(increase)*.

With this particular item, the "better" version also provides a more clearly focused item. The "poor" version could be answered by "validity," "time for testing," "fatigue," and other unintended but clearly correct responses. This again illustrates the great care needed in phrasing short-answer items.

5. *Avoid extraneous clues to the answer.* One of the most common clues in short-answer items is the length of the blank. If a long blank is used for a long word and a short blank for a short word, this is obviously a clue. Thus, all blanks should be uniform in length. Another common clue is the use of the indefinite article "a" or "an" just before the blank. It sometimes gives away the answer, or at least rules out some possible incorrect answers.

EXAMPLE

Poor: The supply-type item used to measure the ability to organize and integrate material is called an *(essay item)*.

Better: Supply-type items used to measure the ability to organize and integrate material are called *(essay items)*.

The "poor" version rules out "short-answer item," the only other supply-type item, because it does not follow the article "an." One solution is to include both articles, using a(an). Another solution is to eliminate the article by switching to plural, as shown in the "better" version.

6. *For numerical answers, indicate the degree of precision expected and the units in which they are to be expressed.* Indicating the degree of precision (e.g., to the nearest whole number) will clarify the task for students and prevent them from spending more time on an item than is required. Indicating the units in which to express the answer will aid scoring by providing a more uniform set of responses (e.g., minutes rather than fractions of an hour). When the learning outcome requires knowing the type of unit in common use and the degree of precision expected, this rule must then be disregarded. See Box 6.2 for a summary checklist.

BOX 6.2 • *Checklist for Evaluating Short-Answer Items*

1. Is this type of item appropriate for measuring the intended learning outcome?
2. Does the item task match the learning task to be measured?
3. Does the item call for a single, brief answer?
4. Has the item been written as a direct question or a well-stated incomplete sentence.
5. Does the desired response relate to the main point of the item?
6. Is the blank placed at the end of the statement?
7. Have clues to the answer been avoided (e.g., "a" or "an," length of the blank)?
8. Are the units and degree of precision indicated for numerical answers?

Essay Questions

The most notable characteristic of the essay question is the freedom of response it provides. As with the short-answer item, students must produce their own answers. With the essay question, however, they are free to decide how to approach the problem, what factual information to use, how to organize the answer, and what degree of emphasis to give each aspect of the response. Thus, the essay question is especially useful for measuring the ability to organize, integrate, and express ideas. These are the types of performance for which selection-type items and short-answer items are so inadequate.

In deciding when and how to use essay questions, it may be desirable to compare their relative merits with those of selection-type items, as shown in Table 6.1. As can be seen in the table, both item types are efficient for certain purposes and inefficient for others. It is also apparent that the two types tend to complement each other in terms of the types of learning outcomes measured and the effect they are most likely to have on learning. Thus, it is not a matter of using either selection-type items or essay questions, but rather

TABLE 6.1 *Summary Comparison of Selection-Type Items and Essay*

	Selection-Type Items	**Essay Questions**
Learning Outcomes Measured	Good for measuring outcomes at the knowledge, comprehension, and application levels of learning; inadequate for organizing and expressing ideas.	Inefficient for measuring knowledge outcomes; best for ability to organize, integrate, and express ideas.
Sampling of Content	The use of a large number of items results in broad coverage, which makes representative sampling of content feasible.	The use of a small number of items limits coverage, which makes representative sampling of content infeasible.
Preparation of Items	Preparation of good items is difficult and time consuming.	Preparation of good items is difficult but easier than selection-type items.
Scoring	Objective, simple, and highly reliable.	Subjective, difficult, and less reliable.
Factors Distorting Scores	Reading ability and guessing.	Writing ability and bluffing.
Probable Effect on Learning	Encourages students to remember, interpret, and use the ideas of others.	Encourages students to organize, integrate, and express their own ideas.

when should each be used. Tests may frequently require both types in order to obtain adequate coverage of the intended learning outcomes.

Types of Essay Questions

The freedom of response permitted by essay questions varies considerably. Students may be required to give a brief and precise response, or they may be given great freedom in determining the form and scope of their answers. Questions of the first type are commonly called *restricted-response questions* and those of the second type are called *extended-response questions.* This is an arbitrary but convenient pair of categories for classifying essay questions.

Restricted-Response Questions.   The restricted-response question places strict limits on the answer to be given. The boundaries of the subject matter to be considered are usually narrowly defined by the problem, and the specific form of the answer is also commonly indicated (by words such as "list," "define," and "give reasons"). In some cases the response is limited further by the use of introductory material or by the use of special directions.

> **EXAMPLE**
>
> Describe the relative merits of selection-type test items and essay questions for measuring learning outcomes at the comprehension level. Confine your answer to one page.

> **EXAMPLE**
>
> Mr. Rogers, a ninth-grade science teacher, wants to measure his students' "ability to interpret scientific data" with a paper-and-pencil test.
>
> 1. Describe the steps that Mr. Rogers should follow.
> 2. Give reasons to justify each step.

Restricting the form and scope of the answers to essay questions has both advantages and disadvantages. Such questions can be prepared more easily, related more directly to specific learning outcomes, and scored more easily. On the other hand, they provide little opportunity for the students to demonstrate their abilities to organize, to integrate, and to develop essentially new patterns of response. The imposed limitations make restricted-response items especially useful for measuring learning outcomes at the comprehension, application, and analysis levels of learning. They are of relatively little value for measuring outcomes at the synthesis and evaluation levels. At these levels the extended-response question provides the more appropriate measure.

Extended-Response Questions.   The extended-response question gives students almost unlimited freedom to determine the form and scope of their responses. Although in some instances rather rigid practical limits may be imposed, such as time limits or page limits, restrictions on the material to be included in the answer and on the form of response are held to a minimum. Students must be given sufficient freedom to demonstrate skills of synthesis and evaluation, and just enough control to assure that the intended intellectual skills and abilities will be called forth by the question. Thus, the amount of structure will vary from item to item depending on the learning outcomes being measured, but the stress will always be on providing as much freedom as the situation permits.

EXAMPLE

Synthesis Outcome: For a course that you are teaching or expect to teach, prepare a complete plan for assessing student achievement. Be sure to include the procedures you would follow, the instruments you would use, and the reasons for your choices.

EXAMPLE

Evaluation Outcome: (The student is given a complete achievement test that includes errors or flaws in the directions, in the test items, and in the arrangement of the items.) Write a critical evaluation of this test using as evaluative criteria the rules and standards for test construction described in your textbook. Include a detailed analysis of the test's strengths and weaknesses and an evaluation of its overall quality and probable effectiveness.

The extended-response question provides for the creative integration of ideas, the overall evaluation of materials, and a broad approach to problem solving. These are all important learning outcomes and ones that cannot be measured by other types of test items. The biggest problem, of course, is to evaluate the answers with sufficient reliability to provide a useful measure of learning. This is a difficult and time-consuming task, but the importance of the outcomes would seem to justify the additional care and effort required (see Box 6.3).

Rules for Writing Essay Questions

The construction of clear, unambiguous easy questions that call forth the desired responses is a much more difficult task than is commonly presumed. The following rules will not make the task any easier, but their application will result in essay items of higher quality.

    1. *Use essay questions to measure complex learning outcomes only.* Most knowledge outcomes profit little from being measured by easy questions.

BOX 6.3 • *Essay Questions*

Strengths
1. The highest level learning outcomes (analysis, synthesis, evaluation) can be measured.
2. Preparation time is less than that for selection-type items.
3. The integration and application of ideas is emphasized.

Limitations
1. There is an inadequate sampling of achievement due to time needed for answering each question.
2. It is difficult to relate to intended learning outcomes because of freedom to select, organize, and express ideas.
3. Scores are raised by writing skill and bluffing and lowered by poor handwriting, misspelling, and grammatical errors.
4. Scoring is time consuming, subjective, and tends to be unreliable.

These outcomes can usually be measured more effectively by objective items that lack the sampling and scoring problems that essay questions introduce. There may be a few exceptions, as when supplying the answer is a basic part of the learning outcome, but for most knowledge outcomes essay questions simply provide a less reliable measure with no compensating benefits.

At the comprehension, application, and analysis levels of learning, both objective tests and essay tests are useful. Even here, though, the objective test would seem to have priority, the essay test being reserved for those situations that require the student to *give* reasons, *explain* relationships, *describe* data, *formulate* conclusions, or in some other way produce the appropriate answer. Where supplying the answer is vital, a properly constructed restricted-response question is likely to be most appropriate.

At the synthesis and evaluation levels of learning, both the objective test and the restricted-response test have only limited value. These tests may be used to measure some specific aspects of the total process, but the production of a complete work (such as a plan of operation) or an overall evaluation of a work (for instance, an evaluation of a novel or an experiment) requires the use of extended-response questions. It is at this level that the essay form contributes most uniquely.

2. *Relate the questions as directly as possible to the learning outcomes being measured.* Essay questions will not measure complex learning outcomes unless they are carefully constructed to do so. Each question should be specifically designed to measure one or more well-defined outcomes. Thus, the place to start, as is the case with objective items, is with a precise description of the performance to be measured. This will help determine both the content and form of the item and will aid in the phrasing of it.

The restricted-response item is related quite easily to a specific learning outcome because it is so highly structured. The limited response expected from the student also makes it possible for the test maker to phrase the question so that its intent is communicated clearly to the student. The extended-response item, however, requires greater freedom of response and typically involves a number of learning outcomes. This makes it more difficult to relate the question to the intended outcomes and to indicate the nature of the desired answer through the phrasing of the question. If the task is prescribed too rigidly in the question, the students' freedom to select, organize, and present the answer is apt to be infringed upon. One practical solution is to indicate to the students the criteria to be used in evaluating the answer. For example, a parenthetical statement such as the following might be added: "Your answer will be evaluated in terms of its comprehensiveness, the relevance of its arguments, the appropriateness of its examples, and the skill with which it is organized." This clarifies the task to the students without limiting their freedom, and makes the item easier to relate to clearly defined learning outcomes.

3. *Formulate questions that present a clear task to be performed.* Phrasing an essay question so that the desired response is obtained is no simple matter. Selecting precise terms and carefully phrasing and rephrasing the question with the desired response in mind will help clarify the task to the student. Since essay questions are to be used as a measure of complex learning outcomes, avoid starting such questions with "who," "what," "when," "where," "name," and "list." These terms tend to limit the response to knowledge outcomes. Complex achievement is most apt to be called forth by such words as "why," "describe," "explain," "compare," "relate," "contrast," "interpret," "analyze," "criticize," and "evaluate." The specific terminology to be used will be determined largely by the specific behavior described in the learning outcome to be measured (see Table 6.2).

There is no better way to check on the phrasing of an essay question than to write a model answer, or at least to formulate a mental answer, to the question. This helps the test maker detect any ambiguity in the question, aids in determining the approximate time needed by the student to develop a satisfactory answer, and provides a rough check on the mental processes required. This procedure is most feasible with the restricted-response item, the answer to which is more limited and more closely prescribed. With the extended-response form it may be necessary to ask one or more colleagues to read the question to determine if the form and scope of the desired answer are clear.

4. *Do not permit a choice of questions unless the learning outcome requires it.* In most tests of achievement, it is best to have all students answer the same questions. If they are permitted to write on only a fraction of the questions, such as three out of five, their answers cannot be evaluated on a comparative basis. Also, since the students will tend to choose those

TABLE 6.2 *Types of Complex Outcomes and Related Terms for Writing Essay Questions*

Outcome	Sample Terms
Comparing	compare, classify, describe, distinguish between, explain, outline, summarize
Interpreting	convert, draw, estimates, illustrate, interpret, restate, summarize, translate
Inferring	derive, draw, estimate, extend, extrapolate, predict, propose, relate
Applying	arrange, compute, describe, demonstrate, illustrate, rearrange, relate, summarize
Analyzing	break down, describe, diagram, differentiate, divide, list, outline, separate
Creating	compose, design, devise, draw, formulate, make up, present, propose
Synthesizing	arrange, combine, construct, design, rearrange, regroup, relate, write
Generalizing	construct, develop, explain, formulate, generate, make, propose, state
Evaluating	appraise, criticize, defend, describe, evaluate, explain, judge, write

questions they are best prepared to answer, their responses will provide a sample of their achievement that is less representative than that obtained without optional questions. As we noted earlier, one of the major limitations of the essay test is the limited and unrepresentative sampling it provides. Giving students a choice among questions simply complicates the sampling problem further and introduces greater distortion into the test results.

In some situations the use of optional questions might be defensible. For example, if the essay is to be used as a measure of writing *skill* only, some choice of topics on which to write may be desirable. This might also be the case if the essay is used to measure some aspects of creativity, or if the students have pursued individual interests through independent study. Even for these special uses, however, great caution must be exercised in the use of optional questions. The ability to organize, integrate, and express ideas is determined in part by the complexity of the content involved. Thus, an indeterminate amount of contamination can be expected when optional questions are used.

5. *Provide ample time for answering and suggest a time limit on each question.* Since essay questions are designed most frequently to measure intellectual skills and abilities, time must be allowed for thinking as well as for writing. Thus, generous time limits should be provided. For example, rather than expecting students to write on several essay questions during one class period, it might be better to have them focus on one or two. There seems to be a tendency for teachers to include so many questions in a single essay test that a high score is as much a measure of writing speed as of achievement. This is probably an attempt to overcome the problem of limited sampling, but it tends to be an undesirable solution. In measuring complex achievement, it is better to use fewer questions and to improve the sample by more frequent testing.

Informing students of the appropriate amount of time they should spend on each question will help them use their time more efficiently; ideally, it will also provide a more adequate sample of their achievement. If the length of the answer is not clearly defined by the problem, as in some extended-response questions, it might also be desirable to indicate page limits. Anything that will clarify the form and scope of the task without interfering with the measurement of the intended outcomes is likely to contribute to more effective measurement.

Rules for Scoring Essay Answers

As we noted earlier, one of the major limitations of the essay test is the subjectivity of the scoring. That is, the feelings of the scorers are likely to enter into the judgments they make concerning the quality of the answers. This may be a personal bias toward the writer of the essay, toward certain areas of content or styles of writing, or toward shortcomings in such extraneous areas as legibility, spelling, and grammar. These biases, of course, distort the results of a measure of achievement and tend to lower their reliability.

The following rules are desired to minimize the subjectivity of the scoring and to provide as uniform a standard of scoring from one student to another as possible. These rules will be most effective, of course, when the questions have been carefully prepared in accordance with the rules for construction.

1. *Evaluate answers to essay questions in terms of the learning outcomes being measured.* The essay test, like the objective test, is used to obtain evidence concerning the extent to which clearly defined learning outcomes have been achieved. Thus, the desired student performance specified in these outcomes should serve as a guide both for constructing the questions and for evaluating the answers. If a question is designed to measure "the ability to explain cause-effect relations," for example, the answer should be evaluated in terms of how adequately the student *explains the particular cause-effect relations presented in the question.* All other factors, such as interesting but extraneous factual information, style of writing, and errors in spelling and grammar, should be ignored (to the extent possible) during the evaluation. In

some cases separate scores may be given for spelling or writing ability, but these should not be allowed to contaminate the scores that represent the degree of achievement of the intended learning outcomes.

2. *Score restricted-response answers by the point method, using a model answer as a guide.* Scoring with the aid of a previously prepared scoring key is possible with the restricted-response item because of the limitations placed on the answer. The procedure involves writing a model answer to each question and determining the number of points to be assigned to it and to the parts within it. The distribution of points within an answer must, of course, take into account all scorable units indicated in the learning outcomes being measured. For example, points may be assigned to the relevance of the examples used and to the organization of the answer, as well as to the content of the answer, if these are legitimate aspects of the learning outcome. As indicated earlier, it is usually desirable to make clear to the student at the time of testing the basis on which each answer will be judged (content, organization, and so on).

3. *Grade extended-response answers by the rating method, using defined criteria as a guide.* Extended-response items allow so much freedom in answering that the preparation of a model answer is frequently impossible. Thus, the test maker usually *grades* each answer by judging its quality in terms of a previously determined set of criteria, rather than *scoring* it point by point with a scoring key. The criteria for judging the quality of an answer are determined by the nature of the question, and thus, by the learning outcomes being measured. If students were asked to "describe a complete plan for preparing an achievement test," for example, the criteria would include such things as (1) the completeness of the plan (for example, whether it included a statement of objectives, a set of specifications, and the appropriate types of items), (2) the clarity and accuracy with which each step was described, (3) the adequacy of the justification for each step, and (4) the degree to which the various parts of the plan were properly integrated.

Typically, the criteria for evaluating an answer are used to establish about five levels of quality. Then as the answer to a question is read, it is assigned a letter grade or a number from 1 to 5, which designates the reader's rating. One grade may be assigned on the basis of the overall quality of the answer, or a separate judgment may be made on the basis of each criterion. The latter procedure provides the most useful information for diagnosing and improving learning and should be used wherever possible.

More uniform standards of grading can usually be obtained by reading the answers to each question twice. During the first reading the papers should be tentatively sorted into five piles, ranging from high to low in quality. The second reading can then serve the purpose of checking the uniformity of the answers in each pile and making any necessary shifts in rating. Beware of student bluffing (see Box 6.4).

BOX 6.4 • *Student Bluffing and Scoring Essays*

Students can obtain higher scores on essay questions by clever bluffing. Although this requires skill in writing and some knowledge of the topic, credit should not be given unless the question is specifically answered. Some common types of bluffing are listed below.

1. Student repeats the question in statement form (slightly paraphrased) and tells how important the topic is (e.g., "The role of assessment in teaching is extremely important. It is hard to imagine effective instruction without it, etc.").
2. Student writes on a well-known topic and fits it to the question (e.g., a student who knows testing well but knows little about performance assessment and is asked to compare testing and performance assessment might describe testing in considerable detail and frequently state that performance assessment is much superior for evaluating the type of learning measured by the test).
3. Student liberally sprinkles the answer with basic concepts whether they are understood or not (e.g., asked to write about any assessment technique the importance of "validity" and "reliability" is mentioned frequently).
4. Student includes the teacher's basic beliefs wherever possible (e.g., "The intended learning outcomes must be stated in performance terms before this type of test is constructed or selected").

Bluffing is most effective where plans have not been made for careful scoring of the answers.

4. *Evaluate all of the students' answers to one question before proceeding to the next question.* Scoring or grading essay tests question by question, rather than student by student, makes it possible to maintain a more uniform standard for judging the answers to each question. This procedure also helps offset the *halo effect* in grading. When all of the answers on one paper are read together, the grader's impression of the paper as a whole is apt to influence the grades assigned to the individual answers. Grading question by question prevents the formation of this overall impression of a student's paper. Each answer is more apt to be judged on its own merits when it is read and compared with other answers to the same question than when it is read and compared with other answers by the same student.

5. *Evaluate answers to essay questions without knowing the identity of the writer.* This is another attempt to control personal bias during scoring. Answers to essay questions should be evaluated in terms of what is written, not in terms of what is known about the writers from other contacts with them. The best way to prevent prior knowledge from biasing our judgment

BOX 6.5 • *Checklist for Evaluating Essay Questions*

1. Is this type of item appropriate for measuring the intended learning outcome?
2. Does the item task match the learning task to be measured?
3. Is the question designed to measure complex learning outcomes?
4. Does the question make clear what is being measured and how the answer will be evaluated?
5. Has terminology been used that clarifies and limits the task (e.g., "describe," not "discuss")?
6. Are all students required to answer the same questions?
7. Has an ample time limit been indicated for each question?
8. Have adequate provisions been made for scoring answers (e.g., model answers or criteria for evaluating)?

is to evaluate each answer without knowing the identity of the writer. This can be done by having the students write their names on the back of the paper or by using code numbers in place of names.

6. *Whenever possible, have two or more persons grade each answer.* The best way to check on the reliability of the scoring of essay answers is to obtain two or more independent judgments. Although this may not be a feasible practice for routine classroom testing, it might be done periodically with a fellow teacher (one who is equally competent in the area). Obtaining two or more independent ratings becomes especially vital where the results are to be used for important and irreversible decisions, such as in the selection of students for further training or for special awards. Here, the pooled ratings of several competent persons may be needed to attain a level of reliability that is commensurate with the significance of the decision being made. See Box 6.5 for a summary checklist for evaluating essay questions.

Summary of Points

1. Use supply-type items whenever producing the answer is an essential element in the learning outcome (e.g., *defines* terms, instead of *identifies* meaning of terms).
2. Supply-type items include short-answer items, restricted-response essay, and extended-response essay.
3. The short-answer item can be answered by a word, number, symbol, or brief phrase.
4. The short-answer item is limited primarily to measuring simple knowledge outcomes.

5. Each short-answer item should be so carefully written that there is only one possible answer, the entire item can be read before coming to the answer space, and there are no extraneous clues to the answer.

6. In scoring short-answer items, give credit for all correct answers and score for spelling separately.

7. Essay questions are most useful to measuring the ability to organize, integrate, and express ideas.

8. Essay questions are inefficient for measuring knowledge outcomes because they provide limited sampling, are influenced by extraneous factors (e.g., writing skills, bluffing, grammar, spelling, handwriting), and scoring is subjective and unreliable.

9. Restricted-response essay questions can be more easily written and scored, but due to limitations on the responses they are less useful for measuring the higher-level outcomes (e.g., integration of diverse material).

10. Extended-response essay questions provide the freedom to select, organize, and express ideas in the manner that seems most appropriate; therefore, they are especially useful for measuring such outcomes.

11. Essay questions should be written to measure complex learning outcomes, to present a clear task, and to contain only those restrictions needed to call forth the intended response and provide for adequate scoring.

12. Essay answers should be scored by focusing on the intended response, by using a model answer or set of criteria as a guide, by scoring question by question, and by ignoring the writer's identity. Be wary of student bluffing. If an important decision is to be based on the results, two or more competent scores should be used.

References and Additional Reading

Linn, R. L., and Gronlund, N. E. *Measurement and Assessment in Teaching*, 8th ed. (Upper Saddle River, NJ: Merrill/Prentice-Hall, 2000).

McMillan, J. H., *Classroom Assessments: Principles and Practices for Effective Instruction*, 2nd ed. (Boston: Allyn and Bacon, 2001).

Osterhoff, A. C. *Classroom Applications of Educational Measurement*, 3rd ed. (Upper Saddle River, NJ: Merrill/Prentice-Hall, 2001).

Stiggins, R. J., *Student-Involved Classroom Assessment*, 3rd ed. (Upper Saddle River, NJ: Merrill/Prentice-Hall, 2001).

7

Traditional Performance Assessments of Skills and Products

Studying this chapter should enable you to

1. Describe how performance assessments differ from paper-and-pencil testing.
2. Identify the strengths and limitation of performance assessments.
3. Write intended performance outcomes for a performance assessment.
4. Distinguish between restricted and extended performance assessment.
5. Describe the general procedure for making a performance assessment.
6. Prepare a plan for arranging, observing, recording, and evaluating a performance task.
7. Construct a checklist that is well stated, relevant, and easy to use.
8. Construct a rating scale that is well stated, relevant, and easy to use.
9. Construct a holistic scoring rubric for some performance outcome.

Paper-and-pencil tests can measure a variety of learning tasks from simple to complex. However, performance assessment is needed when performance skills are not adequately assessed by paper-and-pencil tests alone. These performance outcomes are important in many different types of courses. For example, science courses are concerned with laboratory skills, English and foreign-language courses are concerned with communication skills, mathematics courses are concerned with various types of problem-solving skills, and social studies are concerned with skills such as map and graph construction. In addition, skill outcomes are emphasized heavily in art and music courses, industrial education, business education, agricultural

116

BOX 7.1 • *Performance Assessments of Skills and Products*

Strengths
1. Can evaluate complex learning outcomes and skills that cannot be evaluated with traditional paper-and-pencil tests.
2. Provides a more natural, direct, and complete evaluation of some types of reasoning, oral, and physical skills.
3. Provides greater motivation for students by clarifying goals and making learning more meaningful.
4. Encourages the application of learning to real-life situations.

Limitations
1. Requires considerable time and effort to use.
2. Judgment and scoring performance is subjective, burdensome, and typically has low reliability.
3. Evaluation must frequently be done individually, rather than in groups.

education, home economics courses, and physical education. Thus, in most instructional areas performance assessment provides a useful adjunct to paper-and-pencil tests. Although tests can tell us whether students know what to do in a particular situation, more direct assessments are needed to evaluate their actual performance skills.

This chapter will focus on the assessment of the more traditional and structured performance skills and products (see Box 7.1 for strengths and limitations). The following chapter will focus on the assessment of less structured tasks that provide for the integration of skills and ideas and the use of reasoning ability in solving problems more like those in the real world.

Components of Performance Skills

Although the focus in this chapter is on the assessment of performance skills, it is important to note that successful performance typically has several components that must be considered before and during the assessment (see Figure 7.1).

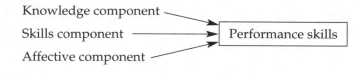

Knowledge component
Skills component → Performance skills
Affective component

FIGURE 7.1   Components of performance skills.

In assessing writing ability, for example, we are concerned with knowledge of vocabulary, grammar, and similar basic elements needed for effective writing, as well as interests and attitudes that support good writing. In assessing laboratory skills we are concerned with the student's knowing the names and uses of the equipment and the procedures to be followed, as well as having an attitude of care in handling the equipment and making accurate measurements. The knowledge components can be measured by tests before the skill is evaluated or made a part of the evaluation. The affective component is typically made a part of the skill assessment (e.g., handles equipment in a careful manner, follows all safety precautions in operating the machine). In any event, all components of the performance must be considered when planning for the performance assessment.

Stating Objectives for Performance Assessment

In planning for instruction, the objectives for performance assessment should be developed at the same time as the objectives are being prepared for the testable learning outcomes. The same two-step procedure of stating the general objectives first and then defining them with a list of specific learning outcomes is followed. A list of objectives for a test construction unit, for example, could be stated as follows.

1. Prepares a table of specifications for an achievement test.
   1.1 Writes a clear description of the achievement domain to be tested.
   1.2 States the intended learning outcomes in performance terms.
   1.3 Lists the content areas to be covered by the test.
   1.4 Constructs a twofold table of specifications that indicates the proportion of items to be devoted to each learning outcome and each area of content.
   1.5 Checks the table of specifications with the achievement domain, to be certain the test measures a representative sample of the desired achievement.

Statements such as these clarify what is involved in preparing a table of specifications and what the final product should be like. An evaluation can be made by using the statements as they are and adding a rating scale to each item to indicate degree of success, or by developing more specific criteria in each area (e.g., Comprehensive description of achievement domain, Intended learning outcomes are clearly stated). In either case the objectives set the stage for performance assessment by focusing attention on what is to be assessed (see Box 7.2).

BOX 7.2 • *Writing Performance Objectives for Skills and Products*

1. State each general objective so that it clearly describes the skill or product to be assessed.
2. List specific performance outcomes for each objective that are most relevant to a successful performance or a satisfactory product.
3. List enough specific performance outcomes to clarify what is meant by an effective performance.
4. State the specific performance outcomes in terms of observable dimensions of the skill or product.
5. State the specific performance outcomes so that they are clear to students.

Restricted and Extended Performance Tasks

Performance tasks may be restricted to fit a specific and limited skill (e.g., measure humidity) or extended to a comprehensive performance that includes numerous specific skills (e.g., predicting weather). Although this dichotomy is somewhat arbitrary, it is useful in planning performance assessments. In some cases, it may be desirable to assess specific skills before putting them together in a more complex performance. In other cases, it may be desirable to use restricted performance tasks to diagnose problems in performing a complex task. For example, students having difficulty with laboratory procedures might benefit from a restricted assessment of measurement skills, and students having difficulty constructing a wood or metal product might need a restricted assessment of how to use a particular tool. Although our major focus is the overall performance, assessing restricted aspects of it can serve as guides for its improvement. This is another example of how teaching and assessment work together to improve learning.

Restricted performance tasks are typically highly restricted and limited in scope, as shown in the following examples.

EXAMPLES

Write a one-page report describing a field trip.
Give a one-minute speech on a given topic.
Read aloud a brief selection of poetry.
Construct a graph from a given set of data.
Demonstrate how to use a measuring instrument.

By limiting the scope of the task, it is easier to focus the observation and to judge the response. It should be recognized, however, that a series of restricted tasks do not provide sufficient evidence of a comprehensive performance. For that we need more extended tasks that integrate the specific skills into a complex pattern of movements or the production of a high quality product.

Extended performance tasks are typically less structured and broader in scope, as illustrated in the following examples.

EXAMPLES

Design and conduct an experiment.
Design and build a wood or metal product.
Write a short story.
Repair a malfunctioning motor.
Paint a picture.
Demonstrate a physical or musical performance.

Extended performance assessments typically give students greater freedom in selecting and carrying out the tasks and greater opportunity for self-assessment and self-improvement. Discussions of the ongoing performance and the final results with the teacher should focus on both the quality of the performance and the development of the students' independent learning skills.

Steps in Preparing Performance Assessments

Effective performance assessments are most likely to result when a systematic approach is used. The following procedural steps outline the main factors to consider when making performance assessments.

1. Specifying the performance outcomes.
2. Selecting the focus of the assessment (procedure, product, or both).
3. Selecting an appropriate degree of realism.
4. Selecting the performance situation.
5. Selecting the method of observing, recording, and scoring.

Each of these steps will be described in turn.

Specifying the Performance Outcomes

If the intended learning outcomes have been prespecified for the instruction, it is simply a matter of selecting those that require the use of performance assessment. If performance outcomes are not available, they should be identified and defined for the areas of performance to be assessed. Restricted performance outcomes, commonly use verbs such as *identify, con-*

struct, and *demonstrate* (and their synonyms). A brief description of these verbs and some illustrative objectives for restricted performance outcomes are shown in Table 7.1.

The specification of performance outcomes typically include a job or task analysis to identify the specific factors that are most critical in the performance. Because it is frequently impossible to focus on all of the specific procedures involved in a particular performance, it is necessary to obtain a representative sample of the most crucial ones. Keeping the list to a reasonable length increases the possibility of more accurate observations and judgments. The following examples illustrate realistic sets of performance tasks for restricted performance assessments.

TABLE 7.1 *Typical Action Verbs and Illustrative Instructional Objectives for Restricted Performance Outcomes*

Action Verbs	*Illustrative Instructional Objectives*
IDENTIFY: Selects the correct objects, part of the object, procedure, or property (typical verbs: identify, locate, select, touch, pick up, mark, describe)	Select the proper tool. Identify the parts of a typewriter. Choose correct laboratory equipment. Select the most relevant statistical procedure. Locate an automobile malfunction. Identify a musical selection. Identify the experimental equipment needed. Identify a specimen under the microscope.
CONSTRUCT: Makes a product to fit a given set of specifications (typical verbs: construct, assemble, build, design, draw, make, prepare)	Draw a diagram for an electrical circuit. Design a pattern for making a dress. Assemble equipment for an experimental study. Prepare a circle graph. Construct a weather map. Prepare an experimental design.
DEMONSTRATE: Performs a set of operations or procedures (typical verbs: demonstrate, drive, measure, operate, perform, repair, set up)	Drive an automobile. Measure the volume of a liquid. Operate a filmstrip projector. Perform a modern dance step. Repair a malfunctioning TV set. Set up laboratory equipment. Demonstrate taking a patient's temperature. Demonstrate the procedure for tuning an automobile.

Demonstrates Skill in Oral Reporting
1. Stands in a natural manner.
2. Maintains good eye contact.
3. Uses appropriate facial expressions.
4. Uses gestures effectively.
5. Speaks clearly and with good volume.
6. Speaks at an appropriate rate.
7. Presents ideas in an organized manner.
8. Uses appropriate language.
9. Maintains interest of the group.

Repairs a Malfunctioning Motor
1. Identifies the nature of the malfunction.
2. Identifies the system causing the malfunction.
3. Selects the tests to be made.
4. Conducts the tests in proper sequence.
5. Locates the malfunctioning component.
6. Replaces or repairs the component.
7. Removes and replaces parts in proper sequence.
8. Uses proper tools in a correct manner.
9. Follows safety precautions throughout procedure.

In some cases, the order in which the performance tasks are listed is unimportant, as illustrated by the first example. In other performance assessments, the sequence of steps provides a systematic approach to be followed. In these cases, as illustrated by the second example, placing the tasks in proper sequence will make it easier to observe and record the performance and to note errors in procedure.

Extended performance outcomes typically involve multiple instructional objectives and it is important to consider all of them when designing a study. A research project, for example, might include intended learning outcomes as follows:

Designs and conducts an experiment.
Writes an accurate account of the study.
States valid conclusions.
Writes a critique of the procedure and findings.
Presents and defends the study in class.

These outcomes would need to be defined in more specific terms, like the two described earlier, but stating the general objectives first and then specifying them in more detail provides a useful procedure. In defining each major outcome, it may be desirable to divide some in two (e.g., Designs an experiment, Conducts an experiment). In other cases some may be combined. For example "States valid conclusions" may be included as part of "Writes an accurate account of the study." In any event, the final list should provide a major list of the intended learning outcomes, each clearly specified by descriptions of what students can do to demonstrate achievement of the outcomes. More detailed descriptions of how to state intended learning outcomes and define them in performance terms can be found in Gronlund (2000).

Selecting the Focus of the Assessment

Performance assessment can focus on the procedure, the product, or some combination of the two. The nature of the performance frequently dictates where the emphasis should be placed, but in some cases there are also other considerations.

Assessing the Procedure

Those types of performance that don't result in a product (e.g., speaking, reading aloud, physical skills, musical performance) require that the performance be evaluated in progress.

In many cases, both procedure and product are important aspects of a performance. For example, skill in locating and correcting a malfunction in a television set involves following a systematic procedure (rather than using trial and error) in addition to producing a properly repaired set. Frequently, procedure is emphasized during the early stages of learning and products later, after the procedural steps have been mastered. In assessing typing skill, for example, proper use of the "touch system" would be evaluated at the beginning of instruction, but later evaluation would focus on the neatness and accuracy of the typed material and the speed with which it was produced. Similarly, in such areas as cooking, woodworking, and painting, correct procedure is likely to be stressed during the early stages of instruction and the quality of the product later. Procedure evaluation may also be used during later stages of instruction, of course, in order to detect errors in procedure that might account for an inferior product.

In general, focus the performance assessment on the procedure when:

1. There is no product, or product evaluation is infeasible (e.g., unavailable or too costly).
2. The procedure is orderly and directly observable.
3. Correct procedure is crucial to later success.
4. Analysis of procedural steps can aid in improving a product.

Assessing the Product

In some areas of performance, the product is the focus of attention and the procedure (or process) is of little or no significance. In evaluating a student's theme, drawing, or insect display, for example, the teacher is not likely to assess the procedures used by the student. This might be because various procedures could lead to an equally good product, or because the product was the result of a take-home project and the process was therefore not observable by the teacher. Also, some in-class activities are nonobservable because they involve primarily mental processes (such as mathematical reasoning). Some elements of the process can be obtained by having students "think aloud" and by using oral questioning, but the main focus is on the product. The quality of the product is typically guided by specific criteria that have been prepared especially for that purpose.

Where both the procedure and product are observable, the emphasis given to each will depend on the skill being assessed and the stage of skill development. However, when the procedure has been sufficiently mastered, product evaluation is favored because it typically provides a more objective basis for judgment, it can be done at a convenient time, and judgments can be rechecked if necessary.

Performance assessment should be focused on the product when:

1. Different procedures can result in an equally good product (e.g., writing a theme).
2. The procedure is not available for observation (e.g., take-home work).
3. The procedural steps have been mastered.
4. The product has qualities that can be clearly identified and judged.

Selecting an Appropriate Degree of Realism

Performance assessment in instructional settings typically falls somewhere between the usual paper-and-pencil test and performance in real-life situations. Although we can't expect to duplicate the natural situation in which the learning will later be used, we can strive for performance assessments that approximate real-world conditions. This, then, is another dimension to consider in preparing performance assessments. How much "realism" can we incorporate into our assessment? The more the better, of course, but authenticity is a matter of degree.

The presence of varying degrees of realism in a performance assessment can be illustrated by the simple example of applying arithmetic skills to the practical problem of determining correct change while shopping in a store (adapted from Fitzpatrick and Morrison, 1971). A simulation of this situation might range from the use of a story problem (low realism) to an actual purchase in a storelike situation (high realism). The various problem situations that might be contrived for this performance measure are shown in Figure 7.2. It should be noted that even though solving a story problem is relatively low in realism, it simulates the criterion situation to a greater degree than simply asking students to subtract 69 from 100. Thus, even with paper-and-pencil testing it is frequently possible to increase the degree of realism to a point where the results are useful in assessing performance outcomes.

The degree of realism selected for a particular situation depends on a number of factors. First, the nature of the instructional objectives must be considered. Acceptable performance in paper-and-pencil applications of skill, or in other measures with a low degree of realism, might be all that the instruction is intended to achieve. This is frequently the case with introductory courses that are to be followed by more advanced courses emphasizing applied performance. Second, the sequence of instruction within a particular course may indicate that it would be desirable to measure paper-and-pencil applications before "hands-on" performance is attempted. Locating the source of a malfunction on a diagram, for example, might precede working with actual equipment. Third, numerous practical constraints, such as time, cost, availability of equipment, and difficulties in administering and scoring, may limit the degree of realism that can be obtained. Fourth, the task itself may restrict the degree of realism in a test situation. In testing first aid skills, for example, it would be infeasible (and undesirable) to use actual patients

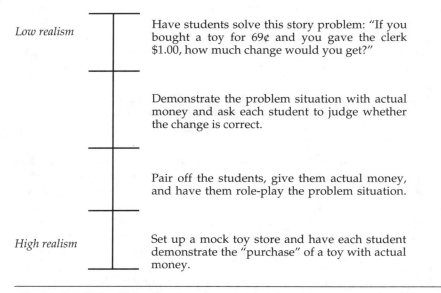

Low realism	Have students solve this story problem: "If you bought a toy for 69¢ and you gave the clerk $1.00, how much change would you get?"
	Demonstrate the problem situation with actual money and ask each student to judge whether the change is correct.
	Pair off the students, give them actual money, and have them role-play the problem situation.
High realism	Set up a mock toy store and have each student demonstrate the "purchase" of a toy with actual money.

FIGURE 7.2 Illustration of various degrees of realism in measuring the ability to determine correct change while making a purchase in a store.

with wounds, broken bones, and other physical conditions needed for realistic assessment. Thus, although we should strive for as high a degree of realism as the performance outcomes dictate, it is frequently necessary to make compromises in preparing performance assessments.

Selecting the Performance Situation

Performance assessments can be classified by the type of situation or setting used. The following classification system closely approximates the degree of realism present in the situation and includes the following types: (1) paper-and-pencil performance, (2) identification test, (3) structured performance test, (4) simulated performance, (5) work sample, and (6) extended research project. Although these categories overlap to some degree, they are useful for describing and illustrating the various approaches used in performance assessment.

Paper-and-Pencil Performance

Paper-and-pencil performance differs from the more traditional paper-and-pencil test by placing greater emphasis on the application of knowledge and skill in a simulated setting. These paper-and-pencil applications might result in desired terminal learning outcomes, or they might serve as an intermediate step to performance that involves a higher degree of realism (for example, the actual use of equipment).

In a number of instances, paper-and-pencil performance can provide a product of educational significance. A course in test construction, for example, might require students to perform activities such as the following:

Construct a set of test specifications for a unit of instruction.
Construct test items that fit a given set of specifications.
Construct a checklist for evaluating an achievement test.

The action verb "construct" is frequently used in paper-and-pencil performance testing. For instance, students might be asked to construct a weather map, bar graph, diagram of an electrical circuit, floor plan, design for an article of clothing, poem, short story, or plan for an experiment. In such cases, the paper-and-pencil product is a result of both knowledge and skill, and it provides a performance measure that is valued in its own right.

In other cases, paper-and-pencil performance might simply provide a first step toward hands-on performance. For example, before using a particular measuring instrument, such as a micrometer, it might be desirable to have students read various settings from pictures of the scale. Although the ability to read the scale is not a sufficient condition for accurate measurement, it is necessary one. In this instance, paper-and-pencil performance would be favored because it is a more convenient method of testing a group of students. Using paper-and-pencil performance as a precursor to hands-on performance might be favored for other reasons. For example, if the performance is complicated and the equipment is expensive, demonstrating competence on paper-and-pencil situations could avoid subsequent accidents or damage to equipment. Similarly, in the health sciences, skill in diagnosing and prescribing for hypothetical patients could avoid later harm to real patients.

Identification Test

The identification test includes a wide variety of situations representing various degrees of realism. In some cases, a student may be asked simply to identify a tool or piece of equipment and to indicate its function. A more complex situation might present the student with a particular performance task (e.g., locating a short in an electrical circuit) and ask him or her to identify the tools, equipment, and procedures needed in performing the task. An even more complex type of identification test might involve listening to the operation of a malfunctioning machine (such as an automobile motor, a drill, or a lathe) and, from the sound, identifying the most probable cause of the malfunction.

Although identification tests are widely used in industrial education, they are by no means limited to that area. The biology teacher might have students identify specimens that are placed at various stations around the room, or identify the equipment and procedures needed to conduct a particular experiment. Similarly, chemistry students might be asked to identify "unknown" substances, foreign-language students to identify correct pronunciation, mathematics students to identify correct problem-solving procedures, English students to identify the "best expression" to be used in writing, and social studies students to identify various leadership roles as they are acted out in a group. Identifying correct procedures is also important, of course, in art, music, physical education, and such vocational areas as agriculture, business education, and home economics.

The identification test is sometimes used as an *indirect* measure of performance skill. The experienced plumber, for example, is expected to have a broader knowledge of the tools and equipment used in plumbing than the inexperienced plumber. Thus, a tool identification test might be used to eliminate the least skilled in a group of applicants for a position as plumber. More commonly, the identification test is used as an instructional device to prepare students for actual performance in real or simulated situations.

Structured Performance Test

A structured performance test provides for an assessment under standard, controlled conditions. It might involve such things as making prescribed measurements, adjusting a microscope, following safety procedures in starting a machine, or locating a malfunction in electronic equipment. The performance situation is structured and presented in a manner that requires all individuals to respond to the same set of tasks.

The construction of a structured performance test follows somewhat the same pattern used in constructing other types of achievement tests but there are some added complexities. The test situation can seldom be fully controlled and standardized, it typically takes more time to prepare and administer, and it is frequently more difficult to score. To increase the likelihood that the test situation will be standard for all individuals, instructions should be used that describe the test situation, the required performance, and the conditions under which the performance is to be demonstrated. Instructions for locating a malfunction in electronic equipment, for example, would typically include the following:

1. Nature and purpose of the test
2. Equipment and tools provided
3. Testing procedure:
   a. Type and condition of equipment
   b. Description of required performance
   c. Time limits and other conditions
4. Method of judging performance

When using performance tests, it may be desirable to set performance standards that indicate the minimum level of acceptable performance. These might be concerned with accuracy (e.g., measure temperature *to the nearest two-tenths of a degree*), the proper sequencing of steps (e.g., adjust a microscope *following the proper sequence of steps*), total compliance with rules (e.g., check *all safety guards* before starting a machine), or speed of performance (e.g., locate a malfunction in electronic equipment *in three minutes*). Some common **standards** for judging performance are shown in Box 7.3.

Performance standards are, of course, frequently used in combination. A particular performance may require correct form, accuracy, and speed. How much weight to give to each depends on the stage of instruction as well as the nature of the performance. In assessing laboratory measurement skills, for example, correct procedure and accuracy might be stressed early in the instruction and concern about speed of performance delayed until the later stages of instruction. The particular situation might also influence the importance of the dimension. In evaluating typing skill, for example, speed might be stressed in typing routine business letters, whereas accuracy would be emphasized in typing statistical tables for economic reports.

BOX 7.3 • *Some Common Standards for Judging Performance*

Type	*Examples*
Rate	Solve ten addition problems in two minutes.
	Type 40 words per minute.
Error	No more than two errors per typed page.
	Count to 20 in Spanish without error.
Time	Set up laboratory equipment in five minutes.
	Locate an equipment malfunction in three minutes.
Precision	Measure a line within one-eighth of an inch.
	Read a thermometer within two-tenths of a degree.
Quantity	Complete 20 laboratory experiments.
	Locate 15 relevant references.
Quality (rating)	Write a neat, well-spaced business letter.
	Demonstrate correct form in diving.
Percentage Correct	Solve 85 percent of the math problems.
	Spell correctly 90 percent of the words in the word list.
Steps Required	Diagnose a motor malfunction in five steps.
	Locate a computer error using proper sequence of steps.
Use of Material	Build a bookcase with less than 10 percent waste.
	Cut out a dress pattern with less than 10 percent waste.
Safety	Check all safety guards before operating machine.
	Drive automobile without breaking any safety rules.

Simulated Performance

Simulated performance is an attempt to match the performance in a real situation—either in whole or in part. In physical education, for example, swinging a bat at an imaginary ball, shadow boxing, and demonstrating various swimming or tennis strokes are simulated performances. In science, vocational, and business courses, skill activities are frequently designed to simulate portions of actual job performance. In mathematics, the use of computers in solving lifelike problems represents simulated performance. Similarly, in social studies, student roleplaying of a jury trial, a city council meeting, or a job interview provides the instructor with opportunities to evaluate the simulated performance of an assigned task. In some cases, specially designed equipment is used for instructional and assessment purposes. In both driver training and flight training, for example, students are frequently trained and tested on simulators. Such simulators may prevent personal injury or damage to expensive equipment during the early stages of skill development. Simulators are also used in various types of vocational training programs.

In some situations, simulated performance testing might be used as the final assessment of a performance skill. This would be the case in assessing students' laboratory performance in chemistry, for example. In many situations, however, skill in a simulated setting simply indicates readiness to attempt actual performance. The student in driver training who has demonstrated driving skill in the simulator, for example, is now ready to apply his or her skill in the actual operation of an automobile.

Work Sample

The work sample requires the student to perform actual tasks that are representative of the total performance to be measured. The sample tasks typically include the most crucial elements of the total performance and are performed under controlled conditions. In being tested for automobile driving skill, for example, the student is required to drive over a standard course that includes the most common problem situations likely to be encountered in normal driving. The performance on the standard course is then used as evidence of the ability to drive an automobile under typical operating conditions.

Performance assessments in business education and industrial education are frequently of the work-sample type. When students are required to take and transcribe shorthand notes from dictation, type a business letter, or operate a computer to analyze business data, a work-sample assessment is being employed. Similarly, in industrial education, a work-sample approach is being used when students are required to complete a metalworking or woodworking project that includes all of the steps likely to be encountered in an actual job situation (steps such as designing, ordering materials, and constructing). Still other examples are the operation of machinery, the repair of equipment, and the performance of job-oriented laboratory tasks. The work-sample approach to assessing performance is widely used in occupations involving performance skills, and many of these situations can be duplicated in the school setting.

Extended Project

One of the most comprehensive types of performance assessments involves the extended project. This approach involves a combination of academic, communication, and thinking skills in the solving of unstructured real-world problems, the construction of a unique product, or both. It typically involves multiple outcomes and criteria for each; student participation in developing criteria, selecting the problem to investigate, designing and carrying out the study, and evaluating the results; and written reports and an oral presentation and defense of the findings. Throughout, the focus is on higher-level learning outcomes used in problem solving (e.g., analysis, synthesis, evaluation), the effective use of communication skills, the development of self-assessment skills, and independent learning. This type of project will be described in the following chapter.

Selecting the Method of Observing, Recording, and Scoring

Whether judging procedures, products, or some combination of the two, some type of guided observation and method of recording and scoring the results is needed. Commonly used procedures include (1) systematic observation and anecdotal records, (2) checklists, and (3) rating scales.

Systematic Observation and Anecdotal Records

Observing students in natural settings is one of the most common methods of assessing performance outcomes. Unfortunately, the observations are typically unsystematic and frequently no record is made of the observation. For minor performance tasks that are easily corrected, like how to hold a paint brush or how to label a graph, informal observation may be all that is needed. For more comprehensive performance situations, however, the observations should be systematic and typically some record of the observation should be made. This will enhance their objectivity, meaningfulness, and usefulness at a later date.

Observations are frequently guided by checklists or rating scales, but there is some advantage in making and recording less structured observations. For example, noting how students approach a task, how persistent they are in completing it, and how carefully they work has significance for evaluating their success in performing the task. Similarly, one student may need assistance on every step of the performance, while another student completes the task early and turns to help others. These important aspects of performance are apt to be overlooked by more structured observational devices but can be described in anecdotal records.

An **anecdotal record** is a brief description of some significant event. It typically includes the observed behavior, the setting in which it occurred, and a separate interpretation of the event. Although keeping anecdotal records can be time consuming, the task can be kept manageable by limiting the records to certain types of behavior (e.g., safety) and to those individuals needing the most help (e.g., slow, careless). The records are likely to be most useful when (1) they focus on meaningful incidents, (2) they are recorded soon after the incident, (3) they contain enough information to be understandable later, and (4) the observed incident and its interpretation are kept separate. What is desired is a brief, objective, self-sufficient description of a meaningful incident and a separate interpretation (if needed) of what the incident means. As these records of events accumulate for a particular individual, a typical pattern of behavior is obtained.

Checklists

The **checklist** is basically a list of measurable dimensions of a performance or product, with a place to record a simple "yes" or "no" judgment. If a checklist were used to evaluate a set of procedures, for example, the steps to be followed might be placed in sequential order on the form; the observer would then simply check whether each action was taken or not taken. Such a checklist for evaluating the proper use of an oral thermometer is shown in Figure 7.3. A checklist for evaluating a product typically contains a list of the dimensions that characterize a good product (size, color, shape, and so on), and a place to check whether each desired characteristic is present or absent. Thus, the checklist simply directs attention to the elements to be observed and provides a convenient means of recording judgments.

Construction of a checklist for performance assessment involves the following steps.

1. List the procedural steps or product characteristics to be evaluated.
2. Add common errors to the list, if such is useful in diagnosing poor performance.
3. Arrange the list in some logical order (e.g., sequence of steps).
4. Provide instructions and a place for checking each item.
5. Add a place for comments at the bottom of the form, if needed.

Directions: Place a check in front of each step as it is performed.

_____ 1. Removes thermometer from container by grasping nonbulb end.
_____ 2. Wipes thermometer downward from nonbulb end with fresh wiper.
_____ 3. Shakes thermometer down to less than 96° while holding nonbulb end.
_____ 4. Places bulb end of thermometer under patient's tongue.
_____ 5. Tells patient to close lips but to avoid biting on thermometer.
_____ 6. Leaves thermometer in patient's mouth for three minutes.
_____ 7. Removes thermometer from patient's mouth by grasping nonbulb end.
_____ 8. Reads temperature to the nearest *two-tenths* of a degree.
_____ 9. Records temperature reading on patient's chart.
_____ 10. Cleans thermometer and replaces in container.

FIGURE 7.3 Checklist for evaluating the proper use of an oral thermometer.

Rating Scales

The **rating scale** is similar to the checklist and serves somewhat the same purpose in judging procedures and products. The main difference is that the rating scale provides an opportunity to mark the degree to which an element is present instead of using the simple "present-absent" judgment. The scale for rating is typically based on the frequency with which an action is performed (e.g., always, sometimes, never), the general quality of a performance (e.g., outstanding, above average, average, below average), or a set of descriptive phrases that indicates degrees of acceptable performance (e.g., completes task quickly, slow in completing task, cannot complete task without help). Like the checklist, the rating scale directs attention to the dimensions to be observed and provides a convenient form on which to record the judgments.

A sample rating scale for evaluating both procedures and product is shown in Figure 7.4. Although this numerical rating scale uses fixed alternatives, the same scale items could be described by descriptive phrases that vary from item to item.

Directions: Rate each of the following items by circling the appropriate number. The numbers represent the following values: 5 — outstanding; 4 — above average; 3 — average; 2 — below average; 1 — unsatisfactory.

PROCEDURE RATING SCALE

How effective was the student's performance in each of the following areas?

5 4 3 2 1 (a) Preparing a detailed plan for the project.
5 4 3 2 1 (b) Determining the amount of material needed.
5 4 3 2 1 (c) Selecting the proper tools.
5 4 3 2 1 (d) Following the correct procedures for each operation.
5 4 3 2 1 (e) Using tools properly and skillfully.
5 4 3 2 1 (f) Using materials without unnecessary spoilage.
5 4 3 2 1 (g) Completing the work within a reasonable amount of time.

PRODUCT RATING SCALE

To what extent does the product meet the following criteria?

5 4 3 2 1 (a) The product appears neat and well constructed.
5 4 3 2 1 (b) The dimensions match the original plan.
5 4 3 2 1 (c) The finish meets specifications.
5 4 3 2 1 (d) The joints and parts fit properly.
5 4 3 2 1 (e) The materials were used effectively.

FIGURE 7.4 Rating scale for a woodworking project.

In this case, each rated item would be arranged as follows:

(a) Plan for the project

1	2	3	4	5
Plan is too general and vague.		Plan is in proper form but needs more detail		Plan is detailed and complete.

A space for comments might also be added under each item, or at the bottom of each set of items, to provide a place for clarifying the ratings or describing how to improve performance.

The construction of a rating scale for performance assessment typically includes the following steps.

1. List the procedural steps or product characteristics to be evaluated.
2. Select the number of points to use on the scale and define them by descriptive terms or phrases.
3. Arrange the items on the rating scale so that they are easy to use.
4. Provide clear, brief instructions that tell the rater how to mark items on the scale.
5. Provide a place for comments, if needed for diagnostic or instructional purposes.

Analytic versus Holistic Scoring

Rating scales are especially useful for **analytic scoring**. That is, when we want a judgment on each criterion by which the performance or product is to be judged. In evaluating writing skill, for example, such things as organization, vocabulary, style, ideas, and mechanics might be judged separately. The rating scale then becomes an instrument for directing observation to these criteria and provides a convenient means of recording and scoring our judgments.

Holistic scoring is based on an overall impression of the performance or product rather than a consideration of the individual elements. The global judgment is made by assigning a numerical score to each performance or product. Typically, between 4 and 8 points are used, and an even number of points is favored to avoid a "middle dumping ground." Evaluation consists of quickly examining the performance or product and assigning the number that matches the general impression of the performance or product. In the case of writing assessment, for example, the reader will read each writing sample quickly for overall impression and place it in one of the piles ranging from 4 to 1. It is assumed that good writing is more than a sum of the individual elements that go into writing and that holistic scoring will capture this total impression of the work.

Holistic scoring can be guided by scoring rubrics that clarify what each level of quality is like. **Scoring rubrics** (i.e., scoring guides) for writing and a

BOX 7.4 • *Sample Scoring Rubric for Writing*

4— Interesting throughout
 Flows smoothly, good transitions
 Well-organized for topic
 Good use of mechanics and sentence structure
3— Interesting most of the time
 Flows smoothly but some poor transitions
 Organized but some weaknesses
 Minor mechanical errors
2— Interest lowered by lapses in focus
 Flow is interrupted by many poor transitions
 Organization weak, strays from topic
 Some serious mechanical errors
1— No clear focus
 Jerky and rambling
 Poorly organized
 Many mechanical errors and weak sentence structure

psychomotor skill are shown in Boxes 7.4 and 7.5. These descriptions of each level do not provide for analysis of the product or the performance but simply list the criteria to keep in mind when making the overall judgment. Another way to clarify the meaning of each score level for a product is to use a *product scale*. This consists of a series of sample products that represent various degrees of quality. In writing assessment, for example, a writing sample representing each level of quality from 4 to 1 are reviewed and each writing product is compared to the sample models and assigned the number of the

BOX 7.5 • *General Scoring Rubric for a Psychomotor Skill*

EXCELLENT	Uses procedure rapidly and skillfully
	Explains function of each step in procedure
	Modifies procedure to fit changing conditions
GOOD	Uses procedure correctly but with some hesitation
	Gives general explanation of steps in procedure
	Modifies procedure but needs some instructor guidance
ACCEPTABLE	Uses procedure correctly but is slow and clumsy
	Explanation of procedure is limited
	Modifies procedures but only after demonstration by instructor
INADEQUATE	Fails to use procedure correctly
	Explanation of procedure shows lack of understanding
	Uses trial and error in adjusting procedure

sample it matches most closely. Product scales are especially useful where the quality of the product is difficult to define (e.g., art, creative writing).

For most instructional purposes, both holistic and analytic scoring are useful. One gives the global judgment of the performance or product and the other provides diagnostic information useful for improving performance. Where both are used, the global judgment should be made first so some specific element does not distort the general impression of the product.

Improving Performance Assessments

Performance assessments can provide useful information concerning student achievement, but they are subject to all of the errors of observation and judgment, such as personal bias, generosity error (tendency to overrate), and halo effect (judging individual characteristics in terms of a general impression). Thus, if performance assessments are to provide valid information, special care must be taken to improve the objectivity, reliability, and meaningfulness of the results. The guidelines listed in Box 7.6 enumerate ways to improve the usefulness of performance assessments.

BOX 7.6 • *Improving Performance Assessments*

1. Specify the intended performance outcomes in observable terms and describe the use to be made of the results.
2. Limit the observable dimensions of the performance to a reasonable number.
3. Provide clear, definite criteria for judging the procedure or product.
4. Select the performance setting that provides the most relevant and realistic situation.
5. If a structured performance situation is used, provide clear and complete instructions.
6. Be as objective as possible in observing, judging, and recording the performance.
7. Observe the performance under various conditions and use multiple observations whenever possible.
8. Make a record as soon as possible after an observation.
9. Use evaluation forms that are clear, relevant, and easy to use.
10. Use a scoring procedure that is appropriate for the use to be made of the results (e.g., holistic for global evaluation, analytic for diagnostic purposes).
11. Inform students of the method and criteria to be used in evaluating the performance.
12. Supplement and verify performance assessments with other evidence of achievement.

Summary of Points

1. Performance assessments provide direct evidence of valued learning outcomes that cannot be adequately assessed by traditional paper-and-pencil testing, but they are time consuming to use and require greater use of judgment in scoring.
2. Performance tasks contain knowledge and affective components as well as the skill component. All three components must be considered when planning performance assessments.
3. Writing performance objectives involves stating each general objective so that it describes a skill or product and then defining it by a list of specific performance outcomes that are relevant, clarify an effective performance, and are stated in observable terms that are easily understood by students.
4. Restricted performance tasks are highly structured and limited in scope (e.g., construct a graph). Extended performance tasks are typically less well structured and broad in scope (e.g., design and conduct an experiment).
5. The first step in performance assessment is to specify the intended performance outcome.
6. Performance assessment may focus on a procedure (e.g., giving a speech), a product (e.g., a theme), or both (e.g., using tools properly in building a bookcase).
7. In some cases, it may be desirable to emphasize procedure evaluation during the early stages of instruction (e.g., touch system in typing) and product evaluation later (typed letter).
8. There are varying degrees of realism in performance assessment, and the aim is to obtain as high a degree of realism as possible within the various constraints operating (e.g., time, cost, availability of equipment).
9. Paper-and-pencil performance assessment is useful as a terminal measure in many areas (e.g., writing, drawing, problem solving) and can serve as a first step toward hands-on performance in others (e.g., procedure for repairing an automobile engine).
10. The identification test is typically concerned with identifying the tools, equipment, and procedures needed for a performance task and serves as an *indirect* measure of performance, or as an instructional device to prepare students for actual performance.
11. A structured performance test provides for an assessment under standard, controlled conditions (e.g., locating a malfunction in electronic equipment). The tools, equipment, conditions, and standards of performance are all carefully prescribed.
12. Performance assessment based on simulated performance (e.g., driver's training simulator) and the work sample (e.g., analyze business data on

a computer) has a high degree of realism. Many performance skills in laboratory courses, business education, and industrial education can be evaluated at this level.

13. Observing students in natural settings and keeping anecdotal records can aid in evaluating aspects of performance that are likely to be overlooked by more structured methods (e.g., work habits).

14. Rating scales provide for analytic scoring, direct attention to the performance dimensions to be observed, and provide a convenient form on which to record the judgments.

15. Holistic scoring rubrics and product scales are especially useful where global judgments are being made (e.g., creative writing, works of art).

16. Improving performance assessments involves making clear what is to be observed, how it is to be observed, how the observations are to be recorded, and how the results are to be scored and used. In addition, any procedure that contributes to more objective observations and records will aid in increasing the reliability and meaningfulness of the results.

References and Additional Reading

Arter, J., and McTighe, J., *Scoring Rubrics in the Classroom* (Thousand Oaks, CA: Corwin Press, 2001).

Chase, C. I., *Contemporary Assessment for Educators* (New York: Longman, 1999).

Fitzpatrick, R., and Morrison, E. J., "Performance and Product Evaluation." Chapter 9 in R. L. Thorndike, Ed., *Educational Measurement*, 2nd ed. (Washington, DC: American Council on Education, 1971).

Gronlund, N. E., *How to Write and Use Instructional Objectives*, 6th ed. (Upper Saddle River, NJ: Merrill/Prentice-Hall, 2000).

Linn, R. L., and Gronlund, N. E. *Measurement and Assessment in Teaching*, 8th ed. (Upper Saddle, NJ: Merrill/Prentice-Hall, 2000).

Oosterhoff, A. C., *Classroom Applications of Educational Measurement*, 3rd ed. (Upper Saddle River, NJ: Merrill/Prentice-Hall, 2001).

8

Expanded Performance Assessments

Studying this chapter should enable you to

1. Describe the nature of expanded performance assessments.
2. Describe ways to expand traditional performance assessments.
3. Prepare a performance-based prompt for use in a subject you are now teaching or plan to teach.
4. Describe how a project can be used to expand performance assessments.
5. Write a plan for a project in a subject you are now teaching or plan to teach.
6. Prepare a rating scale or holistic scoring rubric for a performance-based task and project.

Education has frequently been criticized for putting too much emphasis on *knowing* and too little emphasis on *doing*. This was at least partly due to the wide use of objective tests that were designed primarily to measure the knowledge of facts. Although objective tests can be designed to measure more complex learning outcomes, they were seldom used that way by classroom teachers. With the wider use of criterion-referenced measurement (describing what students can do, rather than just ranking them in order of achievement), there is a greater need for direct assessment of how well students can perform. This has resulted in renewed interest in assessing performance skills in the classroom. All too frequently, however, traditional assessment of performance skill has focused too narrowly on the skill activity, to the neglect of the role of the performance in the general education of students. Limiting the focus to the routine learning and assessment of the skill is appropriate for some training programs and for some classroom activities (e.g., learning to operate a computer or set up laboratory equipment). However, for most educational programs a broader focus is needed—one that emphasizes complex learning outcomes, integrates skills and understandings, and gives students greater responsibility for selecting, organizing, and evaluating educational activities.

This broader conception of performance assessment and its role in the teaching-learning process is supported by the more recent conceptions of how students learn. Modern learning theory emphasizes the need for focusing on more complex learning outcomes, using more comprehensive student activities, engaging students in the activities and obtaining meaning from them, and using more realistic types of problem solving. This emphasis requires more elaborate performance assessments that integrates the various skills and ideas imbedded in the activities. Properly done these expanded assessments can make a significant contribution to the improvement of students' understanding and to their general educational development, in addition to their improvement of the particular skill activity (see Box 8.1).

BOX 8.1 • *Skill Execution versus Expanded Assessment*

Performing a Skill	*Expanded Assessment*
1. Write a short story on a given topic.	1. Plan a short story, outline the plot and characters, write the story, review and critique the story, and rewrite it.
2. Construct a bar graph from a given set of data.	2. Analyze a set of data and select the best type of graph to illustrate it. Construct the graph and give reasons for selecting this type of graph.
3. Set up laboratory equipment and follow the steps of an assigned exercise.	3. Design an experiment for comparing two products, complete the experiment, and write a summary of the findings. Make recommendations concerning the two products and give reasons.
4. Construct a bird house to fit a given set of plans.	4. Make a study of the birds that are most prevalent in your area. Design and build a bird house for one of the most common types. Explain to the class why you selected this model and where would be the best place to locate it.

Ways to Expand Traditional Performance Assessment

In harmony with modern learning theory, performance assessments have been broadened in scope. The newer version is expected to contribute more to the development of cognitive skills, communication skills, problem-solving skills, group-working skills, self-assessment skills, and independent learning—in short, to help move learning toward a higher level of learning outcomes. Following are some ways that the assessment of performance skills can be expanded.

Increase the Emphasis on Cognitive Skills

A common way to increase cognitive skills is to go beyond the *how to do it* aspect of the skill and give more attention to the *why* aspect. For example, why did you select this problem or project to work on, why were these tools or laboratory instruments selected, why use these strategies rather than others, why should this be considered a quality performance or product? These are just a few of the many types of questions that could be asked before, during, and after a performance. Such questions can increase the students' understanding of the performance and move the learning task from limited skill training to an educative activity. A technician may be able to perform a skill expertly, but an educated person should have a conceptual understanding of the process and be able to explain it to others.

Questions are most useful for developing a full understanding if they focus on reflection and thought rather than factual information. For example, asking students to analyze problems or procedures, compare strategies, draw inferences, and evaluate procedures or products is more likely to introduce complex cognitive skills into the process and enhance student reasoning ability. This is a major focus of the trend toward expanded performance assessments.

Increase the Role of Communication Skills

Oral communication can enhance an assessment by asking students to explain what they are doing and why they are doing it. A more comprehensive type of oral communication can also be added by asking students to demonstrate and explain the performance to other students. Requiring students to write an analysis and critique of their performance, to write laboratory reports, to write research reports, and to write other types of relevant reports can also provide a means of broadening performance assessments. Although communication skills are important performance targets in their own right, they also are a useful adjunct to other performance assessments.

They provide opportunities for focusing the performance and the assessment on the more complex learning outcomes and requiring students to reflect on their work.

Increase the Use of Visual Materials

The construction of maps, charts, graphs, slides, posters, and models can be useful for expanding various types of performance assessments. In some cases, the display materials may be part of a written report (e.g., use of graphs with a research report); in others, it may be the main focus with an oral report explaining and interpreting it (e.g., construction of a weather map as part of a weather prediction project). The use of visual materials can aid in analyzing the ability to integrate and express concepts in easily understandable form. In some cases they can also help assess creative abilities, which tend to be neglected in other forms of assessment.

Increase the Participation of Students

There are a number of ways that students can participate in the performance assessment process. They can participate in the development of the criteria to be used, in the preparation of the assessment instruments, and in the use of the instruments (e.g., peer evaluations and self-evaluations). They can compare their self-assessments with the teachers' assessments and peer assessments and discuss the agreements and discrepancies. They can keep a record of progress in the development of a performance and write a paper describing improvement in the performance and factors contributing to it. How much students can, or should, participate is determined by the nature of the performance, the age of the students, and the purpose of the assessment. Where the assessment is to be used to improve learning, students should be encouraged to participate in the process to the extent of their capabilities.

Increase the Realism of Tasks

Assessment **tasks** that are more like those in the real world are apt to be more meaningful to students and to provide understandings, strategies, and skills that are useful in solving other life-like problems (e.g., how to change zoning laws, or how to protect the environment). Real-world problems are likely to be ambiguous and complex, having no set strategies for solving them and no clearly right or wrong solutions. Thus, they can provide for an array of complex learning outcomes that emphasize the integration of cognitive, communication, and problem-solving skills.

Increase the Complexity of Tasks

There are many ways to increase the complexity of the performance tasks that students are expected to master. For restricted performance tasks, a common procedure is to present students with a performance-based prompt and, by means of questions or directions, indicate what the students are expected to do. The tasks are to be complex and thought provoking and may require the use of various skills and strategies. For extended performance tasks, one of the most comprehensive procedures is the use of student projects. An elaborate problem-solving project might involve such things as identifying and defining a problem, consulting many different types of resources, analysis and interpretation of the information, the writing of a report describing possible solutions, preparing visual materials, presenting and defending the project to a group, and critiquing and revising the final report. Such a project might also include an experimental study based on the findings. How elaborate the project is to be depends on the age of the students, the content area, and the instructional objectives.

Using Performance Tasks as Prompts

Direct questions concerning how to solve a problem serve as a type of performance assessment because they ask students to write an answer that requires them to organize, integrate, and express ideas. This role can be enhanced, however, by using performance tasks as prompts for a set of questions. Typically, the performance task describes a problem using a realistic contextual setting with questions based on the problem situation. This makes the questions more meaningful to students because they are based on real situations they are likely to face in the future. The following performance task and questions illustrates this procedure.

> You are employed as a new teacher of science at Jefferson High School. At the beginning of the year the department chairman asks you to describe how the department's assessment program might be improved. The current program uses multiple-choice questions based on the book and ratings of laboratory work, each to count 50 percent of the grade.
>
> What are the weaknesses in the current assessment program? Give reasons you think these are weaknesses.
>
> What procedures would you suggest the department follow in developing an effective assessment program? List the steps that should be taken and the reasons for each step. Describe what the final program should be like. Your responses will be judged using the scoring rubric given to you (see Box 8.2).

BOX 8.2 • *Scoring Rubric for Student Responses*

EXCELLENT 4	Complete analysis of program weaknesses with sound justification for each. Comprehensive and well-organized description of procedures for improving program. Supports each step with sound reasons. Complete and clear description of final program.
ADEQUATE 3	Describes major program weaknesses with good justification. Fairly complete and organized description of procedures for improving program. Supports most steps with sound reasons. Good general description of final program.
MINIMAL 2	Lists several program weaknesses with minimum justification. Describes or lists procedures for improving program, without elaboration. Supports steps with some fairly good reasons. General and limited description of final program.
INADEQUATE 1	States only general and vague program weaknesses. Incomplete description of procedures for improving program. Supports steps with reasons that are general, vague, incomplete, or irrelevant. Description of final program is missing, unclear, or inappropriate.

Using performance tasks as prompts makes the nature of the task clear and yet provides the freedom needed to demonstrate higher level learning outcomes. The scoring rubric lets students know how their responses will be judged.

Guidelines for Preparing Performance Tasks

Effective performance tasks are more time consuming to use and the scoring is subjective, so they need to be constructed with great care. The following guidelines provide the most important factors to consider when writing the performance tasks.

1. *The task should be relevant to the instructional objectives.* The objectives specify the intended learning outcomes in performance terms and thus indicate what performance should be like. Performance tasks frequently involve more than one objective, however, and all of them need to be considered when writing the task (e.g., cognitive skills and communication skills).

2. *The task should focus on complex learning outcomes.* Lower level outcomes (e.g., factual knowledge) can be more effectively measured with objective tests, so performance tasks should be designed for those outcomes that cannot be measured by objective tests. Higher level outcomes such as analysis, synthesis, and evaluation should be the focus of the performance to be assessed.

3. *The task should provide for the integration of understandings and skills.* The task should require the students to combine and use their understanding and skills in new ways. Thus, the task must have enough novelty to prevent students from using ready-made answers to routine problems.

4. *The task should be realistic and meaningful to students.* In performance assessment there is much stress on using real-world problems. This is a worthy goal, but a proviso should be added—providing it is realistic and meaningful to students. Some life-like problems are of little interest or concern to students.

5. *The task should be clearly understood by students.* This means using descriptions that make the problem clear and directions that tell students exactly what to do. Performance tasks should provide the student with some freedom in how to deal with the problem, but the degree of freedom should be clearly indicated in the directions.

6. *The task should be free of factors irrelevant to the task performance.* Students may perform poorly on a performance task because of some factor irrelevant to the learning outcomes being assessed. In a mathematics reasoning problem, for example, keep the demands on computation skills low enough that they don't contaminate the measure of reasoning ability. In final analysis, we want the task performance to provide valid evidence of the intended learning outcomes and not be distorted by irrelevant sources of difficulty.

7. *The task should be feasible in terms of the constraints of time, equipment, and available resources.* This is a rather obvious guideline to apply but performance tasks can vary widely in terms of complexity and the demands on time and other factors. In preparing a performance task, it may be necessary to pare it back to fit the classroom schedule. In other cases, it might be more desirable to assign it as an out-of-class activity so that students have more time and can use community resources.

8. *The task should be developmentally appropriate for the students being assessed.* This means taking into account the students' present knowledge and skill. It's important to strive for difficult and complex performance tasks, but a basic level of knowledge and skill is needed to successfully complete performance tasks. When writing the task, ask yourself whether students have the needed background knowledge, skill in using the equipment, and the like. If not, you will need to modify the task or increase the students' required knowledge and skill before using it.

9. *The task should call forth performance that is generalizable to other similar tasks.* Because of the time required for using performance tasks, relatively few tasks can be used in each area of instruction. Thus, it is important to write tasks so that they have the greatest transfer value. Are the understandings and skills being assessed those that are most likely to be generalizable to comparable tasks? In general, complex learning outcomes (e.g., reasoning ability) tend to have the greatest transferability in problem solving and should receive special attention when writing the task.

10. *The task should be accompanied by the method of scoring the performance.* The scoring involves identifying the criteria to be used in judging the performance and preparing a rating scale or holistic scoring rubric. This needs to be done at the time the task is being developed so that it can be given to students with the task. The scoring procedure lets the students know how the performance will be judged and provides them with an instrument for self-evaluation. Preparing the scoring method at the same time as writing the task provides an opportunity to check on their agreement. It also may require some rewriting of the task to better fit the evaluative criteria.

Developing Criteria for Assessing Performance Tasks

Criteria make clear to teacher and students alike the dimensions of a quality performance. They serve as a guide for both instruction and assessment and a basis for providing feedback to students. Thus, it is important to develop the criteria carefully. The characteristics of sound performance criteria listed in Box 8.3 provide guidelines for this purpose. It may not be possible to match all of these characteristics for some performance tasks (e.g., experts may disagree on the most important aspects of a performance in a given area), but attempts should be made to provide criteria that clearly describe the most important dimensions of the performance.

The best way to start is to review the specific learning outcomes described in the instructional objectives. If the objectives have been well stated, they frequently can be used directly as criteria (e.g., distinguishes between statements of fact and opinion). In other cases the intended learning outcomes may be only slightly modified to become sound criteria. If the objectives are not stated in usable form, it may be necessary to start with the completed task and ask "What are the main attributes that distinguish a satisfactory performance from an unsatisfactory one?" A careful analysis of the task and a review of criteria developed by others should result in a usable list. Just make sure the criteria are in harmony with the instructional objectives, regardless of how the objectives are stated.

BOX 8.3 • *Characteristics of Sound Performance Criteria*

---

1. They describe the components that are most crucial to satisfactory completion of the performance (e.g., beware of peripheral activities that are trivial).
2. They focus on observable aspects of the performance (e.g., "Follows safety procedures," not "Demonstrates safety consciousness").
3. They apply in various contextual settings (e.g., "skill in computation" is applicable in all contexts).
4. They represent aspects of performance that experts would agree are necessary for a successful performance (e.g., "Good organization" would be recognized by experts as basic in all types of writing).
5. They are stated in terms that are readily understood and usable by students in evaluating performance (e.g., for self-evaluation and peer evaluation).
6. They are in harmony with the instructional objectives and the use to be made of the assessment results (e.g., criteria used in judging writing skills and their improvement over time).

The type of scoring method used will also influence how the criteria are stated. For a rating scale, a detailed list of criteria is desired to pinpoint specific areas of strength and weakness. For a holistic scoring rubric, it is desirable to combine specific criteria into broader statements for an overall evaluation. For example, in assessing skills used in analyzing an argument for or against a proposal, the outcomes might be listed as follows: distinguishes between facts and inferences, relevant and irrelevant, cause and effect, consistent and inconsistent, essential and nonessential, and supportive and nonsupportive. Each of these elements might be stated as a criterion for a rating scale. For a scoring rubric, however, it would be necessary to use a broader statement, such as "Evaluates the applicability and validity of statements used to support or refute a proposal." In some cases both a rating scale and holistic scoring rubric are used, so both types of statements might be needed, one to provide a detailed analysis and the other to provide an overall judgment. When both are used, the holistic scoring rubric is responded to first to avoid specific items from distorting the general impression of the performance.

Using Student Projects for Performance Assessment

As noted earlier, a project can provide for a comprehensive form of performance assessment. It can be designed to include a combination of academic, communication, thinking, and related skills that result in a complex performance, product, or problem-solving activity. Ideally, it involves

BOX 8.4 • *Characteristics of a Good Student Project*

1. It focuses on multiple learning outcomes.
2. It includes the integration of understandings, skills, and strategies.
3. It is concerned with problems and activities that relate to out-of-school life.
4. It involves the active participation of students in all phases of the project.
5. It provides for student self-assessment and independent learning.
6. It requires performance skills that are generalizable to similar situations.
7. It is feasible within the constraints of the students' present knowledge, time limits, and available resources and equipment.
8. It is both challenging and motivating to students.
9. It is fair and doable by all students.
10. It provides for collaboration between the students and the teacher.

multiple outcomes and criteria for each and student participation in all phases of the project, including its assessment (see Box 8.4).

To illustrate the use of projects in assessment, we will focus on a problem-solving type of project. Typically, an unstructured problem, like those in the real world, is used so that there is no simple or single solution. This increases the complexity of the problem and provides for greater focus on higher-level learning outcomes (e.g., analysis, synthesis, evaluation). It also provides for the assessment of a greater range of skills useful later in life (e.g., locating resources, writing, speaking, self-assessment).

A common outline for a problem-solving project includes the following items.

1. Establishing criteria and standards.
2. Selecting and stating the problem.
3. Locating and selecting resources.
4. Writing the report.
5. Designing and completing a research study or making a product.
6. Orally presenting and defending the project.

Each of these steps is guided by the teacher and involves considerable student-teacher collaboration.

Establishing Criteria and Standards

Because of the multiple outcomes expected from a project, criteria must be established in many areas. For example, criteria for each of the major areas (i.e., problem selection, research skills, report writing, product design and construction, and oral presentation). Throughout these areas, or as separate categories, criteria must also be established for level of thinking shown and general problem-solving skills. These criteria may be developed by the teacher or they may be cooperatively prepared with the students. The latter procedure tends to provide greater understanding of the criteria by students and tends to be more motivating. The final list of criteria should be checked against the instructional objectives to be sure they are in agreement.

Standards that describe levels of success on each criterion should be set at the same time as the criteria are prepared. These may be stated for use in holistic scoring rubrics or may be included as part of a rating scale to be used in evaluating the project.

Selecting and Stating the Problem

Students should be free to select a problem that interests them, but the selection may require considerable help from the teacher. In a traditional classroom, many students are in the "tell me what to do" mode and one or two conferences may be needed to help them think about possible problems to study. In helping students select a problem, it is important to keep in mind how suitable the problem is for the student. Is it too difficult or too easy for the student? Does it provide an opportunity for new learning, or is it one the student already has studied? Will the problem be motivating to the student or one that is done grudgingly? Will the problem provide significant learning experiences that are in harmony with the intended learning outcomes? These and similar concerns will aid in helping the student select an appropriate and worthwhile problem to study.

Students also typically need help in phrasing the problem so that it is clear, objective, and realistic. Stating the problem in question form usually provides the crux of the problem most effectively. For example, changing "Study of the Environment" to "How Can We Improve the Environment?" helps provide a focus on a major problem. From here it is possible to go to more specific statements, such as "How Can We Improve the Air or Water?" Asking students to put their topics in question form forces them to pose problems. It is then just a matter of helping them refine the statements until they are clear and realistic.

If criteria for selecting and stating a problem have been developed beforehand, as should be done, they can be stated in evaluation form and serve as an aid in the process. They can also, of course, provide a basis for later assessment of the project. Criteria such as the following can be combined with other project criteria and used as a basis for a rating scale.

1. Selects and states a realistic problem.
   1.1. Is the problem in harmony with the student's present knowledge and skill?
   1.2. Does the problem provide opportunities for the student to learn new knowledge and skills?

    1.3. Does the problem provide opportunities for assessing cognitive and communication skills?
    1.4. Does the problem relate to real-world situations?
    1.5. Does the problem have more than one possible solution?
    1.6. Is the problem stated clearly?
    1.7. Is the statement of the problem free from bias and distortion?

In stating the criteria, it is important that they be understandable to the students. This can be accomplished by having the students help develop the criteria. If the problem requires teacher-prepared criteria, they can be presented to the students for clarification and rewording as needed. In any event, criteria should be clear to students and available to them at the beginning of the project. This will provide a focus for doing the project and a guide for self-assessment and peer assessment later.

Locating and Selecting Resources

After stating the problem clearly, the student is expected to go to reference books and other sources to gather information. Other sources might include interviews with knowledgeable people in the community (e.g., banker, accountant, doctor, scientist), observation of a process (e.g., council meeting, trial, bakery operation), or writing a letter to a congressional representative requesting information. The point is, students are expected to obtain information from any source that can provide help with the problem—as we do in real life.
    This phase of the project might include criteria similar to the following.

  2. Selects appropriate resource material.
    2.1. Has a variety of resources been selected?
    2.2. Is the resource material relevant to the problem?
    2.3. Do the resources provide various possible solutions to the problem?
    2.4. Does the resource material include evidence supporting the suggested solutions?
    2.5. Is there enough resource material to provide for valid conclusions?

Writing the Report

The written report provides an opportunity for students to combine ideas from various sources, analyze and interpret the findings, and summarize and draw conclusions. The criteria for judging the report should be used as a guide for writing it. The written report provides an important means of assessing higher-order thinking skills and, thus, they should be reflected in the criteria.
    The following list illustrates how criteria might be stated for the written report.

3. Writes a clear and effective report.
   3.1. Has the problem been clearly stated?
   3.2. Have the study procedures been adequately described?
   3.3. Has the material from various sources been analyzed, compared, and evaluated?
   3.4. Have the findings been integrated into a well-organized report?
   3.5. Have the findings been supported by adequate and relevant information?
   3.6. Does the summary include the main points?
   3.7. Are the conclusions in harmony with the findings and the limits of the study?
   3.8. Does the report exhibit good reasoning ability?

The specific nature of the criteria will, of course, be influenced by the content, instructional objectives, and level of the instruction. Emphasis on reasoning ability might require more specific criteria on the quality of the questions raised, the relevance of the arguments, and distinctions between supported and unsupported statements. Emphasis on communication skills might call for criteria on the clarity of the writing and on grammar and on spelling. At lower grades, the criteria would, of course, need to be modified to fit the age level of the students. Our illustrative criteria are general and simply show how the intended learning outcomes might be stated so that they are most useful for instruction, learning, and assessment. If properly stated, they can be easily converted to a rating scale by adding numbers from 1 to 4, representing different levels of performance, as shown later in the section on Preparing a Rating Scale and in Box 8.5.

In any event, the student should be aware of the completed list of criteria before writing this report, use them to evaluate the report, and then to revise the report as needed. It is helpful for the teacher to evaluate the report and compare the ratings with those of the student in a conference before the student revises the report. Peer evaluations, of course, may also be used.

Designing and Completing a Research Study or Making a Product

In some cases the written report may serve as a basis for a research study. In others, the written report may serve as a basis for constructing a product. This might be a map, poster, chart, graph, model, or some other type of exhibit illustrating the findings. Or it might be a wood or metal product, as in the vocational area. In this case, the focus of the project may be on designing and constructing the product, but the study phase is still important. For a woodworking project, for example, the study phase may involve a comparison of different types of wood, various construction procedures, or a history of the product (e.g., making a replica of an antique chair). The study phase provides for the combining of academic and vocational skills in carrying out the project and increases the opportunity for including higher level thinking skills in the project.

Criteria for assessing the research or product should be stated in the same manner as those listed earlier. The specific nature of the criteria for a research study will depend on the type of problem being studied. However, there are some general criteria that should be considered, such as the use of proper procedures, control of variables, selection and use of equipment, accuracy of measurements, adequacy of interpretation of results, and the validity of conclusions. Adapting these and similar criteria to the specific research project and phrasing them in terms the students can understand provide a sound basis for conducting the research and for its later assessment.

The criteria for a product will depend on the type of product that is being constructed and its relation to the written report. If an exhibit, such as a graph or poster, is being constructed as part of the project, for example, the criteria will include how well it illustrates the findings, its ease of interpretation, and the like. For a woodworking project, the criteria might be concerned with both the procedure (e.g., selection of tools and materials, the use of tools and machines, etc.) and the product (e.g., appearance, meeting specifications, and functioning properly). As indicated earlier, the criteria should be known to students before starting on the construction project. It is also helpful to put the criteria in rating form, as illustrated later in the chapter to clarify how they will be used in the assessment.

Orally Presenting and Defending the Project

Upon completion of the project, it may be desirable to have each student describe the procedures and findings to a group of students, parents, or members of the community. The nature of the group depends on the purpose of the assessment, the type of project, and how the school is organized.

The final presentation gives the student practice in public speaking and in defending his or her work. This, of course, also provides another opportunity to evaluate higher order thinking skills through use of questions that require the student to defend the procedures, findings, and products of the project. As with other phases of the project, evaluation of the presentation is guided by a set of criteria developed at the beginning of the project and fully shared with the students.

The expanded project described here includes multiple outcomes, such as research skills, writing skills, speaking skills, thinking skills, self-assessment skills, and, in some cases, vocational skills. The specific nature of such a project will, of course, vary with the area of instruction and the purpose of the project. It is helpful to review descriptions of how this and other types of expanded performance assessments are functioning in the schools.

The list of references at the end of the chapter provides numerous descriptions and examples of performance assessment in action.

Evaluating Student Projects

Student projects can be evaluated by rating scales or holistic scoring rubrics, depending on the use to be made of the results and the complexity of the project. For diagnosis and correction of specific weaknesses, the rating scale would be favored. The numerous tasks involved in a complex project may also suggest a rating scale for each major phase. A holistic scoring rubric might be favored where the integration of understandings and skills makes a rating scale less useful, or it violates the wholeness of the performance. In some cases it may be desirable to develop a holistic scoring rubric for each phase of the project (e.g., problem identification, using resources, writing the report). If the assessment is for grading or recording purposes, a holistic scoring rubric may be satisfactory for assessing the overall quality of the project or might be used in addition to the rating scale.

Preparing a Rating Scale

If the specific criteria have been listed for each phase of the project, as illustrated earlier, it is simply a matter of adding to each specific criterion the method of rating desired and adding appropriate directions. The use of a four-point scale is fairly common and is illustrated in Box 8.5. The entire scale would have to be completed, of course. All we are doing here is demonstrating how simple the procedure is once the criteria have been specified for the performance or product.

The rating scale provides a focus for judging the project and a convenient place to record the judgments. It is important to state the rating scale items in simple clear language so that they are understandable to students. This makes it a useful device for both student self-evaluation and peer evaluation, as well as teacher evaluation. In some cases, it may be desirable to use all three types of ratings and compare the results in a student-teacher conference. Discussing the agreements and discrepancies should contribute to student learning and to improvement in self-evaluation skills.

Preparing Holistic Scoring Rubrics

Because of the complex nature of the project described earlier, it may be desirable to prepare a holistic scoring rubric for each phase of the project (e.g., selecting and stating the problem, locating and selecting resources, writing the report, etc.). A sample scoring rubric for the first phase of a project

BOX 8.5 • *Sample Rating Scale Form for a Project*

Directions: Rate each item by circling the appropriate number. The numbers represent the following values: 4—excellent; 3—good; 2—satisfactory, 1—weak (needs modification).

Selecting and Stating the Problem

4 3 2 1   (a) Is the problem in harmony with the student's present knowledge and skill?

4 3 2 1   (b) (add others)

Locating and Selecting Resources

4 3 2 1   (a) Has a variety of resources been selected?

4 3 2 1   (b) (add others)

Writing the Report

4 3 2 1   (a) Has the problem been clearly stated?

4 3 2 1   (b) (add others)

Conducting a Research Study

4 3 2 1   (a) Have proper procedures been followed?

4 3 2 1   (b) (add others)

Building a Product

4 3 2 1   (a) Did the product match the specifications?

4 3 2 1   (b) (add others)

Oral Presentation of Project

4 3 2 1   (a) Did the oral presentation reflect understanding of the problem studied?

4 3 2 1   (b) (add others)

---

is shown in Box 8.6. A similar type rubric for each of the other phases of project would then provide a profile of judgments on each phase of the project, as shown below.

Problem selection	— Good
Use of resources	— Acceptable
Written report	— Excellent
Research study	— Acceptable
Constructed product	— Good
Oral report	— Inadequate

Such a profile would help identify where improvement is most needed, but a more detailed study of the inadequate area would be required. The criteria listed in the scoring rubric would help focus on the nature of the problem.

BOX 8.6 • *Scoring Rubric for Selecting and Stating a Problem for a Project*

EXCELLENT 4	Selects a complex problem that is solvable. Selects a problem that challenges his or her knowledge and skill. States the problem clearly and objectively.
GOOD 3	Selects a fairly complex problem that is solvable. Selects a problem that is appropriate but could be more challenging. States the problem clearly and objectively.
ACCEPTABLE 2	Selects a solvable problem that is not very complex. Selects a problem of moderate difficulty. States the problem fairly clearly and objectively.
INADEQUATE 1	Selects a problem that is too simple or too complex. Selects a problem that is unchallenging or beyond his or her knowledge or skill. Statement of problem lacks clarity and objectivity.

Summary of Points

1. Expanded performance assessments focus on complex learning outcomes that integrate skills and understandings and involve students' active participation in the learning process.
2. Expanded performance assessments are supported by modern learning theory.
3. Traditional performance assessment can be expanded by increasing the emphasis on cognitive skills, communication skills, visual materials, realism of tasks, complexity of tasks, and student participation in the assessment process.
4. Two common ways of expanding performance assessments are through the use of performance tasks as prompts and through the use of student projects.
5. Performance tasks provide useful prompts for performance assessment. They typically present a realistic problem situation that describes the type of performance to be assessed and the method of scoring to be used.
6. Performance tasks should be relevant to the instructional objectives; focus on complex learning outcomes; provide for the integration of understandings and skills; be realistic and meaningful, clear, free of irrelevant factors, feasible, and developmentally appropriate for students;

be based on generalizable performance; and be accompanied by the method of scoring.

7. Criteria make clear the dimensions of a quality performance and, thus, play a key role in performance assessment. Effective performance criteria describe the crucial components of the performances, focus on observable elements, apply in various contexts, are agreed upon by experts, are stated in understandable and usable terms, and are in harmony with the instructional objectives and use to be made of the results.

8. Preparing assessment criteria involves reviewing the instructional objectives and relevant specific learning outcomes, analyzing the performance called forth by the task, consulting criteria developed by others, and considering the type of scoring method to be used.

9. Student projects provide for the assessment of multiple learning outcomes (e.g., research, writing, speaking, thinking, and self-assessment skills), are adaptable to various areas of instruction, and typically use realistic problems.

10. A problem-solving project includes the establishing of criteria and standards for assessing the project, selecting and stating the problem, locating and selecting resources, writing the report, designing and completing a research study or making a product (e.g., model), and orally presenting and defending the project.

11. The criteria for evaluating the project should be converted into a rating scale or holistic scoring rubric for assessment purposes.

12. Students should actively participate in stating the criteria and preparing the assessment instruments, to the extent possible. The completed assessment instruments should be available to students before starting work on the project.

References and Additional Reading

Airasian, P. W., *Classroom Assessment*, 3rd ed. (New York: McGraw Hill, 1997).

Arter, J., and McTighe, J., *Scoring Rubrics in the Classroom* (Thousand Oaks, CA: Corwin Press, 2001).

Darling-Hammond, L., Ancess, J., and Falk, B., *Authentic Assessment in Action: Studies of Schools and Students at Work* (New York: Teachers College Press, Columbia University, 1995).

Johnson, B., *Performance Assessment Handbook: Volume 2, Performances and Exhibitions* (Princeton, NJ: Eye on Education, 1996).

McMillan, J. H., *Classroom Assessment: Principles and Practices for Effective Instruction*, 2nd ed. (Boston: Allyn and Bacon, 2001).

Stiggins, R. J., *Student-Involved Classroom Assessment*, 3rd ed. (Upper Saddle River, NJ: Merrill/Prentice-Hall, 2001).

Wiggins, G. P. *Educative Assessment: Designing Assessments to Inform and Improve Student Performance* (San Francisco, CA: Jossey-Bass, 1998).

9

Portfolio Assessment

Studying this chapter should enable you to

1. Describe the advantages of using a portfolio as a means of assessment.
2. Distinguish between a developmental portfolio and a showcase portfolio.
3. List the types of portfolio entries that should be considered in your teaching area.
4. Describe the factors to consider in planning a portfolio.
5. Describe a procedure for getting started in the use of a portfolio in the classroom.
6. Prepare a rating scale for the structural evaluation of a portfolio in your teaching area.
7. Prepare a rating scale for evaluating a student's learning progress shown in a portfolio in your teaching area.
8. Prepare a holistic scoring rubric for evaluating a student's final level of performance shown in a portfolio, in your teaching area.

Portfolios are becoming an important means of assessment in many schools. In some cases, they are used as a basic, or sole, method of performance assessment. In others, they provide another useful tool in the teacher's assessment kit. A portfolio is a collection of student work that has been selected and organized to show student learning progress (developmental portfolio) or to show samples of the student's best work (showcase portfolio). A common practice is to use the developmental portfolio throughout an instructional program and the showcase portfolio at the end. Thus, the showcase portfolio provides a collection of work that indicates the student's final level of performance. Some schools have used the showcase portfolio as a basis for high school graduation. Some states have used them on a statewide basis as a means of assessing performance in basic skills. Our focus will be on **portfolio assessment** in the classroom instructional program.

BOX 9.1 • *What a Student Portfolio Can Show*

1. Learning progress over time.
2. Student's current best work.
3. Comparison of best work to past work.
4. Development of self-assessment skills.
5. Development of reflective learning.
6. Individual's level and pace of work.
7. Clear evidence of learning to parents and others.
8. The amount of teacher-student collaboration involved.

The assessment value of portfolios is found in the variety of types of evidence that are available for judging student performance. They typically include various types of independent work (e.g., writing samples, drawings, research reports, computer worksheets, projects) as well as assessment results in the form of written comments, checklists, rating scales, test scores, and conference reports. The assessment data is also likely to include the student's self-assessments, peer assessments, and teacher's assessments. See Box 9.1 for what portfolios can show.

Students play an active role in selecting the entries and maintaining the portfolio. This provides for another important item to be included in a portfolio—that is, the student's reflections on such things as why the entry was chosen, what it illustrates, what was learned, and what might be done to improve performance. These written reflections cause students to focus on the learning process, the changes taking place, and the growth in their learning.

The active participation of students in selecting entries for the portfolio helps them focus on the criteria of successful performance, and their reflections on the criteria provides a basis for developing critical thought and deeper understanding. The criteria also make students aware of their responsibility for participating fully in the learning process, an important step toward becoming independent learners.

Advantages of Using Classroom Portfolios

Portfolios have a number of specific advantages as a means of assessing classroom learning.

1. Learning progress over times can be clearly shown (e.g., changes in writing, thinking, or research skills).
2. Focus on students' best work provides a positive influence on learning (e.g., best writing samples, best examples of reasoning and problem solving).

3. Comparing work to past work provides greater motivation than comparison to the work of others (e.g., growth in knowledge and skills).
4. Self-assessment skills are increased due to the student selection of best samples of work (e.g., focus is on criteria of good performance).
5. Reflective learning is encouraged as students are asked to comment on each portfolio entry (e.g., why do you consider this your best work?)
6. Providing for adjustment to individual differences (e.g., students work at their own levels but work toward common goals).
7. Providing for clear communication of learning progress to students, parents, and others (e.g., work samples obtained at different times can be shown and compared).
8. Increasing teacher-student collaboration in the teaching-learning-assessment process.

Despite the numerous advantages of using portfolios, they are time consuming to maintain and use. Assisting students in the selection of portfolio entries, providing feedback on the students' work, and periodically reviewing the students' learning progress requires considerable student-teacher conference time. Simply collecting samples of student work and putting it in a file does not constitute a portfolio. Much greater care is required in the development of a portfolio that will be useful in instruction and assessment.

Planning for the Use of Portfolios

There are a number of factors to keep in mind when planning for the use of portfolios in the classroom. A careful consideration of them will increase a portfolio's value as an instructional and assessment tool. The major considerations are:

1. Purpose of the portfolio.
2. Types of entries to include.
3. Guidelines for selecting and evaluating the entries.
4. Maintaining and using the portfolio.
5. Evaluating the portfolio.

Each of these will be discussed in turn.

Purpose of the Portfolio

The main purpose of the classroom portfolio, as with any method of assessment, is to improve student learning. As noted earlier, it provides unique contributions to this goal by showing actual samples of student work, providing for comparisons of work in different areas and progress over time, providing opportunities for students to evaluate their own work and reflect on it, conveying clear evidence of learning to all interested persons, and increasing students' participation in the learning process.

Although the main purpose of the assessment portfolio is to improve student learning, a secondary purpose is to help students become responsible for their own learning. This means active participation of the students in selecting the samples to be included in the portfolios, in assessing the quality of entries, in reflecting on what was learned and how to improve performance, in maintaining the portfolio and evaluating it. All of this is done under the guidance of the teacher, of course, but there should be a weaning away of control as students become increasingly capable of independent learning.

In some schools the students have limited opportunity to participate because of the requirements set by the department, school, or district. All a teacher can do in these cases, obviously, is to provide the students with as much freedom of choice as is allowed by the constraints. For example, if the nature of the task and the criteria for the assessment are predetermined, provide students with a limited choice of tasks within that framework.

Portfolios may be set up for more specific purposes than the assessment portfolio we have been discussing. For example, a portfolio may be used to showcase only the student's best work for use in grading, accountability, or placement in permanent school records. A portfolio may be limited to evidence that shows the development of student self-assessment skills and growth toward becoming an independent learner. A portfolio may be limited to the development of research skills only. We have been stressing the comprehensive use of portfolios in assessing student learning, but portfolios can serve a variety of purposes. Thus, it is important to be clear about the purpose of the portfolio. This will help answer the following basic questions.

1. What understandings and skills should result from the use of the portfolio?
2. What types of performance tasks are best for providing the needed evidence?
3. Who are the users of the portfolio and how will they use them?

Types of Entries to Include

The selection of entries for the portfolio is guided by the purpose, the intended learning outcomes, and the use to be made of the results. If the portfolio is limited to a specific area such as writing skill, the entries might be limited to one type of writing (e.g., narrative) or include different types of writing tasks (e.g., letters, essays, poetry). They might also include writing on different topics or in specific content areas (e.g., scientific writing). Both the first draft of the writing and later revisions also might be included. The specific types of entries will depend on the goals of instruction, how the information is to be used in the instructional programs, and with whom the information will be shared.

A more comprehensive portfolio will include samples of various types of student work, depending on the area of instruction. In math, for example, entries might include samples of problem solving, written explanations of how to solve problems, mathematical charts and graphs, and computer printouts of problem solving. Science entries might include examples of experimental studies, laboratory skills, evidence of conceptual understandings, student-designed projects, and field studies. The types of entries to include will, of course, vary with the purpose of the portfolio, the grade level, the instructional objectives, and any school requirements concerning the nature of the portfolio.

As noted earlier, each entry should be accompanied by the students' reflections on the entry. A brief form can be designed that provides questions and a space for answering. For example, What did I do? What did I learn? How would I improve it? Such questions cause students to think about their learning and their need to take responsibility for it.

In addition to the other entries, portfolios should also include test scores, checklists, rating scales, and other types of relevant data used for assessing learning (see Box 9.2).

Guidelines for Selecting and Evaluating the Entries

The portfolio should not be a repository for all of the student's work. If this is done, it becomes too cumbersome and unmanageable. Its content should be a sample of the student's best work, or latest work in progress, in selected areas. The areas may be determined by the teacher or by school requirements. In any event, the selection and evaluation of the portfolio entries should be determined by guidelines such as the following.

BOX 9.2 • *What Types of Entries Should Be Included*

---

1. Entries selected by students (e.g., work samples, writing samples, drawings, performance tasks, projects, assessment results).
2. Student reflections on the entries:
   2.1 Why was this entry selected?
   2.2 What was done to accomplish it?
   2.3 What was learned from it?
   2.4 What changes would improve it?

1. Entries should be in harmony with the goals of instruction and the use to be made of the portfolio (e.g., to improve learning, for use in parent-teaching conferences, as part of a schoolwide assessment).
2. Entries should provide a variety of types of evidence (e.g., written, oral, exhibits, projects).
3. Entries should be selected in terms of the criteria to be used in judging them.
4. Entries should be selected by students, or at least they should be involved in the process.
5. Entries should be complex enough to allow for students' self-evaluations and their reflections on the learning that resulted.
6. Entries should be started early in the instructional program to better show growth in learning.
7. Entries should be evaluated by using the criteria and standards established for the performance tasks.

The procedure for developing criteria for evaluating the portfolio entries is the same here as for any performance task, like those discussed in the last two chapters. The criteria should specify the types of performance we are willing to accept as evidence of a quality product, and the standards should identify the various levels of acceptable performance. These are then used in preparing rating scales or holistic scoring rubrics to be used in the assessments.

The criteria can aid students in selecting, preparing, and evaluating the samples to be entered in the portfolio by focusing their attention on the elements to be included in the product. In working on a problem-solving project, for example, criteria like those discussed in the last chapter make clear to the students that the project requires a realistic problem, the selection and use of various resources, a written report, the preparation of an exhibit, and an oral report to a group. The specific criteria in each area make clear how the project will be judged and thus provide direction for student learning. Within the framework provided by the criteria, the students are still free to select a problem that interests them.

Our discussion makes clear why the criteria and standards must be shared with students at the beginning of the instruction. They provide guidelines for the preparation of the portfolio entries, for the students' self-assessments and reflections, and for the final assessment of the performance.

Maintaining and Using the Portfolios

The portfolio entries are typically placed in file folders or notebooks and stored in a cabinet. As noted earlier, it is important to keep the portfolio entries down to a manageable number, so that they can be arranged in an orderly and useful manner. A hodgepodge collection of material is apt to defeat the purpose of using portfolios. Arranging the entries by sections and placing a table of contents in front of the file makes it easier to maintain the file and to locate material when evaluating learning progress or reporting to parents. Each entry should be dated and labeled before placing it in the file.

Students should actively participate in the maintenance of the portfolio. It is a collection of their work, so they should aid in setting the guidelines for what goes into the portfolio, selecting the portfolio samples, and evaluating the progress reflected in the samples of work. Unless a student is an active participant, he or she is likely to feel that it is not a personal portfolio.

The portfolio is to be reviewed periodically during a student-teacher conference. Here, student and teacher can view the content together, compare evaluations, and discuss strengths in learning progress and areas where improvement is needed. The portfolio is also used in parent-teacher conferences to demonstrate and discuss student achievement. There is no better way to make clear to parents what a student is learning than by the use of actual samples of student work.

If portfolios have not been used in the school before, one might start on a small scale. A safe approach is to start with one specific area such as writing, drawing, problem solving, laboratory work, or some other relevant learning activity. This makes it possible to obtain practice in use of the procedure with a limited and clearly defined task. The goals and criteria can be more easily specified, the nature of the entries are more readily identifiable, and the entire process is more manageable. Once experience is obtained in helping students select entries, evaluate and reflect on their work, and maintain the portfolio, other content and skills can be added.

The specific nature of the portfolio entries varies so widely from one instructional area to another and one level of instruction to another that it is wise to consult some of the numerous references on portfolio design and use before getting started. Especially useful are those illustrating the criteria, forms, and procedures used in specific content areas. The references at the end of this chapter provide a sample of helpful resource material.

Evaluating the Portfolio

As noted earlier, criteria for each performance task that is to serve as an entry should be clearly specified beforehand, as is done with any performance assessment. The criteria provide guidelines for preparing and evaluating the entry and should be shared with students early in the process. They are typically converted to rating scales or other scoring rubrics that can be used in self-assessment, peer assessment, and teacher assessment. The specification of criteria and their use in task assessment have been discussed and illustrated earlier and need not be repeated here. In addition to these specific performance assessments, however, there is a need to evaluate the portfolio structure and the students' overall performance.

Evaluating the Portfolio Structure

The criteria for evaluating the structure of the portfolio should clarify the main features of an effective portfolio. Although these will vary somewhat with the content and level of instruction, there are some general criteria that should apply to all portfolios. The list in Box 9.3 includes some of main ones to be considered.

General criteria, such as these, provide guidelines for both developing a portfolio and for detecting shortcomings in its makeup. Criteria for evaluating a portfolio in a given content area could be made more specific and content oriented. For example, in a science course, item 2 might be stated as "Does the portfolio provide evidence of understandings, laboratory skills, and research skills?" Thus, the general criteria can serve as a guide for developing a more content-relevant set of criteria.

Evaluating the Student's Overall Portfolio Performance

In addition to the evaluation of individual samples as they are entered in the portfolio, there is a need to evaluate the student's overall performance. Criteria concerning the improvement in performance during the year and the final level of performance can provide the basis for a rating scale or holistic scoring rubric.

BOX 9.3 • *General Criteria for Evaluating the Portfolio's Structure*

---

1. Has the purpose of the portfolio been clearly stated?
2. Does the portfolio provide evidence of various types of student learning?
3. Does the portfolio include evidence of complex learning in realistic settings?
4. Does the portfolio include enough entries in each area to make valid judgments?
5. Does the portfolio include students' self-evaluations and their reflections on what was learned?
6. Does the portfolio enable one to determine learning progress and current level of learning?
7. Does the portfolio provide clear evidence of learning to users of the portfolio?
8. Does the portfolio provide for student participation and responsibility?
9. Does the portfolio provide guidelines for the student participation?
10. Does the portfolio present the entries in a well-organized and useful manner?
11. Does the portfolio include assessments based on clearly stated criteria of successful performance?
12. Does the portfolio provide for greater interaction between instruction and assessment?

Evaluating Student Improvement.   For evaluating student's improvement over the school year, a rating scale is typically favored because it can focus attention on the student's strengths and weaknesses. A rating scale based on general criteria is shown in Box 9.4.

The items in our illustrative rating scale are, obviously, very general but they illustrate the types of items to consider when preparing this form of assessment instrument. The specific items to include would be determined by the instructional area, the intended learning outcomes of the instruction, and the purpose of the portfolio. A set of items for a writing portfolio, for example, would focus on the improvement of specific writing skills (e.g., word choice, sentence structure, organization, flow of ideas, etc.). A language arts portfolio would not only include specific items on writing skills but also on reading skills, reading comprehension, and speaking and listening skills. In addition to the specific items needed to fit the nature of the instruction, however, some of the general criteria still should be considered. Growth in self-assessment skills, reflective skills, and independent learning should be of interest in all areas of instruction.

The unique advantage of the portfolio in assessing student growth is that the entries over the school year provide sequential evidence of changes in student performance that can be examined and reexamined, if needed, when judging the degree of improvement. The rating scale simply provides

---

BOX 9.4 • *Portfolio Ratings of Student Improvement*

Directions: Rate each of the following items by circling the appropriate number. The numbers represent the following values: 4—outstanding progress; 3—good progress; 2—satisfactory progress; 1—unsatisfactory progress.

To what extent does the student show improvement in:

4	3	2	1	Understanding of concepts
4	3	2	1	Application of information
4	3	2	1	Reasoning ability
4	3	2	1	Writing skills
4	3	2	1	Speaking skills
4	3	2	1	Problem-solving skills
4	3	2	1	Performance skills
4	3	2	1	Computational skills
4	3	2	1	Computer skills
4	3	2	1	Self-assessment skills
4	3	2	1	Reflection skills
4	3	2	1	Work-study skills
4	3	2	1	Independent learning

a convenient place to record the judgments. As with the assessment of individual entries, the students can also use the rating scale to rate their own overall improvement and, if desired, compare it to the teacher's ratings.

Evaluating the Student's Final Level of Performance.   For an evaluation of the student's final level of performance, a holistic scoring rubric is preferred. Here we are interested in an overall impression of each student's terminal performance. If the portfolio is focused on one limited area of instruction such as narrative writing, a single scoring rubric may suffice. However, for most courses of instruction several scoring rubrics would be needed. In science, for example, a separate scoring rubric for understanding science concepts, application of concepts and methods, scientific research skills, and process skills may be needed. In math, separate scoring rubrics for conceptual understanding, problem solving, reasoning ability, and using math in communications might be needed.

The preparation of scoring rubrics for an overall evaluation of a student's final level of performance is time consuming but the following outline of steps should help.

1. *Prepare a list of criteria for each scoring rubric to be prepared.* A review of the instructional objectives and the criteria used for portfolio entries should help here. For overall assessment of a student's final level of performance in the portfolio, however, there is a problem of selecting a limited number of criteria. A list of six or fewer is desirable so that the scoring rubric does not become too cumbersome. This means focusing on the most important criteria for judging the quality of the performance. A common procedure is to state the criteria you think are most important and then consult the literature to get help on how to combine them into a list of major criteria.
2. *Select the number of categories of performance to be used.* A good procedure is to start with four categories and expand it to six or eight if finer distinctions are needed. It is frequently difficult to describe more than four discrete levels of performance. A guide for preparing holistic scoring rubrics, using four categories, is presented in Box 9.5. The commonly used category labels and the frequently used terms for stating criteria were gleaned from currently used scoring rubrics in various content areas. The lists are not meant to be exhaustive and should not be used in a perfunctory manner, but they should be helpful in getting started.
3. *Adapt scoring rubrics from published sources.* The literature on portfolios and scoring rubrics provide numerous examples of scoring rubrics in various areas of instruction that might be adapted for use in an overall evaluation of student performance. Because of the difficulty of preparing holistic scoring rubrics, selecting those rubrics that seem most

BOX 9.5 • *Guide for Preparing Holistic Scoring Rubrics*

Level Number	Category Labels	Frequently Used Terms When Stating Criteria	
4	Exemplary	Sophisticated	Thorough
	Superior	Extensive	Deep
	Distinguished	Comprehensive	Elegant
	Excellent	Unique	Perceptive
		Clear	Efficient
3	Satisfactory	Appropriate	Mostly
	Adequate	Consistent	Clear
	Competent	Relevant	Accurate
	Good	Acceptable	Broad
		Detailed	Variety
2	Minimal	Paraphrases	Inconsistent
	Borderline	Shallow	Incomplete
	Marginal	Limited	Basic
	Fair	Weak	Minor
		Minimal	Conventional
1	Unsatisfactory	Trivial	Incoherent
	Inadequate	Unclear	Lacks
	Incomplete	Vague	Disorganized
	Poor	General	Irrelevant
		Inaccurate	Superficial

appropriate and then adapting them by modifying the criteria to fit your particular instructional situation and type of portfolio can provide a good way to start. When completed, check to be sure they are appropriate for your use.

4. *Check your prepared scoring rubrics to see if they work as intended.* When you have completed the sets of scoring rubrics, try them out by evaluating students' sample portfolios. This will help you determine if the criteria focus on the most important areas of performance and provide clear distinctions between the various levels of performance. At this point you might just need some fine-tuning.

Summary of Points

1. A portfolio is a collection of student work that has been selected and organized to show learning progress (developmental portfolio) or to show the student's best work (showcase portfolio).

2. Both types of portfolios are useful in the classroom—the developmental to show student growth during the school year and the showcase to indicate final level of learning.

3. The assessment value of portfolios is found in the vast array of evidence of learning they provide, the actual use of students' samples of work, the active participation of students in selecting entries and maintaining the portfolio, and the variety of types of assessment data included.

4. The specific advantages of using a portfolio in the classroom are that it shows actual samples of student work, provides for comparisons of work in different areas and growth over time, provides students with an opportunity to evaluate and reflect on their work, provides clear evidence of learning to all interested persons, and provides for increased participation of students in the teaching-learning-assessment process.

5. Planning for the use of portfolios involves determining the purpose, the types of entries to include, the guidelines for selecting and evaluating the entries, the procedures for maintaining and using the portfolio, and the criteria for an overall evaluation of the portfolio.

6. Although the main purpose of using a portfolio is to improve student learning, a secondary purpose is to encourage students to participate more actively in the learning process and become more responsible for their own learning. This is an important step in becoming independent learners.

7. The structural evaluation of a portfolio can be accomplished by considering a series of questions concerning its makeup, organization, and content.

8. The overall evaluation of student progresses shown in the portfolio can be determined by a rating scale that focuses on the learning outcomes being assessed by the portfolio.

9. The final level of student performance can best be determined by holistic scoring rubrics for each of the major areas of instruction included in the portfolio.

References and Additional Reading

Arter, J., and McTighe, J., *Scoring Rubrics in the Classroom* (Thousand Oaks, CA: Corwin Press, 2001).

Cole, D. J., Ryan, C. W., Kick, F., and Mathies, B. K., *Portfolios across the Curriculum and Beyond*, 2nd ed. (Thousand Oaks, CA: Corwin Press, 2000).

Johnson, B., *Performance Assessment Handbook: Volume 1, Portfolios and Socratic Seminars* (Princeton, NJ: Eye on Education, 1996).

Linn, R. L., and Gronlund, N. E., *Measurement and Assessment in Teaching*, 8th ed. (Upper Saddle River, NJ: Merrill/ Prentice-Hall, 2000).

McMillan, J. H., *Classroom Assessment: Principles and Practices for Effective Instruction*, 2nd ed. (Boston: Allyn and Bacon, 2001).

10

Grading and Reporting

Studying this chapter should enable you to

1. Distinguish between absolute grading and relative grading.
2. Describe how to select a proper frame of reference, or standard, for assigning grades.
3. Explain why learning ability, improvement, and effort provide a poor basis for grading.
4. Describe and defend the grading system you would use in your area of instruction.
5. Demonstrate how to properly weight components to be included in a grade.
6. Describe a rationale for making the pass-fail decision.
7. Write a statement, to be given to students, that describes your grading procedures.
8. Report learning progress to students and parents.

Grades assigned to student work should represent the extent to which the instructional objectives (i.e., the intended learning outcomes) have been achieved and should be in harmony with the grading policies of the school. Some schools have both clearly defined objectives and grading policies; many schools have neither. With or without the guidance of clear-cut policies and procedures, the assigning of grades is a difficult and frustrating task. It is somewhat easier if valid evidence of achievement has been gathered throughout the course.

Assessment of learning during instruction might include the use of objective and essay tests, ratings, papers, and various types of performance assessment. The problem of grading is that of summarizing this diverse collection of information into a single letter grade or brief report. Because the single letter grade (e.g., A, B, C, D, F) is the most widely used grading system, we shall focus on how best to assign such grades. This involves several important considerations: (1) What frame of reference, or standard, should be used to report level of performance? (2) How should the performance data be combined for grading? (3) What guidelines should be followed to provide the most effective and fair grading system? Each of these will be discussed in turn.

Selecting the Basis for Grading

Letter grades are typically assigned by comparing a student's performance to a prespecified standard of performance (absolute grading) or to the performance of the members of a group (relative grading). In some cases, grades are based on or modified by the learning ability of the student, the amount of improvement shown over a given instructional period, or student effort. As we shall see later, these factors provide an inadequate basis for assigning grades.

Absolute Grading

A common type of absolute grading is the use of letter grades defined by a 100-point system. Whether assigning grades to an individual set of test scores or as a basis for the final grades in a course, the set of grades might be expressed as one of the following:

	Points	Points	Points
A =	90–100	95–100	91–100
B =	80–89	85–94	86–90
C =	70–79	75–84	81–85
D =	60–69	65–74	75–80
F =	below 60	below 65	below 75

In the case of an individual test, this 100-point system might represent the percentage of items correct or the total number of points earned on the test. When used as a final grade, it typically represents a combining of scores from various tests and other assessment results. In any event, it provides an absolute basis for assigning letter grades.

Which set of points provides the best basis for assigning grades? There is no way of knowing. The distribution of points is arbitrary. Whatever distribution is used, however, should be based on the teacher's experience with this and past groups of students, knowledge concerning the difficulty of the intended learning outcomes, the difficulty of the tests and other assessments used, the conditions of learning, and the like. These are all subjective judgments, however, and shifts in the proportion of students getting the letter grade of A or F are difficult to evaluate. Do a larger number of grades of A represent improved instruction and better study habits by students, or easier tests and less rigid grading of papers and projects? Do more failures indicate poor teaching, inadequate study, or assessments that have inadvertently increased in difficulty?

Despite the problem of setting meaningful standards for an absolute grading system, this method is widely used in schools. It is most appropriate in programs where the set of learning tasks has been clearly specified, the standards have been defined in terms of the learning tasks, and the tests and other assessment techniques have been designed for criterion-referenced interpretation. All too frequently, however, absolute grading is based on some hodgepodge of ill-defined achievement results. When the distribution of points does not fit the grading scale, the points are adjusted upward or downward by some obscure formula to get a closer fit. Needless to say, such grades do not provide a meaningful report of the extent to which the intended learning outcomes have been achieved.

Relative Grading

When assigning grades on a relative basis, the students are typically ranked in order of performance (based on a set of test scores or combined assessment results) and the students ranking highest receive a letter grade of A, the next highest receive a B, and so on. What proportion of students should receive each grade is predetermined and might appear as one of the following:

	Percent of Students	*Percent of Students*
A	15	10–20
B	25	20–30
C	45	40–50
D	10	10–20
F	5	0–10

The percent of students to be assigned each grade is just as arbitrary as the selection of points for each grade in the absolute grading system. The use of a range of percents (e.g., A = 10–20 percent) should probably be favored because it makes some allowance for differences in the ability level of the class. It does not make sense to assign 15 percent As to both a regular class and a gifted class. Likewise, in an advanced course a larger proportion of As and Bs should be assigned and fewer (if any) Fs because the low-achieving students have been "weeded out" in earlier courses. When these percentages have been set by the school system, one has little choice but to follow the school practice—at least until efforts to change it are successful.

Older measurement books recommended using the normal curve to assign grades. This resulted in the same percent of As and Fs (e.g., 7 percent) and Bs and Ds (e.g., 38 percent). Although some teachers may still use such a system, its use should be discouraged. Measures of achievement in classroom groups seldom yield normally distributed scores. Also, to maintain the same proportion of grades, especially failures, at different grade levels does not take into account that the student population is becoming increasingly select as the failing students are held back or drop out of school.

The relative grading system requires a reliable ranking of students; thus, it is most meaningful when the achievement measures provide a wide range of scores. This makes it possible to draw the lines between grades with greater assurance that misclassifications will be kept to a minimum. Ideally, of course, the spread of scores should be based on the difficulty and complexity of the material learned. For example, an A should not simply represent more knowledge of factual material, but a higher level of understanding, application, and thinking skills. Thus, although norm-referenced interpretation is being utilized, the real meaning of the grades comes from referring back to the nature of the achievement that each grade represents. See Box 10.1 for a summary comparison of absolute and relative grading.

BOX 10.1 • *Absolute Grading and Relative Grading*

ABSOLUTE GRADING

Strengths
1. Grades can be described directly in terms of student performance, without reference to the performance of others.
2. All students can obtain high grades if mastery outcomes are stressed and instruction is effective.

Limitations
1. Performance standards are set in an arbitrary manner and are difficult to specify and justify.
2. Performance standards tend to vary unintentionally due to variations in test difficulty, assignments, student ability, and instructional effectiveness.
3. Grades can be assigned without clear reference to what has been achieved (but, of course, they should not be).

RELATIVE GRADING

Strengths
1. Grades can be easily described and interpreted in terms of rank in a group.
2. Grades distinguish among levels of student performance that are useful in making prediction and selection decisions.

Limitations
1. The percent of students receiving each grade is arbitrarily set.
2. The meaning of a grade varies with the ability of the student group.
3. Grades can be assigned without clear reference to what has been achieved (but, of course, they should not be).

Learning Ability, Improvement, and Effort

In some cases, attempts are made to base grades on achievement in relation to learning ability, the amount of improvement in achievement, or the amount of effort a student puts forth. All of these procedures have problems that distort the meaning of grades.

Grading on the basis of *learning ability* has sometimes been used at the elementary level to motivate students with less ability. At first glance, it seems sensible to give a grade of A to students who are achieving all that they are capable of achieving. There are two major problems with this procedure, however. First, it is difficult, if not impossible, to get a dependable measure of learning ability apart from achievement. Both tests have similar type items and measure similar concepts. Second, the meaning of the grades become distorted. A low-ability student with average performance might receive an A, whereas a high-ability student with average performance receives a grade of C. Obviously, the grades are no longer very meaningful as indicators of achievement.

Using the amount of *improvement* as a basis for grading also has its problems. For one, the difference scores between measures of achievement over short spans of time are very unreliable. For another, students who score high on the entry test cannot possibly get a high grade because little improvement can be shown. Students who know about this grading procedure ahead of time can, of course, do poorly on the first test and be assured of a fairly good grade. This is not an uncommon practice where grades are based on improvement. Finally, the grades lack meaning as indicators of achievement when increase in achievement becomes more important than level of achievement. For example, a low-achieving student with considerable improvement might receive an A, while a high-achieving student with little improvement receives a B or C.

Grading on the basis of *effort,* or adjusting grades for effort, also distorts the meaning of the results. Low-achieving students who put forth great effort receive higher grades than their achievement warrants and high-achieving students who put forth little effort are likely to receive lower grades than deserved. Although such grading seems to serve a motivational function for low-achieving students, the grades become meaningless as measures of the extent to which students are achieving the intended learning outcomes.

In summary, assigning grades that take into account learning ability, amount of improvement, or effort simply contaminates the grades and distorts their meaning as indicators of student achievement. A letter grade is most useful when it represents achievement and only achievement. Other factors may be rated separately on a report card, but they should not be allowed to distort the meaning of the letter grade.

A Combination of Absolute and Relative Grading

Grades should represent the degree of which instructional objectives (i.e., intended learning outcomes) are achieved by students. Some of the objectives of instruction are concerned with minimum essentials that must be mastered if a student is to proceed to the next level of instruction. Other objectives are concerned with learning outcomes that are never fully achieved but toward which students can show varying degrees of progress. The first are called minimal objectives and the second developmental objectives.

Minimal objectives are concerned with the knowledge, skill, and other lower-level learning outcomes that represent the minimum essentials of the course. In order to receive a passing grade, a student must demonstrate that this basic knowledge and skill, which are prerequisite to further learning in the area, have been learned to a satisfactory degree. *Developmental objectives* are concerned with higher-level learning outcomes such as understanding, application, and thinking skills. Although we can identify degrees of progress toward these objectives, we cannot expect to ever fully achieve them. In science, for example, we might expect all students to master basic terms, concepts, and skills, but encourage each student to proceed as far as he or she can in understanding and applying the scientific process and in developing the intellectual skills used by scientists. Similarly, all students in math might be expected to master the fundamental operations, but show wide diversity in problem-solving ability and mathematical reasoning. In all instructional areas there are lower-level objectives that should be mastered by all students and higher-level objectives that provide goals that never can be fully achieved. Thus, with minimal objectives we attempt to obtain a uniformly high level of performance for all students, and with developmental objectives we encourage each student to strive for maximum development.

As indicated earlier, the pass-fail decision should be based on whether the minimal objectives have been mastered. Students demonstrating that they have achieved the minimal objectives, and thus have the necessary prerequisites for success at the next level of instruction, should be passed. Those who do not should fail. This requires an *absolute* judgment, not a relative one. Students should not be failed simply because their achievement places them near the bottom of some group. It is the nature of the achievement that is significant.

Above the pass-fail cutoff point, grades should be assigned on a relative basis. This is because students' scores will tend to be spread out in terms of their degree of development beyond the minimal level. Students cannot be expected to master the more complex learning outcomes described by developmental objectives, but they can show varying degrees of progress toward their attainment. Although it would be ideal to have a scale of achievement ranging from simple to complex so that absolute grading could be used, this is not possible at this time. The best we can do is obtain a spread of student achievement scores in terms of the complexity of the learning outcomes attained and use relative grading. If properly done, a grade of A would represent greater achievement of the higher-level learning outcomes and not simply a high relative position in the group. This would assume, of course, that tests and other assessment techniques would measure a range of achievement from simple to complex, and not just knowledge of factual information and simple skills.

In most cases the school will dictate the grading policy, including the basis on which the grades are to be assigned. Regardless of the system used, it is important to relate the grades back to student achievement so that different grades represent different levels of performance. Letter grades without an achievement referent tend to have little meaning.

Combining Data for Grading

Assigning grades typically involves combining results from various types of assessment, including such things as tests, projects, papers, and laboratory work. If each element is to be included in the grade in terms of its relative importance, the data must be combined in a way that proper weights are used. For example, if we want test scores to count 50 percent, papers 25 percent, and laboratory work 25 percent of the grade, we need a method that will result in grades that reflect this emphasis. The process is simplified if all assessment results are converted to numerical scores first. It is then simply a matter of following a systematic procedure of combining scores.

The method of combining scores so that proper weights are obtained for each element is not as simple as it seems. A common procedure is simply to add scores together if they are to have equal weight and to multiply by 2 if an element is to count twice as much as the other. This typically will not result in each element receiving its proper weight, even if the highest possible scores is the same for all sets of scores. How much influence each element has in a composite score is determined by the spread, or variability, of scores and not the number of total points.

The problem of weighting scores when combining them can be best illustrated with a simple example. Let's assume we only have two measures of achievement and we want to give them equal weight in a grade. Our two sets of achievement scores have score ranges as follows:

Test scores	20 to 100
Laboratory work	30 to 50

If we simply added together a student's test score and score on laboratory work, the grade the student received would be determined largely by the test score because of its wide spread of scores. This can be shown by comparing a student who had the highest test score and lowest laboratory score (Student 1) with a student who had the lowest test score and highest laboratory score (Student 2).

	Student 1	Student 2
Test score	100	20
Laboratory score	30	50
Composite score	130	70

It is quite obvious from the difference in composite scores that the weighting is not equal.

With sets of scores like those for our test and laboratory work, it is not uncommon for teachers to attempt to give them equal weight by making the top possible score equal. This can be done, of course, by multiplying the score on laboratory work by 2, making the highest possible score 100 for both measures. Here is how the two composite scores for our hypothetical students would compare under this system:

	Student 1	Student 2
Test score	100	20
Laboratory score (× 2)	60	100
Composite score	160	120

Our composite scores make clear that equalizing the maximum possible score does not provide equal weights either. As noted earlier, the influence a measure has on the composite score depends on the spread, or variability, of scores. Thus, the greater the spread of scores, the larger the contribution to the composite score.

We can give equal weight to our two sets of scores by using the **range** of scores in each set. Because our test scores have a range of 80 (100–20) and our laboratory scores have a range of 20 (50–30), we must multiply each laboratory score by 4 to equalize the spread of scores and, thus, given them equal weight in the composite score. Here are the composite scores for our two hypothetical students:

	Student 1	Student 2
Test score	100	20
Laboratory score (× 4)	120	200
Composite score	220	220

At last we have a system that gives the two measures equal weight in the composite score. Note that if we wanted to count our test score *twice* as much as the laboratory score, we would multiply it by 2 and the laboratory score by 4. However, if we wanted to have our laboratory score count twice as much as the test score, we would have to multiply each laboratory score by 8. Thus, when we originally multiplied our laboratory scores by 4, we simply adjusted the spread of those scores to match the spread of the test scores. When the two sets of scores have the same range of scores, we can then assign additional weights in terms of their relative importance (see Box 10.2).

The range of scores provides only a rough approximation of score variability but it is satisfactory for most classroom grading purposes. A more dependable basis for weighting grade components can be obtained with the standard deviation.

BOX 10.2 • *Computing Composite Scores for Grading*

1. Select assessments to be included in the composite score and assign percentages.
2. Record desired weight for each assessment.
3. Equate range of scores by using multiplier.
4. Determine weight to apply to each score by multiplying "desired weight" by "multiplier to equate ranges."

Components		Desired Weight	Range of Scores	Multiplier to Equate Ranges	Weight to Apply to Each Score
1. Test scores	50%	2	20 to 100	1	$2 \times 1 = 2$
2. Laboratory work	25%	1	30 to 50	4	$1 \times 4 = 4$
3. Homework	25%	1	0 to 10	8	$1 \times 8 = 8$

COMPUTING THE COMPOSITE SCORES

Students	Raw Scores			Weighted Scores			Composite
	1	2	3	1(×2)	2(×4)	3(×8)	1(w)+2(w)+3(w)
Nguyen	93	42	8	186	168	64	418
Derek	84	45	10	168	180	80	428
Maria	85	47	7	170	188	56	414
Jonus	95	35	10	190	140	80	410

Note that Derek had the highest composite score but would have had the lowest if the raw scores were simply added together, or even if the test score was multiplied by 2 (the desired weight). That is because the measure with the biggest range of scores has the greatest influence on the combined scores unless adjustments are made to equate the spread of scores. Compare Jonus's raw scores and composite scores to Derek's.

Some teachers obtain a composite grade by converting all test scores and other assessments to letter grades, converting the letter grades to numbers (e.g., A = 4, B = 3, C = 2, D = 1, F = 0) and then averaging them for a final grade. When this procedure is followed, information is lost because the data are reduced to only five categories. For example, a student with a high A and high B would receive the same average grade as a student with a low A and a low B. To overcome this problem, pluses and minuses are sometimes added (e.g., A+ = 12, A = 11, A– = 10, B+ = 9, B = 8, B– = 7, etc.). This provides more categories but some information is still lost. A better solution is to use numerical scores on all assessments and then combine these numerical scores into a composite score before assigning grades.

Guidelines for Effective and Fair Grading

Assigning grades that provide a valid measure of student achievement, that have a meaning beyond the classroom in which they are given, and that are considered to be fair by students is a difficult but important part of teaching. The following guidelines provide a framework that should help clarify and standardize the task.

1. *Inform students at the beginning of instruction what grading procedures will be used.* This should include what will be included in the final grade (e.g., tests, projects, laboratory work) and how much weight will be given to each element. It should also include a description, in achievement terms, of what each letter grade represents. A descriptive handout may be helpful.

2. *Base grades on student achievement, and achievement only.* Grades should represent the extent to which the intended learning outcomes were achieved by students. They should *not* be contaminated by student effort, tardiness, misbehavior, or other extraneous factors. These can be reported on separately, but they should not influence the achievement grade. If they are permitted to become a part of the grade, the meaning of the grade as an indicator of achievement is lost.

3. *Base grades on a wide variety of valid assessment data.* All too frequently, grades are based primarily, if not entirely, on test scores. If grades are to be sound indicators of achievement, all important learning outcomes must be assessed and the results included in the final grade. Evaluations of papers, projects, and laboratory work are not as reliable as objective test scores but to eliminate them lowers the validity of the grades.

4. *When combining scores for grading, use a proper weighting technique.* As noted earlier, the influence of a component on the overall grade is determined by the spread, or variability, of the scores. Thus, in combining scores to obtain a composite for assigning grades, be sure the spread of scores is equalized before weighting and combining them.

5. Select an appropriate frame of reference for grading. If the entire instruction is based on mastery learning, it is necessary to use an *absolute* standard for grading and to define the grades in mastery terms. For conventional classroom instruction, the pass-fail distinction should be described in absolute terms and the grades above that determined by relative position in the group. However, these relative letter grades should have achievement referents representing learning outcomes ranging from simple to complex.

6. Review borderline cases by reexamining all achievement evidence. When setting cutoff points for each grade, there is typically a student or two just below the cutoff line. Measurement errors alone might be responsible for a student being just below (or above) the line. Also, the composite score may contain a clerical error, or one low test score contributing to the composite score may be due to illness or some other extraneous factor. In any event, it is wise to review the data for borderline cases and make any needed adjustments. When in doubt, fair grading would favor giving the student the higher grade.

Although in this chapter we focused on assigning grades, it does not imply that all student assignments and activities should be graded. Using brief tests, written assignments, and projects as learning tools is frequently more effective if the focus is on detecting and overcoming learning errors rather than on assigning grades. Formative assessment emphasizes this function of assessment results. Whether graded or not, however, all assessments of student achievement should include plans for the effective feedback of results along with suggestions for improving learning. Grading is an important and necessary task in teaching but it is secondary to our main purpose—improving student learning.

Reporting to Students and Parents

The letter grade is typically required for school records, but a more elaborate report is needed for describing achievement to students and parents. One method is to use a reporting system that provides a rating of performance on each of the major learning outcomes of a course of instruction. The example of a Science Performance Report shown in Box 10.3 illustrates a form for this purpose. The report could be made more informative by listing the specific learning outcomes for each major outcome. If the instructional objectives and specific learning outcomes are specified at the beginning of instruction, as they should be, the report form can be easily arranged and shared with students when instruction begins. Just don't make the list so long and

BOX 10.3 • *Science Performance Report*

The circled number indicates the student's level of performance on each of the major learning outcomes being evaluated. The numerical ratings are defined as follows:

4 — Outstanding performance.
3 — Good performance, some improvement needed.
2 — Inadequate performance, needs additional work.
1 — Did not achieve the intended outcome.

4   3   2   1   (a) Knows scientific terms and facts.
4   3   2   1   (b) Understands science concepts and processes.
4   3   2   1   (c) Applies science learning to new situation.
4   3   2   1   (d) Demonstrates reasoning ability.
4   3   2   1   (e) Demonstrates research skills.
4   3   2   1   (f) Demonstrates laboratory proficiency.
4   3   2   1   (g) Solves math problems needed in science.

cumbersome that it overwhelms students and confuses parents. It may be helpful to have a committee of teachers, students and parents work out a satisafactory report form for your grade level, department, or the entire school.

A comprehensive report form should contain a place for an achievement grade (uncontaminated by effort, tardiness, misbehavior, or similar factors), a separate grade for effort (if desired), and a list of the intended learning outcomes, work habits, and personal characteristics to be rated. The letter grade is useful as an overall measure of achievement and is easily recorded for administrative uses. But the ratings of intended learning outcomes and related characteristics provide the most valuable information for improving learning and instruction, and reporting progress to students and parents.

Using a Portfolio

As noted in Chapter 9, there is no better way of reporting student achievement than the use of a portfolio. The collected samples of work make clear to students and parents alike what students are learning and how well they are learning it. In conference with students and parents, you can present a summary of the students' achievements and then support it by showing actual samples of the students' work. This provides as comprehensive and complete a report of student achievement as is possible. The conference also provides for two-way communication that permits the student or parent to ask for clarification and to discuss ways to improve performance.

If portfolios are not used in the school, it is still wise to use samples of student work when discussing learning progress and level of achievement with students and parents. Combined with a report form, like the one described earlier, work samples can be very useful in clarifying student achievement.

Summary of Points

1. Grades should represent achievement of the intended learning outcomes and be uncontaminated by other factors.
2. Grades should be assigned in accordance with the grading policies and procedures of the school.
3. Absolute grading requires predetermined standards based on clearly specified learning tasks and measures designed for criterion-referenced interpretation.
4. If instruction is based on a mastery learning program, absolute grading should be used with defined cutoff points and a stated rationale for the selection of the cutoff points.
5. Relative grading is based on the ranking of individuals in a group but relative grades also should have content meaning. Higher grades should represent higher levels of understanding, application, thinking skills, and performance skills.
6. Where relative grading is used, the pass-fail decision still should be determined on an absolute basis. The important question is: Does this student have the minimum knowledge and skill needed to succeed at the next level of instruction?
7. A grading system based on minimal objectives (to determine the pass-fail decision) and developmental objectives that spread students out in terms of the difficulty and complexity of the material learned, provides a good compromise between absolute and relative grading for use in conventional classroom instruction.
8. Basing grades on achievement in relation to learning ability, amount of improvement, or effort will only distort the meaning of grades as measures of achievement.
9. Grades should be based on valid measures of achievement. Validity is built in during the construction of tests and other assessment procedures by designing instruments that measure the intended outcomes of instruction.
10. Grades should be based on a variety of achievement assessments. Test scores should be supplemented by various types of performance assessment that measure the intended outcomes of instruction more directly (e.g., writing samples, laboratory work).

11. Components entering into an overall grade should be adjusted for the spread of scores before weighting them in terms of their importance.
12. Borderline cases should be given the benefit of the doubt and assigned the higher grade, unless a review of the achievement data indicates otherwise.
13. Attitude, effort, misbehavior, and other nonachievement factors might be rated separately but should not be allowed to influence the achievement grade.
14. Some tests and assessment procedures can be used for learning purposes and need not be assigned a grade (e.g., formative use of learning assessments).
15. Reporting to students and parents involves informing them of the extent to which the intended learning outcomes are being achieved. Both detailed performance reports and portfolios are useful for this purpose.
16. Whatever grading and reporting system is used, the procedures should be made clear to students at the beginning of instruction. A descriptive handout may be useful for this.

References and Additional Reading

Airasian, P. W., *Classroom Assessment*, 3rd ed. (New York: McGraw-Hill, 1997).

Linn, R. L., and Gronlund, N. E., *Measurement and Assessment in Teaching*, 8th ed. (Upper Saddle River, NJ: Merrill/Prentice-Hall, 2000).

McMillan, J. H., *Classroom Assessment: Principles and Practices for Effective Instruction.* 2nd ed. (Upper Saddle River, NJ: Merrill/Prentice-Hall, 2001).

Oosterhoff, A. C., *Classroom Applications of Educational Measurement*, 3rd ed. (Upper Saddle River, NJ: Merrill/Prentice-Hall, 2001).

11

Interpreting Standardized Achievement Test Scores

Studying this chapter should enable you to

1. Distinguish between norm-referenced and criterion-referenced interpretation of standardized test results.
2. Describe the basic features of a standardized achievement test.
3. Explain the meaning of each of the scores used in norm-referenced interpretation and list the cautions when interpreting each one.
4. Describe how standard scores are derived from the mean and standard deviation.
5. Convert standard scores to each other and to percentile ranks, using the normal curve.
6. Explain the stanine system and describe the advantages of using stanine scores.
7. Describe the procedures for making criterion-referenced interpretations with standardized tests.
8. List the cautions to observe when making criterion-referenced interpretations with standardized tests.

Standardized achievement tests have been widely used in the schools as a means of determining how well schools are doing. These tests have been primarily norm-referenced tests that compared local student performance to the performance of a representative sample of students in a norm group (e.g., a group of students at the national, regional, or state level). In the past, the test items were selection-type items, primarily multiple choice. In recent years, the tests have been modified to provide for criterion-referenced interpretations as well (e.g., by including more items per task, using open-ended tasks, and providing for interpretation by clusters of tasks). Both types of interpretation will be discussed in turn.

Being able to interpret the various types of norm-referenced test scores and understand how criterion-referenced interpretations are used in standardized tests is important, if the tests are to play a role in the instructional program. It is also important, of course, to understand them well enough to be able to explain them to students and parents. To start with, it is important to keep in mind that norm-referenced interpretation indicates a student's relative level of performance in comparison to others and criterion-referenced interpretation describes the tasks a student can perform.

Features of Standardized Achievement Tests

Standardized achievement tests are designed to determine how well students are achieving a common set of broadly based goals. Well-constructed standardized achievement tests typically have the following features.

1. The content of the test is based on widely used textbooks and curriculum guides.
2. The test items are written by test experts in consultation with subject-matter experts, and are based on a clear set of specifications.
3. The test items are tried out, reviewed, analyzed for difficulty and discriminating power, and either revised or eliminated.
4. The final set of items is selected on the basis of the test specifications.
5. Directions for administering and scoring the test are rigidly prescribed.
6. The test is administered to select groups of students to establish national, regional, or statewide norms for interpretation of the test scores.
7. The final version of the test is published along with a test manual that describes the test's technical qualities and the procedures for administering, scoring, interpreting, and using the results.

Thus, a standardized test measures a standard set of broadly based educational outcomes, uses standard directions and standard scoring procedures, and provides for a comparison of a student's score to that of similar students who have taken the same test under the same conditions. If a **battery of tests** is used, and all tests have been standardized on the same norm group, a student's performance on the different tests can also be compared. On a basic skill battery, for example, we can determine a student's relative level of performance in reading, language, and mathematics. With comparable forms of the test, we can also examine learning progress over a series of grade levels. All of these norm-referenced interpretations and comparisons of standardized test scores requires an understanding of the various types of test scores that are used in describing students' test performance.

Interpreting Norm-Referenced Scores

The score a student receives when a test has been scored according to the directions is called the **raw score.** On a classroom test, this is typically the number of items a student answers correctly. Although raw scores are used in classroom testing, the interpretations and comparisons made with standardized tests require that the raw scores be converted to some type of **derived score.** Comparison of performance on two different tests (e.g., reading and math), for example, require that both tests be on the same scale. Raw scores won't work because the two tests may differ in the number of items in the test and the difficulty of the items. By converting both sets of raw scores to the same derived score scale, we provide a common basis for comparing relative performance. Although there are many different types of derived scores, the most common types used in school achievement testing are:

1. Percentile ranks
2. Grade equivalent scores
3. Standard scores

The raw scores on a standardized test are converted to derived scores during the norming of the test. Attempts are made to obtain norm groups that contain a sample of students like those for whom the test is intended. National **norms,** for example, typically include students from the various geographic regions of the United States, urban and rural schools, and schools of different size. A balance of boys and girls, socioeconomic levels, and ethnic groups is also sought. Thus, national norms should approximate as closely as possible the student population throughout the United States. The same care is typically also followed in obtaining regional, state, and special group norms (e.g., private schools). Despite the care in obtaining norm groups, however, the obtained sample of students only approximates the ideal sample, due to such constraints as the needed cooperation of selected schools to administer the tests and the time limits for obtaining the norm sample.

After the norm groups have been selected and the tests administered and scored, the raw scores are converted to derived scores and presented in the test manual in tables of norms. These tables present the raw scores and derived scores in columns so that a raw score can be converted into a derived score by going across the parallel columns from the raw score to the derived score. Of course, the printout from machine scoring will give both the raw score and the derived score.

Before using the derived scores from a standardized test, it is wise to consider the nature of the norm group. Does the norm group provide a relevant basis for interpreting student performance? How was the norm group obtained? When were the norms obtained? We can obtain the most meaningful norm-referenced interpretation of test scores when the norms are relevant, representative, and up to date.

A final caution. The scores in the norm group should not be viewed as goals or standards. They are simply the scores that a representative group of students have earned on the test. They aid in interpreting and comparing test performance but they do not represent levels of performance to strive for. They are average or typical scores obtained in average or typical schools.

Percentile Ranks

The percentile rank is one of the easiest scores to understand and to interpret to parents. A percentile rank indicates a student's relative position in a group in terms of the percentage of group members scoring at or below the student's raw score. For example, if a raw score of 33 equals a percentile rank of 80, it means 80 percent of the group members had raw scores equal to or lower than 33. By converting raw scores to percentile ranks, the raw scores are put on a scale that has the same meaning with different size groups and for different length tests.

To further clarify the meaning of percentile ranks, Table 11.1 illustrates how raw scores are converted to percentile ranks. The following steps illustrate the procedure.

1. The raw scores are ranked from high to low (column 1).
2. The number of students obtaining each score is listed in the frequency column (column 2).
3. The score frequencies are added from the bottom up (i.e., adding each score frequency to the total frequency of all lower scores) to obtain the cumulative frequency (column 3).
4. Applying the following formula at each score level to get the percentile rank for that raw score (column 4).

$$PR = \frac{CF \text{ below score} + 1/2 \text{ of frequency at score}}{\text{number in group } (N)} \times 100$$

where PR = percentile rank
CF = cumulative frequency

To illustrate the computation, let's compute the percentile ranks for two scores.

Score 33 $\quad PR = \dfrac{23 + 1}{30} \times 100 = 80$

Score 30 $\quad PR = \dfrac{17 + .5}{30} \times 100 = 58.3$

TABLE 11.1 *Frequency Distribution and Percentile Ranks for an Objective Test of 40 Items*

1 Test Score	2 Frequency	3 Cumulative Frequency	4 Percentile Rank*
38	1	30	98
37	1	29	95
36	0	28	93
35	2	28	90
34	1	26	85
33	2	25	80
32	3	23	72
31	2	20	63
30	1	18	58
29	4	17	50
28	2	13	40
27	2	11	33
26	2	9	27
25	3	7	18
24	1	4	12
23	0	3	10
22	1	3	8
21	1	2	5
20	0	1	3
19	1	1	2
	$N = 30$		

*Rounded to nearest whole number.

Percentile ranks are rounded to the nearest whole number, so the percentile rank for the raw score of 30 is listed in Table 11.1 as 58. To be sure you understand this procedure, you can compute the percentile ranks of other raw scores in the table and check your answers.

When interpreting percentile ranks there are a number of cautions to be kept in mind. (1) Percentile ranks describe test performance in terms of the *percentage of persons* earning a lower score and *not* the percentage of items answered correctly. The **percentage correct score** is a criterion-referenced interpretation; **percentile rank** indicates relative standing and, therefore, is a norm-referenced score. (2) Percentile ranks are always specific to a particular group. For example, a percentile rank of 90 in a gifted group represents higher test performance than a percentile rank of 90 in an average group. Thus, whenever we are describing a student's relative performance, knowing the nature of the group is just as important as knowing the student's relative standing. (3) Percentile ranks are not equally spaced on the scale. A difference of 5 percentile ranks near the middle of the distribution of scores represents a smaller difference in test performance than a 5 percentile rank difference at the ends of the distribution. This is because percentile ranks are based on the percentage of persons being surpassed and there is a larger percentage of persons in the middle of a score distribution to surpass than at the ends of the distribution. For example, at the high end of the distribution, a raw score difference of several points will make little difference in percentile rank because there are so few high scores. Although this limits some uses of percentile ranks (e.g., they can't be directly averaged), they remain one of the most useful and easiest to interpret types of derived scores.

Percentile Bands

Some test manuals use **percentile bands** in presenting test norms. Instead of a specific percentile rank for each raw score, a range of percentile ranks is presented. For example, a table of norms may show that a raw score of 52 has a percentile band of 60–64. This allows for the possible error in the test score. The band tells us that we can be fairly certain that a student who earns a raw score of 52 on the test has a relative standing that falls somewhere between the 60th and 64th percentile rank. We cannot be more precise than this because our estimates of test performance (i.e., raw scores) always contain some error, due to such factors as fluctuations in attention, memory, effort, and luck in guessing during testing.

The width of the percentile band is determined by the reliability of the test. With a highly reliable test the band is narrow. With a test of low reliability the band is wide. The width of the band is computed by using the **standard error of measurement.** This is a statistic computed from the reliability coefficient and used to estimate the amount of error in an individual test score (see Chapter 12). These *error* bands can, of course, be computed for raw scores or for any type of derived score. They are sometimes called *confidence* bands because they indicate how much confidence we can have in the score representing a person's test performance. With a narrow band, we are more confident that the score represents the person's "true" or "real" level of achievement.

In addition to using percentile bands to interpret an individual's test performance, percentile bands can also be used to interpret differences in test performance on a battery of tests. In comparing percentile bands for the different tests, we can conclude that where the bands do *not* overlap there is probably a "real" difference in test performance and where they do overlap, the differences are likely to be due to error. For example, the following percentile bands from a test battery for Maria indicate that there is no "real" difference in her performance in reading and language, but she is lower in math.

	Reading	*Language*	*Math*
Maria's percentile bands	70–75	74–79	63–68

The use of percentile bands prevents us from over interpreting small differences in test scores. Test publishers that use percentile bands typically plot them as bars on students' test profiles, making it easy to determine when the ends of the bands overlap and when they don't.

Grade Equivalent Scores

Grade equivalent scores provide another widely used method of describing test performance. They are used primarily at the elementary school level. With these scores, a student's raw score on the test is converted to the grade level at which the score matches the average raw score of students in the norm group. As with other derived scores, tables in the test manual present parallel columns of raw scores and grade equivalents. Thus, all we need to do is consult the table and obtain the grade equivalent for any given raw score. Although it is easy to obtain and is apparently easy to interpret, it is probably one of the most misinterpreted types of score. Let's take a look at what the grade equivalent score means and what it doesn't mean.

To clarify the meaning of grade equivalents, let's assume that we obtained the following grade equivalent scores from a test battery for Dave, who is in the middle of the fourth grade.

Reading	4.5
Language	6.5
Math	7.8

First note that the grade equivalent score is expressed in terms of the grade level and the month in that school year. Thus, Dave's score in reading is equal to the average score earned by students (in the norm group) in the middle of the fourth grade. Because Dave is in the middle of the fourth grade, we interpret his performance in reading as average. In language, Dave is two years advanced, and in math, he is more than three years advanced. Does that mean that Dave can do the work at these levels? No, it most likely means that he does fourth-grade work in these areas faster and more efficiently than other fourth-graders. The tests probably did not include sixth- and seventh-grade material. The same misinterpretations can occur with low grade equivalents. If Dave had a math score of 2.0, for example, it wouldn't mean he could only do second-grade math problems. It would more likely mean that he did fourth-grade problems slower and with more errors than other fourth-graders. High and low grade equivalent scores are typically obtained by extrapolation and do not represent average scores earned by those groups. This is often necessary because students at lower grade levels may not have the knowledge and skill needed to take the test and students at higher grade levels may have moved beyond the types of skills measured by the test.

Grade equivalent scores provide a simple method of interpreting test performance, but when using them and interpreting them to parents, the following common misinterpretations should be avoided.

1. They are *not* standards to be achieved but simply the average scores of students in the norm group.
2. They do *not* indicate the grade level at which a student can do the work.
3. Extremely high and low grade equivalent scores are *not* as dependable indicators of test performance as those near the student's grade level.

In addition to these cautions to be observed when interpreting an individual's grade equivalent scores, a comparison of scores on tests in a test battery requires an additional caution. Growth in basic skills, for example, is uneven. In reading, growth is more rapid than in math, which depends more directly on the skills taught in school. Thus, a difference of a year in grade equivalent scores represents a larger difference in achievement on a reading test than on a math test. In addition, growth in achievement tends to slow down at different times for different skills, and when growth slows down, the differences in achievement between grade equivalent scores become smaller. Both the variations in growth of skills from one area to another and the variations in patterns of growth over time contribute to the unevenness of the units on our grade equivalent score scale. In comparing a student's grade equivalent scores on different tests from a test battery, it may be wise to look at the norm table to see how the raw scores spread out on each test. A high or low grade equivalent score might be discounted if the difference from other grade equivalent scores is based on relatively few raw score points.

Standard Scores

A **standard score** describes test performance in terms of how far a raw score is above or below average. It is expressed in units that are computed from the mean and the standard deviation of a set of scores. We are all familiar with the use of the **mean** as an average. It is obtained by summing the test scores and dividing by the number of scores. The standard deviation indicates the spread of scores in a set. The computation for obtaining the standard deviation is shown in Box 11.1, but that does not help us understand its meaning or its use in interpreting standard scores. This can best be done by describing its properties and showing how it is used as the basic unit for the various types of standard scores.

BOX 11.1 • *Computation of the Standard Deviation Using a Hand Calculator*

Steps to Follow
1. Square each score in the set.
2. Add these squared values to obtain a total.
3. Divide the total by the number of scores in the set.
4. Square the mean of the set of scores.
5. Subtract the squared mean in step 4 from the result obtained in step 3.
6. Take the square root of the difference obtained in step 5. This is the standard deviation (*SD* or *s*).

Formula for the Computational Steps

$$SD = \sqrt{\frac{\Sigma X^2}{N} - M^2}$$

where
Σ = "sum of"
X = a test score
N = number of scores
M = mean
$\sqrt{}$ = "square root of"

The standard deviation (*SD* or *s*) is an important and widely applicable statistic in testing. In addition to its use as a basic unit in standard scores, it also serves as a basis for computing reliability coefficients and the standard error of measurement, as we shall see in the next chapter.

The Mean, Standard Deviation, and Normal Curve

The mean and the standard deviation can probably be best understood in terms of the **normal curve,** although a normal distribution is not required for computing them. The normal curve is a symmetrical bell-shaped curve based on a precise mathematical equation. Scores distributed according to the normal curve are concentrated near the mean and decrease in frequency the further one departs from the mean. A sample normal curve is presented in Figure 11.1.

It will be noted in Figure 11.1 that the mean falls at the exact center of a normal distribution. Note also that when the normal curve is divided into standard deviation (*SD*) units, which are equal distances along the baseline of the curve, each portion under the curve contains a fixed percentage of cases. Thus, 34 percent of the cases fall between the mean and +1 *SD*, 14 percent

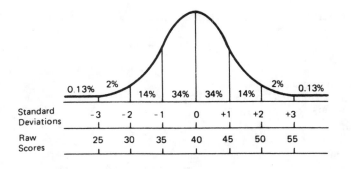

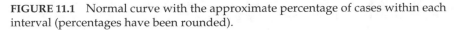

FIGURE 11.1   Normal curve with the approximate percentage of cases within each interval (percentages have been rounded).

between +1 *SD* and +2 *SD,* and 2 percent between +2 *SD* and +3 *SD*. Since the curve is symmetrical, the same percentages, of course, apply to the intervals below the mean. These percentages have been rounded to the nearest whole number, but only a small fraction of a percent (0.13 percent) of the cases fall above and below three standard deviations from the mean. Thus, from a practical standpoint, a normal distribution of scores falls between –3 and +3 standard deviations from the mean.

To aid in understanding the meaning of standard deviation, a set of raw scores with a mean of 40 and a standard deviation of 5 has been placed below the baseline of the curve in Figure 11.1. Note that the mean raw score of 40 has been placed at the zero point and that the distance of one standard deviation is 5 raw score points everywhere along the baseline of the curve. Thus, the point one standard deviation above the mean equals 45 (40 + 5) and the point one standard deviation below the mean equals 35 (40 – 5). In this particular set of scores, then, approximately 68 percent of the scores (about two-thirds) fall between 35 and 45, approximately 96 percent fall between 30 and 50, and approximately 99.7 percent fall between 25 and 55 (the figure shows 100 percent because numbers are rounded).

When the standard deviation is being computed for a set of normally distributed scores, we are essentially determining how far we need to go above (or below) the mean in raw score points to include 34 percent of the cases. The scores obtained with standardized tests typically approximate a normal distribution or are normalized by statistical means and thus permit the types of interpretations we are making here.

z-Scores

A number of standard scores are based on the standard deviation unit. The simplest of these and the one that is basic to the others is the z-score. This score simply indicates, in standard deviation units, how far a given raw score is above or below the mean. The raw score of 45 in Figure 11.1, for example, would be assigned a z-score of 1.0 because it is one standard deviation above the mean. The raw score of 30 in Figure 11.1 would be given a z-score of −2.0 because it is two standard deviations below the mean. The formula for z-scores is:

$$z\text{-score} = \frac{\text{Raw score} - \text{Mean}}{\text{Standard deviation}}$$

For example, z-scores for raw scores of 47 and 36 in Figure 11.1 would be computed as follows:

$$z\text{-score} = \frac{47 - 40}{5} = 1.4 \qquad z\text{-score} = \frac{36 - 40}{5} = -.8$$

Thus, a raw score of 47 is 1.4 standard deviations above the mean and a raw score of 36 is .8 of a standard deviation below the mean.

While used in research, z-scores are seldom used directly in test interpretation because of the use of decimal points and minus signs. Instead, z-scores are converted to other types of standard scores that use only whole numbers and positive values. Such scores are more convenient to use and avoid the possibility of misinterpretation due to a forgotten minus sign.

There are a number of different types of standard scores used in test interpretation. All one needs to do is select an arbitrary mean and standard deviation and convert the z-scores into the standard score units. To illustrate, we will describe the procedure for some common standard scores.

T-Scores

***T*-scores** have a mean of 50 and a standard deviation of 10. They are obtained from z-scores by multiplying the z-score by 10 and adding the result to 50, as shown in the following formula.

$T\text{-score} = 50 + 10\,(z\text{-score})$

Applying the formula to the various z-scores discussed earlier (1.0, −2.0, 1.4, −.8) we would obtain *T*-scores as follows:

$T = 50 + 10\,(1.0) = 60 \qquad T = 50 + 10\,(-2.0) = 30$

$T = 50 + 10\,(1.4) = 64 \qquad T = 50 + 10\,(-.8) = 42$

T-scores can be easily interpreted because they always have the same mean and standard deviation. A *T*-score of 60 always means one standard deviation above the mean and a *T*-score of 30 always means two standard deviations below the mean. Thus, with the use of *T*-scores, an individual's performance on different tests can be directly compared, and the scores can be combined or averaged without the distortion of different size standard deviations, which occur with the raw scores.

Where a normal distribution can be assumed, *T*-scores can also be interpreted in terms of percentile ranks because, in this case, there is a direct relationship between the two as shown in Figure 11.2. Note that a *T*-score of 30 is equivalent to a percentile rank of 2, a *T*-score of 40 is equivalent to a percentile rank of 16, and so on. This relationship makes it possible to use standard scores for those purposes where equal units are

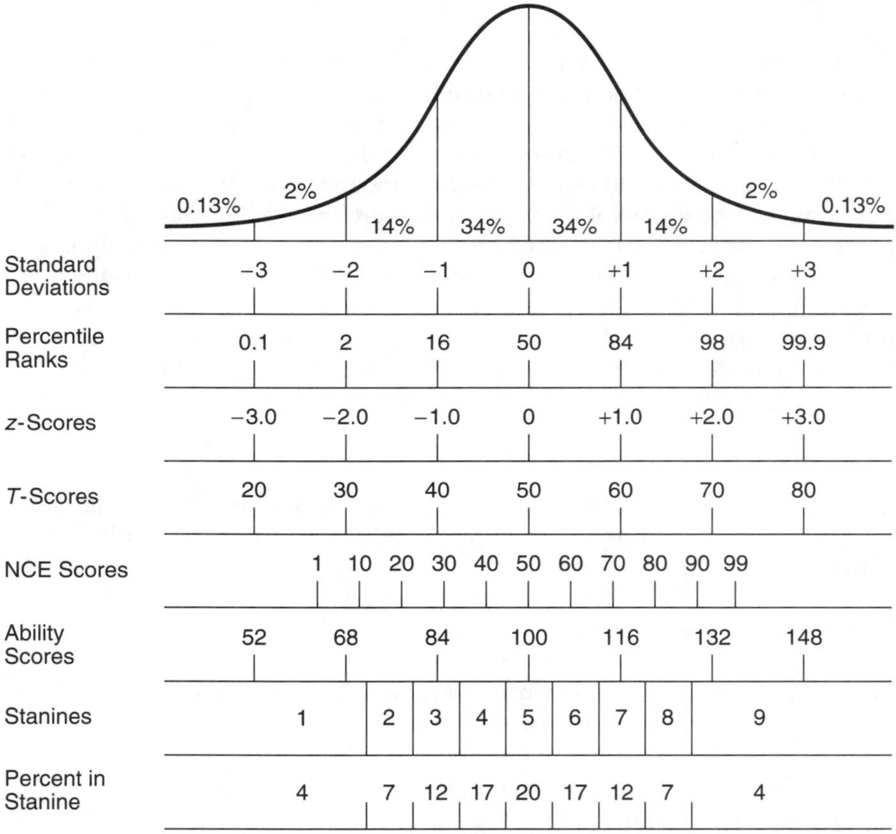

FIGURE 11.2   Corresponding percentile ranks, z-scores, *T*-scores, NCE scores, ability scores, and stanines in a normal distribution.

needed and to use percentile ranks when interpreting test performance to students and parents.

Because *T*-scores and percentile ranks both have a mean of 50 and use similar two-digit numbers, the two types of scores are often confused by those inexperienced in test interpretation. Thus, it is important to keep in mind that percentile rank indicates the percentage of individuals who fall at or below a given score, while a *T*-score indicates how many standard deviation units a given score falls above or below the mean. Note in Figure 11.2 that although percentile ranks and *T*-scores have the same mean value of 50, below the mean percentile ranks are smaller than *T*-scores and above the mean they are larger than *T*-scores. This is accounted for, of course, by the fact that percentile ranks are crowded together in the center of the distribution and spread out at the ends, while *T*-scores provide equal units throughout the distribution of scores.

Normal-Curve Equivalent Scores (NCE)

Another standard score that might be confused with both *T*-scores and percentile ranks is the **normal-curve equivalent score** (NCE). This set of scores also has a mean of 50, but a standard deviation of 21.06. This provides a set of scores with equal units, like the *T*-score, but the scores range from 1 to 99. Percentile ranks also range from 1 to 99, but they do not provide equal units. As can be seen in Figure 11.2, percentile ranks are smaller at the middle of the distribution (e.g., one SD = 34%) than at the ends (e.g., one SD = 2%). Thus, when interpreting NCE scores, don't confuse them with *T*-scores, which have a more restricted range of scores (typically 20 to 80), or with percentile ranks that have the same range of scores (1 to 99) but are based on unequal units.

Ability Scores

Publishers of achievement test batteries typically administer a test of learning ability (also called cognitive ability, school ability, or intelligence) to the same norm groups as the achievement battery to make comparisons of learning ability and achievement possible. The scores on these tests are now reported as standard scores with a mean of 100 and standard deviation of 16 (15 on some tests). These scores are to be interpreted like any other standard score (see Figure 11.2). A score of 116 means one standard deviation above the mean (percentile rank = 84). These scores were originally called deviation IQs, because they replaced the old ratio IQ (i.e., $\frac{MA}{CA} \times 100$). More recently, however, to avoid the confusion surrounding IQ scores, they have been given more appropriate names, such as school ability scores and standard age scores.

Stanine Scores

Test scores can also be expressed by single-digit standard scores called stanines (pronounced *stay-nines*). The stanine scale divides the distribution of raw scores into nine parts (the term **stanine** was derived from *standard nines*). The highest stanine score is 9, the lowest is 1, and stanine 5 is located in the center of the distribution. Each stanine, except 9 and 1, includes a band of raw scores *one-half of a standard deviation wide*. Thus, stanines are standard scores with a mean of 5 and a standard deviation of 2. The distribution of stanines and the percentage of cases in each stanine are shown in Figure 11.2.

The nine-point scale is simple to interpret to students and parents because of the single-digit score. It is easy to visualize where a person falls on a nine-point scale, where 5 is average. Because each stanine includes a band of raw scores, there is also less chance that test performance will be overinterpreted. When comparing scores on two different tests in a test battery, a difference of two stanines is typically significant. Thus, in interpreting the following scores for a student, we would conclude that the student is higher in math but there is no difference between reading and language.

Reading stanine   = 5
Language stanine = 4
Math stanine   = 7

In addition to the ease of interpretation, stanines provide a simple method for combining and averaging test scores. The conversion of raw scores to stanines puts the scores from different tests on the same standard score scale, with equal units. Thus, they have uniform meaning from one part of the scale to another and from one test to another. A difference between stanine 5 and stanine 7 is the same as a difference between a stanine of 4 and a stanine of 6. A difference of two stanines is also the same, if we are referring to a reading test, a language test, a math test, or any other test. Like other standard scores, they provide equal units that can be readily combined. Unlike other standard scores, they are easy to interpret and to explain to others. See Box 11.2 for suggestions on how to interpret test results.

Criterion-Referenced Interpretation

To make standardized achievement test batteries more useful for instructional purposes, some test publishers have modified the multiple-choice items to include more real-life situations, added open-ended performance tasks, and made provisions for criterion-referenced interpretation of test performance.

BOX 11.2 • *Interpreting Standardized Test Results to Students and Parents*

1. Describe in general terms what the test measures and how it relates to the local curriculum (e.g., The test measures computational skills only. It does not include measures of math reasoning, which is the main focus of our curriculum.).
2. When interpreting percentile ranks, keep the description simple (e.g., The percentile rank of 87 means 87 percent of students in the norm group had lower scores. It is not a percentage-correct score.).
3. When interpreting grade equivalents, make statements that are unlikely to be misinterpreted (e.g., The grade equivalent of 6.5 for a fifth-grader means he can do fifth-grade work as rapidly and efficiently as students in the middle of the sixth grade.).
4. When interpreting stanines, use brief, simple statements (e.g., The stanine of 6 on the reading test is one stanine above average on a scale from 1 to 9, and the stanine of 4 on the math test is one stanine below average.).
5. When interpreting differences between test scores use percentile bands or other ways to take error into account (e.g., The percentile bands for reading and math do not overlap, so there is probably a "real" difference in performance. Or, the stanines indicate a "real" difference because they differ by two stanines.).

One of the best known methods of reporting criterion-referenced test results is the *percentage-correct score*. This simply reports the percentage of test items in a test, or subtest, answered correctly. The report can be for individual students, the class, the school, or the entire school district. Percentage-correct scores for the various school groups are compared to the percentage-correct scores in the national norm sample as one basis for evaluating the schools.

Scores for individuals can also be presented by clusters of items representing a content area, skill, or objective, with an indication of the level of performance (e.g., above average, average, below average). Care must be taken in interpreting these results where a small number of items is included in the item clusters.

Some test batteries provide reports that include standards of performance. The standards are typically set by panels of educators and the report indicates a student level of performance by categories ranging from lack of mastery to superior performance.

When making criterion-referenced interpretations of test performance there are a number of questions to keep in mind.

1. Do the objectives the tests were designed to measure match the school's objectives for these subjects (e.g., routine skills versus reasoning)?
2. Are the skills and content measured by the tests appropriate for the grade levels tested?
3. Did elimination of the easy items from the test, to obtain greater discrimination among students for norm-referenced interpretation, result in inadequate description of what low-achieving students can do?
4. Was there a sufficient number of test items in each item cluster to permit criterion-referenced interpretation?
5. Was the procedure in setting performance standards adequate for this type of interpretation?

Criterion-referenced interpretation of standardized tests can be useful in classroom instruction but they must be cautiously made.

Summary of Points

1. Standardized achievement tests have been widely used in the schools to determine how student performance compared to that of a sample of students (i.e., a norm group) at the national, regional, or state level.
2. Standardized tests were carefully constructed to fit a set of test specifications, tried out and improved, and administered to a norm group for norm-referenced test interpretation.
3. The most common types of norm-referenced scores used with standardized tests are percentile ranks, grade equivalent scores, and various types of standard scores.
4. A percentile rank indicates relative position in a group in terms of the percentage of group members scoring at or below a given score. It should not be confused with the percentage of items answered correctly (a criterion-referenced interpretation).
5. Percentile bands are used in reporting test performance to allow for possible error in test scores. The width of the band indicates the amount of error to allow for during interpretation, and it prevents the overinterpretation of small differences in test scores.
6. A grade equivalent score indicates relative test performance in terms of the grade level at which the student's raw score matches the average score earned by the norm group. Thus, a grade equivalent score of 4.5 indicates performance equal to the average student in the middle of the fourth grade. Grade equivalent scores are easy to interpret but they are subject to numerous misinterpretations.

7. Standard scores are based on the mean (*M*) and standard deviation (*SD*) of a set of scores. To fully understand them it is necessary to understand the meaning of these statistics.

8. Standard scores indicate the number of standard deviations a raw score falls above and below the mean. They are more difficult to understand and interpret to others but they have the advantage of providing equal units.

9. The standard scores discussed in this chapter have the following means (*M*) and standard deviations (*SD*). The third column shows the score for one standard above the mean.

	M	*SD*	*+1SD*
z-scores	0	1	1
T-scores	50	10	60
NCE scores	50	21.06	71
Ability scores	100	16	116
Stanines	5	2	7

10. In a normal distribution, any standard score can be converted to percentile rank for easy interpretation. For example, one standard deviation above the mean (see column 3) has a percentile rank of 84, no matter what type of standard score is used to express test performance.

11. Because *T*-scores, NCE scores, and percentile ranks all have a mean of 50 and use similar two-digit numbers, care must be taken not to confuse them when interpreting test performance.

12. Stanines are single-digit standard scores that range from 1 to 9. They are easily explained to students and parents and a difference of two stanines typically indicates a significant (i.e., "real") difference in test performance.

13. Stanines and percentile ranks using percentile bands are the two types of scores that are favored when interpreting test results to others and judging differences between test scores.

14. Criterion-referenced interpretations of test performance have been added to many standardized tests. These include percentage correct scores, the use of performance standards and interpretation by item clusters representing a content area, skill, or objective.

15. Criterion-referenced interpretations of standardized tests require a check on how well the objectives, content, and skills of the test match the local instructional program; whether the construction of the test favors criterion-referenced interpretation; whether there is a sufficient number of test items for each type of interpretation; and how the performance standards are determined.

References and Additional Reading

American Educational Research Association, *Standards for Educational and Psychological Testing* (Washington, DC: AERA, 1999).

Chase, C. I., *Contemporary Assessment for Educators* (New York: Longman, 1999).

Linn, R. L., and Gronlund, N. E., *Measurement and Assessment in Teaching*, 8th ed. (Upper Saddle River, NJ: Merrill/Prentice-Hall, 2000).

Lyman, H. B., *Test Scores and What They Mean*, 6th ed. (Boston: Allyn and Bacon, 1998).

Oosterhoff, A. C. *Classroom Applications of Educational Measurement*, 3rd ed. (Upper Saddle River, NJ: Merrill/Prentice-Hall, 2001).

12

Validity and Reliability

Studying this chapter should enable you to

1. Distinguish between validity and reliability.
2. Describe the essential features of the concept of validity.
3. Describe how content-related evidence of validity is obtained.
4. List factors that can lower the validity of achievement assessments.
5. Describe procedures for obtaining criterion-related evidence of validity.
6. Describe procedures for obtaining construct-related evidence of validity.
7. Describe the role of consequences of using an assessment procedure on its validity.
8. Describe the methods for estimating test reliability and the type of information provided by each.
9. Describe how the standard error of measurement is computed and interpreted.
10. Explain how to determine the reliability of a performance-based assessment.

The two most important questions to ask about a test or other assessment procedure are: (1) to what extent will the interpretation of the results be appropriate, meaningful, and useful?, and (2) to what extent will the results be free from errors? The first question is concerned with *validity*, the second with *reliability*. An understanding of both concepts is essential to the effective construction, selection, interpretation, and use of tests and other assessment instruments. Validity is the most important quality to consider in the preparation and use of assessment procedures. First and foremost, we want the results to provide a representative and relevant measure of the achievement domain under consideration. Our second consideration is reliability, which refers to the consistency of our assessment results. For example, if we tested individuals at a different time, or with a different sample of equivalent items, we would like to obtain approximately the same results. This consistency of results is important for two reasons. (1) Unless the results are fairly stable we cannot expect them to be valid. For example, if an individual scored high on a test one time and low another time, it would be impossible to validly describe the achievement. (2) Consistency of results indicates smaller errors of measurement and, thereby, more dependable results. Thus, reliability provides the consistency needed to obtain validity and enables us to interpret assessment results with greater confidence.

Although it is frequently unnecessary to make elaborate validation and reliability studies of informal assessment procedures, an understanding of these concepts provides a conceptual framework that can serve as a guide for more effective construction of assessment instruments, more effective selection of standardized tests, and more appropriate interpretation and use of assessment results.

Validity

Validity is concerned with the interpretation and use of assessment results. For example, if we infer from an assessment that students have achieved the intended learning outcomes, we would like some assurance that our tasks provided a relevant and representative measure of the outcomes. If we infer that the assessment is useful for predicting or estimating some other performance, we would like some credible evidence to support that interpretation. If we infer that our assessment indicates that students have good "reasoning ability," we would like some evidence to support the fact that the results actually reflect that construct. If we infer that our use of an assessment had positive effects (e.g., increased motivation) and no adverse effects (e.g., poor study habits) on students, we would like some evidence concerning the consequences of its use. These are the kinds of considerations we are concerned with when considering the validity of assessment results (see the summary in Figure 12.1).

The meaning of *validity* in interpreting and using assessment results can be grasped most easily by reviewing the following characteristics.

1. Validity is *inferred* from available evidence (not measured).
2. Validity depends on *many different types* of evidence.
3. Validity is expressed by *degree* (high, moderate, low).
4. Validity is specific to a particular *use*.
5. Validity refers to the *inferences drawn*, not the instrument.
6. Validity is a *unitary concept*.
7. Validity is concerned with the *consequences of using the assessments*.

Describing validity as a unitary concept is a basic change in how validity is viewed. The traditional view that there were several different "types of

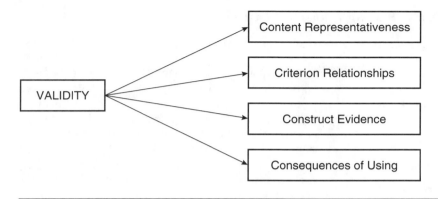

FIGURE 12.1   Types of considerations in determining the validity of assessment results.

validity" has been replaced by the view that validity is a single, unitary concept that is based on various forms of evidence. The former "types of validity" (content, criterion-related, and construct) are now simply considered to be convenient categories for accumulating evidence to support the validity of an interpretation. Thus, we no longer speak of "content validity," but of "content-related evidence" of validity. Similarly, we speak of "criterion-related evidence" and "construct-related evidence."

For some interpretations of assessment results only one or two types of evidence may be critical, but an *ideal* validation would include evidence from all four categories. We are most likely to draw valid inferences from assessment results when we have a full understanding of: (1) the nature of the assessment procedure and the specifications that were used in developing it, (2) the relation of the assessment results to significant criterion measures, (3) the nature of the psychological characteristic(s) or construct(s) being assessed, and (4) the consequences of using the assessment. Although in many practical situations the evidence falls short of this ideal, we should gather as much relevant evidence as is feasible within the constraints of the situation. We should also look for the various types of evidence when evaluating standardized tests (see Table 12.1).

Content-Related Evidence

Content-related evidence of validity is critical when we want to use performance on a set of tasks as evidence of performance on a larger domain of tasks. Let's assume, for example, that we have a list of 500 words that we expect our students to be able to spell correctly at the end of the school year. To test their spelling ability, we might give them a 50-word spelling test. Their performance on these words is important only insofar as it provides

TABLE 12.1   *Basic Approaches to Validation*

Type of Evidence	Question to Be Answered
Content-Related	How adequately does the sample of assessment tasks represent the domain of tasks to be measured?
Criterion-Related	How accurately does performance on the assessment (e.g., test) predict future performance (predictive study) or estimate present performance (concurrent study) on some other valued measure called a criterion?
Construct-Related	How well can performance on the assessment be explained in terms of psychological characteristics?
Consequences	How well did use of the assessment serve the intended purpose (e.g., improve performance) and avoid adverse effects (e.g., poor study habits)?

evidence of their ability to spell the 500 words. Thus, our spelling test would provide a valid measure to the degree to which it provided an adequate sample of the 500 words it represented. If we selected only easy words, only difficult words, or only words that represented certain types of common spelling errors, our test would tend to be unrepresentative and thus the scores would have low validity. If we selected a balanced sample of words that took these and similar factors into account, our test scores would provide a representative measure of the 500 spelling words and thereby provide for high validity.

It should be clear from this discussion that the key element in content-related evidence of validity is the adequacy of the *sampling*. An assessment is always a sample of the many tasks that could be included. Content validation is a matter of determining whether the sample of tasks is representative of the larger domain of tasks it is supposed to represent.

Content-related evidence of validity is especially important in achievement assessment. Here we are interested in how well the assessment measures the intended learning outcomes of the instruction. We can provide greater assurance that an assessment provides valid results by (1) identifying the learning outcomes to be assessed, (2) preparing a plan that specifies the sample of tasks to be used, and (3) preparing an assessment procedure that closely fits the set of specifications. These are the best procedures we have for ensuring the assessment of a representative sample of the domain of tasks encompassed by the intended learning outcomes.

Although the focus of content-related evidence of validity is on the adequacy of the sampling, a valid interpretation of the assessment results assumes that the assessment was properly prepared, administered, and scored. Validity can be lowered by inadequate procedures in any of these areas (see Box 12.1). Thus, validity is "built in" during the planning and preparation stages and maintained by proper administration and scoring. Throughout this book we have described how to prepare assessments that provide valid results, even though we have not used the word validity as each procedure was discussed.

The makers of standardized test follow these same systematic procedures in building achievement tests, but the content and learning outcomes included in the test specifications are more broadly based than those used in classroom assessment. Typically, they are based on the leading textbooks and the recommendations of various experts in the area being covered by the test. Therefore, a standardized achievement test may be representative of a broad range of content but be unrepresentative of the domain of content taught in a particular school situation. To determine relevance to the local situation, it is necessary to evaluate the sample of test items in light of the content and skills emphasized in the instruction.

In summary, content-related evidence of validity is of major concern in achievement assessment, whether you are developing or selecting the assessment procedure. When constructing a test, for example, content relevance and representativeness are built in by following a systematic procedure for specifying and selecting the sample of test items, constructing high quality items, and arranging the test for efficient administration and scoring. In test selection, it is a matter of comparing the test sample to the domain of tasks to be measured and determining the degree of correspondence between them. Similar care is needed when preparing and using performance assessments. Thus, content-related evidence of validity is obtained primarily by careful, logical analysis.

BOX 12.1 • *Factors That Lower the Validity of Assessment Results*

1. Tasks that provide an inadequate sample of the achievement to be assessed.
2. Tasks that do not function as intended, due to use of improper types of tasks, lack of relevance, ambiguity, clues, bias, inappropriate difficulty, or similar factors.
3. Improper arrangement of tasks and unclear directions.
4. Too few tasks for the types of interpretation to be made (e.g., interpretation by objective based on a few test items).
5. Improper administration—such as inadequate time allowed and poorly controlled conditions.
6. Judgmental scoring that uses inadequate scoring guides, or objective scoring that contains computational errors.

Criterion-Related Evidence

There are two types of studies used in obtaining criterion-related evidence of validity. These can be explained most clearly using test scores, although they could be used with any type of assessment result. The first type of study is concerned with the use of test performance to predict future performance on some other valued measure called a *criterion*. For example, we might use scholastic aptitude test scores to predict course grades (the criterion). For obvious reasons, this is called a *predictive* study. The second type of study is concerned with the use of test performance to estimate current performance on some criterion. For instance, we might want to use a test of study skills to estimate what the outcome would be of a careful observation of students in an actual study situation (the criterion). Since with this procedure both measures (test and criterion) are obtained at approximately the same time, this type of study is called a *concurrent* study.

Although the value of using a predictive study is rather obvious, a question might be raised concerning the purpose of a concurrent study. Why would anyone want to use test scores to estimate performance on some other measure that is to be obtained at the same time? There are at least three good reasons for doing this. First, we may want to check the results of a newly constructed test against some existing test that has a considerable amount of validity evidence supporting it. Second, we may want to substitute a brief, simple testing procedure for a more complex and time-consuming measure. For example, our test of study skills might be substituted for an elaborate rating system if it provided a satisfactory estimate of study performance. Third, we may want to determine whether a testing procedure has *potential* as a predictive instrument. If a test provides an unsatisfactory estimate of current performance, it certainly cannot be expected to predict future performance on the same measure. On the other hand, a satisfactory estimate of present performance would indicate that the test may be useful in predicting future performance as well. This would inform us that a predictive study would be worth doing.

The key element in both types of criterion-related study is the *degree of relationship* between the two sets of measures: (1) the test scores and (2) the criterion to be predicted or estimated. This relationship is typically expressed by means of a correlation coefficient or an expectancy table.

Correlation Coefficients.   Although the computation of correlation coefficients is beyond the scope of this book, the concept of correlation can easily be grasped. A **correlation coefficient** (r) simply indicates the degree of relationship between two sets of measures. A *positive* relationship is indicated when high scores on one measure are accompanied by high scores on the other; low scores on the two measures are similarly associated. A *negative* relationship is indicated when high scores on one measure are accompanied by low scores on the other. The extreme degrees of relationship it is possible to obtain between two sets of scores are indicated by the following values:

1.00 = perfect positive relationship
.00 = no relationship
−1.00 = perfect negative relationship

When a correlation coefficient is used to express the degree of relationship between a set of test scores and some criterion measure, it is called a *validity coefficient.* For example, a validity coefficient of 1.00 applied to the relationship between a set of aptitude test scores (the predictor) and a set of achievement test scores (the criterion) would indicate that each individual in the group had exactly the same relative standing on both measures, and would thereby provide a perfect prediction from the aptitude scores to the achievement scores. Most validity coefficients are smaller than this, but the extreme positive relationship provides a useful bench mark for evaluating validity coefficients. The closer the validity coefficient approaches 1.00, the higher the degree of relationship and, thus, the more accurate our predictions of each individual's success on the criterion will be.

A more realistic procedure for evaluating a validity coefficient is to compare it to the validity coefficients that are *typically* obtained when the two measures are correlated. For example, a validity coefficient of .40 between a set of aptitude test scores and achievement test scores would be considered small because we typically obtain coefficients in the .50 to .70 range for these two measures. Therefore, validity coefficients must be judged on a relative basis, the larger coefficients being favored. To use validity coefficients effectively, one must become familiar with the size of the validity coefficients that are typically obtained between various pairs of measures under different conditions (e.g., the longer the time span between measures, the smaller the validity coefficient).

Expectancy Table. The expectancy table is a simple and practical means of expressing criterion-related evidence of validity and is especially useful for making predictions from test scores. The **expectancy table** is simply a twofold chart with the test scores (the predictor) arranged in categories down the left side of the table and the measure to be predicted (the criterion) arranged in categories across the top of the table. For each category of scores on the *predictor,* the table indicates the percentage of individuals who fall within each category of the *criterion.* An example of an expectancy table is presented in Table 12.2.

Note in Table 12.2 that of those students who were in the above-average group (stanines 7, 8, and 9) on the test scores, 43 percent received a grade of A, 43 percent a B, and 14 percent a C. Although these percentages are based on this particular group, it is possible to use them to predict the future performance of other students in this science course. Hence, if a student falls in

TABLE 12.2 *Expectancy Table Showing the Relation between Scholastic Aptitude Scores and Course Grades for 30 Students in a Science Course*

Grouped Scholastic Aptitude Scores (Stanines)	Percentage in Each Score Category Receiving Each Grade				
	E	D	C	B	A
Above Average (7, 8, 9)			14	43	43
Average (4, 5, 6)		19	37	25	19
Below Average (1, 2, 3)	57	29	14		

the above-average group on this scholastic aptitude test, we might predict that he or she has 43 chances out of 100 of earning an A, 43 chances out of 100 of earning a B, and 14 chances out of a 100 of earning a C in this particular science course. Such predictions are highly tentative, of course, due to the small number of students on which this expectancy table was built. Teachers can construct more dependable tables by accumulating data from several classes over a period of time.

Expectancy tables can be used to show the relationship between any two measures. Constructing the table is simply a matter of (1) grouping the scores on each measure into a series of categories (any number of them), (2) placing the two sets of categories on a twofold chart, (3) tabulating the number of students who fall into each position in the table (based on the student's standing on both measures), and (4) converting these numbers to percentages (of the total number in that row). Thus, the expectancy table is a clear way of showing the relationship between sets of scores. Although the expectancy table is more cumbersome to deal with than a correlation coefficient, it has the special advantage of being easily understood by persons without knowledge of statistics. Thus, it can be used in practical situations to clarify the predictive efficiency of a test.

Construct-Related Evidence

The construct-related category of evidence focuses on assessment results as a basis for inferring the possession of certain psychological characteristics. For example, we might want to describe a person's reading comprehension, reasoning ability, or mechanical aptitude. These are all hypothetical qualities, or *constructs*, that we assume exist in order to explain behavior. Such theoretical constructs are useful in describing individuals and in predicting how they will act in many different specific situations. To describe a person as being highly intelligent, for example, is useful because that term carries with it a series of associated meanings that indicate what the individual's behavior is likely to be under various conditions. Before we can interpret assessment results in terms of these broad behavior descriptions, however, we must first establish that the constructs that are presumed to be reflected in the scores actually do account for differences in performance.

Construct-related evidence of validity for a test includes (1) a description of the theoretical framework that specifies the nature of the construct to be measured, (2) a description of the development of the test and any aspects of measurement that may affect the meaning of the test scores (e.g., test format), (3) the pattern of relationship between the test scores and other significant variables (e.g., high correlations with similar tests and low correlations with tests measuring different constructs), and (4) any other type of evidence that contributes to the meaning of the test scores (e.g., analyzing the mental process used in responding, determining the predictive effectiveness of the test). The specific types of evidence that are most critical for a particular test depend on the nature of the construct, the clarity of the theoretical framework, and the uses to be made of the test scores. Although the gathering of construct-related evidence of validity can be endless, in practical situations it is typically necessary to limit the evidence to that which is most relevant to the interpretations to be made.

The construct-related category of evidence is the broadest of the three categories. Evidence obtained in both the content-related category (e.g., representativeness of the sample of tasks) and the criterion-related category (e.g., how well the scores predict performance on specific criteria) are also relevant to the construct-related category because they help to clarify the meaning of the assessment results. Thus, the construct-related category encompasses a variety of types of evidence, including that from content-related and criterion-related validation studies (see Figure 12.2).

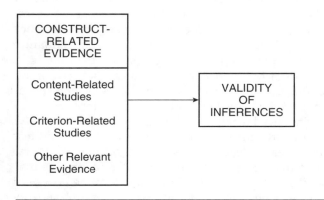

FIGURE 12.2 Construct validation includes all categories of evidence.

The broad array of evidence that might be considered can be illustrated by a test designed to measure mathematical reasoning ability. Some of the evidence we might consider is:

1. Compare the sample of test tasks to the domain of tasks specified by the conceptual framework of the construct. Is the sample relevant and representative (content-related evidence)?
2. Examine the test features and their possible influence on the meaning of the scores (e.g., test format, directions, scoring, reading level of items). Is it possible that some features might distort the scores?
3. Analyze the mental process used in answering the questions by having students "think aloud" as they respond to each item. Do the items require the intended reasoning process?
4. Determine the internal consistency of the test by intercorrelating the test items. Do the items seem to be measuring a single characteristic (in this case mathematical reasoning)?
5. Correlate the test scores with the scores of other mathematical reasoning tests. Do they show a high degree of relationship?
6. Compare the scores of known groups (e.g., mathematical majors and nonmajors). Do the scores differentiate between the groups as predicted?
7. Compare the scores of students before and after specific training in mathematical reasoning. Do the scores change as predicted from the theory underlying the construct?
8. Correlate the scores with grades in mathematics. Do they correlate to a satisfactory degree (criterion-related evidence)?

Other types of evidence could be added to this list, but it is sufficiently comprehensive to make clear that no single type of evidence is adequate. Interpreting test scores as a measure of a particular construct involves a comprehensive study of the development of the test, how it functions in a variety of situations, and how the scores relate to other significant measures.

Assessment results are, of course, influenced by many factors other than the construct they are designed to measure. Thus, construct validation is an attempt to account for all possible influences on the scores. We might, for example, ask to what extent the scores on our mathematical reasoning test are influenced by reading comprehension, computation skill, and speed. Each of these factors would require further study. Were attempts made to eliminate such factors during test development by using simple vocabulary, simple computations, and liberal time limits? To what extent do the test scores correlate with measures of reading comprehension and computational skill? How do students' scores differ under different time limits? Answers to these and similar questions will help us to determine how well the test scores reflect the construct we are attempting to measure and the extent to which other factors might be influencing the scores.

Construct validation, then, is an attempt to clarify and verify the inferences to be made from assessment results. This involves a wide variety of procedures and many different types of evidence (including both content-related and criterion-related). As evidence accumulates from many different sources, our interpretations of the results are enriched and we are able to make them with great confidence.

Consequence of Using Assessment Results

Validity focuses on the inferences drawn from assessment results with regard to specific uses. Therefore, it is legitimate to ask, What are the consequences of using the assessment? Did the assessment improve learning, as intended, or did it contribute to adverse effects (e.g., lack of motivation, memorization, poor study habits)? For example, assessment procedures that focus on simple learning outcomes only (e.g., knowledge of facts) cannot provide valid evidence of reasoning and application skills, are likely to narrow the focus of student learning, and tend to reinforce poor learning strategies (e.g., rote learning). Thus, in evaluating the validity of the assessment used, one needs to look at what types of influence the assessments have on students. The following questions provide a general framework for considering some of the possible consequences of assessments on students.

1. Did use of the assessment improve motivation?
2. Did use of the assessment improve performance?
3. Did the use of the assessment improve self-assessment skills?
4. Did the use of the assessment contribute to transfer of learning to related areas?
5. Did the use of the assessment encourage independent learning?
6. Did the use of the assessment encourage good study habits?
7. Did the use of the assessment contribute to a positive attitude toward schoolwork?
8. Did use of the assessment have an adverse effect in any of the above areas?

Judging the consequences of using the various assessment procedures is an important role of the teacher, if the results are to serve their intended purpose of improving learning. Both testing and performance assessments are most likely to have positive consequences when they are designed to assess a broad range of learning outcomes, they give special emphasis to complex learning outcomes, they are administered and scored (or judged) properly, they are used to identify students' strengths and weaknesses in learning, and the students view the assessments as fair, relevant, and useful for improving learning.

Reliability

Reliability refers to the consistency of assessment results. Would we obtain about the same results if we used a different sample of the same type task? Would we obtain about the same results if we used the assessment at a different time? If a performance assessment is being rated, would different raters rate the performance the same way? These are the kinds of questions we are concerned about when we are considering the reliability of assessment results. Unless the results are generalizable over similar samples of tasks, time periods, and raters, we are not likely to have great confidence in them.

Because the methods for estimating reliability differ for tests and performance assessments these will be treated separately.

Estimating the Reliability of Test Scores

The score an individual receives on a test is called the *obtained score, raw score,* or *observed score.* This score typically contains a certain amount of error. Some of this error may be *systematic error,* in that it consistently inflates or lowers the obtained score. For example, readily apparent clues in several test items might cause all students' scores to be higher than their achievement would warrant, or short time limits during testing might cause all students' scores to be lower than their "real achievement." The factors causing systematic errors are mainly due to inadequate testing practices. Thus, most of these errors can be eliminated by using care in constructing and administering tests. Removing systematic errors from test scores is especially important because they have a direct effect on the validity of the inferences made from the scores.

Some of the error in obtained scores is *random error,* in that it raises and lowers scores in an unpredictable manner. Random errors are caused by such things as temporary fluctuations in memory, variations in motivation and concentration from time to time, carelessness in marking answers, and luck in guessing. Such factors cause test scores to be inconsistent from one measurement to another. Sometimes an individual's obtained score will be higher than it should be and sometimes it will be lower. Although these errors are difficult to control and cannot be predicted with accuracy, an estimate of their influence can be obtained by various statistical procedures. Thus, when we talk about estimating the *reliability* of test scores or the amount of *measurement error* in test scores, we are referring to the influence of random errors.

Reliability refers to the *consistency* of test scores from one measurement to another. Because of the ever present measurement error, we can expect a certain amount of variation in test performance from one time to another, from one sample of items to another, and from one part of the test to another. Reliability measures provide an estimate of how much variation we might expect under different conditions. The reliability of test scores is typically reported by means of a *reliability coefficient* or the *standard error of measurement* that is derived from it. Since both methods of estimating reliability require score variability, the procedures to be discussed are useful primarily with tests designed for norm-referenced interpretation.

As we noted earlier, a correlation coefficient expressing the relationship between a set of test scores and a criterion measure is called a *validity coefficient*. A *reliability coefficient* is also a correlation coefficient, but it indicates the correlation between two sets of measurements taken from the same procedure. We may, for example, administer the same test twice to a group, with a time interval in between (*test-retest* method); administer two equivalent forms of the test in close succession (*equivalent-forms* method); administer two equivalent forms of the test with a time interval in between (*test-retest with equivalent forms* method); or administer the test once and compute the consistency of the response within the test (*internal-consistency* method). Each of these methods of obtaining reliability provides a different type of information. Thus, reliability coefficients obtained with the different procedures are not interchangeable. Before deciding on the procedure to be used, we must determine what type of reliability evidence we are seeking. The four basic methods of estimating reliability and the type of information each provides are shown in Table 12.3.

TABLE 12.3 *Methods of Estimating Reliability of Test Scores*

Method	*Type of Information Provided*
Test-retest method	The stability of test scores over a given period of time.
Equivalent-forms method	The consistency of the test scores over different forms of the test (that is, different samples of items).
Test-retest with equivalent forms	The consistency of test scores over *both* a time interval and different forms of the test.
Internal-consistency methods	The consistency of test scores over different parts of the test.

Note: Scorer reliability should also be considered when evaluating the responses to *supply-type* items (for example, essay tests). This is typically done by having the test papers scored independently by two scorers and then correlating the two sets of scores. Agreement among scorers, however, is not a substitute for the methods of estimating reliability shown in the table.

Test-Retest Method   The test-retest method requires administering the same form of the test to the same group after some time interval. The time between the two administrations may be just a few days or several years. The length of the time interval should fit the type of interpretation to be made from the results. Thus, if we are interested in using test scores only to group students for more effective learning, short-term stability may be sufficient. On the other hand, if we are attempting to predict vocational success or make some other long-range predictions, we would desire evidence of stability over a period of years.

Test-retest reliability coefficients are influenced both by errors within the measurement procedure and by the day-to-day stability of the students' responses. Thus, longer time periods between testing will result in lower reliability coefficients, due to the greater changes in the students. In reporting test-retest reliability coefficients, then, it is important to include the time interval. For example, a report might state: "The stability of test scores obtained on the same form over a three-month period was .90." This makes it possible to determine the extent to which the reliability data are significant for a particular interpretation.

Equivalent-Forms Method   With this method, two equivalent forms of a test (also called **alternate forms** or **parallel forms**) are administered to the same group during the same testing session. The test forms are equivalent in the sense that they are built to measure the same abilities (that is, they are built to the same set of specifications), but for determining reliability it is also important that they be constructed independently. When this is the case, the reliability coefficient indicates the adequacy of the test sample. That is, a high reliability coefficient would indicate that the two independent samples are apparently measuring the same thing. A low reliability coefficient, of course, would indicate that the two forms are measuring different behavior and that therefore both samples of items are questionable.

Reliability coefficients determined by this method take into account errors within the measurement procedures and consistency over different samples of items, but they do not include the day-to-day stability of the students' responses.

Test-Retest Method with Equivalent Forms   This is a combination of both methods. Here, two different forms of the same test are administered with time intervening. This is the most demanding estimate of reliability, since it takes into account all possible sources of variation. The reliability coefficient reflects errors within the testing procedure, consistency over different samples of items, and the day-to-day stability of the students' responses. For most purposes, this is probably the most useful type of reliability, since it enables us to estimate how generalizable the test results are over the various conditions. A high reliability coefficient obtained by this method would indicate that a test score represents not only present test performance but also what test performance is likely to be at another time or on a different sample of equivalent items.

Internal-Consistency Methods   These methods require only a single administration of a test. One procedure, the *split-half* method, involves scoring the odd items and the even items separately and correlating the two sets of scores. This correlation coefficient indicates the degree to which the two arbitrarily selected halves of the test provide the same results. Thus, it reports on the internal consistency of the test. Like the equivalent-forms method, this procedure takes into account errors within the testing procedure and consistency over different samples of items, but it omits the day-to-day stability of the students' responses.

Since the correlation coefficient based on the odd and even items indicates the relationship between two halves of the test, the reliability coefficient for the total test is determined by applying the Spearman-Brown prophecy formula. A simplified version of this formula is as follows:

$$\text{Reliability of total test} = \frac{2 \times \text{reliability for } \frac{1}{2} \text{ test}}{1 + \text{reliability for } \frac{1}{2} \text{ test}}$$

Thus, if we obtained a correlation coefficient of .60 for two halves of a test, the reliability for the total test would be computed as follows:

$$\text{Reliability of total test} = \frac{2 \times .60}{1 + .60} = \frac{1.20}{1.60} = .75$$

This application of the Spearman-Brown formula makes clear a useful principle of test reliability; the reliability of a test can be increased by lengthening it. This formula shows how much reliability will increase when the length of the test is doubled. Application of the formula, however, assumes that the test is lengthened by adding items like those already in the test.

Another internal-consistency method of estimating reliability is by use of the **Kuder-Richardson Formula 20** (KR-20). Kuder and Richardson developed other formulas but this one is probably the most widely used with standardized tests. It requires a single test administration, a determination of the proportion of individuals passing each item, and the standard deviation of the total set of scores. The formula is not especially helpful in understanding how to interpret the scores, but knowing what the coefficient means is important. Basically, the KR-20 is equivalent to an average of all split-half coefficients when the test is split in all possible ways. Where all items in a test are measuring the same thing (e.g., math reasoning), the result should approximate the split-half reliability estimate. Where the test items are measuring a variety of skills or content areas (i.e., less homogeneous), the KR-20 estimate will be lower than the split-half reliability estimate. Thus, the KR-20 method is useful with homogeneous tests but can be misleading if used with a test designed to measure heterogeneous content.

Internal-consistency methods are used because they require that the test be administered only once. They should not be used with speeded tests, however, because a spuriously high reliability estimate will result. If speed is an important factor in the testing (that is, if the students do not have time to attempt all the items), other methods should be used to estimate reliability.

Standard Error of Measurement   The standard error of measurement is an especially useful way of expressing test reliability because it indicates the amount of error to allow for when interpreting individual test scores. The standard error is derived from a reliability coefficient by means of the following formula:

Standard error of measurement $= s\sqrt{1 - r_n}$

where s = the standard deviation and r_n = the reliability coefficient. In applying this formula to a reliability estimate of .60 obtained for a test where s = 4.5, the following results would be obtained.

$$
\begin{aligned}
\text{Standard error of measurement} &= 4.5\sqrt{1 - .60} \\
&= 4.5\sqrt{.40} \\
&= 4.5 \times .63 \\
&= 2.8
\end{aligned}
$$

The standard-error of measurement shows how many points we must add to, and subtract from, an individual's test score in order to obtain "reasonable limits" for estimating that individual's true score (that is, a score free of error). In our example, the standard error would be rounded to 3 score points. Thus, if a given student scored 35 on this test, that student's *score band,* for establishing reasonable limits, would range from 32 (35 − 3) to 38 (35 + 3). In other words, we could be reasonably sure that the score band of 32 to 38 included the student's true score (statistically, there are two chances out of three that it does). The standard errors of test scores provide a means of allowing for error during test interpretation. If we view test performance in terms of score bands (also called *confidence bands*), we are not likely to overinterpret small differences between test scores.

For the test user, the standard error of measurement is probably more useful than the reliability coefficient. Although reliability coefficients can be used in evaluating the quality of a test and in comparing the relative merits of different tests, the standard error of measurement is directly applicable to the interpretation of individual test scores.

Reliability of Criterion-Referenced Mastery Tests As noted earlier, the traditional methods for computing reliability require score variability (that is, a spread of scores) and are therefore useful mainly with norm-referenced tests. When used with criterion-referenced tests, they are likely to provide misleading results. Since criterion-referenced tests are not designed to emphasize differences among individuals, they typically have limited score variability. This restricted spread of scores will result in low correlation estimates of reliability, even if the consistency of our test results is adequate for the use to be made of them.

When a criterion-referenced test is used to determine mastery, our primary concern is with how consistently our test classifies masters and nonmasters. If we administered two equivalent forms of a test to the same group of students, for example, we would like the results of both forms to identify the same students as having mastered the material. Such perfect agreement is unrealistic, of course, since some students near the cutoff score are likely to shift from one category to the other on the basis of errors of measurement (due to such factors as lucky guesses or lapses of memory). However, if too many students demonstrated mastery on one form but nonmastery on the other, our decisions concerning who mastered the material would be hopelessly confused. Thus, the reliability of mastery tests can be determined by computing the percentage of consistent mastery-nonmastery decisions over the two forms of the test.

The procedure for comparing test performance on two equivalent forms of a test is relatively simple. After both forms have been administered to a group of students, the resulting data can be placed in a two-by-two table like that shown in Figure 12.3. These data are based on two forms of a 25-item test administered to 40 students. Mastery was set at 80 percent correct (20 items), so all students who scored 20 or higher on both forms of the test were placed in the upper right-hand cell (30 students), and all those who scored below 20 on both forms were placed in the lower left-hand cell (6 students). The remaining students demonstrated mastery on one form and nonmastery on the other (4 students). Since 36 of the 40 students were con-

| | | FORM B | |
		NONMASTERS	MASTERS
FORM A	MASTERS	2	30
	NONMASTERS	6	2

FIGURE 12.3 Classification of 40 students as masters or nonmasters on two forms of a criterion-referenced test.

sistently classified by the two forms of the test, we apparently have reasonably good consistency.

We can compute the percentage of consistency for this procedure with the following formula:

$$\% \text{ Consistency } = \frac{\text{Masters (both forms) + Nonmasters (both forms)}}{\text{Total number in group}} \times 100$$

$$\% \text{ Consistency } = \frac{30 + 6}{40} \times 100 = 90\%$$

This procedure is simple to use but it has a few limitations. First, two forms of the test are required. This may not be as serious as it seems, however, since in most mastery programs more than one form of the test is needed for retesting those students who fail to demonstrate mastery on the first try. Second, it is difficult to determine what percentage of decision consistency is necessary for a given situation. As with other measures of reliability, the greater the consistency, the more satisfied we will be, but what constitutes a minimum acceptable level? There is no simple answer to such a question because it depends on the number of items in the test and the consequences of the decision. If a nonmastery decision for a student simply means further study and later retesting, low consistency might be acceptable. However, if the mastery-nonmastery decision concerns whether to give a student a high school certificate, as in some competency testing programs, then a high level of consistency will be demanded. Since there are no clear guidelines for setting minimum levels, we will need to depend on experience in various situations to determine what are reasonable expectations.

More sophisticated techniques have been developed for estimating the reliability of criterion-referenced tests, but the numerous issues and problems involved in their use go beyond the scope of this book. See Box 12.2 for factors that lower reliability of test scores.

BOX 12.2 • *Factors That Lower the Reliability of Test Scores*

1. Test scores are based on too few items. (*Remedy:* Use longer tests or accumulate scores from several short tests.)
2. Range of scores is too limited. (*Remedy:* Adjust item difficulty to obtain larger spread of scores.)
3. Testing conditions are inadequate. (*Remedy:* Arrange opportune time for administration and eliminate interruptions, noise, and other disrupting factors.)
4. Scoring is subjective. (*Remedy:* Prepare scoring keys and follow carefully when scoring essay answers.)

Estimating the Reliability of Performance Assessments

Performance assessments are commonly evaluated by using scoring rubrics that describe a number of levels of performance, ranging from high to low (e.g., outstanding to inadequate). The performance for each student is then judged and placed in the category that best fits the quality of the performance. The reliability of these performance judgments can be determined by obtaining and comparing the scores of two judges who scored the performances independently. The scores of the two judges can be correlated to determine the consistency of the scoring, or the proportion of agreement in scoring can be computed.

Let's assume that a performance task, such as writing sample, was obtained from 32 students and two teachers independently rated the students' performance on a four-point scale where 4 is high and 1 is low. The results of the ratings by the two judges are shown in Table 12.4. The ratings for Judge 1 are presented in the columns and those for Judge 2 are presented in the rows. Thus, Judge 1 assigned a score of 4 to seven students and Judge 2 assigned a score of 4 to eight students. Their ratings agreed on six of the students and disagreed by one score on three of the students. The number of rating agreements can be seen in the boxes on the diagonal from the upper righthand corner to the lower lefthand corner. The percentage of agreement can be computed by adding the numbers in these diagonal boxes (6 + 7 + 6 + 5 = 24), dividing by the total number of students in the group (32), and multiplying by 100.

$$\text{Rater agreement} = \frac{24}{32} \times 100 = 75\%$$

TABLE 12.4 *Classification of Students Based on Performance Ratings by Two Independent Judges*

		Ratings by Judge 1				
	Scores	*1*	*2*	*3*	*4*	*Row Totals*
	4			2	6	8
Ratings by Judge 2	**3**		3	7	1	11
	2	2	6			8
	1	5				5
Column Totals		7	9	9	7	32

By inspection, we can see that all ratings were within one score of each other. The results also indicate that Judge 2 was a more lenient rater than Judge 1 (i.e., gave more high ratings and fewer low ratings). Thus, a table of this nature can be used to determine the consistency of ratings and the extent to which leniency can account for the disagreements.

Although the need for two raters will limit the use of this method, it seems reasonable to expect two teachers in the same area to make periodic checks on the scoring of performance assessments. This will not only provide information on the consistency of the scoring, but will provide the teachers with insight into some of their rating idiosyncrasies. See Box 12.3 for factors that lower the reliability of performance assessment.

The percentage of agreement between the scores assigned by independent judges is a common method of estimating the reliability of performance assessments. It should be noted, however, that this reports on only one type of consistency—*the consistency of the scoring*. It does not indicate the consistency of performance over similar tasks or over different time periods. We can obtain a crude measure of this by examining the performance of students over tasks and time, but a more adequate analysis requires an understanding of **generalizability** theory, which is too technical for treatment here.

BOX 12.3 • *Factors That Lower the Reliability of Performance Assessments*

---

1. Insufficient number of tasks. (*Remedy:* Accumulate results from several assessments. For example, several writing samples.)
2. Poorly structured assessment procedures. (*Remedy:* Define carefully the nature of the tasks, the conditions for obtaining the assessment, and the criteria for scoring or judging the results.)
3. Dimensions of performance are specific to the tasks. (*Remedy:* Increase generalizability of performance by selecting tasks that have dimensions like those in similar tasks.)
4. Inadequate scoring guides for judgmental scoring. (*Remedy:* Use scoring rubrics or rating scales that specifically describe the criteria and levels of quality.)
5. Scoring judgments that are influenced by personal bias. (*Remedy:* Check scores or ratings with those of an independent judge. Receive training in judging and rating, if possible.)

Summary of Points

1. Validity is the most important quality to consider in assessment and is concerned with the appropriateness, meaningfulness, and usefulness of the specific inferences made from assessment results.

2. Validity is a *unitary concept* based on various forms of evidence (content-related, criterion-related, construct-related, and consequences).

3. Content-related evidence of validity refers to how well the sample of tasks represents the domain of tasks to be assessed.

4. Content-related evidence of validity is of major concern in achievement assessment and is built in by following systematic procedures. Validity is lowered by inadequate assessment practices.

5. Criterion-related evidence of validity refers to the degree to which assessment results are related to some other valued measure called a *criterion.*

6. Criterion-related evidence may be based on a predictive study or a concurrent study and is typically expressed by a correlation coefficient or expectancy table.

7. Construct-related evidence of validity refers to how well performance on assessment tasks can be explained in terms of psychological characteristics, or constructs (e.g., mathematical reasoning).

8. The construct-related category of evidence is the most comprehensive. It includes evidence from both content-related and criterion-related studies plus other types of evidence that help clarify the meaning of the assessment results.

9. Consequences of using the assessment is also an important consideration in validity—both positive and negative consequences.

10. Reliability refers to the consistency of scores (i.e., to the degree to which the scores are free from measurement error).

11. Reliability of test scores is typically reported by means of a reliability coefficient or a standard error of measurement.

12. Reliability coefficients can be obtained by a number of different methods (e.g., test-retest, equivalent-forms, internal-consistency) and each one measures a different type of consistency (e.g., over time, over different samples of items, over different parts of the test).

13. Reliability of test scores tends to be lower when the test is short, range of scores is limited, testing conditions are inadequate, and scoring is subjective.

14. The standard error of measurement indicates the amount of error to allow for when interpreting individual test scores.

15. Score bands (or *confidence bands*) take into account the error of measurement and help prevent the over interpretation of small differences between test scores.

16. The reliability of criterion-referenced mastery tests can be obtained by computing the percentage of agreement between two forms of the test in classifying individuals as masters and nonmasters.
17. The reliability of performance-based assessments are commonly determined by the degree of agreement between two or more judges who rate the performance independently.

References and Additional Reading

American Educational Research Association, *Standards for Educational and Psychological Testing* (Washington, DC: AERA, 1999).

Linn, R. L., and Gronlund, N. E., *Measurement and Assessment in Teaching*, 8th ed. (Upper Saddle River, NJ: Merrill/Prentice-Hall, 2000).

Oosterhoff, A. C., *Classroom Applications of Educational Measurement*, 3rd ed. (Upper Saddle River, NJ: Merrill/Prentice-Hall, 2001).

Thorndike, R., *Measurement and Evaluation in Psychology and Education*, 6th ed. (Upper Saddle River, NJ: Prentice-Hall, 1997).

Glossary

This glossary of assessment terms focuses primarily on the terms used in this book.

Achievement Assessment A procedure that is used to determine the degree to which individuals have achieved the intended learning outcomes of instruction. It includes both paper-and-pencil tests and performance assessments, plus judgments concerning learning progress.

Achievement Test An instrument that typically uses sets of items designed to measure a domain of learning tasks and is administered under specified conditions (e.g., time limits, open or closed book).

Alternate Forms Two or more forms of a test or assessment that are designed to measure the same abilities (also called *equivalent* or *parallel forms*).

Alternative Assessment An assessment procedure that provides an alternative to paper-and-pencil testing.

Analytic Scoring The assignment of scores to individual components of a performance or product (e.g., Evaluate a writing sample by using separate scores for organization, style, mechanics, etc.).

Anecdotal Record A brief description of some significant student behavior, the setting in which it occurred, and an interpretation of its meaning.

Authentic Assessment An assessment procedure that emphasizes the use of tasks and contextual settings like those in the real world.

Battery of Tests Two or more tests standardized on the same sample of students, so that performance on the different tests can be compared using a common norm group.

Checklist A list of dimensions of a performance or product that is simply checked present or absent.

Content Standard A broad educational goal that indicates what a student should know and be able to do in a subject area.

Correlation Coefficient A statistic indicating the degree of relationship between two sets of test scores or other measures.

Criteria A set of qualities used in judging a performance, a product, or an assessment instrument.

Criterion-Referenced Interpretation A description of an individual's performance in terms of the tasks he or she can and cannot perform.

Derived Score A score that results from converting a raw score to a different score scale (e.g., percentile rank, standard score).

Difficulty Index Percentage of individuals who obtain the correct answer on a test item or task.

Discrimination Index The degree to which a test item or task discriminates between high and low scorers on the total test.

Expectancy Table A twofold chart that shows the relationship between two sets of scores. It can be used to predict the chances of success on one measure (the criterion) for any given score on the other measure (the predictor), and it can be used for obtaining criterion-related evidence of validity.

Generalizability The extent to which an assessment procedure provides comparable results over different samples of similar tasks, different settings, and different administrations.

Grade Equivalent Score A derived score that indicates the grade level at which an individual's score matches the average score (e.g., a grade equivalent score of 4.5 indicates the raw score matches the average score of students in the middle of the fourth grade).

Holistic Scoring The assignment of a score based on an overall impression of a performance or product rather than a consideration of individual elements. The overall judgment is typically guided by descriptions of the various levels of performance or scoring rubrics.

Item Analysis Traditionally, a method for determining the difficulty and discriminating power of test items. It can also be used to determine the responsiveness of test items to instructional effects.

Kuder-Richardson Formula 20 (KR-20) A method for estimating reliability based on the internal consistency of a test (i.e., on the extent to which the test items correlate with each other).

Mastery Test An assessment method used to determine whether an individual has met some predetermined level of performance.

Mean The arithmetic average that is determined by adding together a set of scores and dividing by the number of scores.

Norm-Referenced Interpretation A description of an individual's performance in terms of how it compares to the performance of others (typically those in a norm group).

Normal Curve A symmetrical bell-shaped curve based on a precise mathematical equation. It is widely used in interpreting standardized test scores because of its fixed mathematical properties (e.g., when standard deviations are plotted along the baseline of the curve, each portion of the curve contains a fixed percentage of scores).

Normal-Curve Equivalent Score A normalized standard score that ranges from 1 to 99 with a mean of 50. It is used for reporting performance on standardized achievement tests.

Norms Data that describe the performance of individuals in some reference group (e.g., national norms, local norms). Norms represent average or typical performance and are not to be interpreted as standards.

Objective Test A test that can be consistently scored by equally competent scorers (i.e., they obtain the same scores). This contrasts with subjective tests where the scores are influenced by scorer judgment (e.g., essay tests).

Percentage Correct Score The percentage of items that an individual answers correctly on a test, or the percentage of tasks an individual performs correctly on a performance assessment.

Percentile Band A range of percentile ranks that sets reasonable limits within which an individual's true score is likely to fall. It takes into account the inconsistency of obtained scores due to errors of measurement (also called an *error band* or *confidence band*).

Percentile Rank The percentage of individuals in a group scoring at or below a given score. Not to be confused with the percentage-correct score.

Performance Assessment A procedure that requires individuals to perform tasks and the process or product of the performance is judged using prespecified criteria.

Portfolio Assessment A preplanned collection of samples of student work, assessment results, and other data that represent the student's accomplishments. It is viewed by some as a basic type of performance assessment and by others as merely a convenient method for accumulating evidence of student performance.

Range The difference between the highest score and the lowest score in a distribution of scores.

Rating Scale A systematic procedure for guiding and recording judgments concerning the degree to which the characteristics of a performance or behavior are present.

Raw Score The score that is obtained when first scoring a test or performance task (also called an obtained score). The raw score is frequently converted to some type of derived score for interpretation (e.g., percentile rank or standard scores).

Reliability The degree to which assessment results are consistent from one measurement (or assessment) to another. Reliability estimates typically indicate the consistency of scores or judgments over different forms, different time periods, different parts of the instrument, or different raters. High reliability indicates greater freedom from error.

Scoring Rubric A set of scoring guidelines that describe the characteristics of the different levels of performance used in scoring or judging a performance.

Standard A prespecified level of performance that is considered satisfactory for the use to be made of the assessment results (e.g., minimum standards, mastery standards).

Standard Error of Measurement A method of expressing reliability that estimates the amount of error in test scores. It is the standard deviation of the errors of measurement and is used to compute the error bands (e.g., percentile bands) used in interpreting test scores.

Standard Score A term used to describe a variety of derived scores that convert raw scores to a standard scale for a more useful interpretation of test results.

Standardized Achievement Test A test constructed to fit detailed specifications, administered under prescribed conditions to selected groups, and scored using definite rules of scoring. Published standardized tests typically include a test manual that contains rules for administration and scoring, norms for interpretation, and validity and reliability data.

Stanine A standard score that ranges from 1 to 9 with a mean of 5. Each stanine is one-half of a standard deviation wide, except 1 and 9 at the ends of the distribution.

T-Score A standard score with a mean of 50 and standard deviation of 10.

Table of Specifications A two-way chart that specifies the number or proportion of test items (or assessment tasks) to be designed for each area of content and each type of intended learning outcome when planning a test (or other assessment procedure).

Task An assessment exercise that requires students to demonstrate a knowledge, skill, or combination of attributes, by means of a performance or product (see *performance assessment*).

Validity The extent to which inferences made from assessment results are appropriate, meaningful, and useful in terms of the purpose for the assessment. Validity is a unitary concept that depends on a variety of types of evidence, is expressed by degree (high, low), and refers to the inferences drawn (not the instrument itself).

Index

Appendix A

A Framework for Communicating Student Learning

A Framework for Student Assessment

How to Develop and Use Performance Assessments in the Classroom

A Framework for Communicating Student Learning

Contents

1. Context and Issues

Framework Model—Communicating Student Learning • Purpose of the framework • On communicating student learning • Underlying questions • Real people, real issues • Purpose of grading • Balanced assessment program • Perspectives on grading

2. Basis for Communicating Student Learning

Legal basis for communicating student learning • Ethical basis for communicating student learning • Guidelines for communicating student learning • Perspectives on communicating student learning • What are the roles of teacher, student and parent?

3. Approaches to Communicating Student Learning

From report cards to portfolios • Effective report cards, conferencing and portfolios • Developing a school assessment, evaluation and communication plan

Glossary

Selected Bibliography

Appendices

Appendix I
 School Act • More on the legal and ethical basis for communicating student learning • Alberta Education policies • Principles of Fair Student Assessment Practices for Education in Canada

Appendix II
 Reporting for students with special needs

FRAMEWORK MODEL -
COMMUNICATING STUDENT LEARNING *

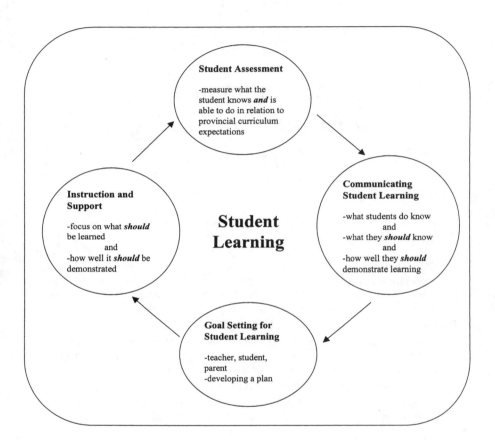

*Designed by Greg Hall, Student Evaluation Branch, Alberta Education (1999)

Context and Issues

Purpose of the framework

This framework is intended as a resource to help teachers and administrators think through the many difficult and diverse issues related to communicating student learning. It is a resource for those occasions when new report cards, portfolios and conferencing models are being examined. We hope that this document will also help parents better understand the processes associated with communicating student learning.

> *Read this framework* to explore and discuss ideas with colleagues about
> key questions and issues
> grading
> effective report card design
> student involvement in conferencing
> portfolios to celebrate student learning
> special needs reporting
> developing a school plan for assessment, evaluation
>   and communication
> legal and ethical dimensions
> role of teacher, student and parent
>
> *Visit the AAC Web site* (www.aac.ab.ca) to find
> best practices in communicating student learning
> possible questions for parents to ask during a conference
> how to develop school-level communication tools
> communication samples including report cards
> an overview of ways to communicate student learning
>   (PowerPoint presentation)

On communicating student learning

Working with students on a day-to-day basis gives us tremendous insight into their capabilities, and we experience a wide range of emotions as we watch them grow and develop. We delight when a student remarks, "I understand that now!"; we smile to ourselves when we observe students finally accomplishing tasks that had previously foiled them; we brim with pride when they share projects they have worked hard to complete. We also have to deal with disappointments and sometimes feel discouraged when students perform poorly on tests when we know they can do better.

As part of our duties, we are also charged with the task of collecting information about our students' performance. We use a variety of methods over a period of time in a process of information collecting referred to as **assessment.** When a student's performance is judged against a standard, the process is called **evaluation.** Communicating the information gathered through assessment and evaluation, in a manner that is clear and meaningful, is not an easy task. **Report cards, parent conferences, student-led conferences and portfolios** are all means to share information about what students are learning, and for the students themselves to provide demonstrations of what they know and can do.

> The most crucial part of the communication process is to ensure a shared understanding between the person providing the information and the information receiver. Letter grades, percentages, percentiles, or comments from an activity, test, or assignment must be clear and comprehensive.
>
> Effective communication informs the student, parent, and others about what has been accomplished and what the next steps are in the learning process. The communication process involves all the key players. However, the greater the role students are given in this process, the richer the information that is shared and the greater the impact on future student learning.
>
> —*A Framework for Student Assessment,*
> Alberta Assessment Consortium, 1997

Underlying questions in communicating student learning

Have you ever wrestled with how to report the progress of your students? Teachers have been reporting on student progress for years, but continue to struggle with important issues that have no easy answers:

- What kind of feedback is most helpful to students in order to improve learning?
- How do students determine how well they are doing?
- Students learn a great deal in school. Should all of this be reported?
- How often should students receive feedback, formally or informally, on how well they are doing?
- How important is it to have consistency in the way student learning is reported or communicated?
- What kinds of information (letter grades, marks, anecdotal comments, observations) best communicate what and how well a student is learning?
- What do marks and letter grades really mean? Is there a more meaningful way to communicate student learning?

- What if a student neglects to complete assignments and assessment tasks? What are the consequences of non-performance? Does the teacher assign a zero for each incomplete task and, in the end, say that the student failed to meet the standard?
- How should effort and attitude be assessed and evaluated? Where does participation fit in?
- How does a teacher know if the student is achieving at grade level in language arts, mathematics, science and social studies?

Communicating student learning is one of a teacher's most important responsibilities and consumes a fair amount of teacher time. Indeed, Guskey (1996) states that *teachers engage in some form of reporting nearly every hour* they are in the classroom.

In his 1996 ASCD yearbook, Guskey recounts the stories of three students and the issues he encountered when trying to assign them grades.

> I first entered education as a middle school teacher. Every nine weeks I was required to reduce to a single symbol all the impressions and information I had gathered on the learning of each of my students. I recorded this symbol on a report card that was carried home by students, signed by one of their parents, and then returned to the school until the end of the next nine-week cycle. When the year drew to a close, I tallied, summarized, and then recorded yet another symbol that was to represent my students' accumulated accomplishments.
>
> Initially I approached the process of grading and reporting rather casually, with little doubt I could be fair and objective ... The first time I sat down to complete report cards, however, I quickly discovered the process to be far more complex than I ever anticipated.

Real people, real issues

One of the top students in the class was Angela; she clearly deserved a high mark.

> She consistently attained the highest score on examinations, and all of her work was well organized and exceptionally neat. But I also knew that none of what we worked on in class required serious effort from Angela, and I had not done a very good job of challenging her capabilities. Still, I recorded the mark and moved on.

Stephen was a hard worker and exceptionally creative on assignments, but had not done well on tests.

> I certainly did not want to give him a mark that would discourage the extra effort he was putting forth. Since I would need to consider his case more carefully, I set his report card aside with the intention of coming back to it later.

Finally, Elizabeth had struggled initially, but had recently made remarkable progress.

> Somehow the mark I gave her needed to reflect her most recent work and show how far she had come. I set her report card aside too.

These stories illustrate what teachers already know—representing student learning and achievement in one simple symbol is a challenge.

What is the purpose of grading?

Parents ask us, *"So, how's my kid doing?"* and we respond with a mark, a letter grade or a comment. Sometimes we even provide them with some form of comparison, such as the class average, performance relative to provincial standards or the extent of the progress the student has made since the last formal evaluation.

But, what do we mean by the term *grading?* It can mean the number or letter we assign to a student at a given moment to represent how well he or she has performed on a specific task or series of tasks, tests, projects and other activities. Alternatively, it can be an average of the marks derived from a number of performances.

In any case, the information that is condensed in this symbolic representation is enormous.

In addition to grades that reflect performance in subject areas, teachers also continually evaluate students in terms of their social and emotional progress and behaviour. This information, which comprises a teacher's assessment of effort, attitude, behaviour, participation and attendance, should be reported separately from academic information.

> Parents are interested in how their children get along with their peers, in their work habits and efforts toward learning, and in their attitudes toward, level of interest in and motivation toward their studies. Assessing behaviour, effort, motivation and interest and including them in a grading system are problematic. Such traits are difficult to define and assess objectively. As much as possible, teachers should use systematic, dependable methods when assessing student attitude and behaviour.
>
> Often a student's achievement is affected by behaviour and, as an indirect result, the letter grade will be affected. However, reducing grades as a deterrent is unfair and self-defeating. Behaviours and personal traits are best reported to parents through written comments and conferences.
>
> —*Guidelines for Student Reporting for the Kindergarten to Grade 12 Education Plan (1994)*, British Columbia Ministry of Education

Balanced assessment program

A *balanced assessment program* incorporates the results of large-scale assessment (provincial achievement tests and diploma examinations and district assessments) and classroom assessments to communicate student learning. According to Stiggins (1997), "If we are to establish a more balanced set of assessment priorities, we must give far greater attention to ensuring the quality of classroom assessments. Having said this, let me remind you that a balanced perspective encourages the use of all of the assessment tools at our disposal. This includes standardized (large-scale) tests."

Alberta Education supports the use of multiple assessments in a balanced assessment program and takes the position that a single test is not intended as the final word. (See also "Legal Basis for Communicating Student Learning" on page A1-9.)

The challenge is to ensure that grades reflect what students *know* and *can do* relative to provincial curriculum standards. It is vital that teachers, students and parents be well prepared to understand, interpret and use test results, knowing the strengths and limitations of the scores. Otherwise, as Dressel (1997) stated,

> A grade [could be regarded only as] an inadequate report of an inaccurate judgement by a biased and variable judge of the extent to which a student has attained an undefined level of mastery of an unknown proportion of an indefinite amount of material.

> *Remember, it is vital that teachers, students and parents be well prepared to understand, interpret and use test results knowing the strengths and limitations of the scores.*

Keeping grading in perspective

Grading succeeds as a means of communicating student learning to the extent that students are provided meaningful feedback that encourages further growth and development. After all, as Phillip Gammage of the Faculty of Education at the University of Nottingham once asked, "Whoever got taller by [only] being measured?"

> If the greater value is given the score,
> Then value the score.

> If the greater value is intrinsic,
> Then value the child.

> There is, I think, a far greater value in teaching the
> intrinsic desire to learn than in
> teaching to achieve a score.

If the desire to learn is in its place,
Then achievement will find its place.

—Bob Stanish, The Giving Book

Further perspective on grading

In 1996, Wiggins said that "trying to get rid of familiar letter (or number) grades . . . gets the matter backwards while leading to needless political battles . . . Parents have reasons to be suspicious of educators who want to tinker with a 120-year-old system they think they understand—even if we know traditional grades are often of questionable worth." He went on to say that it is more productive to make grades better: "What critics of grading must understand [is] that the symbol is not the problem; the lack of stable and clear points of reference in using the symbols is the problem."

Basis for Communicating Student Learning

Legal basis for communicating student learning

The *legal cornerstones* for communicating student achievement are found in provincial legislation, Alberta Education policies and jurisdiction policies. Assessment of student progress is based on the learning outcomes in the programs of study.

School and jurisdiction policies for communicating student learning should be based on regulations authorized under the Province of Alberta *School Act* (see Appendix I). The Act outlines evaluation, reporting and recording requirements, as well as the roles and responsibilities of Alberta Education, school boards, administrators and teachers with respect to implementation of policy.

Ethical basis for communicating student learning

Ethics of Assessment, Evaluation and Communication of Student Learning

Student achievement is communicated and reported *ethically* to the extent that there is a reasonable relationship between

- the expectations of the curriculum (general and specific outcomes) *and* classroom instruction
- classroom instruction *and* student assessment
- student assessment *and* the communication of student learning

Guidelines for communicating student learning

The following assumptions about reporting student progress, as stated by Wright and Kiernan (1996) and Armstrong (1999), provide guidelines for communicating student learning:

1. The primary purpose of reporting is to improve learning.
2. Reporting student progress should be based on curricular outcomes.
3. Communication of student achievement should be timely and should involve multiple reporting strategies.
4. Parents and students must be active participants in the process of reporting. The home-school partnership is enhanced by comprehensive reporting.
5. Reporting techniques should reflect a school's philosophy about learning, instruction and assessment.

Perspectives on communicating student learning

Communicating student learning should be carried out so that it supports continuous learning and development. O'Connor (1999) has put forth the following guidelines to help ensure that the meaning of grades is clear and that grades support learning and encourage student success.

Make achievement the only factor in assessments.
- Achievement of the curriculum outcomes should be the only basis for grades.
- Effort, participation, attitudes and other personal and social characteristics should be reported separately.

In 1994, Kohn went so far as to suggest that teachers should never give a rating for effort. "The fatal paradox is that, while coercion can sometimes elicit resentful obedience, it can never create desire. A low grade for effort is more likely to be read as 'You're a failure even at trying.' On the other hand, a high grade for effort combined with a low grade for achievement says 'You're just too dumb to succeed.'"

Sample student performance—don't mark everything.
- Provide feedback on formative assessment to help students know what to do to improve their knowledge and skills.
- Include only summative assessment results in report card grades.

A wide variety of assessment approaches should be used to take account of different learning styles and multiple intelligences.

Grade in pencil and use up-to-date information.
- Brightly coloured pen marks on paper can look aggressive and judgemental—always use pencil. Also, be sure to use the most recent information. Be prepared to replace old information with more recent information that better demonstrates each student's real achievement.
- Provide second (or more) assessment opportunities. Students may need multiple opportunities to perform at their best, but there should also be some evidence of students using feedback about past mistakes to enhance future success.

Relate grading procedures to intended learning.
Teachers must have a clear understanding of what learning results are expected—grading must be related to these results. It is also critical that teachers evaluate learning on clear, preestablished standards. Therefore, the use of detailed rubrics or scoring guides is essential.

Use care when crunching numbers.
The arithmetic mean may not be the best way to calculate a score. Consider using medians—they provide more opportunities for success by diminishing the impact of a few high or low marks.

Use absolute or preset standards to distribute marks.
There should be no artificial rationing of high grades. "The number of good grades should not be artificially limited so that one student's success makes another's unlikely." (Kohn, 1994) Do not mark on a curve.

Properly record evidence from quality assessment instruments.
Grades are meaningful only if they are based on quality assessment instruments that are both valid and reliable. Record and date results; do not rely on your memory.

Describe assessment and evaluation practices to students at the beginning of the course.
Students must receive clear, concise information on how grades for each course will be determined. Whenever possible, students should be involved in the development of criteria against which their work will be judged.

What are the roles of teacher, student and parent?

The *role of the teacher* is to
- ensure that students know what is expected of them
- establish clear and fair criteria and standards (with involvement of the student when appropriate)

- provide an evaluation process of student performance based on these criteria and standards
- communicate this information in a manner that is meaningful and understandable

The *role of the student* is to
- know what is expected of him or her
- "be diligent in pursuing his/her studies" (*School Act*) as demonstrated by completion of assigned work and achievement of curriculum standards
- participate in developing criteria and standards where appropriate
- self-evaluate based on these criteria and standards
- learn from the feedback obtained from self-evaluation, that of the teacher, and others, if provided
- communicate this information in a manner that indicates his or her responsibility for learning

The *role of the parent* is to
- support learning at home with time, study space and support
- join the child in the discussion about learning during formal conferences
- ask teachers and students about the goals set for the child
- ask the teacher what to look for in the child's portfolio
- spend time assisting with student work, portfolio management, personal learning plans and student self-evaluation
- look for and acknowledge progress rather than perfection. Doing this encourages the child to take risks in his or her learning.

Parent role adapted from *Partners in Learning*
(Alberta Teachers' Association, 1996)

Approaches to Communicating Student Learning

From report cards to portfolios

There is a growing emphasis on communicating the results of performance forms of assessment, complemented by better and more appropriate reporting systems. This moves communicating student learning beyond basic academic skills to embrace other essential competencies in problem solving, higher-order thinking skills, interpersonal skills and teamwork.

A variety of communicating practices have been created for inclusion in school communication plans to clearly communicate student accomplishments and to advise students of the next steps to be taken in the instructional process. The diversity of communication practices parallels the variety in assessment practices necessary to determine the performance levels of students with greatest validity and reliability.

Practices for communicating student learning may include:

phone calls (positive as well as negative)

home response journals (three-way communication journals for regular dialogue between student, parent and teacher)

newsletters

individual program plans (IPP)

home video (a videotape of class activities circulated among the homes of the students)

portfolios

student self-reflections

goal setting

student-led conferences

open classroom (periodic, student-planned, evening open houses)

celebrations of learning

report cards

homework hotline (a voice-mail system with pre-recorded messages and messages that may be recorded)

> adapted from *Reporting Student Progress*. Video and Facilitator's Guide. ASCD: Alexandria, VA. 1996.

Effective Report Cards

Report cards are central to the reporting process. "Today's report card celebrates learning. It tells the parent and child what the child can do." (Armstrong, 1990)

Report cards should be based on the curriculum and aligned with programming, assessment and the school philosophy. Since report cards communicate many messages, they must be designed carefully. The amount of space assigned to a particular course suggests its importance in the school. Too much information is confusing for parents; too little doesn't tell them enough.

J. McTighe observed that clearly defined reporting standards are necessary to increase the communication value of a reporting document. According to McTighe, reporting documents should distinguish between the following factors:

• *achievement*—performance relative to identified learning outcomes based on collected evidence and judged against established criteria

An effective reporting document	An ineffective reporting document
• promotes a student's feelings of success and positive self-worth	• leaves the student feeling inadequate
• encourages further student learning	• is viewed as an endpoint
• promotes home-school communication	• provides only one-way communication
• provides a context for judgements	• reports numbers in isolation from learning
• is clearly understood by students and parents	• includes a confusing assortment of codes, numbers and jargon
• provides information on student achievement and growth	• provides only sorting and ranking information
• is aligned to provincial curriculum standards	• is based on inconsistent grading scales and criteria with little similarity from classroom to classroom
• tells what individual students know and can do	• tells only what the teacher taught
• ensures that the mark awarded is an accurate and current reflection of student learning	• shows an over-reliance on averaging to come up with a final mark
• factors out elements not related to the curriculum, or not reflective of the student's typical achievement level	• includes non-academic factors such as effort, behaviour, and attendance as part of the student's mark
• acknowledges actions that need to be taken by partners in learning—students, parents and teachers	• blames others for poor student performance

- *progress*—degree of growth toward mastery of the learning outcomes, based on a performance continuum
- *work habits*—includes effort, completion of assignments, behaviour and attendance

McTighe also noted that each of these factors should be reported separately.

The *School Act* does not specifically address report cards. The Alberta Education *Guide to Education* includes the requirement to report student learning on a regular basis.

Effective Conferencing

The main purpose of a formal conference is to establish communication links between students, parents and teachers. Conferencing provides explanations

An effective conference	An ineffective conference
• includes the student as an active participant	• excludes the student from the conversation
• uses student products to demonstrate achievement and growth	• expects parents to accept that "expert opinion" is sufficient justification for judgements
• focuses clearly on individual student learning and includes specific strategies for improvement	• provides little or no insight into how to increase student learning
• expands upon the information provided in the report card	• repeats the same information as the report card
• engages all participants in discussing achievement and setting goals	• provides few ideas about what the student has done, can or could do
• includes a discussion of the successes and difficulties the student is experiencing	• focuses only on what the student can't or won't do
• provides an opportunity for open and relevant sharing of information between participants	• is dominated by one participant who does most of the talking
• establishes an atmosphere in which everyone feels welcome to participate	• conveys to the parent the idea that keeping to the scheduled time is more important than sharing information
• provides information about curriculum	• deals primarily with non-academic issues
• includes an action plan that is supportive of student learning	• provides little or no direction about what each participant is to do by the next reporting period
• ends on a positive note	• ends with parents and/or students being frustrated and discouraged

and insights into teacher evaluations, student progress and the grade level achieved. Conferencing also gives parents an opportunity to share their perspectives on their child's performance, needs, interests and concerns.

Formal conferences should be pre-planned and organized so that there are no surprises for any of the participants. The teacher must establish the parameters of the conference and explain the role of each participant. Students should have opportunities to practise conferencing during classroom activities so that they are prepared to engage in the discussion. Parents must know what is expected of them during the conferencing process, and they also must be able to ask questions. Through conferencing, the parental role

An effective portfolio	An ineffective portfolio
• is a planned and organized collection of student work	• is a random collection of student work, undated and unrelated
• tells detailed stories about a variety of student outcomes that would otherwise be difficult to document	• is uni-dimensional with an over-abundance of knowledge and recall activities
• includes self-reflections that describe the student as both a learner and an individual	• shows little evidence of the student's participation in the learning process
• serves as a guide for future learning by illustrating a student's present level of achievement	• acts as a repository for student work that is never revisited
• includes a selection of items that are representative of curriculum outcomes and what the student knows and can do	• includes work representing only a narrow slice of curriculum
• includes the criteria against which the student work was judged	• provides no guidelines to assist the reader in interpreting judgements
• supports the assessment, evaluation and communication of student learning	• is not an integral part of the student's learning and is viewed as an "add on" by the teacher
• documents learning in a variety of ways—process, product, growth and achievement	• provides a snapshot in time with little connection to what has come before or what is to follow

in the educational process becomes more clearly defined, and the parents are more likely to value this process as a means of finding out what their child knows and can do.

As Stiggins noted at the National Conference on Standards and Assessment in April 1999, "Student-led parent conferences are considered to be the breakthrough of the century as a path to greater student motivation and achievement."

Effective Portfolios

A portfolio is a purposeful collection of student work that provides a visual representation of a student's learning. The samples of work in a portfolio record growth and achievement in one or more subject areas over time. Although there are no rigid guidelines as to what should be included in a portfolio, selections should be representative samples that really reflect the child.

We must constantly remind ourselves that the ultimate purpose of evaluation is to enable students to evaluate themselves.

—Arthur L. Costa

Developing a school assessment, evaluation and communication plan

A school assessment, evaluation and communication plan establishes a common understanding among staff, parents and students of the assessment and reporting components of the instructional process. Edmonton Public Schools has developed a checklist which addresses seven elements that may comprise a school plan. The following attributes of an effective plan are adapted from this checklist.

Attributes of an Effective School Assessment, Evaluation and Communication Plan

School identification and beliefs
- includes distinctive identification of school and key information such as names, logos (school and jurisdiction), address; communication links, such as phone and fax numbers, Web site URL and e-mail address
- provides a clear statement of school beliefs about communicating student achievement and growth integrated with other school activities

Methods of Assessment
Explanation of the relationship between the methods of assessment and student information including
- process of collecting information with supporting examples
- specific information about what methods are used by whom; identifies those with whom assessment measures and interpretation of results may be discussed

Process of Evaluation
Explanation of the process of evaluation including
- illustration of processes and resources used by staff and students
- information about where resources may be viewed and who may explain them

Methods of Communication
Description and explanation of methods of communication including
- dates of progress reports with an explanation of what to expect at each reporting period
- description of procedures for parents who wish to meet with any staff to discuss assessments, student goals and results, and curriculum expectations

- dates for curriculum information session(s) and explanation of the use of newsletters to convey curriculum information
- Scheduling and explanation of parent-teacher conferences, and/or student-led conferences, and/or celebrations of learning
- description and explanation of student recognition practices

Parent and Student Input
Explanation of
- processes into which students and parents have input
- avenues of appeal

Overall Tone, Audience
- clear sense of audience is conveyed (user friendly)
- plan is clear whether read by teachers, students, parents or community members
- tone is personal and inviting—when specific examples or explanations are not included, the plan makes it clear that inquiries are welcome and readily responded to

Purpose
- serves as notice of, and rationale for, school information sessions and conferences
- serves as information for a variety of audiences

Further thoughts on planning, assessment and communication

When we deal in generalities,
    we will never succeed.
When we deal in specifics,
    we will rarely have a failure.
When performance is assessed,
    performance improves.
When performance is assessed and the learning is communicated,
        the rate of improvement accelerates.

                    —adapted from T. S. Monson, former publisher and printer

Glossary

achievement a student's demonstration of knowledge, skills and attitudes relative to grade level curriculum standards

assessment process of collecting information on student achievement and performance. A balanced assessment includes a variety of assessment tasks. Ongoing diagnostic assessment provides information to inform instruction and improve student performance.

assessment task a complex assessment activity requiring multiple responses to a challenging question or problem

criteria guidelines, rules or principles by which student responses, products or performances are judged

curriculum statement of both general and specific outcomes and expectations for student achievement:
- general learner outcomes are the intended knowledge, skills and attitudes students demonstrate as a result of schooling
- specific learner outcomes are the knowledge, skills and attitudes which students demonstrate at specific grades

curriculum standards what students should know and be able to demonstrate based on the curriculum

evaluation judgement of how well a student has done based on a number of assessment indicators; the overall quality, value, or worth of a response, product or performance based on curriculum standards

grade (mark) level of achievement; a summary statement of student achievement based on demonstrated performance relative to curriculum standards

grades a term widely used to refer to judgments of student performance in relation to the curriculum

grading a process to determine a student's level of achievement within a subject area or course

outcome a goal statement specifying desired knowledge, skills and attitudes to be achieved as a result of educational experiences

performance assessment an assessment activity that requires students to construct a response, create a product or demonstrate something they have learned or created

portfolio a collection of work that provides a concrete representation of a student's learning and progress

rubric/scoring guide a set of criteria used to evaluate a student's performance. A rubric or scoring guide consists of a fixed measurement scale (for example, 4-point) and a list of criteria that describe the characteristics of products or performances for each score point.

self-assessment a process in which a student engages in a systematic review of a performance, usually for the purpose of improving future performance. Self-assessments involve comparison with established criteria, and they often involve comparison with past performance.

subjectivity an element of assessment and evaluation by which the impression or opinion of the assessor influences the score or evaluation of performance

Selected Bibliography

Alberta Assessment Consortium. *A Framework for Student Assessment.* AAC: Edmonton, AB. 1997.

Alberta Education. *Guide to education: ECS to grade 12.* Crown in Right of Alberta: Edmonton, AB. 1998.

Alberta Teachers' Association. *Partners in Learning.* ATA: Edmonton, AB. 1996.

Allan, J., and Little, N. *Student-Led Parent Conferences.* Lugus Production: Toronto, ON. 1988.

Arter, J., and Spandel, V. *Using Portfolios of Student Work in Instruction and Assessment.* Northwest Regional Educational Laboratory: Portland, OR. 1991.

Austin, T. *Changing the View, Student-Led Parent Conferences.* Heinemann: Portsmouth, NH. 1994.

Azwell, T, and Schmar, E. editors. *Report Card on Report Cards: Alternatives to Consider.* Heinemann: Portsmouth, NH. 1995.

Board of Education for the City of Etobicoke— Writing Committee. *Making the Grade— Evaluating Student Progress.* Prentice-Hall Canada: Scarborough, ON. 1987.

Burke, K., Fogarty, R., and Belgrade, S. *The Portfolio Connection.* Skylight: Arlington, VA. 1994.

Canady, R. L. and Hotchkiss, P. R. "It's a Good Score: Just a Bad Grade." *Phi Delta Kappan* Vol. 71 No. 1, September, 1989.

Clemmons, J., and Lase, L. *Portfolios in the Classroom.* Scholastic: Toronto, ON. 1993.

Cooper, D. and Wakeman-Jones, N. *Getting Assessment Right: Language.* DataBased Directions: Barrie, ON. 1998.

Cooper, D., Wakeman-Jones, N., and Blake, P. *Getting Assessment Right: Mathematics.* DataBased Directions: Barrie, ON. 1998.

Daggett, W. and Kruse, B. *Education is NOT a Spectator Sport.* Northwest Regional Laboratory: Portland, OR. 1991.

Davies, A., Cameron, C., Politano, C., et al. *Together is Better: Collaborative Assessment and Reporting.* Pequis: Winnipeg, MB. 1992.

Dressel, P. *Basic College Quarterly, Winter 1957.* Michigan State University: East Lansing, MI. 1957.

Educational Leadership. Theme Issue: "Reporting What Students are Learning." Vol. 52, No. 2, Association for Supervision and Curriculum Development (ASCD), October, 1994.

Frisbie, D. and Waltman, K. "Developing a personal grading plan." In *Instructional topics in educational measurement.* National Council on Measurement in Education: Washington, DC. 1992.

Government of Alberta. *School Act, Statutes of Alberta, 1988, Chapter S-3.1 with amendments in force as of June 18, 1997.* Queen's Printer, Edmonton, AB. 1997.

Government of British Columbia, Ministry of Education. *Guidelines for Student Reporting for The Kindergarten to Grade 12 Education Plan.* Victoria, BC. 1994.

Grant, J., Heffler, B., and Mereweather, K. *Student-Led Conferences—Using portfolios to share learning with parents.* Pembroke: Markham, ON. 1995.

Grant, J.M. *Student-Led Conferences.* Pembroke: Markham, ON. 1995.

Graves, D. and Sunstein, B.S. *Portfolio Portraits.* Irwin: Toronto, ON. 1992.

Guskey, T. editor. *Communicating Student Learning.* ASCD Yearbook: Alexandria, VA. 1996.

Haley, B. *The Report Card Trap.* Betterway: White Hall, VA. 1986.

Hebert, E. "Portfolios Invite Reflection from Students and Staff" *Educational Leadership,* ASCD: Alexandria, VA. May, 1992.

Jasmine, J. *Portfolio Assessment for Your Whole Language Classroom.* Teacher Created Materials: Huntington Beach, CA. 1992.

Joint Advisory Committee. *Principles for Fair Student Assessment Practices for Education in Canada.* Centre for Research in Applied Measurement and Evaluation, University of Alberta, Edmonton, AB. 1993.

National Forum on Assessment. *Principles and Indicators for Student Assessment Systems.* National Centre for Fair and Open Testing (FairTest): Cambridge, MA. 1995.

Neill, D.M. "What is Authentic Evaluation?" Brochure. National Centre for Fair and Open Testing (Fair Test): Cambridge, MA. 1992.

McTighe, J. "What happens between assessments?" *Educational Leadership,* ASCD: Alexandria, VA. December 1997.

O'Connor, K., *The Mindful School: How to Grade for Learning.* Skylight: Arlington Heights, IL. 1999.

Ory, J. and Ryan, K. *Tips for Improving Testing and Grading.* Sage: Newbury Park, CA. 1993.

Picciotto, L. *Evaluation—A Team Effort.* Scholastic: Toronto, ON. 1992.

Reporting Student Progress. Video and Facilitator's Guide. ASCD: Alexandria, VA. 1996.

Rolheiser, C. editor. *Self-Evaluation . . . Helping Students Get Better At It!* CLEAR Group: Toronto, ON. 1996.

Stiggins, R. *A Practical Guide for Developing Sound Grading Practices.* Northwest Regional Laboratory: Portland, OR. 1991.

Stiggins, R. *Student-Centered Classroom Assessment (Second Edition).* Prentice-Hall: Upper Saddle River, NJ. 1997.

Stiggins, R. and Knight, T. *But Are They Learning.* Assessment Training Institute. Portland, OR. 1998.

Tierney, R., Carter, M., and Desai, L. *Portfolio Assessment in the Reading-Writing Classroom.* Christopher Gordon: Norwood, MA. 1991.

Wiggins, G. and McTighe, J. *Understanding by Design.* ASCD: Alexandria, VA. 1998.

Wolf, D. "Portfolio Assessment: Sampling Student Work." *Educational Leadership* ASCD: Alexandria, VA. April, 1989.

Appendix I

School Act

Legal basis for communicating student learning

Teachers   **13** A teacher while providing instruction or supervision must . . .

(e) regularly evaluate students and periodically report the results of the evaluation to the students, the students' parents and the board; . . .

Principals   **15** A principal of a school must . . .

(c) evaluate or provide for the evaluation of programs offered in the school;

(c. 1) ensure that students in the school have the opportunity to meet the standards of education set by the Minister; . . .

More on the legal basis for communicating student learning

Students   **7** A student shall conduct himself so as to reasonably comply with the following code of conduct:

(a) be diligent in pursuing his studies . . .

School council   **17** (4) A school council may, at its discretion, . . .

(c) consult with the principal so that the principal may ensure that students in the school have the opportunity to meet the standards of education set by the Minister, . . .

Student records   **18** (1) A board shall establish and maintain pursuant to the regulations a student record for each student enrolled in its schools.

(2) Subject to subsection (3),

(a) if a student is younger than 16 years of age, his parent,

(b) if a student is 16 years of age or older, the student, his parent or both of them, or

(c) if an individual has access to the student under an order made under the *Divorce Act* (Canada), that individual

may review the student record maintained in respect of that student.

Requests to pro-   **60.** 1 (1) A board shall provide the Minister with any infor-
vide information   mation the Minister requests in writing.

(2) The Minister may publish or otherwise disseminate any information the Minister receives under subsection (1).

Accountability   **60.2** (1) A board shall develop a reporting and accountability
of board   system on any matter the Minister prescribes.

(2) A board shall disseminate any information in the reports and accounts reproduced under the reporting and accountability system it develops under subsection (1) to students, parents, electors or the Minister in the manner the Minister prescribes.

(3) A board shall use any information in the reports and accounts produced under the reporting and accountability system it develops under subsection (1) in the manner the Minister prescribes.

Standards for Teacher Competence in Educational Assessment of Students (1990)

More on the ethical basis for communicating student learning

The standards, originating in the United States, formed the conceptual framework for the *Principles for Fair Student Assessment Practices for Education in Canada*.

The assessment competencies included here are the knowledge and skills critical to a teacher's role as educator. It is understood that there are many competencies beyond assessment competencies which teachers must possess.

1. *Teachers should be skilled in choosing assessment methods appropriate for instructional decisions.*

2. *Teachers should be skilled in developing assessment methods appropriate for instructional decisions.*

3. *The teacher should be skilled in administering, scoring and interpreting the results of both externally produced and teacher-produced assessment methods.*

4. *Teachers should be skilled in using assessment results when making decisions about individual students, planning teaching, developing curriculum, and school improvement.*

5. *Teachers should be skilled in developing valid pupil grading procedures that use pupil assessments.*

   Grading students is an important part of professional practice for teachers. Grading is defined as indicating both a student's level of performance and a teacher's valuing of that performance. The principles for using assessments to obtain valid grades are known, and teachers should employ them.

   Teachers who meet this standard will have the conceptual and application skills that follow:

   Teachers will be able to devise, implement, and explain a procedure for developing grades composed of marks from various assignments, projects, in-class activities, quizzes, tests, and/or other assessments that they may use.

Teachers will understand and be able to articulate why the grades they assign are rational, justified, and fair, acknowledging that such grades reflect their preferences and judgements.

Teachers will be able to recognize and to avoid faulty grading procedures such as using grades as punishment.

Teachers will be able to evaluate and to modify their grading procedures in order to improve the validity of the interpretations made from them about students' attainments.

6. *Teachers should be skilled in communicating assessment results to students, parents, other lay audiences, and other educators.*

Teachers who meet this standard will have the conceptual and application skills that follow:

Teachers will understand and be able to give appropriate explanations of how the interpretation of student assessments must be moderated by the student's socioeconomic, cultural, language, and other background factors.

Teachers will explain that assessment results do not imply that such background factors limit a student's ultimate educational development.

Teachers will communicate to students and to their parents or guardians how they may assess the students educational progress.

Teachers will explain the importance of taking measurement errors into account when using assessments to make decisions about individual students.

Teachers will explain the limitations of different informal and formal assessment methods.

Teachers will explain printed reports of the results of pupil assessments at the classroom, school district, provincial, and national levels.

7. *Teachers should be skilled in recognizing unethical, illegal, and otherwise inappropriate assessment methods and uses of assessment information.*

Alberta Education policies

Policy on Provincial Large-Scale Assessment

The Government of the Province of Alberta has mandated the annual administration of Achievement Tests to all students in selected subject areas for Grades 3, 6, and 9. The results from these tests may be used by teachers to contribute to the final mark for students. For Grade 12 students, Provincial

Diploma Examinations results contribute 50% of students' final grades in the key diploma courses.

Background from *Policy 2.1.3 - Use and Reporting of Results on Provincial Assessments*

Results from provincial assessments provide only part of the overall picture of the province's, a school authority's, a school's or an individual student's performance. Although the achievement tests and diploma exams are designed to assess the achievement of provincial standards as reflected in the *Program of Studies,* many important learning outcomes cannot be measured by time-limited, paper-and-pencil tests. In addition, many factors affect student achievement. The analysis, interpretation, use and communication of results from provincial assessments need to take these into account.

Provincial assessments provide a common measure of achievement for students throughout the province. The tests support the classroom teacher in carrying out the responsibility for evaluating students' progress and communicating to students and parents the full range and richness of students' achievement. (italics added)

Policy on Assessment as the Basis for Communicating Individual Student Achievement

(also applies to students on home education programs—ECS to grade 9)

Teachers shall ensure that information is made available to parents about:

- what their child knows and can do in the programs she or he is studying
- how well their child is doing in those programs
- the grade level(s) the child has achieved in relation to the grade levels of the provincial programs of study for language arts, mathematics, science and social studies.

The policy does not restrict the communicating of achievement to written reports, nor does it require schools to use a particular type of instructional grouping or placement policy.

Teaching Quality Standards in Alberta

The following is the ninth standard in Permanent Professional Certification, Appendix III (page 6):

9. *Teachers gather and use information about students' learning needs and progress.*

Teachers help students, parents and other educators interpret and understand the results of diagnoses and assessments, and the implications for students. They also help students develop the ability to diagnose their own learning needs and to assess their progress toward learning goals.

Principles for Fair Assessment Practices for Education in Canada (1993)

The *Principles* is "a set of principles and guidelines generally accepted by professional organizations as indicative of fair assessment practice within the Canadian educational context." The following sections from Part A of the *Principles* relate specifically to communicating student learning:

IV. Summarizing and Interpreting Results

Principle

Procedures for summarizing and interpreting assessment results should yield accurate and informative representations of a student's performance in relation to the goals and objectives of instruction for the reporting period.

1. Procedures for summarizing and interpreting results for a reporting period should be guided by a written policy.

2. The way in which summary comments and grades are formulated and interpreted should be explained to students and their parents/guardians.

3. The individual results used and the process followed in deriving summary comments and grades should be described in sufficient detail so that the meaning of a summary comment or grade is clear.

4. Combining disparate kinds of results into a single summary should be done cautiously. To the extent possible, achievement, effort, participation, and other behaviours should be graded separately.

5. Summary comments and grades should be based on more than one assessment result so as to ensure adequate sampling of broadly defined learning outcomes.

6. The results used to produce summary comments and grades should be combined in a way that ensures that each result receives its intended emphasis or weight.

7. The basis for interpretation should be carefully described and justified.

8. Interpretations of assessment results should take account of the backgrounds and learning experiences of the students.

9. Assessment results that will be combined into summary comments and grades should be stored in a way that ensures their accuracy at the time they are summarized and interpreted.

10. Interpretations of assessment results should be made with due regard for limitations in the assessment methods used, problems encountered in collecting the information and judging or scoring it, and limitations in the basis used for interpretation.

V. Reporting Assessment Findings

Principle

Assessment reports should be clear, accurate, and of practical value to the audiences for whom they are intended.

1. The reporting system for a school or jurisdiction should be guided by a written policy. Elements to consider include such aspects as audiences, medium, format, content, level of detail, frequency, timing, and confidentiality.

2. Written and oral reports should contain a description of the goals and objectives of instruction to which the assessments are referenced.

3. Reports should be complete in their descriptions of strengths and weaknesses of students, so that strengths can be built upon and problem areas addressed.

4. The reporting system should provide for conferences between teachers and parents/guardians. Whenever it is appropriate, students should participate in these conferences.

5. An appeal process should be described to students and their parents/guardians at the beginning of each school year or course of instruction that they may use to appeal a report.

6. Access to assessment information should be governed by a written policy that is consistent with applicable laws and with basic principles of fairness and human rights.

7. Transfer of assessment information from one school to another should be guided by a written policy with stringent provisions to ensure the maintenance of confidentiality.

Appendix II

Reporting For Students With Special Needs

Students on the graded curriculum

When a student with special needs is expected to achieve or surpass the learning outcomes set out in the provincial curriculum, regular grading and reporting procedures should be followed. To achieve expected learner outcomes, modifications may have to be made to the instruction or assessment methods. It is important to remember that some students take longer to complete the requirements for a given grade or program than others.

Students not on the graded curriculum

If it is determined that a student with special needs is not capable of achieving the learning outcomes set out in the provincial curriculum and that substantial course or program modification is necessary, specific individual goals and objectives will be established for the student in the individual program plan (IPP). The use of letter grades and percentages for reporting the progress of these students is generally inappropriate. Structured written comments should be used to communicate student learning.

Often, a professional support person, together with the classroom teacher, is responsible for providing some portion of the student's education program (for example, speech pathologist, orientation and mobility instructors). Assessment information from these support people should be included in the process of communicating student learning.

Evaluation and Communication Practices

1. Grading should be based on the academic requirements specified in the IPP and linked to curricular outcomes at the grade level at which the student is functioning.
2. The student should be involved in activities that encourage self-assessment including celebrations of learning and portfolios.
3. Information on specific areas of strength and relative weaknesses, suggestions for further study and areas for peer/parent tutor assistance should be included.

APPENDIX

A-2

A Framework for Student Assessment

Contents

Assessing Student Learning in the Classroom

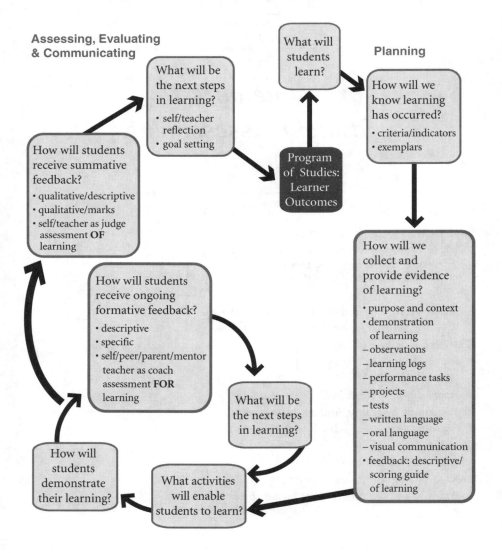

Setting the Stage

When I think about assessment . . . Key Visual [link] 🔗 **Planning**

> What image(s) does classroom assessment bring to your mind?
>
> Assessment is like _____
>
> because _____

The figure below shows images that reflect beliefs about assessment expressed by educators in the AAC study *The Power of Assessment* FOR *Learning* (2003). You will see that teachers expressed both positive and negative attitudes about assessment. On the one hand, assessment can be seen as a celebration of student learning and an opportunity to help students choose the right path in life; on the other hand, it can be seen in a negative light, as a pair of pliers squeezing the joy in learning out of children.

When teachers are asked to discuss their feelings and concerns about assessment, their responses often conflict over assessment that focuses on important learning processes and assessment that demonstrates results. In other words, the conflict between summative and formative assessment.

The assessments that drive **academic learning** and **self-concept** are those used by teachers in classrooms.
—Richard J. Stiggins, Assessment Training Institute,
Portland, Oregon

IMAGES THAT REFLECT BELIEFS ABOUT ASSESSMENT

Source: Adapted from the AAC study *The Power of Assessment* FOR *Learning* (2003), pp. 35–37

The Teacher's Role in Assessment

In 1997 the Teaching Quality Standard (TQS) became part of the *School Act*. This standard clearly outlines teachers' classroom responsibilities and provides nine descriptive statements pertaining to student assessment.

Teachers gather and use information about students' learning needs and progress

Teachers

1. monitor students' actions on an ongoing basis to determine and respond to their learning needs.
2. use a variety of diagnostic methods that include observing students' activities, analyzing students' learning difficulties and strengths, and interpreting the results of assessments and information provided by students, their parents, colleagues and other professionals.
3. select and develop a variety of classroom assessment strategies and instruments to assess the full range of learning objectives.
4. differentiate between classroom and large-scale instruments such as provincial achievement tests, administer both and use the results for the ultimate benefit of students.
5. record, interpret and use the results of their assessments to modify their teaching practices and students' learning activities.
6. help students, parents and other educators interpret and understand the results of diagnoses and assessments, and the implications for students.
7. help students develop the ability to diagnose their own learning needs and to assess their progress toward learning goals.
8. use their interpretations of diagnoses and assessments as well as students' work and results to guide their own professional growth.
9. assist school councils and members of the community to understand the purposes, meanings, outcomes and implications of assessments.

Policy 4.2.1 Teaching Quality Standard Applicable to the Provision of Basic Education in Alberta. Approved: May 14, 1997

Transcending Polarization: The Importance of Achieving a Holonomous Perspective

When confronted with new ideas about teaching, learning and assessing, and daunting expectations for our own learning, we can easily fall into polarized ways of thinking and see different purposes of and approaches to assessment as contradictory rather than as complementary. It is easy to adopt an adversarial stance, seeing external testing as a constraint or arguing for a singular focus on traditional methods of assessment, or advocating their abandonment in favour of other methods.

Fortunately, we are capable of transcending these polarized viewpoints and adopting a *holomonous* viewpoint, a term coined by Arthur Koestler and adapted by Costa and Garmston (2001). The word *holonomous* is derived from the Greek *holo*, meaning *whole*, and the suffix *on*, which means *part*. Holonomy, then, refers the study of the relationship between wholes and parts.

From an assessment perspective, a *holonomous* view enables us to gather information from a variety of assessment sources, both external to the classroom (from international, national, provincial and jurisdictional testing, for example) and within the classroom (from tests, observations, personal conversations, projects, journals, performances, students' evaluations of themselves and peer evaluations, etc.) and to make judicious use of that information to evaluate, support and enhance student learning. It is this *holonomous* perspective that the Alberta Assessment Consortium seeks to foster among educators, parents and other community members. It will take time, patience and collaboration to achieve this view of assessment. We trust that this framework takes us a little closer to the realization of that goal.

Changing views of learning, teaching and assessing

The turmoil around assessment is not surprising. We are in the midst of an important shift in our thinking about learning and teaching. The traditional view of the learner as a passive recipient of information has given way to an emerging view of the learner as an active participant in his or her own learning.

The need for a multidimensional approach to assessment

Changing views of teaching, learning and assessing require a shift from a single focus on paper-and-pencil tests that traditionally come at the end of the learning process to a multidimensional approach that

- encompasses other forms of assessment designed to accomplish a variety of purposes;
- provides teachers, students, parents and members of the community with clear and accurate information about
  student achievement; and
- enables students, parents and members of the community to become involved as partners in the assessment process

Cognitive Learning Theory—Implications for Assessing Student Learning

Cognitive learning theory recognizes the links between instruction and assessment. The chart below describes the theory and how teachers can put the theory into practice.

Theory	How Teachers Put Theory Into Practice
Knowledge is constructed. Learning is a process of creating personal meaning from new information and prior knowledge.	• Encourage discussion of new ideas. • Encourage divergent thinking, multiple links and solutions, not just one right answer. • Encourage multiple modes of expression, for example, role playing, simulations, debates and explanations to others. • Emphasize critical thinking skills: analyze, compare, generalize, predict, synthesize, hypothesize. • Relate new information to personal experience, prior knowledge. • Encourage students to apply information to a new situation.
All ages/abilities can think and solve problems. Learning isn't necessarily a linear progression of discrete skills.	• Engage all students in problem solving. • Don't make problem solving, critical thinking, or discussion of concepts contingent on mastery of routine basic skills.
There is a great variety in learning styles, attention spans, memory, the pace of development and intelligences.	• Provide choices in tasks (not all reading and writing). • Provide choices in how to show mastery/competence. • Provide time for students to think about and do assignments. • Don't overuse timed tests. • Provide opportunities to revise, rethink. • Include concrete experiences (manipulatives, links to prior personal experience).

Theory	How Teachers Put Theory Into Practice
People perform better when they know the goal, see models and know how their performance compares to the standard.	• Discuss goals; let students help define them (personal and class). • Provide a range of examples of student work; discuss characteristics. • Provide students with opportunities for self-reflection and peer feedback. • Discuss criteria for judging performance. • Allow students to have input into setting criteria.
It's important to know when to use knowledge, how to adapt it, how to manage one's own learning.	• Give real-world opportunities (or simulations) to apply/adapt new knowledge. • Have students self-evaluate; think about how they learn well/poorly; set new goals; understand why they like certain work.
Motivation, effort and self-esteem affect learning and performance.	• Motivate students with real-life tasks and connections to personal experience. • Encourage students to see connections between effort and results.
Learning has social components. Group work is valuable.	• Provide group work. • Make sure that student groups are heterogeneous. • Enable students to take on a variety of roles. • Consider group products and group processes.

From Herman, J. L. et al. (1992) *A Practical Guide to Alternative Assessment*, p. 20–21, reprinted with permission from the Association for Supervision and Curriculum Development, a worldwide community of educators advocating sound policies and sharing best practices to achieve the success of each learner. To learn more, visit ASCD at www.ascd.org.

Cultivating my ideas

1. Which of my beliefs about assessment have been confirmed as a result of reading "Setting the Stage"?
2. As I was reading, I was puzzled by . . .
3. As I was reading, I was surprised by . . .

Collecting Evidence of Learning

Why should teachers be concerned with assessment?

Assessment involves collecting evidence of learning that provides the basis for sound decision making regarding teaching and learning. Planning for assessment and using assessment data to modify teaching are essential parts of the instructional cycle.

The purposes of assessment

The primary purpose of assessment is to provide ongoing feedback to educators, students and parents to enhance teaching and learning. Teachers assess to gather information about what students know and can do, to monitor student progress, to evaluate achievement and to evaluate their instruction. The major purposes of assessment are often described as assessment **for** learning (diagnostic and formative) and assessment **of** learning (summative). Both kinds of assessment play an important role in a balanced assessment program.

Assessment FOR Learning—Diagnostic and Formative Assessment

Assessment **for** learning is ongoing communication with students about their progress in relation to clearly specified learning goals. It should happen in the classroom on a daily basis and should take the form of quality, detailed descriptive feedback from teachers to students. It might be useful to use a sports analogy to understand assessment **for** learning. In competitive sports, the assessment of an athlete's fitness is a form of diagnostic assessment. That is, the coach asks questions to obtain information about the athlete's fitness and uses this information to give the athlete specific guidance about appropriate diet, exercise and attitude. During training sessions, the coach and the athlete's peers observe the athlete's performance and give specific feedback about what the athlete is doing well and what the athlete needs to do to improve. The athlete will also be encouraged to self-assess and make changes to improve performance. This formative assessment will be repeated many times over as the athlete prepares for competition.

There are two types of assessment for learning: diagnostic and formative.

Diagnostic assessment

Diagnostic assessment may occur at the beginning of a term, a unit of study or whenever information about a student's prior learning is useful or needed. Various types of diagnostic assessments (observations, tests, journals, performance-based assessments, etc.) may be used to collect information.

Educators may use diagnostic assessment to

- find out what students know and can do;
- identify student strengths and plan instruction that builds on and extends those strengths;
- target weak areas, identify their precise nature, and plan instruction to respond to the needs; and
- make informed decisions about where to focus instructional time and effort.

Formative assessment

Formative assessment differs from diagnostic assessment in that it provides ongoing feedback to the teacher about the effectiveness of instruction. Formative assessment encompasses a variety of strategies to help teachers accomplish one or more of the following goals:

- monitoring student learning and providing feedback to students and parents
- identifying areas of growth
- motivating students and providing incentives to study
- helping students to focus their attention and make concentrated efforts
- emphasizing what is important to learn
- helping students practice in applying, demonstrating and extending knowledge, skills and attitudes
- encouraging student self-reflection, peer coaching, goal setting and monitoring achievement of goals
- reflecting on program structure and effectiveness, and modifying or adjusting teaching as necessary

It should be noted that data/information gathered from diagnostic and formative assessments should not be part of a student's grade.

Key Visual ◔ʒʔ **—How will students receive ongoing formative feedback?**

Assessment OF Learning—Summative Assessment

Assessment **of** learning is the process of summarizing information collected about learning at a given point in order to share that information with those outside the classroom. In essence, assessment **of** learning is the process of establishing learning milestones.

To continue the sports analogy, the assessment **of** learning comes on the day of the competition. The athlete will receive summative feedback on his or her performance, usually in numerical form—the time taken to complete an event, the score awarded by judges in relation to a set of criteria, etc. Even though this summative assessment is a final judgment for that particular competition, it is also the beginning of a new cycle of diagnostic and formative assessment; the athlete will self-assess, and with the assistance of his or her coach, set new goals for training to improve performance at the next competition. For an athlete, and for that matter any learner, there is always a next time, another chance to improve achievement.

Summative assessment

Summative assessment is usually carried out at the end of a unit or term, or whenever students need to demonstrate their achievement of learning outcomes. At the classroom level, summative assessment can include tests, projects, demonstrations, performances, classroom assessment materials (CAMP), etc. Examples of types of summative assessment external to the classroom are provincial achievement tests and diploma examinations.
Summative assessment

- provides feedback to educators, students, parents, post-secondary institutions, and so on about achievement;
- helps parents and teachers make decisions about appropriate placement or programs for students;
- helps students make decisions regarding further study; and
- determines program effectiveness and where improvement may be required.

It should be noted that the data/information gathered from summative assessment simply reflects student achievement at a given moment in a specific context. This information is then used to determine a grade for communicating student learning.

Key Visual —**How will students receive summative feedback?**

Choosing Assessment Strategies

Assessment must be part of the process of planning for instruction. To choose appropriate assessment strategies, a teacher must first consider what purposes the assessment will serve and the kinds of assessment information that must be gathered to fulfill those purposes. A balanced and comprehensive assessment of student learning includes a judicious selection of diagnostic, formative and summative assessments.

Clarifying the Purposes of Assessment

Educators must understand that there is a difference between assessment **of** learning and assessment **for** learning. Ruth Sutton (adapted from an unpublished document, 2001, and used with permission) looks at it this way:

Assessment **of** *Learning* (**summative** *assessment*)	*Assessment* **for** *Learning* (**formative** *assessment*)
Checks what has been learned to date.	Checks learning to decide what to do next, then provides suggestions of what to do. Teaching and learning are indistinguishable from assessment.
Is designed to provide information to those not directly involved in daily learning and teaching (for example, school administration, parents, school boards, Alberta Education, post-secondary institutions) in addition to educators and students.	Is designed to assist educators and students in improving learning.
Is presented in a periodic report.	Provides continual descriptive feedback.
Usually compiles data into a single number, score or mark as a formal report.	Usually uses detailed, specific and descriptive feedback in a formal or informal report.
Must be reported as part of an achievement grade.	Must not be reported as part of an achievement grade.
Usually compares a student's learning either with other students' learning (norm-referenced, making learning highly competitive) or the standard for a grade level (criterion-referenced, making learning more collaborative and individually focused).	Usually focuses on improvement and compares a student's present performance with his or her previous best (self-referenced, making learning more personal).
Does not always involve the student.	Must involve the student.

Types of Assessment Strategies

There are many sources of information about student achievement, and no one source is necessarily better than another. Each can provide useful and different information about student achievement. However, interpretation of the findings is valid only when linked to the circumstances under which performance was assessed. The most accurate profile of student achievement is based on the findings gathered from assessing student performance in a variety of contexts. The key is the match between the specific learner outcomes and the selected assessments to ensure reliable (consistent) and valid (trustworthy) results.

Source of Information	Strategy	What It Meausres
Observations	• Anecdotal records • Conferences	immediate evaluation and feedback of learning, focus on specific learner expectations, social skills and behaviours, teamwork, interactions, knowledge into context, levels of understanding, relationships, attitude, oral language skills, listening skills, ability to synthesize, cooperation, leadership skills, tolerance, respect
Learning Logs	• Reflective journals • Personal response journals • Dialogue journals	understanding, written ability, conventions, organization, pre and post comparisons, feedback to teachers, personal connections, social skills, connection to concepts in literature, understanding of story elements, internalization of literature, personal experience, goal setting, understanding process, affective mode, background knowledge
Performance Tasks	• Simulations • Demonstrations • Labs • Video productions • Presentations —drama/music/ dance • Computer-based software	creativity, understanding, end product, public speaking and performing, group work, organization skills, application of skills to new situations, reasoning skills, analysis, real-life application, process, procedures, ability to handle equipment

Source of Information	Strategy	What It Meausres
Projects	• Models • Experiments • Work samples • Investigations • Surveys • Scrapbooks	knowledge, application, motor skills, planning and research skills, demonstration, organization, process, procedures, formulating and testing hypotheses, perseverance, ability to gather and process information to create meaning, cooperation
Tests	• Multiple choice • True/false • Short answer • Paper and pencil • Matching • Extended response	pre and post test of knowledge, content mastery, ability to make inferences, recall, recognition, memorization, content, problem-solving abilities
Written Language	• Lab reports • Essays • Research papers • Script • Brochure • Word puzzles • Articles • Stories • Proposals	logical organization, ability to make hypotheses, comprehension, ability to follow directions, writing skills, use of logic, interpersonal relations, expression, vocabulary, style, understanding different writing structures/genres, research skills, evaluation, initiative
Oral Language	• Retelling • Debate • Story boards • Interviewing • Poetry reading • Questions/responses • Audiotapes • Teaching a lesson • Games	comprehension, ability to synthesize and paraphrase, speaking and listening skills, substantiation of positions, development of counter argument, reasoning, assessment of background knowledge, perspective, organization, decision-making skills, personal information, attitude, ability to analyze, memorization, interpretation, composure, confidence, enunciation, articulation
Visual Communication	• Story boards • Illustrations • Design • Advertisements • Photographs • Videotapes • Dioramas • Collages • Maps	assessment of background knowledge, comprehension, organization, creativity, growth and maturity level, depth of conceptualization, application, ability to synthesize, process, application of knowledge and skills, equipment use, decision-making abilities

Key Visual ⌬—**How will we collect and provide evidence of learning?**

CURRICULAR PRIORITIES AND ASSESSMENTS

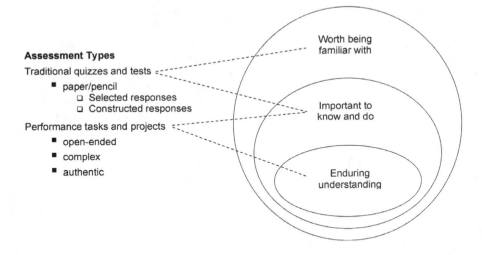

Assessment Types

Traditional quizzes and tests

- paper/pencil
  - Selected responses
  - Constructed responses

Performance tasks and projects

- open-ended
- complex
- authentic

Worth being familiar with

Important to know and do

Enduring understanding

From Wiggins, G and J. McTighe (1998) *Understanding by Design* Figure 1.5-**Curricular Priorities and Assessments**. Used with permission from the Association for Supervision and Curriculum Development, a worldwide community of educators advocating sound policies and sharing best practices to achieve the success of each learner. To learn more, visit ASCD at www.ascd.org.

Cultivating my ideas

1. How do my assessment practices help every student to succeed?
2. How do I ensure that my assessments gather evidence of all the learner outcomes of a course?
3. To what extent are the assessment strategies I use congruent with instruction? In other words, do my assessment and my teaching complement each other?
4. To what extent do the assessment tasks that I require of my students merit their time and energy to complete?
5. How do I provide student feedback that is encouraging, **not** discouraging?

Implementing a Quality Student Assessment Program

Thinking
Consider beliefs and underlying principles.

It has been said that assessment drives instruction. This is often true and is not necessarily a bad thing.

Current research continues to shed light on what constitutes good assessment. During the planning process teachers are challenged to put some of this research into practice.

Collaboration with other educators, and collaboration amongst educators, students and parents, enhances the planning process. Teachers can develop valuable knowledge, skills and attitudes, and a sense of the big picture by participating in assessment- related activities external to the school, such as

- marking jurisdiction and/or provincial achievement tests and diploma examinations;
- developing test items;
- attending conferences; and
- attending AAC summer development workshops.

For further information, investigate published assessment tools such as provincial achievement tests, diploma examinations, and information bulletins (blueprints) at www. learning.gov.ab.ca and performance tasks at www.aac. ab.ca.

(See also the Selected Bibliography and Webography at the end of this document)

Planning
Consider curriculum, learner outcomes and exemplars.

Key Visual ⌘—Program of Studies: Learner Outcomes
A quality assessment program results from extensive short- and long-term planning, and must answer two critical questions:

- Are my programming and assessment based on the provincial program of studies?
- Am I assessing the big ideas covered in the program of studies?

A quality assessment program includes

- a variety of assessment strategies

gathering information about student achievement on all aspects of the curriculum (knowledge, skills, and

For further information, look in the provincial Programs of Studies and the Illustrative Examples. www.l earning.gov.ab.ca/ k_12/curriculum/ bySubject/

attitudes), not just those easiest to
measure.

- considering various audiences that
will use the information:
- students
- educators
- parents or guardians
- district staff
- provincial staff
- elected officials
- employers
- post-secondary education staff
- general public

A quality balanced assessment program includes a wide range of assessment strategies that demonstrate what
students know, understand and
can do.

Constructing
Consider pur-
poses and types
of assessment.

The specificity and formality of an
assessment strategy and the information gathered will vary depending on
who uses the data and the purpose of
the assessment (diagnostic, formative,
summative). Each assessment chosen
should start with a plan or blueprint
that specifies

- learner outcome(s); that is, what is
being targeted;
- level of thinking required;
- criteria; that is, what evidence will
be accepted;
- exemplary responses that demonstrate the criteria;
- method for eliciting student products or behaviours (context and task
development); and
- process for providing feedback, and
for recording and communicating
results.

A comprehensive picture of a student,
school or jurisdiction requires the synthesis of data derived from a variety of
sources. For example, some assessments

For further infor-
mation, refer to
the AAC resource
*How To . . .
Develop and Use
Performance
Assessments in the
Classroom.*

demonstrate acquisition of knowledge. Other assessments provide teachers with information about students' thinking skills and learning processes. The challenge for teachers is to ensure that classroom assessments capture information about student achievement and performance that cannot be derived from external measures.

Conducting
Consider curriculum, instruction and assessment *for* learning.

There must be a strong alignment between curriculum, instruction, assessment, evaluation and communication of results. Effective assessment and evaluation reflect and promote good instruction, and provide data that can be used meaningfully by some or all of the stakeholders. Assessment should mirror as closely as possible what we want students to be able to do. Engage students in meaningful, contextualized reading, writing, science and mathematics rather than inauthentic proxy activities. Provide specific, descriptive feedback that is positive and constructive so that students are motivated to persevere. Avoid making critical and discouraging comments.

For further information refer to the AAC resource *Refocus: Looking at Assessment for Learning.*

Interpreting
Consider evaluation and assessment *of* learning.

The process of making judgments about student performance gives rise to many questions:

- Should all the students in my class be expected to reach the same standard?
- Are my standards the same as other teachers' standards?
- How can I determine what standards my students are achieving?
- How do I know if the learning I am assessing is consistent with what students are expected to know and do?

The concept of standards is complex and not easily defined. For example, a

For further information, refer to the AAC resource *Smerging Data: Grading . . . More Than Just Number Crunching.*

standard is often considered to be the highest level of achievement that has been accomplished in a particular endeavour, such as an Olympic event. The definitions that are often applied to student achievement and performance defy common understanding and agreement. We must acknowledge the ambiguities, complexities and nuances that keep us from developing a shared understanding, and we need to share our thoughts, ask questions, listen to each other and explore the issues. To develop a shared understanding of expectations and standards, there is a need for continued dialogue and an examination of the implications for student learning and openness.

Communicating Consider reporting student achievement and growth.

The most crucial part of the communication process is to ensure a shared understanding between the person providing the information and the information receiver. Letter grades, percentages and comments resulting from an activity, test or assignment must be clear and comprehensive. Effective communication informs the student, parents and others about what the student has accomplished and what the next steps are in the learning process. Just as a variety of assessment strategies are essential to telling the story of a student's educational accomplishments, a variety of communication methods are essential to provide the whole achievement story. For example, a list of subjects with only percentage marks is more meaningful to teachers than to parents and community members because the teacher brings a background of information about the courses of study. To keep all stakeholders informed, additional information must be shared, ideally in a parent–student–teacher conference.

For further information, refer to the AAC resource *A Framework for Communicating Student Learning.*

Such information includes curriculum information, products and student exemplars of acceptable and excellent work. The communication process must involve all the key players. However, the greater the role students are given in this process, the richer the information about the student's achievement and the greater the impact on future learning and success.

Paul Black, based on the research of Butler (1988), asserts that comment-only marking (descriptive feedback) during the course of formative assessment results in significantly better achievement for all students in subsequent assessment experiences, thereby making a strong case for refraining from assigning marks at the coaching stage in the interest of increasing student achievement and inspiring continued learning.

Reflecting
Consider the next steps in the teaching–learning continuum.

Assessment, evaluation and communication of student achievement are integral parts of schooling. Each part of the process should be a positive experience for students and should promote growth. Practices should be carried out in such a way that they support continuous learning.

Just as students are in a continuous learning cycle, so too are teachers. Looking back on an assessment program provides insights teachers can use when planning future instruction and assessments. Reflective questions a teacher might ponder to determine what worked, what could be improved and what should be discontinued include

• Were the students aware of what they know and can do? Were parents?

For further information, refer to the AAC resource *Refocus: Looking at Assessment for Learning.*

- Were new goals for learning established? By the students? By me (the teacher)?
- Do I have sufficient information to know if students need me to review, re-teach, enrich, reassess or move on?
- Did what was assessed actually align with the curriculum and did it provide valid (trustworthy) results?

Key Visual 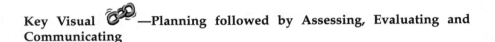—Planning followed by Assessing, Evaluating and Communicating

Cultivating my ideas

1. After reading this section, what I would like to investigate further is . . .
2. How do I make my current assessment practices ongoing and use the information gathered to plan effective programming for all students?
3. In what ways are my students taking an active role in the assessment, evaluation and communication of their learning?
4. How do I communicate information about students' performance to parents, students and non-educators so that it can be easily understood?
5. How can we set up our learning opportunities so that learning continues while assessment occurs?

Glossary

Achievement a student's demonstration of knowledge, skills and attitudes relative to grade level curriculum standards

Assessment the collection of information on student achievement and performance to improve student learning

Assessment for **Learning** ongoing exchange of information between students and teachers about student progress toward clearly specified learning goals (formative assessment)

Assessment of **Learning** summarizing information collected about learning in order to share that information with those outside classrooms (summative assessment)

Criteria what one would accept as evidence that a student has achieved a learning outcome

Descriptive Feedback part of an ongoing, hopeful conversation about learning that relates directly to the expected learning outcomes

Evaluation judgment regarding the quality, value or worth of a response

Formative Assessment provides information about student progress and direction for improvement and/or adjustment to a program for individual students or for a whole class, but is not part of an achievement grade (adapted from O'Connor, 1999)

Grade (mark) a summary statement of student achievement relative to curriculum standards

Learner Outcomes what we expect students to learn; the knowledge, skills and attitudes we expect students to demonstrate as a result of schooling

Peer Coaching a cooperative activity of providing feedback to a peer in a nonthreatening and supportive way to help improve performance

Self-Reflection considering the quality of one's work by applying performance standards when one feels safe and able to be honest in making objective observations about the work (also referred to as *self-assessment* or *self-evaluation*) (adapted from Stiggins, 2001)

Summative Assessment provides information to make judgments about student achievement at the end of a period of instruction and for determining an achievement grade (adapted from O'Connor, 1999)

Selected Bibliography

Alberta Assessment Consortium. *A Framework for Communicating Student Learning.* Edmonton, AB: AAC, 1999.

Alberta Assessment Consortium. *Smerging Data: Grading . . . More Than Just Number Crunching.* Edmonton, AB: AAC, 2001.

Alberta Assessment Consortium. *How to Develop and Use Performance Assessments in the Classroom.* Edmonton, AB: AAC, revised edition, 2003a.

Alberta Assessment Consortium. *The Power of Assessment FOR Learning: Final Report.* Edmonton, AB: AAC, 2003b.

Alberta Assessment Consortium. *Refocus: Looking at Assessment for Learning. Second Edition.* Edmonton, AB: AAC, 2005.

Alberta Education. *Guide to Education: ECS to Grade 12.* Edmonton, AB: Alberta Education, 1998.

Alberta Learning. *Classroom Assessment Tool Kit for the Information and Communication Technology (ICT) Program of Studies.* Edmonton, AB: Alberta Learning, 2003.

Arter, J. A. and K. Busick. *Practice with student-involved classroom assessment.* Portland, OR: Assessment Training Institute, 2001.

Black, P., et al. *Working inside the black box: Assessment for learning in the classroom.* London: King's College, 2002.

Black, P., et al. *Assessment for Learning: Putting It into Practice.* Berkshire, U.K.: Open University Press, 2003.

Black, P., and D. Wiliam. *Inside the Black Box: Raising standards through classroom assessment.* London: King's College, 1998.

Butler, R. "Enhancing and Undermining Intrinsic Motivation: the Effects of Task-involving and Ego-involving Evaluation on Interest and Performance," *British Journal of Educational Psychology*, 58: 1–14, 1988.

Chappuis, S., R. Stiggins, J. Arter, and L. Chappuis. *Assessment FOR Learning: An Action Guide for School Leaders.* Portland, OR: Assessment Training Institute, 2004.

Committee on the Foundations of Assessment (J. Pelligrino, N. Chudowsky, and R. Glaser, editors) *Knowing What Students Know: The Science and Design of Educational Assessment.* Washington, D.C.: National Academy Press, 2001.

Costa, A and R. Garmston. *Cognitive Coaching: A Foundation for Renaissance Schools.* Norwood, MA: Christopher Gordon Publishers, 2001.

Davies, A. *Making Classroom Assessment Work.* Merville, BC: Connections International, 2000.

Davies, A. *A Facilitator's Guide to Classroom Assessment.* Merville, BC: Classroom Connections International, 2003.

Educational Leadership. *Teaching for Meaning* 62, no. 1 (September 2004).

Educational Leadership. *Closing Achievement Gaps* 62. no. 3 (November 2004).

Eisner, E. "The Uses and Limits of Performance Assessment." *Phi Delta Kappan* 80, no. 9 (May 1999).

Graves, D. H. *Testing Is Not Teaching: What Should Count in Education.* Portsmouth, N.H.: Heinemann, 2002.

Guskey, T. R. "How Classroom Assessments Improve Learning." *Educational Leadership*, ASCD: Alexandria, VA: Feb 2003.

Johnston, P. H. *Choice Words: How our language affects children's learning.* Portland, ME: Stenhouse, 2004.

Joint Advisory Committee. *Principles for Fair Student Assessment Practices for Education in Canada.* Edmonton, AB: Centre for Research in Applied Measurement and Evaluation, University of Alberta, 1993.

Marzano, R., D. J. Pickering, and J. E. Pollock. *Classroom Instruction That Works: Research-Based Strategies for Increasing Student Achievement.* Alexandria, VA: ASCD, 2001.

McTighe, J. "What happens between assessments?" *Educational Leadership*, ASCD. December 1997.

National Research Council, *Knowing What Students Know: The Science and Design of Educational Assessment.* Washington, D.C.: National Academy Press, 2001.

Northwest Regional Educational Laboratory, *Improving classroom assessment: A toolkit for professional developers (Toolkit 98)*: Portland, OR: Northwest Regional Educational Laboratory, 1998.

Popham, W. J. *The Truth about Testing: An educator's call to action.* Alexandria, VA: ASCD, 2001.

Popham, W. J. *Test Better, Teach Better: The Instructional Role of Assessment.* Alexandria, VA: ASCD, 2003.

Popham, W.J. Classroom Assessment: What Teachers Need to Know. Boston, MA: Pearson, 2005.

Rolheiser, C. (ed.). *Self-Evaluation . . . Helping Students Get Better At It!* Toronto, ON: CLEAR Group, 1996.Shepard, L. "The Role of Assessment in a Learning Culture." *Educational Researcher* 29, no. 7, 2000.

Stiggins, R. "Assessment, Student Confidence, and School Success." *Educational Leadership*, ASCD, November 1999.

Stiggins, R. *Student-Involved Classroom Assessment (Third Edition).* Upper Saddle River, N.J.: Merrill Prentice Hall, 2001.

Stiggins, R. "Assessment Crisis: The Absence of Assessment *for* Learning". Phi Delta Kappan, Phi Delta Kappa International, June 2002.

Stiggins, R., et al. *Classroom Assessment for Student Learning: Doing it Right—Using it Well.* Portland, OR: Assessment Training Institute, 2004.

Stiggins, R. and T. Knight. *But Are They Learning?.* Portland, OR: Assessment Training Institute, 1998.

Sutton, R. *The Learning School.* Salford, U.K.: RS Publications, 1997.

Sutton, R. *Assessment for Learning.* Salford, U.K.: RS Publications, 2001.

University of Cambridge School of Education. *Assessment for Learning: Beyond the Black Box*: London: University of Cambridge, 1999.

Wiggins, G. and J. McTighe. *Understanding by Design.* Alexandria, VA: ASCD, 1998.

*Selected Webography*_____

Alberta Assessment Consortium (AAC): www.aac.ab.ca

Alberta Learning. *Classroom Assessment Tool Kit For the Information and Communication Technology (ICT) of Studies.* www. learning.gov.ab.ca/k_12/curriculum/ bySubject/ict/

Assessment Reform Group, *Assessment for Learning: Beyond the Black Box*. University of Cambridge School of Education, www.assessment-reform-group.org.uk/ AssessInsides.pdf

Assessment Training Institute: www.assessmentinst.com/index.html

Classroom Connections: www.connect2learning.com

APPENDIX

A-3

How to Develop and Use Performance Assessments in the Classroom

Contents

This document, *How to Develop and Use Performance Assessments in the Classroom*, is the third in a series of resources produced by the Alberta Assessment Consortium (AAC). The intent of these resources is to provide teachers with practical approaches for assessing, evaluating and communicating student learning.

While the first two resources in the series, *A Framework for Student Assessment* (1997) and *A Framework for Communicating Student Learning* (1999), provide the foundation for implementing an effective classroom assessment program, the present document, *How to Develop and Use Performance Assessments in the Classroom,* is designed to enable teachers to build on the foundation and to develop and use performance assessments for improving student achievement in the classroom.

Research* indicates that learning is driven by what teachers and students do in classrooms. Student confidence and school success are positively affected through "enhanced classroom assessment."

Learning is enhanced when

- assessment strategies match the learner outcomes and are aligned to instruction
- assessment is integrated with instruction (unit and lesson planning)
- assessment relates new concept(s) to previous learning
- students are involved with their own assessment
- students get immediate, meaningful feedback
- students of all ability levels are able to demonstrate what they know and what they can do
- assessment engages and motivates students

Tips for School Success

Needed improvements

Effective schools use assessment in the service of student success. Black and William, *Inside the Black Box . . . Raising standards through classroom assessment* (see *References and Resources (R&R)* on page A 3-74), note that learning can be increased significantly by involving students in their own assessment and by increasing the amount of feedback students receive on their performance. When these things happen, all students show significant gains, but lower performing students show the largest gains overall. Clearly, classroom assess-

---

* See *References and Resources (R&R)* for supporting research

ment and evaluation make the difference in student learning and performance.

Black and William indicate that the following areas need improvement
in order for the educational benefits of enhanced classroom assessment to be
realized

- **assessment accuracy**—teacher accuracy in judging student performance, i.e., consistency in scoring
- **quality of feedback**
  - to students and parents—enhances student confidence and encour-
    ages further development
  - to the teacher—feedback guides teaching and learning
- **student involvement**—students can help set criteria, complete assessment tasks that reveal what they know and can do, and they can self-
  evaluate
- **teacher development**—teachers need professional development to acquire the knowledge and skills needed to integrate enhanced assessment
  practices into instructional processes. This professional development
  applies to both pre-service teacher education and in-service programs.

We have all but ignored day-to-day classroom assessments in our journey to
school improvement.

Richard J. Stiggins

About Performance Assessment

Relationship between assessment and evaluation

Assessment	Evaluation
Assessment is the process of collecting information on student achievement and performance. Assessment information provides the basis for sound decision making regarding teaching and learning.	*Evaluation* is a judgment regarding the quality, value or worth of a response, product or performance based on established criteria and curriculum standards.
The *assessment process* reveals what a student knows, understands and can do.	*Evaluation* gives students a clear indication of how well they are performing based on the curriculum (learner outcomes).
Assessment provides the basis for feedback on a student's learning to encourage further development.	The payoff of an effective evaluation is that students know how they can improve their performance.

Assessment and evaluation always go together.

Assessment and evaluation provide information to teachers, students and parents that can be used to enhance student learning. Assessment and evaluation occur when teachers

- gather information about what students know, understand and can do
- monitor student progress
- evaluate achievement of the learner outcomes for the purpose of report card marks

Assessment always has more to do with helping students grow than with cataloguing their mistakes.

Carol Ann Tomlinson

Performance assessment

"Performance Assessment = Task + Rubric"

Instructional Internet, Chicago Public Schools

A performance assessment is an activity that requires students to construct a response, create a product or demonstrate a skill they have acquired. Rubrics are scoring guides that help define what students are expected to demonstrate. Teachers use rubrics to evaluate the quality of student performance based on selected criteria. Students use rubrics to ensure that they know what they need to do to meet or exceed the learner outcomes and to self-evaluate.

According to a Chicago Public Schools document (2000), many classroom instructional activities can be transformed into a performance assessment.

Identify *instructional activities* you have used that could be transformed into a performance assessment.

- e.g. write and present a research/lab report
-
-
-
-

Benefits of using performance assessment

Performance assessment provides *teachers* **with a tool that will help**
- identify a focus for instruction
- involve students in setting criteria, resulting in increased student motivation and understanding
- increase the level of consistency in evaluating student performance
- clarify what students know and can do
- generate specific and informative comments for students and parents
- identify outcomes to be reviewed or taught again (that is, highlight student strengths and weaknesses)

Performance assessment provides *students* **with**
- an opportunity to increase their learning
- clear performance targets and the opportunity to achieve excellence
- an opportunity to be involved in setting the criteria
- an assessment that motivates and should have a real-world context
- an assessment that enables them to demonstrate what they know and can do
  - in more than one way
  - with more than one possible solution
- a way to reflect on their learning and set goals for improved performance

Performance assessment provides *parents and the community* **with**
- information about what is important in a subject area
- a basis for working with students and the school to help improve performance

Adapted from the *Physical Education Guide to Implementation to Grade 12*, Alberta Learning, 2000

Performance assessments may be time-consuming so it stands to reason that time should be well-spent. Instead of being an "add-on" to regular instruction, the assessment should be part of it.

Chicago Public Schools

Performance assessment is an effective tool for meeting standards established in the *School Act.*

According to the *Teaching Quality Standards Applicable to the Provision of Basic Education in Alberta* (1997) teachers are to "gather and use information about students' learning needs and progress."

Furthermore *"Teachers*
• select and develop a variety of classroom assessment strategies and instruments to assess the full range of learning objectives.
• record, interpret and use the results of their assessments to modify their teaching practices and students' learning activities.
• help students develop the ability to diagnose their own learning needs and to assess their progress toward learning goals."

Numerous education researchers note that performance assessments improve teaching and learning, but only if teachers receive sufficient training and support.

About Using Performance Assessment in the Classroom

Beginning to use performance assessments in my class

Collaborate with colleagues
• Select and use common assessment language.
• Share insights and accomplishments.
• Develop performance assessments with scoring guides (e.g., checklists, rating scales or rubrics).
• Discuss what does and does not work.

Prepare students
• Include frequent activity-based learning experiences for students.
• Provide one self-reflective and one peer evaluation activity for students each week.
• Provide exemplary student samples with the scoring guide.
• Have students assist in developing scoring guides or write their own.
• Use simple, clear and relevant language with students.

Simplify implementation
• Use sample performance assessments with scoring guides as models for your performance assessments (refer to the Alberta Assessment Consortium website at *www.aac.ab.ca*).
• Try one performance assessment in an area you are familiar with and confident in during each reporting period.
• Provide immediate feedback to students, but limit marking time by using student self-evaluation or peer evaluation.
• Mark selected samples, not every performance.
• Make necessary revisions or changes in teaching and assessment practices soon after using a performance assessment.

- Increase consistency in scoring by using scoring guides based on learner outcomes, not on effort, participation, ability, or comparing and ranking of student work.

Backward design . . . begin *with the end in mind*

Backward design, originated by Wiggins and McTighe, is a process of first identifying a desired learner outcome then deciding on a series of steps that will lead to that outcome.

> To begin with the end in mind means to start with a clear understanding of your destination. It means to know where you are going so that you better understand where you are now so that the steps you take are always in the right direction.
>
> *Stephen R. Covey*

Teachers who have adopted a backward design approach for their unit and lesson design report that it provides a clear understanding of learner outcomes, more focused teaching and learning, and improvement in student performance.

To use backward design

1. Begin with selected, specific learner outcomes.
2. Determine what you will accept as evidence that students have attained the desired understandings and proficiencies.
3. Determine what lessons, learning experiences and activities are needed to help students develop and practise new skills.
4. Determine what assessment tasks will enable students to reveal what they *know* and demonstrate what they *can do,* and how these assessments will be evaluated (for example, will you use a checklist, rating scale, rubric, paper and pencil test, etc.?).
5. Use the information obtained through the assessment and evaluation process to determine what to teach next.

Assessment Framework Model, *A Framework for Student Assessment,* (AAC, 1997)

Backward design requires the teacher to think like an *assessor* as well as an *activity designer.*

Two Complementary Approaches to Teaching

Thinking Like an Assessor	Thinking Like an Activity Designer
What would be sufficient and revealing evidence of understanding?	What would be interesting and engaging activities on this topic?
What performance tasks must anchor the unit and focus the instructional work?	What resources and materials are available on this topic?
How will I be able to distinguish between those who really understand and those who don't (though they may seem to do so?)	What will students be doing in and out of class? What assignments will be given?
What criteria will I use to evaluate student work?	How will I give students a mark (and justify it to parents)?
What misunderstandings are likely? How will I check for those misunderstandings?	Did the activities work? Why, or why not?

Adapted from Grant Wiggins and Jay McTighe, *Understanding by Design,* Association for Supervision & Curriculum Development (ASCD), 1998. p. 68

Backward Design Model

When developing unit and lesson plans, teachers decide how student performance will be assessed. When developing performance assessments, teachers move between thinking and working in the role of an assessor and thinking and working in the role of an activity developer.

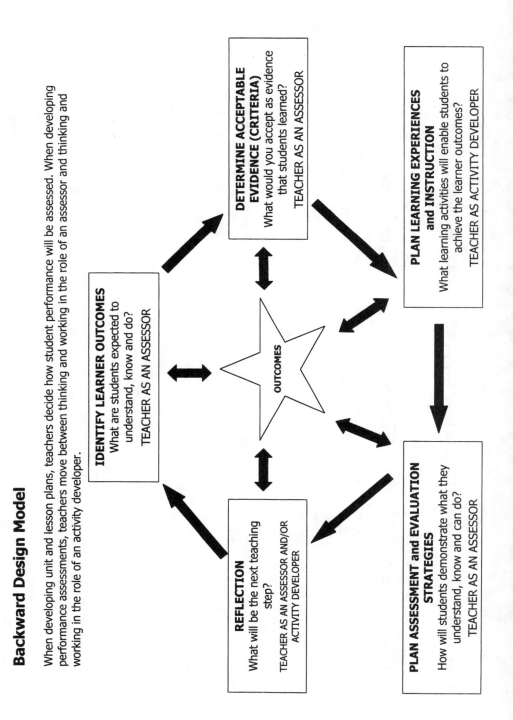

Five Steps for Developing and Using Performance Assessments

STEP 1   IDENTIFY LEARNER OUTCOMES

CLASSROOM VIGNETTE	BACKWARD DESIGN	QUESTIONS TO ASK YOURSELF
Ms. Jenkins is working with Grade 8 students in the measurement unit (shape and space) and is ready to introduce the concepts of surface area and volume. She wants her students to be able to apply the concepts in the real world and has begun to think of real life contexts. She begins by identifying and listing the learner outcomes appropriate for performance assessment (PA).	• Begin to complete the Performance Assessment Template (see **R&R** on page 37) • Select learner outcomes appropriate for the performance assessment. • Choose General Outcomes, supported by additional Specific Outcomes from the Program of Studies.	• What will I evaluate? (What are the important, enduring ideas in the curriculum?) • Which of the important, enduring ideas would be best assessed using a performance assessment?

SAMPLE	TRY ONE OF YOUR OWN
Subject <u>Mathematics</u>	Subject _____
Strand <u>Shape and Space</u> (Measurement)	Strand _____
Grade <u>8</u>	Grade _____
General Outcome(s) Generalize measurement patterns and procedures, and solve problems involving area, perimeter, surface area and volume. Apply indirect measurement procedures to solve problems.	**General Outcome(s)**
Specific Outcome(s) Estimate, measure and calculate the surface area and volume of any right prism or cylinder. Communicate mathematical ideas clearly and effectively orally and in writing.	**Specific Outcome(s)**

DETERMINE ACCEPTABLE EVIDENCE (CRITERIA)

CLASSROOM VIGNETTE	BACKWARD DESIGN	QUESTIONS TO ASK YOURSELF
Having selected the learner outcomes, Ms. Jenkins now determines the criteria for success; that is, what students will need to do to demonstrate understanding and proficiency. She lists these criteria on the template.	• Identify possible criteria using action verbs such as "describe," "construct," "design," and "defend" that will demonstrate student knowledge and skill of the selected outcomes. (see **R&R** for suggested action verbs)	• What evidence would convince me that my students know and can do what is expected?
Ms. Jenkins decides to have the students determine the volume of a large room so that they will have to apply a general rule for determining volume and will use calculations to find the answer.	• Avoid verbs such as "understand," "learn," "know," and "appreciate" because they are difficult to observe or measure.	
The students will present their findings by writing an extension to the story *Popcorn,* by Frank Asch.	• Predict what products or performances best demonstrate a student's learning.	• What products/performances would best demonstrate the students' learning? (see **R&R** for additional ideas)
	• Look for authentic (real world) applications such as ⋏ simulations ⋏ demonstrations ⋏ labs ⋏ video productions ⋏ presentations ⋏ computer based software (packaged presentation software)	

SAMPLE	TRY ONE OF YOUR OWN
<u>Criteria</u>	<u>Criteria</u>
The student • demonstrates an understanding of the concept of volume • solves a problem involving calculations of volume • demonstrates accurate calculations using equations • presents findings in writing to an audience • presents findings orally to an audience	

PLAN LEARNING EXPERIENCES AND INSTRUCTION

CLASSROOM VIGNETTE	BACKWARD DESIGN	QUESTIONS TO ASK YOURSELF
Ms. Jenkins now identifies the prior knowledge and skills students bring to the new learning by having them show what they know about surface area and volume. She determines what their prior experience has been working in groups.	• Identify students' prior knowledge and skills.	• What math do the students need to know to be prepared for the new concept?
Ms. Jenkins discusses the criteria with her students.	• Provide students with the criteria to enable them to be confident and successful.	• What social skills (e.g., listening) do students need to complete the performance assessment?
Ms. Jenkins is ready to engage students in new learning experiences by having them complete a series of new activities on estimating, measuring and calculating the surface area and volume of various shapes.	• Design a series of meaningful activities around the identified outcomes.	• How will I share the criteria with my students?
		• What learning activities will I use to teach the concepts to the students?
		• How will I ensure that learning activities result in a fair and valid assessment of performance?
		• How will I gather information about what I intend to evaluate?

SAMPLE	TRY ONE OF YOUR OWN
Ms. Jenkins determines that students • know what surface area means and how to calculate it • do not know what volume means or how to calculate it • are capable of working in groups	What do my students know (and not know) about the concept(s)?
She shares, reviews and clarifies the criteria with students.	How will I present the criteria to the students?
The students • estimate the volume of tin cans, cylinders and boxes by filling them with rice, beans, jelly beans or dried peas • measure the volume of the containers • brainstorm how to calculate volumes *without* filling them (need to come up with a rule to find volumes of these containers) • find and verify the rule for finding volume • demonstrate the use of the rule by calculating volume two or three times	What learning experiences will I plan for them?

PLAN ASSESSMENT AND EVALUATION STRATEGIES

CLASSROOM VIGNETTE	BACKWARD DESIGN	QUESTIONS TO ASK YOURSELF
Ms. Jenkins decides to use the book *Popcorn* by Frank Asch as an introduction to her performance assessment. She reads the story, which is about a small bear whose home fills with popcorn, aloud to her students.	**To design a performance assessment task** • Begin with the **criteria**, be clear about what the students need to be able to do.	• What products or performances will provide evidence of what students know and can do? (see **R&R** for specific ideas)
Ms. Jenkins then presents her students with the performance assessment. She has the students read the task in partners and ask questions.	• Determine a **meaningful context.** Contexts could be issues/problems (real or hypothetical) or themes. The context must engage the student, be interesting and be worth doing with connections to the real world (see **R&R** for specific ideas).	• Is this the kind of issue/problem that adults face?
Ms. Jenkins then tells the students that their work will be evaluated with a rubric (scoring guide) based on the criteria. She gives each student the rubric, carefully reviews the criteria and shows samples of student work at each level.	Performance tasks and projects are **authentic** when they mirror the issues and problems faced by adults.	
She instructs the students to refer to the rubric often as they complete the performance assessment.	• Include **higher level thinking** skills such as induction, deduction, analysis, synthesis, error analysis, or comparisons.	• What thinking skills and processes will I emphasize?
The students choose working teams of two and begin the assessment. Students take two periods to complete		

PLAN ASSESSMENT AND EVALUATION STRATEGIES

CLASSROOM VIGNETTE	BACKWARD DESIGN	QUESTIONS TO ASK YOURSELF
the investigation and are given two additional evenings to write the story. Students individually submit completed performance assessments with attached stories. The rubric is used to evaluate the assessment.	• Ensure that **student learning** is enhanced as a result of completing the performance assessment. • Ensure that the student **product** or **performance** is meaningful. • Provide meaningful **integration** of subject areas. **To build a rubric** • Begin with the learner outcomes and criteria in Steps 1 and 2. • Decide how many levels are needed to evaluate the performance or product. • Describe what the criteria look like at each level of performance.	• How will I know that student learning has been enhanced? • What activities will be included in the performance assessment? • What other subject areas can I integrate? • What are the most important criteria for evaluating student responses? • How many levels will I need to clearly distinguish performances? • How can I involve students in developing the scoring guide? (see **R&R** for specific ideas)

PLAN ASSESSMENT AND EVALUATION STRATEGIES

CLASSROOM VIGNETTE	BACKWARD DESIGN	QUESTIONS TO ASK YOURSELF
	• Ensure that each level of the rubric ➢ specifies what students are expected to know and do ➢ addresses the same criteria using the same number of descriptors ➢ conveys the quality of learning at each level, by using descriptors of quality, not quantitative statements ➢ clearly distinguishes one level of performance from all others on the continuum **To use a rubric** • Create or select samples of student responses.	• Am I clear on what each level means? • Do the descriptors clearly convey my expectations in a manner that students will understand? • Are the descriptors statements of quality? • Will the levels enable me to definitively decide on the quality of the product or performance? • What should a product or performance look like for each level?

PLAN ASSESSMENT AND EVALUATION STRATEGIES

CLASSROOM VIGNETTE	BACKWARD DESIGN	QUESTIONS TO ASK YOURSELF
	• Share the criteria, scoring guide and samples with students and parents. • Decide who will evaluate the product or performance and what preparation they will require in order to apply the scoring guide.	• What is an effective way to share criteria, scoring guides and samples? • Who will complete the evaluation and what preparation will they need?

SAMPLE	TRY ONE OF YOUR OWN
Working in groups of two as story writers and using the materials provided, calculate how much popcorn you will need to fill the classroom. Create an extension to the *Popcorn* story using your findings. The story must include the volume calculations, procedures and conclusions used to determine the answer. The audience for your oral presentation of the story could be a small group of your peers or younger students. Be prepared to answer questions.	Design a performance assessment.
Your story will be evaluated using the rubric by ■ your peers ■ your teacher ■ you	Design a rubric.

Rubric/Scoring Guide – Popcorn Story

Level	Description
4 **Excellent**	• demonstrates insightful analysis and application of mathematical information to fulfill task requirements • takes initiative in trying new methods and techniques to solve the problem • demonstrates a high degree of accuracy • extends the story line and provides an insightful and original communication of the mathematical concepts involved • explains and discusses ideas clearly, precisely and confidently
3 **Proficient**	• analyzes and applies mathematical information as required for the task • chooses appropriate methods and techniques to solve the problem • demonstrates overall accuracy • extends the story line and effectively communicates the mathematical concepts using appropriate terms • explains ideas in a logical, sequential way
2 **Adequate**	• uses mathematical information as required for the task • uses predictable methods and techniques to solve the problem • makes accurate calculations generally, with occasional errors • extends the story line and communicates with sufficient information to fulfill task requirements • explains and discusses ideas simply and may be in an incomplete way

Rubric/Scoring Guide – Popcorn Story

Level	Description
1 * **Limited**	• shows minimal mathematical information as required for the task • demonstrates little evidence of appropriate methods or techniques for solving the problem • makes calculations with frequent and erratic errors • extends the story line with few, if any, mathematical connections • has difficulty explaining and discussing ideas
Insufficient / Blank *	No score is awarded because there is insufficient evidence of student performance based on the requirements of the assessment task.

* When work is judged limited or insufficient, the teacher makes decisions about appropriate intervention to help the student improve.

Try One of Your Own
Rubric/Scoring Guide

Level	Description
4 **Excellent**	•
3 **Proficient**	•
2 **Adequate**	•
1 **Limited ***	•
Insufficient / Blank *	No score is awarded because there is insufficient evidence of student performance based on the requirements of the assessment task.

* When work is judged limited or insufficient, the teacher makes decisions about appropriate intervention to help the student improve.

REFLECTION

CLASSROOM VIGNETTE	BACKWARD DESIGN	QUESTIONS TO ASK YOURSELF
Ms. Jenkins reflects on the learning and assessment activity.	• Analyze the learning. Ask and answer a series of questions that will help determine if the learning and assessment experience was successful.	• Were students actively engaged in the learning and assessment activities?
The performance assessment took place in the afternoon of the Friday before Halloween. Ms. Jenkins is impressed with the engagement level of the students in the class especially considering the day and the length of the activity. Many students told her they liked being tested this way and were able to give solid reasons why.		• What was student reaction to the performance assessment and rubric?
	• Review the gathered information and decide what the next step in teaching should be.	• Were instructions for the performance assessment clear?
Classroom management was easy and she was able to circulate to all groups, noting positive interactions and conversations.		• Were the students able to demonstrate knowledge and understanding of the identified concepts?
	• Make necessary changes in the instructional activities, performance assessment and scoring guide.	• Did students perform better or differently than before?
The students understood and were able to complete the task with varying degrees of success.		• Was I able to distinguish between those who clearly understood and those who did not?
The rubric worked reasonably well but, for the next use, she would change a few words that were unclear to her students. She would use student input		• Did the rubric successfully distinguish degrees of understanding by students?

REFLECTION

to determine what the new words would be.		• What misunderstandings were apparent?
She decides that in the future she will ask for student help in the development of the rubric so that the descriptors will be easier to understand. This will help ensure that students will know what success looks like.		• How will I re-teach or clarify misunderstandings?
She discovered which students understood the process of determining volume and noted that three of the students still struggle with the concept.	• Involve students in designing performance assessments and scoring guides.	• How does this guide my future teaching? How will I make connections to prior knowledge and new learning experiences?
She established a re-teaching time for the three students who were having problems.		• How can I involve students in designing future performance assessments and scoring guides? (see **R&R** on student involvement)
Ms. Jenkins intends to include performance assessment in future units of study.		

References and Resources (R&R)

Supporting Research

Educational research indicates the importance of student-centered class-room assessment in building student confidence and increasing success in school. AAC is dedicated to the implementation of these research findings for improving student learning in Alberta. Davies (2000)[1] and Khattri, Kane, and Reeve (1995)[2] have reviewed and summarized a number of studies that demonstrate the impact of student-centred classroom assessment on student achievement.

> *When students are involved in their own assessment and evaluation, they are required to think about their learning and articulate their understandings which helps them learn.*[1]
>
> (Schon 1983, 1990; Walters, Seidel, and Gardner 1994;
> Wolf 1987, 1989; Young 2000; Zessoules and Gardner 1991)

> *Self-assessment asks students to make choices about what to focus on next in their learning. When students make choices about their learning, achievement increases: when choice is absent, achievement decreases.*[1]
>
> (Purkey and Novak 1984; deCharms 1968, 1972;
> Kovalik 1994; Lepper and Green 1974, 1978; Maehr 1974;
> Mahoney 1974; Deci and Ryan 1985; Deci, Vallerand,
> Pelletier, and Ryan 1991; Mager and McCann 1963)

> *When students are involved in their own assessment, mistakes become feedback they can use to adjust what they are doing. When students' mistakes are identified by others and feedback limited to marks or letters, students are less likely to know what to do differently next time.*[1]
>
> (Butler and Nisan 1986, 1987; Buttersworth and
> Michael 1975; Kohn, 1993; Seagoe 1970;
> Shepard and Smith 1986, 1987)

> *Involving students in assessment and increasing the amount of descriptive feedback while decreasing evaluative feedback increases student learning. While all students show significant gains, students who usually achieve the least show the largest gains overall.*[1]
>
> (Black and Wiliam 1998)

> *Performance assessments provide the means for improving teaching and learning, but only if teachers receive sufficient training and support.*[2]
>
> (Borko et al. 1993; Falk and Darling-Hammond 1993;
> Gearhard et al. 1993; Kentucky Institute for Educational
> Research 1995; Koretz et al. 1993; Smith et al 1994)

Classroom assessment and performance assessment

There are many sources of information about student performance. No one source or strategy is necessarily better than another. Each strategy can provide useful and different information about the student. The most accurate profile of student performance is based on the findings gathered from assessing student performance in a variety of contexts and using a variety of strategies over a period of time. *The key to valid and meaningful results is the match between the specific learner outcome(s) and the selected assessment strategy.*

Adapted from the *Physical Education Guide to Implementation to Grade 12,*
Alberta Learning, 2000

Assessment strategies may also include

- *Selected or brief constructed response*—(multiple choice, true-false, completion, matching) typically used to assess recall, recognition, or content mastery
- *Oral communication*—(constructed responses including interviews, questions and responses, peer teaching/coaching, conferencing) typically to assess speaking and listening skills, ability to support/defend a position, information gathering, synthesizing concepts/methods
- *Written language*—(constructed responses, including essays, learning logs, journals) typically to assess writing and organization skills, research skills, progress over time, goal setting, recording of personal experiences, and vocabulary

See also, *Types of Assessment Strategies,* A Framework for Student Assessment, AAC. 1997, pp. 20–21.

Student involvement

Students do better when they know the goal, see models and know how their performance compares to learner outcomes.

Rationale

- *Learning increases when students are involved in the assessment process.*

  Underlying the various approaches to improving classroom assessment are assumptions about what makes for effective learning, in particular that students are to be actively involved in the assessment process.

  Richard J. Stiggins

- *Learner outcomes are clarified when students assist in describing the criteria used to evaluate the performance.*

  Kids can hit any target as long as it holds still for them . . . we must eliminate the mystery.

  Richard J. Stiggins

- *Students are motivated to learn when they are involved in determining the performance criteria and setting goals.*

  Giving youngsters a voice . . . provides them with a clear understanding of what is expected of them and the assurance that their accomplishments will be recognized.

  Andi Stix

- *Students understand how they learn when they assess their own learning.*

  When students assess themselves they develop insights into their own learning.

  Gregory, Cameron and Davies

Strategies to Involve Students in Assessment

Continual self-reflection throughout the performance assessment enables students to assess progress, identify areas of difficulty, define learning and reassess goals. Self-reflection is the key to continued, powerful learning.

> We must constantly remind ourselves that the ultimate purpose of evaluation is to have students become self-evaluating. If students graduate from school still dependent on others to tell them when they are adequate, good or excellent, then we've missed the whole point of what education is about.
>
> *Art Costa and Bena Kallack*

Developing Criteria and/or Rubrics

Students can help

- identify/determine the important criteria for a task (use brainstorming and discussions that analyze student samples to develop a critical elements list)
- write descriptors in student-friendly language
- create their own rubric for an open-ended task (begin by having students write criteria for simple things like the ideal birthday party, being a good friend or expected classroom behaviors)
- generate/choose samples for each performance level

Initiating Teacher-Student Communication

As the teacher moves about the classroom during the administration of a performance assessment, communication between teacher and student can be used to

- provide continual feedback to students and teacher
- observe student progress on the performance assessment
- encourage students to continuously self-assess
- assist students with difficulties

Facilitating Self-Reflection and Goal Setting

Using Pause-and-Think

Have students briefly pause, think or reflect about their work and what they have learned. The reflection should be guided and specific. Students could reflect on their progress, their learning, what they did not understand, what comes next or changing goals.

After pause-and-think students could complete the following activities.

- *Pause, Think and Share*—Turn to a partner and describe what they have learned.
- *Look for Proof*—Select and comment on a work sample that demonstrates an aspect of their learning.
- *Connect to Criteria*—Explain how they have met the criteria.
- *Relate the Learning*—Connect current concepts to past learning or find examples of the concept in other contexts.
- *Self/Peer Assessment*—Use the rubric to evaluate their own or another student's product or performance and then suggest what works, what doesn't and what's missing.

PAUSE-AND-THINK TEMPLATES

<u>**Progress Self-Reflection**</u>   **Name** _____   **Date** _____

The steps I have completed in this performance assessment include _____

_____

_____

The steps I still have to complete include _____

_____

_____

_____

Stumbling Blocks Self-Reflection   **Name** _____   **Date** _____

Something I did not understand about ___(name of the performance assessment)_ was _____

_____

_____

Now What? Self-Reflection   Name_____   Date_____

Something I am going to change/correct/add to/remove from (name of performance assessment) is:

_____

_____

_____

Learning Self-Assessment   Name_____   Date_____

One concept I have learned from (name of performance assessment) is _____

_____

_____

_____

This piece of work demonstrates that I can _____

Check

_____   (list the criteria)

_____   (list the criteria)

_____ (list the criteria) _____

I can improve my work by _____

_____

My Changing Goals Self-Assessment   Name_____   Date_____

After reviewing this assessment, I would now like to achieve (define revised goals).

_____

_____

I would like to do this because (explanation).

_____

_____

_____

Assessment choices

Selected Response	Constructed Response	
	Products	**Performances**
Multiple Choice	Simulation	Demonstration
True/False	Story/script	Oral presentation
Completion	Poem	Debate
Matching	Video production	Dance/movement
	Model	Dramatic reading
	Project (individual and group)	Video production
	Report	Teach a lesson
	Portfolio	Interview
	Learning log/journal	Speech
	Paragraph	Role play
	Essay	Mime
	Research paper	Sports drill

Adapted from Jay McTighe, 1998

PERFORMANCE ASSESSMENT TEMPLATE (with highlighted design process steps 1-4)

Title _____

OVERVIEW

RECOMMENDED GRADE LEVEL ____

TIME SUGGESTED

Specify Course and Strand or Topic

1

GENERAL OUTCOMES

No.	Description

SPECIFIC OUTCOMES

No.	Description

2

CRITERIA for assessing student products/performances *based on specific learner outcomes that will be evaluated*

Each student
•

3

PRIOR LEARNING EXPERIENCES AND INSTRUCTION

•

4

STUDENT PRODUCTS/PERFORMANCES

•

DESCRIPTION OF PERFORMANCE ASSESSMENT

Title:

Purpose:

Assessment Activity:

Student Role:

Audience:

MATERIALS AND RESOURCES NEEDED

ASSESSMENT HANDOUT

RUBRIC

(Holistic Type)

Level	Description
4 **Excellent**	•
3 **Proficient**	•
2 **Adequate**	•
1 **Limited ***	•
Insufficient **/ Blank ***	No score is awarded because there is insufficient evidence of student performance based on the requirements of the assessment task.

* When work is judged limited or insufficient, the teacher makes decisions about appropriate intervention to help the student improve.

(Analytic Type)

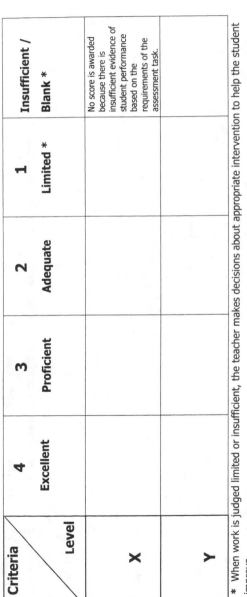

Criteria \ Level	4 Excellent	3 Proficient	2 Adequate	1 Limited *	Insufficient / Blank *
X					No score is awarded because there is insufficient evidence of student performance based on the requirements of the assessment task.
Y					

* When work is judged limited or insufficient, the teacher makes decisions about appropriate intervention to help the student improve.

STUDENT REFLECTION / EVALUATION

Students should be invited to evaluate and support their own performance based on the criteria from the rubrics provided. The self-evaluation as well as the teacher evaluation may be included in a notebook or portfolio.

LINK AND LEARN

Adaptations/extensions for other subject areas or setting

Suggested action verbs

adapt	contrast	find	predict
adjust	construct	gather (evidence)	present
advise	correct	generalize	prioritize
analyze	create	give (reasons, examples)	produce
announce	decide	help	pursue
apply	deduce	honour	question
appraise	defend	identify	rate
argue	define	imagine	reason
articulate	demonstrate	incorporate	recognize
ask	describe	induce	reflect
assess	design	inquire	represent
build	detect	inspect	research
calculate	develop	instruct	respond
challenge	devise	integrate	retrieve
check	differentiate	interact	review
classify	discover	interpret	revise
clarify	discuss	invent	search
coax	display	investigate	seek
collect	distinguish	justify	select
combine	engage	label	show
compare	establish	locate	solve
complain	estimate	list	structure
complete	evaluate	make	support
compute	examine	modify	synthesize
conceive	exhibit	monitor	teach
conclude	experiment	organize	test
conduct	explain	participate	use
connect	explore	perform	utilize
consider	express	plan	write

Adapted from *Maryland Assessment Consortium* document, 1995

Criteria for Designing a Performance Assessment

The following analytic rating scale provides a guide to help you ensure that important elements are included in a performance assessment. It also provides an indicator of the extent to which each element is present.

	To what extent does the performance assessment	fully	partially	not at all
1	assess student performance on **high priority** *and* **relevant outcomes** – what is important for a student *to know and be able to do* based on student learning needs and interests together with the priorities of the community, school and jurisdiction?			
2	establish a **meaningful context** (based on issues/problems, themes and/or student interests) that is authentic?			
3	require the application of a range of **thinking skills** *or* **processes**?			
4	contain **age/grade appropriate** activities that are *sufficiently challenging*?			
5	contain accurate and credible **information** or instructions?			
6	allow for **ease of implementation** in the classroom?			
7	call for products/performances directed to a specific **audience**?			
8	establish clear **criteria** for assessing student learning (related to specified learner outcomes)? These criteria form the basis of evaluating and communicating student learning.			

9	elicit responses that reveal **levels of performance** (rather than simply correct or incorrect answers)?		
10	provide an **evaluation rubric** matched with the criteria?		
11	provide students with the criteria and opportunities **to reflect on, self-evaluate** *and* **improve their performance?**		
12	allow for students of **varying ability levels** to complete tasks?		
13	provide opportunity for **student revision** based on feedback?		
14	provide for **purposeful integration** of subject areas?		
15	allow for a **variety** of products/performances?		
16	require a **demonstration/application** of outcome(s) *in more than one way?*		
17	provide **clear directions** for students?		
18	**engage the students** so that their interest and enthusiasm will be sustained?		
19	**merit the time and energy required to complete it?**		

Adapted from *Maryland Assessment Consortium*

About rubrics

Rubric

A rubric is a set of criteria used to evaluate a student's performance on a continuum. It consists of a fixed measurement scale (for example, 4-point) and a list of qualitative criteria that describe the characteristics of products or performances for each score point.

Rubrics
- list the criteria for successfully completing a piece of work (what counts)
- articulate graduations of *quality* (*how well* based on criteria and illustrated by samples) for each criterion from "Excellent" to "Limited." Criteria that specify *quantity* (*how many* paragraphs, answers, examples, etc.) are *not* encouraged.

Adapted from Heidi Goodrich, "Understanding Rubrics", *Educational Leadership*, 54(4), 14–17

Why use performance assessment *criteria* and *rubrics*

According to Guskey, rubrics

are powerful tools for teaching *and* assessment

help students become more thoughtful judges of their own work

reduce the time teachers spend evaluating students' work

allow teachers to recognize and respond to performance differences in heterogeneous classes

are easy to use and explain

improve consistency in scoring

Adapted from Thomas R. Guskey, *Using Assessments to Improve Student Learning*, National Conference on Standards and Assessment, 1999

If a teacher fails to have a clear sense of the full dimensions of performance, ranging from poor or unacceptable to exemplary, he or she will not be able to teach students to perform at the highest levels or help students to evaluate their own performance.

Richard J. Stiggins

Some tips for writing and using rubrics
- Look at sample rubrics (see *R&R* samples and bibliography, and refer to the Alberta Assessment Consortium website at *www.aac.ab.ca*).

- Start with a project that you have used before.
- Work with colleagues.
- Develop an even number of levels of performance.
- Start writing a rubric using an excellent performance.
- Use language that is easily understood by the people who will use the rubric.
- During the development of the rubric use samples of student work that clearly represent all levels defined in the rubric.
- Inform students about the criteria that their work will be judged against prior to the activity.
- Show students samples of work at each of the levels before they begin.
- Revise the rubric after the evaluation has been completed. Don't expect perfection the first time.

Meaning of each performance level

[Holistic Scale]

Level	Meaning	Commentary
4 **Excellent**	The student meets the standard of excellence for the grade, demonstrates exemplary performance or understanding; shows creativity.	This is a "**Wow!**"
3 **Proficient**	The student meets the acceptable standard for the grade by demonstrating solid performance or understanding.	This is a "**Yes.**"
2 **Adequate**	The student just meets the acceptable standard for the grade. Performance and understanding are emerging or developing; errors are being made; grasp is not thorough.	This is an "**On the right track, but ...** " The teacher needs to make decisions about appropriate teacher intervention to help the student improve.
1 **Limited** *	The student is not yet meeting the acceptable standard for the grade, and has serious errors, omissions or misconceptions.	This is a "**No, but there is some basis for making improvement.**" The teacher needs to make decisions about appropriate teacher intervention to help the student improve.

Level	Meaning	Commentary
Insufficient / Blank *	No score is awarded because there is insufficient evidence of student performance based on the requirements of the assessment task.	This is a **"No judgement can be made."** The teacher must decide whether to have the student • redo the task if the student is capable • provide more time to complete the task • complete a different task at the student's ability level • receive further instruction that will lead to retesting or • scrap it – the task is inappropriate for the student at this time

* When work is judged limited or insufficient, the teacher needs to make decisions about appropriate intervention to help the student improve.

What students say about rubrics

"We use rubrics a lot and they are very helpful. You can just read the 4-column, do what it says, and get a better mark".

"I think if teachers used rubrics instead of oral directions, students would get better grades because they could just look at the rubric instead of constantly asking the teacher."

"All I can say is that rubrics act almost like the brain because they both collect information for us. They are reminders of what I should improve on."

"Rubrics are an easier way of grading. There is less guilt, favorites or decisions. This is a more fair way of grading. Also you can see why you got that grade."

"In the end they help make things fair so that a student can't complain about his grade, and it also gives the teacher back-up for the grade he/she gave. A student can also use it for them if they feel they have been unfairly graded."

Sample rubrics

1) Fun Rubric

DINING OUT (rubric designed by Anne Mulgrew, Supervisor, Student Assessment, Edmonton Public Schools)

Level	Description
4 **Scrumptious!** **First Class!**	• you are ushered immediately to a table in a desirable location in the restaurant • the table is set with immaculate white linen • your wine and water glasses are sparkling clean crystal • your order is taken after a comfortable amount of time with the menu • each course of your meal is placed before you just when you expect it • your waiter is considerate yet unobtrusive • the food is attractively presented and tasty • the price is more than fair • you leave a 20% tip and feel good about it
3 **Tasty.** **Will come** **back!**	• you wait 10 minutes before a desirable table becomes available • the tablecloth has a few stains but the napkin is immaculate • a crystal wine glass graces your table but you have to request water • your order is taken after a reasonable time • your meal is nicely paced and there are few waits • your waiter is considerate, but asks once or twice too often if everything is all right • the food is pleasingly presented and flavourful, but your mother has been known to cook better • price is reasonable • you leave a 15% tip, but wonder about it later

Level	Description
2 **Edible. May come back.**	• you wait 15 minutes and are finally ushered to a table in a dark corner • the linen tablecloth has seen better days and the napkins are definitely paper • both water and wine glasses are in evidence but the waiter thinks they are strictly decorative • your order is taken after a considerable time • the meal arrives after a considerable wait • your waiter hovers in the vicinity of your table watching your every mouthful • the food is edible, but your mother generally cooks better • price seems a bit steep • you leave a 10% tip, but halfway out reconsider and go back to pick up half of what you left
1 **Lost my appetite! May never come back!**	• you wait 30 minutes to get a table just outside the swinging door to the kitchen • your paper tablecloth still has pen doodling from the previous customer and there is no napkin in sight • your glass has a definite lipstick smear • you wait another 25 minutes to place your order • your entrée arrives exactly 37 seconds after your soup is placed before you • your waiter has left the restaurant and you wait another 30 minutes for your cheque • there is a distinct thumbprint in your mashed potatoes and your other vegetables are still frozen in the center • price is excessive given the quality of service and food • you leave, asking the management to give you a tip

2) Another Fun Rubric

Simply Scrumptious Kabobs!

Sample Performance Assessment (rubric designed by Student Assessment, Edmonton Public Schools)

As party host you decide to serve kabobs as a dessert item at a fancy party. Based on Madame Benoit's standards for high quality and attractive kabobs, prepare a sample kabob for the serving crew to follow as they prepare them.

Criteria / Level	4 Superb	3 Delectable	2 Yummy	1 Edible	Insufficient / Blank
Use of colour	uses creative arrangement of colour and pattern	uses variety of colour with alternation to establish a consistent pattern	uses some colours to establish a discernible pattern; may bunch colours together	uses minimum variety of colours that are bunched together randomly	No score is awarded because there is insufficient evidence of student performance based on the requirements of the assessment task.
Use of shape	uses creative arrangement of shapes to establish an eye-pleasing pattern	uses a variety of shapes with alternation to establish a consistent pattern	uses a few different shapes to establish a discernible pattern	uses limited number of shapes with no evidence of patterning	
Taste	has a palate-pleasing range of flavours and textures	has a tasty assortment of flavours and a variety of textures	demonstrates some variety of flavours and some attention to texture	repeats flavours to maximize sugar content	

Criteria ⟍ Level	4 Superb	3 Delectable	2 Yummy	1 Edible	Insufficient / Blank
Visual presentation/ aesthetic appeal	is a work of art that viewer is reluctant to eat	displays a variety of fruits in an attractive presentation	constructs kebab using premise that eating is more important than aesthetics	has a piece of fruit on a skewer	
Health connections	contains a variety of vitamin content; 100% fruit	is primarily constructed of fruit	is mostly fruit but includes several candies	has more candy than fruit	

3) Science - research report and demonstration

Sample Performance Assessment (adapted from performance assessment developed by University of Alberta students, Tony Benge, John Chase, and Jonathan Sharek in Educational Psychology 303 (1999))

An anonymous donor has given a local museum a valuable collection of silver coins. Unfortunately, the coins have not been stored carefully and have become tarnished. The museum would like to have the tarnish removed so the collection can be ready for public display, but want to avoid using cleaning processes that might remove the silver under the tarnish and leave the coins damaged. You have been invited to prepare and present a research report on removing tarnish from coins together with a recommended cleaning method.

Criteria ＼ Level	4 Excellent	3 Proficient	2 Adequate	1 Limited *	Insufficient / Blank *
Research report	Well-organized and thoroughly detailed report with few, if any, grammatical or spelling mistakes. Pros and cons of various cleaning methods are explored in detail and used as a basis	Organized and detailed report with few grammatical and spelling mistakes. Pros and cons of various cleaning methods are outlined and used as a basis for selecting the	Partially organized and detailed report with several grammatical and spelling errors. Pros and cons of various cleaning methods are explored briefly and have reference to recommended.	Poorly organized report with many grammatical and spelling errors. A method may be recommended, but without comparing the pros and cons of various methods.	No score is awarded because there is insufficient evidence of student performance based on the requirements of the assessment task.

Criteria \ Level	4 Excellent	3 Proficient	2 Adequate	1 Limited *	Insufficient / Blank *
	for selecting the recommended method.	recommended method.	Method.		
Demonstration of method	Effective, efficient and comprehensive demonstration with clearly visible results	Complete demonstration with visible results	Partially complete demonstration with somewhat visible results	Incomplete demonstration or inappropriate to the requirements of the task	
Effectiveness of method	Tarnish is removed without damage to silver finish.	Most of tarnish is removed with little or no damage to silver finish.	Some of tarnish is removed with little or no damage to silver finish.	Little or no tarnish is removed.	

* When work is judged limited or insufficient, the teacher needs to make decisions about appropriate intervention to help the student improve.

4) Physical Education - Sample General Outcomes "A", "C" and "D" Rubric

Physical Education Guide to Implementation to Grade 12, Alberta Learning, 2000

Criteria \ Level	4 Excellent	3 Proficient	2 Adequate	1 Limited *	Insufficient / Blank *
Following the rules of the activity or game	Consistently follows the rules	Frequently follows the rules	Occasionally follows the rules	Demonstrates little or no willingness to comply with the rules	No score is awarded because there is insufficient evidence of student performance based on the requirements of the assessment task.
Skills	Consistently demonstrates skills appropriate to the activity or game	Frequently demonstrates skills appropriate to the activity or game	Demonstrates skills appropriate to the game or activity, but lacks consistency	Rarely demonstrates skills appropriate to the activity or game	
Ready position	Consistently in the ready position	Frequently in the ready position	In the ready position some of the time	Rarely in the ready position	

Criteria \\ Level	4 Excellent	3 Proficient	2 Adequate	1 Limited *	Insufficient / Blank *
Participation	Eagerly engages in activities and helps lead the group in goal setting	Participates fully in activities	Participates when interested	Participates only when encouraged	
Attitude	Displays a positive attitude and enthusiasm towards the activities	Displays a positive attitude	Displays an indifferent attitude	Shows little or no interest	
Initiative	Takes initiative and tries new activities	Tries new activities and is developing a sense of confidence	Tries new activities when given peer or teacher support	Reluctant to try new activities	
Cooperation	Works cooperatively providing encouragement and support for others	Works cooperatively with others	Needs reminders in order to work cooperatively	Needs supervision in order to work cooperatively	

Criteria \ Level	4 Excellent	3 Proficient	2 Adequate	1 Limited *	Insufficient / Blank *
Leadership	Takes on various roles and responsibilities enthusiastically	Takes on various roles and responsibilities	Takes on roles and responsibilities reluctantly	Avoids or refuses to take on various roles and responsibilities	
Fair play	Consistently plays fair and shows proper etiquette	Frequently plays fair and shows proper etiquette	Occasionally plays fair and shows proper etiquette	Rarely, if ever, plays fair and shows proper etiquette	
Safety	Considers the well-being and safety of others, and consistently follows safe practices	Considers the well-being and safety of others, and frequently follows safe practices	Usually considers the well-being and safety of others, and usually follows safe practices	Rarely, if ever, considers the well-being and safety of others, but sometimes follows safe practices	

* When work is judged limited or insufficient, the teacher needs to make decisions about appropriate intervention to help the student improve.

5) Language Arts - Response to Reading (the following is a verbatim rubric written by students in Judy Moen's grade 4 class at Windsor Park School, Edmonton Public Schools, 1995)

Level	Description
4 **Excellent**	• asks thoughtful questions; tries to provide reasonable answers • makes logical predictions • checks back to see if prediction was correct and, therefore, adds to understanding of story • uses information and quotes from story to explain thoughts and feelings in detail • shows personal involvement by relating story to own experiences and giving specific detail • makes comparisons to other authors, titles, characters, themes; specific details are given • comments in detail on author's writing style and techniques; provides examples • states title, author, chapters or pages read
3 **Proficient**	• asks predictable questions; some attempt to answer them • makes predictions • may attempt to check back to see if prediction was correct • some attempt to use information or quotes from story to explain thoughts and feelings • shows personal involvement; connections to own experience lack detail • makes comparisons to other authors, titles, characters, themes by noting similarities, but explanation lacks detail • comments on author's writing techniques; limited examples are given • states title and author

Level	Description
2 **Adequate**	• asks questions; no answers are provided • few logical predictions are made • no attempt to check back to see if prediction was correct • states thoughts and feelings but use of information or quotes is limited; connections are weak and lack detail • shows some personal involvement; attempts to connect to specific events in own life are limited • attempts to make comparisons to other authors, titles, characters, themes; little or no specific detail • attempts to comment on author's writing technique; no examples are given • may state title or author
1 **Limited**	• no questions are asked • does not make predictions • has no prediction to check out • limited expression of thoughts or feeling; no information or quotes from story are used to explain • no personal involvement; only gives a retelling of what was read • no comparisons are made • does not discuss author's writing technique • does not include title or author

6) Language Arts - Quality of Writing

Adapted from Edmonton Public Schools Highest Level of Achievement Tests (HLAT) Writing (Jobs)

Level	Description
4 **Excellent**	• writer fulfills the task and purposefully controls details and language to shape the writing • piece shows overall unity and artistry of communication • writing is focused, sustains reader's interest and engages audience • content is insightful, memorable and topic is thoroughly developed • vocabulary and usage are especially well chosen for form and purpose • organization and style create a sense of voice unique to writer • spelling, grammar, capitalization and punctuation applications are controlled to enhance impact of the piece; errors are hardly noticeable
3 **Proficient**	• writer fulfills the task and uses supportive details and effective language • piece reads smoothly and is clear and consistent throughout • an awareness of audience is maintained throughout the writing • content is clear; topic is effectively developed • evidence of precise vocabulary and usage suitable for form and purpose • organization of piece is coherent, and voice and style are appropriate

Level	Description
3 **Proficient**	• spelling, grammar, capitalization and punctuation applications are effective; errors are few and do not interfere with writer's intended meaning
2 **Adequate**	• writer addresses the task and uses sufficient details and some language control • piece generally reads smoothly, but may have a few awkward parts • an awareness of audience is conveyed, but may not be sustained throughout • content is appropriate; topic developed satisfactorily • evidence of generally suitable vocabulary and usage for form and purpose • organization is logical, but the piece may ramble • spelling, grammar, capitalization and punctuation applications are uncomplicated; errors are evident, but do not significantly interfere with writer's intended meaning
1 **Limited**	• writer generally addresses the task and demonstrates minimal language control • piece is awkward to read • consideration of audience may be vague • content and topic development are sketchy • vocabulary and usage choices are within a narrow range • there is evidence of difficulty in organizing ideas • spelling, grammar, capitalization and punctuation applications are inconsistent; errors may interfere with writer's intended meaning

7) Language Arts - Oral Presentation (rubric designed by Wendy Mathieu, teacher at Mary Butterworth School, Edmonton Public Schools, 1994)

Criteria / Level	4 Excellent	3 Proficient	2 Adequate	1 Limited *	Insufficient / Blank *
Interaction (sense of audience, appearance, gestures, posture, movement)	Speaker is sensitive to and controls audience response using oral language with power and proficiency. Eye contact and gestures engage audience. Presentation is confident, clear, effective and entertaining.	Speaker is conscious of audience and adjusts presentation in response to cues from audience. Eye contact and gestures hold audience interest. Presentation is confident and clear.	Speaker is aware of audience, but makes little overt effort to include it. Eye contact and gestures do not vary to engage audience. Presentation is clear.	Speaker attention to audience is sporadic or speaker excludes audience. Eye contact and gestures are minimal, inappropriate, lacking or distracting. Presentation falters or interferes with or prevents communication.	No score is awarded because there is insufficient evidence of student performance based on the requirements of the assessment task.

Criteria \ Level	4 Excellent	3 Proficient	2 Adequate	1 Limited *	Insufficient / Blank *
Content	Speaker controls details and language to achieve a specific purpose. Ideas are thoroughly developed. Planning and suitable sequencing are evident.	Speaker's purpose is clear. Details and language are appropriate to the purpose. Ideas are developed. Organization is clear and purposeful.	Speaker presents ideas and details methodically and clearly. Development is on topic and sufficient can be understood. Some disorganization is evident.	Speaker's ideas lack a central focus, or the development of ideas may be incomplete, inadequate or confusing. Disorganization contributes to a general lack of clarity.	
Performance (language and voice)	Vocabulary is rich, effective and precise. Pace, inflection, pitch, tone and volume are appropriate to audience.	Vocabulary is appropriate to the topic. Diction, emphasis, volume and inflection are adjusted appropriately to	Vocabulary is simple, but correct. Diction, emphasis, volume and inflection are acceptable to convey the	Vocabulary is simple, but incomplete or inaccurate for the topic and audience. Lack of control of diction, emphasis,.	

Criteria / Level	4 Excellent	3 Proficient	2 Adequate	1 Limited *	Insufficient / Blank *
	Pronunciation is highly articulate.	convey speaker's intent. Pronunciation is clear and precise.	speaker's intent. Pronunciation is generally clear and correct.	volume and inflection may interfere with the speaker's intent. Pronunciation errors may be evident	

* When work is judged limited or insufficient, the teacher needs to make decisions about appropriate intervention to help the student improve.

8) Self Management - organizes efficiently and effectively for the best results

Level	Description
4 **Excellent**	• plans and makes highly effective use of time; anticipates needs • consistently uses a personal, well-equipped study area • selects and effectively and efficiently uses most appropriate available resources
3 **Proficient**	• plans and makes effective use of time • uses a personal study area • finds and uses available resources
2 **Adequate**	• generally makes effective use of time • occasionally uses of a personal study area • uses resources that are pre-selected
1 **Limited**	• makes inconsistent connection between time and task completion • makes little or no use a personal study area • requires coaching and encouragement to find available resources

9) Skills Outcomes - initiating and planning an investigation

Criteria / Level	4 Excellent	3 Proficient	2 Adequate	1 Limited *	Insufficient / Blank *
Questioning	Asks relevant, clear questions about task	Asks questions that clarify task and focus the investigation	Asks simple questions that partially focus the investigation	Asks few questions about task or questions are vague	No score is awarded because there is insufficient evidence of student performance based on the requirements of the assessment task.
Hypothesizing	Generates an insightful and fully testable hypothesis based on theory	Generates a testable hypothesis based on theory	Generates a questionable hypothesis based on intuition	Generates an untestable hypothesis	
Planning	Develops procedures that are efficient and complete	Develops a complete set of procedures that may lack efficiency and clarity	Develops a partial set of simple procedures	Develops unworkable procedures	

Criteria\Level	4 Excellent	3 Proficient	2 Adequate	1 Limited *	Insufficient / Blank *
Planning	Develops a practical and appropriate plan	Develops a workable and appropriate plan	Develops a workable, but incomplete, plan	Develops a plan that is not workable	
Identifying variables	Identifies and controls all variables	Identifies and controls most variables	Identifies and controls some variables	Identifies and controls few, if any, variables	

* When work is judged limited or insufficient, the teacher needs to make decisions about appropriate intervention to help the student improve.

10) Skills Outcomes - performing and recording an investigation, project or lab

Criteria Level	4 Excellent	3 Proficient	2 Adequate	1 Limited *	Insufficient / Blank *
Carrying out plan	Sets up and carries out investigation that is a complete and valid test of the hypothesis	Sets up and carries out investigation that is a fair test of the hypothesis	Sets up and carries out investigation that addresses some aspects of the hypothesis	Sets up and carries out investigation that is unable to test the hypothesis	
Using equipment	Uses tools, equipment and materials correctly and independently	Uses tools, equipment and materials correctly with only occasional assistance	Uses tools, equipment and materials correctly with assistance	Uses tools, equipment and materials correctly with guidance and assistance	

Criteria \ Level	4 Excellent	3 Proficient	2 Adequate	1 Limited *	Insufficient / Blank *
Safety	Considers the well-being and safety of others and consistently follows safe practices	Considers the well-being and safety of others and frequently follows safe practices	Usually considers the well-being and safety of others and usually follows safe practices	Rarely, if ever, considers the well-being and safety of others, but sometimes follows safe practices	
Recording	Consistently records data in an organized, skillful way. Record is accurate and uses units of measure.	Records most relevant data in an organized way and is generally accurate with units of measure.	Records data, but organization is lacking, with some inconsistencies, or may omit units of measure.	Records little data and data is irrelevant, inaccurate or missing units of measure.	
Observing	Makes insightful observations	Makes sufficient observation to generate data	Makes observations, but they are insufficient to generate data	Makes few, if any, observations	

* When work is judged limited or insufficient, the teacher needs to make decisions about appropriate intervention to help the student improve.

Suggested performances and products

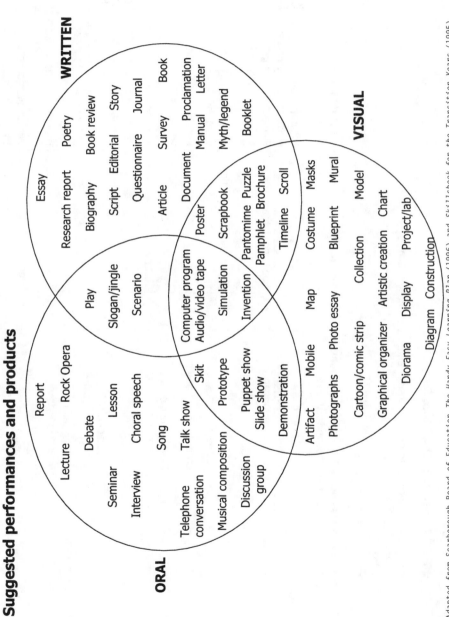

Adapted from Scarborough Board of Education *The Handy Easy Learning Plan* (1996) and *Skillsbook for the Transition Years* (1995).

Suggested meaningful contexts

In developing performance assessments, consider authentic contexts such as

❖ real issues and problems
❖ themes
❖ student interests

Possible categories and higher order performance contexts for performance assessments that may be especially applicable at the secondary level

Category	Higher order performance contexts
Arts & Aesthetics	Polish a performance
	Create an insightful model
	Achieve an intended aesthetic effect
	Critique a piece of work
Basic needs	Debate the merits of legislation on health, education and housing for seniors
	Advocate for kind treatment of animals
Communication	Explore and report fairly on a controversy
	Successfully mediate a dispute

Category	Higher order performance contexts
Food and Nutrition	Plan a nutritious meal for a birthday party
Government and Politics	Thoroughly re-think an issue
	Rate proposals made by candidates
History	Judge the adequacy of an appealing/unpopular idea
	Discern a pattern
	As a soldier in World War I, write a letter to your parents describing the conditions in the trenches
Medicine	Pursue alternative answers to a health issue

Category	Higher order performance contexts
Community	Analyze a water treatment issue
	Develop an anti-froshing policy
Crime/Corrections	Prepare a school map for new students
	Conduct a study on the merits of a police services helicopter to reduce crime
Economics	Pursue alternative answers to a community problem
	Complete a cost-benefit analysis
Education	Develop and effectively implement a plan
	Investigate mandated bus passes
	As Romeo, write a sonnet to Juliet suggesting engagement

Category	Higher order performance contexts
Pollution	Analyze a community's water supply
Recreation and Sports	Create a game
	Develop a fitness plan for overweight teenagers
	As a basketball, write a list of instructions for the team captain promoting better ball handling
Science and Technology	Build a self-propelled vehicle
	Invent a tool to simplify a task
	Design an innovative enclosure for elk
	As an oxygen molecule, write a script outlining your reaction with hydrogen in the formation of water
Transportation	Design, develop and operate an experimental vehicle

Category	Higher order performance contexts
Education (cont.)	You are a television viewer. Write a letter or e-mail message to the manager of the Public Broadcasting System network praising educational television
Environment	Conduct an impact study on new transportation routes near environmentally sensitive areas

Category	Higher order performance contexts

Alberta Education. Curriculum Support Branch. *The Writing Process: Using the Word Processor: Inservice Leader's Reference Manual,* 1988

and

Grant Wiggins

Suggested audiences and student roles

Audiences	Student Roles
• advertisers	• (as an) animal (mouse, frog, horse, amoeba)
• ancestors	• advertiser
• architect	• adviser
• author (novelist, poet, playwright)	• alien
• babysitter	• artist
• banker	• astronaut
• bicycle	• auctioneer
• bigot	• author
• board or council (city, town, recreation, school trustees, chamber of commerce)	• banker
• boss/employer	• baker (chef)
• celebrities (athletes, actors, musicians)	• biographer
• citizens (neighbors)	• boss (owner, supervisor, executive officer)
• coach	• cartoon character
• customers/consumers	• caterer
• editor (magazine, newspaper)	• citizen (community member)
• experts in (_____)	• coach
• family members (immediate–parents, siblings; relatives–grandparents, uncles, aunts)	• composer
	• council member (city, town, sports team, school board)
• fans	• counselor (guidance, minister/priest)
• feminist	• curator (museum)
• friends	• customer
• ghost	• detective
• government official (mayor, premier, prime minister)	• doctor
• historical character	• editor
• hockey star	• eye witness

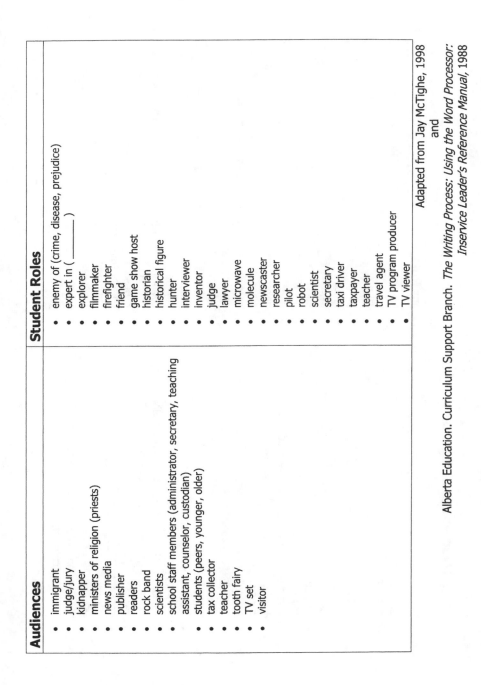

Audiences	Student Roles
• immigrant	• enemy of (crime, disease, prejudice)
• judge/jury	• expert in (_____)
• kidnapper	• explorer
• ministers of religion (priests)	• filmmaker
• news media	• firefighter
• publisher	• friend
• readers	• game show host
• rock band	• historian
• scientists	• historical figure
• school staff members (administrator, secretary, teaching assistant, counselor, custodian)	• hunter
	• interviewer
• students (peers, younger, older)	• inventor
• tax collector	• judge
• teacher	• lawyer
• tooth fairy	• microwave
• TV set	• molecule
• visitor	• newscaster
	• researcher
	• pilot
	• robot
	• scientist
	• secretary
	• taxi driver
	• taxpayer
	• teacher
	• travel agent
	• TV program producer
	• TV viewer

Adapted from Jay McTighe, 1998
and
Alberta Education. Curriculum Support Branch. *The Writing Process: Using the Word Processor: Inservice Leader's Reference Manual,* 1988

Selected bibliography

Alberta Education. Curriculum Support Branch. *The Writing Process: Using the Word Processor: Inservice Leader's Reference Manual.* Edmonton, AB. 1988.

Alberta Assessment Consortium. *A Framework for Student Assessment.* AAC: Edmonton, AB. 1997.

Alberta Assessment Consortium. *A Framework for Communicating Student Learning.* AAC: Edmonton, AB. 1999.

ASCD. *Educational Leadership: Redirecting Assessment.* Vol. 46, No. 7 (1998).

ASCD. *Educational Leadership: Teaching for Authentic Student Performance.* Vol. 54, No. 4 (1996).

Black, P. and Wiliam, D. *Inside the Black Box.* A monograph published by Kings College: London, England. 1998.

Burke, K. *The Mindful School: How to Assess Thoughtful Outcomes.* Skylight: Palatine. IL. 1999.

Covey, S. *The 7 Habits of Highly Effective People,* Simon & Schuster: New York, NY. 1989.

Davies, A. *How Classroom Assessment Works.* Connections Publishing: Merville, BC. 2000.

Goodrich, H. "Understanding Rubrics". *Educational Leadership,* ASCD: Alexandria, VA. 1996.

Gregory, K., Cameron, C., and Davies, A. *Knowing What Counts Book One: Setting and Using Criteria.* Connections Publishing: Merville, BC. 2000.

Gregory, K., Cameron, C., and Davies, A. *Knowing What Counts Book Two: Self-Assessment and Goal Setting.* Connections Publishing: Merville, BC. 2000.

Joint Advisory Committee. *Principles for Fair Student Assessment Practices for Education in Canada.* Centre for Research in Applied Measurement and Evaluation, University of Alberta, Edmonton, AB. 1993.

Khattri, N., Kane, M., and Reeve, A. "How Performance Assessments Affect Teaching and Learning" *Educational Leadership,* ASCD: Alexandria, VA. November 1995.

Linton Professional Development Corporation, *Video Journal of Education: Designing Performance Assessments.* Videotape. Sandy, UT. 1999.

McTighe, J. "What happens between assessments?" *Educational Leadership,* ASCD: Alexandria, VA. December 1997.

McTighe, J. and Ferrara, S. Assessing Learning in the Classroom. National Education Association: Washington, DC. 1998.

Olson, T. and Peters, C. Classroom Criteria From A to Z. Student Centered Publications: Kamloops, BC. 2000.

Rolheiser, C. *Self-Evaluation . . . Helping Students Get Better at It!* VISUTroniX: Ajax, ON. 1997.

Stiggins, R. "Assessment, Student Confidence, and School Success". Phi Delta Kappan, November, 1999. Vol. 81, No. 3

Stiggins, R. *Student-Centered Classroom Assessment* (Second Edition). Prentice-Hall: Upper Saddle River, NJ. 1997.

Stiggins, R. and Knight, T. *But Are They Learning.* Assessment Training Institute. Portland, OR. 1998.

Stix, A. *Stix Picks: Stratigies for Student-Centered Assessment.* Interactive Classroom 1996.

Tomlinson, C. *The Differentiated Classroom: Responding to the Needs of All Learners.* ASCD: Alexandria, VA 1999.

Wiggins, G. *Standards, Not Standardization.* Videotape. Greater Insights Productions (CLASS): Genesco, NY. 1991.

Wiggins, G. and McTighe, J. *Understanding by Design.* ASCD: Alexandria, VA. 1998.

Web Sites _____

AAC About Classroom Assessment (Q&A)
http://www.aac.ab.ca/class.html

AAC Related Links on Classroom Assessment
www.aac.ab.ca/related.html

ASCD Tutorial on Performance Assessment
www.ascd.org/frametutorials.htmI

Assessment in a Constructivist Classroom
httg://www.ncrel.orci/sdrs/areas/issues/methods/assment/as7const.htm

Assessment Tools Links
www.2learn.ca/currlinks/Netsteps/Public/Netstepyiew.asp?page=878&retu

Backward Design—*Understanding by Design,* Excerpt
http://www.ascd.org/readingroom/books/wigains98book.html#chap

Best Practice Resources
http://www.teachermentors.com/RSOD%20Site/PerfAssmt/P.AssmtLinks.htmI

Black and Wiliam Research
http://www.pdkintl.org/kappan/kbla9810.htm

Can Performance-Based Assessments Improve Student Learning?
http://www.ericae.net/db/edo/ED327612.htm

Contextual Teaching and Learning: Authentic Assessment
http://www.bgsu.edu/organizations/ctl/aa.html

CRESST Center for Research on Evaluation, Standards and Student Testing
http://cresst96.cse.ucla.edu/index.htm

Designing Performance Assessment: Challenges for the Three Story Intellect
http://geocities.com/Athens/Parthenon/8658/

Elliott Eisner—The Uses and Limits of Performance Assessment Phi Delta Kappan, May 1999
http://www.pdkintl.org/kappan/keis9905.htm

Ideas and Rubrics (Chicago Public Schools, Instructional Internet)
http://intranet.cps.k12.il.us/Assessments/Ideas and Rubrics/ideas and rubrics.html

Performance Tasks in Science: an interactive resource bank for science performance assessment tasks.
http://www.ctl.sri.com/pals/

Rubrics
http://school.discovery.com/schrockguide/assess.html

Rubrics for Web Lessons
http://edweb.sdsu.edu/webquest/rubrics/weblessons.htm

Appendix B

Principles for Fair Student Assessment Practices for Education in Canada

Guidelines for Student Reporting

B-1

Principles for Fair Student Assessment Practices for Education in Canada

The *Principles for Fair Student Assessment Practices for Education in Canada* contains a set of principles and related guidelines generally accepted by professional organizations as indicative of fair assessment practice within the Canadian educational context. Assessments depend on professional judgment; the principles and related guidelines presented in this document identify the issues to consider in exercising this professional judgment and in striving for the fair and equitable assessment of all students.

Assessment is broadly defined in the *Principles* as the process of collecting and interpreting information that can be used (i) to inform students, and their parents/guardians where applicable, about the progress they are making toward attaining the knowledge, skills, attitudes, and behaviors to be learned or acquired, and (ii) to inform the various personnel who make educational decisions (instructional, diagnostic, placement, promotion, graduation, curriculum planning, program development, policy) about students. Principles and related guidelines are set out for both developers and users of assessments. Developers include people who construct assessment methods and people who set policies for particular assessment programs. Users include people who select and administer assessment methods, commission assessment development services, or make decisions on the basis of assessment results and findings. The roles may overlap, as when a teacher or instructor develops and administers an assessment instrument and then scores and interprets the students' responses, or when a ministry or department of education or local school system commissions the development and implementation of an assessment program and scoring services and makes decisions on the basis of the assessment results.

The *Principles for Fair Student Assessment Practices for Education in Canada* is the product of a comprehensive effort to reach consensus on what constitutes sound principles to guide the fair assessment of students. The principles and their related guidelines should be considered neither exhaustive nor mandatory; however, organizations, institutions, and individual professionals who endorse them are committing themselves *to endeavor to follow their intent and spirit* so as to achieve fair and equitable assessments of students.

Organization and Use of the Principles

The principles and their related guidelines are organized in two parts. Part A is directed at assessments carried out by teachers at the elementary and secondary school levels. Part A is also applicable at the post-secondary level with some modifications, particularly with respect to whom assessment results are reported. Part B is directed at standardized assessments developed external to the classroom by commercial test publishers, provincial and territorial ministries and departments of education, and local school jurisdictions[1].

Five general principles of fair assessment practices are provided in each Part. Each principle is followed by a series of guidelines for practice. In the case of Part A where no prior sets of standards for fair practice exist, a brief comment accompanies each guideline to help clarify and illuminate the guideline and its application.

The Joint Advisory Committee recognizes that in the field of assessment some terms are defined or used differently by different groups of

The *Principles of Fair Student Assessment Practices for Education in Canada* was developed by a Working Group guided by a Joint Advisory Committee. The Joint Advisory Committee included two representatives appointed by each of the following professional organizations: Canadian Education Association, Canadian School Boards Association, Canadian Association for School Administrators, Canadian Teachers' Federation, Canadian Guidance and Counselling Association, Canadian Association of School Psychologists, Canadian Council for Exceptional Children, Canadian Psychological Association, and Canadian Society for the Study of Education. In addition, the Joint Advisory Committee included a representative of the Provincial and Territorial Ministries and Departments of Education.

Financial support for the development and dissemination of the *Principles* was provided principally by the Walter and Duncan Gordon Charitable Foundation, with additional support provided by various Faculties, institutes, and Colleges of Education and Provincial and Territorial Ministries and Departments of Education in Canada. This support is gratefully acknowledged.

The Joint Advisory Committee invites users to share their experiences in working with the *Principles* and to submit any suggestions that could be used to revise and improve the *Principles*. Comments and suggestions should be sent to the Joint Advisory Committee at the address shown below.

The *Principles for Fair Student Assessment Practices for Education in Canada* is not copyrighted. Reproduction and dissemination are encouraged. Please cite the *Principles* as follows:

Principles for Fair Student Assessment Practices for Education in Canada. (1993). Edmonton, Alberta: Joint Advisory Committee. (Mailing Address: Joint Advisory Committee, Centre for Research in Applied Measurement and Evaluation. 3-104 Education Building North. University of Alberta. Edmonton, Alberta. T6G 2G5).

[1]Boards, boroughs, counties, and school districts.

people. To maintain as much consistency in terminology as possible, an attempt has been made to employ generic terms in the *Principles.*

A. Classroom Assessments

Part A is directed toward the development and selection of assessment methods and their use in the classroom by teachers. Based on the conceptual framework provided in the *Standards for Teacher Competence in Educational Assessment of Students* (1990), it is organized around five *interrelated* themes:

> I. Developing and Choosing Methods for Assessment
> II. Collecting Assessment Information
> III. Judging and Scoring Student Performance
> IV. Summarizing and Interpreting Results
> V. Reporting Assessment Findings

The Joint Advisory Committee acknowledges that not all of the guidelines are equally applicable in all circumstances. However, consideration of the full set of principles and guidelines within Part A should help to achieve fairness and equity for the students to be assessed.

I. Developing and Choosing Methods for Assessment

Assessment methods should be appropriate for and compatible with the purpose and context of the assessment.

> Assessment method is used here to refer to the various strategies and techniques that teachers might use to acquire assessment information. These strategies and techniques include, but are not limited to, observations, text- and curriculum-embedded questions and tests, paper-and-pencil tests, oral questioning, benchmarks or reference sets, interviews, peer- and self-assessments, standardized criterion-referenced and norm-referenced tests, performance assessments, writing samples, exhibitions, portfolio assessment, and project and product assessments. Several labels have been used to describe subsets of these alternatives, with the most common being "direct assessment," "authentic assessment," "performance assessment," and "alternative assessment." However, for the purpose of the *Principles,* the term assessment method has been used to encompass all the strategies and techniques that might be used to collect information from students about their progress toward attaining the knowledge, skills, attitudes, or behaviors to be learned.

> 1.   Assessment methods should be developed or chosen so that inferences drawn about the knowledge, skills, attitudes, and behaviors possessed by each student are valid and not open to misinterpretation.

Validity refers to the degree to which inferences drawn from assessments results are meaningful. Therefore, development or selection of assessment methods for collecting information should be clearly linked to the purposes for which inferences and decisions are to be made. For example, to monitor the progress of students as proofreaders and editors of their own work, it is better to assign an actual writing task, to allow time and resources for editing (dictionaries, handbooks, etc.), and to observe students for evidence of proofreading and editing skill as they work than to use a test containing discrete items on usage and grammar that are relatively devoid of context.

2.   Assessment methods should be clearly related to the goals and objectives of instruction, and be compatible with the instructional approaches used.

To enhance validity, assessment methods should be in harmony with the instructional objectives to which they are referenced. Planning an assessment design at the same time as planning instruction will help integrate the two in meaningful ways. Such joint planning provides an overall perspective on the knowledge, skills, attitudes, and behaviors to be learned and assessed, and the contexts in which they will be learned and assessed.

3.   When developing or choosing assessment methods, consideration should be given to the consequences of the decisions to be made in light of the obtained information.

The outcomes of some assessments may be more critical than others. For example, misinterpretation of the level of performance on an end-of-unit test may result in incorrectly holding a student from proceeding to the next instructional unit in a continuous progress situation. In such "high-stake" situations, every effort should be made to ensure the assessment method will yield consistent and valid results. "Low stake" situations, such as determining if a student has correctly completed an in-class assignment, can be less stringent. Low stake assessments are often repeated during the course of a reporting period using a variety of methods. If the results are aggregated to form a summary comment or grade, the summary will have greater consistency and validity than its component elements.

4.   More than one assessment method should be used to ensure comprehensive and consistent indications of student performance.

To obtain a more complete picture or profile of a student's knowledge, skills, attitudes, or behaviors, and to discern consistent patterns and trends, more than one assessment method should be used. Student knowledge might be assessed using completion items; process or reasoning skills might be assessed by observing performance on a relevant task; evaluation skills might be assessed by reflecting upon the discussion with a student about what materials to include in a portfolio. Self-assessment may help to clarify and add meaning to the assessment of a written communication, science project, piece of art work, or an attitude. Use of more than one method will also help minimize inconsistency brought about by different sources of measurement error (for example, poor performance because of an "off-day"; lack of agreement among items included in a test, rating scale, or questionnaire; lack of agreement among observers; instability across time).

5.   Assessment methods should be suited to the backgrounds and prior experiences of students.

Assessment methods should be free from bias brought about by student factors extraneous to the purpose of the assessment. Possible factors to consider include culture, developmental stage, ethnicity, gender, socio-economic background, language, special interests, and special needs. Students' success in answering questions on a test or in an oral quiz, for example, should not be dependent upon prior cultural knowledge, such as understanding an allusion to a cultural tradition or value, unless such knowledge falls within the content domain being assessed. All students should be given the same opportunity to display their strengths.

6.   Content and language that would generally be viewed as sensitive, sexist, or offensive should be avoided.

The vocabulary and problem situation in each test item or performance task should not favour or discriminate against any group of students. Steps should be taken to ensure that stereotyping is not condoned. Language that might be offensive to particular groups of students should be avoided. A judicious use of different roles for males and females and for minorities and the careful use of language should contribute to more effective and, therefore, fairer assessments.

7.   Assessment instruments translated into a second language or transferred from another context or location should be accompanied by evidence that inferences based on these instruments are valid for the intended purpose.

Translation of an assessment instrument from one language to another is a complex and demanding task. Similarly, the adoption or modification of an instrument developed in another country is often not simple and straightforward. Care must be taken to ensure that the results from translated and imported instruments are not misinterpreted or misleading.

II. Collecting Assessment Information

Students should be provided with a sufficient opportunity to demonstrate the knowledge, skills, attitudes, or behaviors being assessed.

Assessment information can be collected in a variety of ways (observations, oral questioning, interviews, oral and written reports, paper-and-pencil tests). The guidelines which follow are not all equally applicable to each of these procedures.

1.   Students should be told why assessment information is being collected and how this information will be used.

Students who know the purpose of an assessment are in a position to respond in a manner that will provide information relevant to that purpose. For example, if students know that their participation in a group activity is to be used to assess cooperative skills, they can be encouraged to contribute to the activity. If students know that the purpose of an assessment is to diagnose strengths and weaknesses rather than to assign a grade, they can be encouraged to reveal weaknesses as well as strengths. If the students know that the purpose is to assign a grade, they are well advised to respond in a way that will maximize strength. This is especially true for assessment methods that allow students to make choices, such as with optional writing assignments or research projects.

2.   An assessment procedure should be used under conditions suitable to its purpose and form.

Optimum conditions should be provided for obtaining data from and information about students so as to maximize the validity and consistency of the data and information collected. Common conditions include such things as proper light and ventilation, comfortable room temperature, and freedom from distraction (e.g., movement in and out of the room, noise). Adequate workspace, sufficient materials, and adequate time limits appropriate to the purpose and form of the assessment are also necessary. For example, if the intent is to assess student participation in a small group, adequate work space should be provided for each student group, with sufficient space between subgroups so that the groups do not interfere with or otherwise influence one another and so that the teacher has the same opportunity to observe and assess each student within each group.

3.   In assessments involving observations, checklists, or rating scales, the number of characteristics to be assessed at one time should be small enough and concretely described so that the observations can be made accurately.

Student behaviors often change so rapidly that it may not be possible simultaneously to observe and record all the behavior components. In such instances, the number of components to be observed should be reduced and the components should be described as concretely as possible. One way to manage an observation is to divide the behavior into a series of components and assess each component in sequence. By limiting the number of components assessed at one time, the data and information become more focused, and time is not spent observing later behavior until prerequisite behaviors are achieved.

4.   The directions provided to students should be clear, complete, and appropriate for the ability, age and grade level of the students.

Lack of understanding of the assessment task may prevent maximum performance or display of the behavior called for. In the case of timed assessments, for example, teachers should describe the time limits, explain how students might distribute their time among parts for those assessment instruments with parts, and describe how students should record their responses. For a portfolio assessment, teachers should describe the criteria to be used to select the materials to be included in a portfolio, who will select these materials, and, if more than one person will be involved in the selection process, how the judgments from the different people will be combined. Where appropriate, sample material and practice should be provided to further increase the likelihood that instructions will be understood.

5.   In assessments involving selection items (e.g., true-false, multiple-choice), the directions should encourage students to answer all items without threat of penalty.

A correction formula is sometimes used to discourage "guessing" on selection items. The formula is intended to encourage students to omit items for which they do not know the answer rather than to "guess" the answer. Because research evidence indicates that the benefits expected from the correction are not realized, the use of the formula is discouraged. Students should be encouraged to use whatever partial knowledge they have when choosing their answers, and to answer all items.

6.   When collecting assessment information, interactions with students should be appropriate and consistent.

Care must be taken when collecting assessment information to treat all students fairly. For example, when oral presentations by students are assessed, questioning and probes should be distributed among the students so that all students have the same opportunity to demonstrate their knowledge. While writing a paper-and-pencil test, a student may ask to have an ambiguous item clarified, and, if warranted, the item should be explained to the entire class.

7.   Unanticipated circumstances that interfere with the collection of assessment information should be noted and recorded.

Events such as a fire drill, an unscheduled assembly, or insufficient materials may interfere in the way in which assessment information is collected. Such events should be recorded and subsequently considered when interpreting the information obtained.

8.   A written policy should guide decisions about the use of alternate procedures for collecting assessment information from students with special needs and students whose proficiency in the language of instruction is inadequate for them to respond in the anticipated manner.

It may be necessary to develop alternative assessment procedures to ensure a consistent and valid assessment of those students who, because of special needs or inadequate language, are not able to respond to an assessment method (for example, oral instead of written format, individual instead of group administered, translation into first language, providing additional time). The use of alternate procedures should be guided by a written policy developed by teachers, administrators, and other jurisdictional personnel.

III. Judging and Scoring Student Performance

Procedures for judging or scoring student performance should be appropriate for the assessment method used and be consistently applied and monitored.

Judging and scoring refers to the process of determining the quality of a student's performance, the appropriateness of an attitude or behavior, or the correctness of an answer. Results derived from judging and scoring may be expressed as written or oral comments, ratings, categorizations, letters, numbers, or as some combination of these forms.

1.   Before an assessment method is used, a procedure for scoring should be prepared to guide the process of judging the quality of a performance or product, the appropriateness of an attitude or behavior, or the correctness of an answer.

To increase consistency and validity, properly developed scoring procedures should be used. Different assessment methods require different forms of scoring. Scoring selection items (true-false, multiple-choice, matching) requires the identification of the correct or, in some instances, best answer. Guides for scoring essays might include factors such as the major points to be included in the "best answer" or models or exemplars corresponding to different levels of performance at different age levels and against which comparisons can be made.

Procedures for judging other performances or products might include specification of the characteristics to be rated in performance terms and, to the extent possible, clear descriptions of the different levels of performance or quality of a product.

2.   Before an assessment method is used, students should be told how their responses or the information they provide will be judged or scored.

Informing students prior to the use of an assessment method about the scoring procedures to be followed should help ensure that similar expectations are held by both students and their teachers.

3.   Care should be taken to ensure that results are not influenced by factors that are not relevant to the purpose of the assessment.

Various types of errors occur in scoring, particularly when a degree of subjectivity is involved (e.g., marking essays, rating a performance, judging a debate). For example, if the intent of a written communication is to assess content alone, the scoring should not be influenced by stylistic factors such as vocabulary and sentence structure. Personal bias errors are indicated by a general tendency to rate all students in approximately the same way (e.g., too generously or too severely). Halo effects can occur when a rater's general impression of a student influences the rating of individual characteristics or when a previous rating influences a subsequent rating. Pooled results from two or more independent raters (teachers, other students) will generally produce a more consistent description of student performance than a result obtained from a single rater. In combining results, the personal biases of individual raters tend to cancel one another.

4.   Comments formed as part of scoring should be based on the responses made by the students and presented in a way that students can understand and use them.

Comments, in oral and written form, are provided to encourage learning and to point out correctable errors or inconsistencies in performance. In addition, comments can be used to clarify a result. Such feedback should be based on evidence pertinent to the learning outcomes being assessed.

5.   Any changes made during scoring should be based upon a demonstrated problem with the initial scoring procedure. The modified procedure should then be used to rescore all previously scored responses.

Anticipating the full range of student responses is a difficult task for several forms of assessment. There is always the danger that unanticipated responses or incidents that are relevant to the purposes of the assessment may be overlooked. Consequently, scoring should be continuously monitored for unanticipated responses and these responses should be taken into proper account.

6.   An appeal process should be described to students at the beginning of each school year or course of instruction that they may use to appeal a result.

Situations may arise where a student believes a result incorrectly reflects his/her level of performance. A procedure by which students can appeal such a situation should be developed and made known to them. This procedure might include, for example, checking for addition or other recording errors or, perhaps, judging or scoring by a second qualified person.

IV. Summarizing and Interpreting Results

Procedures for summarizing and interpreting assessment results should yield accurate and informative representations of a student's performance in relation to the goals and objectives of instruction for the reporting period.

Summarizing and interpreting results refers to the procedures used to combine assessment results in the form of summary comments and grades which indicate both a student's level of performance and the valuing of that performance.

1.   Procedures for summarizing and interpreting results for a reporting period should be guided by a written policy.

Summary comments and grades, when interpreted, serve a variety of functions. They inform students of their progress. Parents, teachers, counsellors, and administrators use them to guide learning, determine promotion, identify students for special attention (e.g., honours, remediation), and to help students develop future plans. Comments and grades also provide a basis for reporting to other schools in the case of school transfer and, in the case of senior high school students, post-secondary institutions and prospective employers. They are more likely to serve their many functions and those functions are less likely to be confused if they are guided by a written rationale or policy sensitive to these different needs. This policy should be developed by teachers, school administrators, and other jurisdictional personnel in consultation with representatives of the audiences entitled to receive a report of summary comments and grades.

2.   The way in which summary comments and grades are formulated and interpreted should be explained to students and their parents/guardians.

Students and their parents/guardians have the "right-to-know" how student performance is summarized and interpreted. With this information, they can make constructive use of the findings and fully review the assessment procedures followed.

It should be noted that some aspects of summarizing and interpreting are based upon a teacher's best judgment of what is good or appropriate. This judgment is derived from training and experience and may be difficult to describe specifically in advance. In such circumstances, examples might be used to show how summary comments and grades were formulated and interpreted.

3.   The individual results used and the process followed in deriving summary comments and grades should be described in sufficient detail so that the meaning of a summary comment or grade is clear.

Summary comments and grades are best interpreted in the light of an adequate description of the results upon which they are based, the relative emphasis given to each result, and the process followed to combine the results. Many assessments conducted during a reporting period are of a formative nature. The intent of these assessments (e.g., informal observations, quizzes, text-and-curriculum embedded questions, oral questioning) is to inform decisions regarding daily learning, and to inform or otherwise refine the instructional sequence. Other assessments are of a summative nature. It is the summative assessments that should be considered when formulating and interpreting summary comments and grades for the reporting period.

4.   Combining disparate kinds of results into a single summary should be done cautiously. To the extent possible, achievement, effort, participation, and other behaviors should be graded separately.

A single comment or grade cannot adequately serve all functions. For example, letter grades used to summarize achievement are most meaningful when they represent only achievement. When they include other aspects of student performance such as effort, amount (as opposed to quality) of work completed, neatness, class participation, personal conduct, or punctuality, not only do they lose their meaningfulness as a measure of achievement, but they also suppress information concerning other, important aspects of learning and invite inequities. Thus, to more adequately and fairly summarize the different aspects of student performance, letter grades for achievement might be complemented with alternate summary forms (e.g., checklists, written comments) suitable for summarizing results related to these other behaviors.

5.   Summary comments and grades should be based on more than one assessment result so as to ensure adequate sampling of broadly defined learning outcomes.

More than one or two assessments are needed to adequately assess performance in multi-facet areas such as Reading. Under-representation of such broadly defined constructs can be avoided by ensuring that the comments and grades used to summarize performance are based on multiple assessments, each referenced to a particular facet of the construct.

6.   The results used to produce summary comments and grades should be combined in a way that ensures that each result receives its intended emphasis or weight.

When the results of a series of assessments are combined into a summary comment, care should be taken to ensure that the actual emphasis placed on the various results matches the intended emphasis for each student.

When numerical results are combined, attention should be paid to differences in the variability, or spread, of the different sets of results and appropriate account taken where such differences exist. If, for example, a grade is to be formed from a series of paper-and-pencil tests, and if each test is to count equally in the grade, then the variability of each set of scores must be the same.

7.   The basis for interpretation should be carefully described and justified.

Interpretation of the information gathered for a reporting period for a student is a complex and, at times, controversial issue. Such information, whether written or numerical, will be of little interest or use if it is not interpreted against some pertinent and defensible idea of what is good and what is poor. The frame of reference used for interpretation should be in accord with the type of decision to be made. Typical frames of reference are performance in relation to pre-specified standards, performance in relation to peers, performance in relation to aptitude or expected growth, and performance in terms of the amount of improvement or amount learned. If, for example, decisions are to be made as to whether or not a student is ready to move to the next unit in an instructional sequence, interpretations based on pre-specified standards would be most relevant.

8.   Interpretations of assessment results should take account of the backgrounds and learning experiences of the students.

Assessment results should be interpreted in relation to a student's personal and social context. Among the factors to consider are age, ability, gender, language, motivation, opportunity to learn, self-esteem, socio-economic background, special interests, special needs, and "test-taking" skills. Motivation to do school tasks, language capability, or home environment can influence learning of the concepts assessed, for example. Poor reading ability, poorly developed psycho-motor or manipulative skills, lack of test-taking skills, anxiety, and low self-esteem can lead to lower scores. Poor performance in an assessment may be attributable to a lack of opportunity to learn because required learning materials and supplies were not available, learning activities were not provided, or inadequate time was allowed for learning. When a student performs poorly, the possibility that one or more factors such as these might have interfered with a student's response or performance should be considered.

9. Assessment results that will be combined into summary comments and grades should be stored in a way that ensures their accuracy at the time they are summarized and interpreted.

Comments and grades and their interpretations, formulated from a series of related assessments, can be no better than the data and information upon which they are based. Systematic data control minimizes errors which would otherwise be introduced into a student's record or information base, and provides protection of confidentiality.

10. Interpretations of assessment results should be made with due regard for limitations in the assessment methods used, problems encountered in collecting the information and judging or scoring it, and limitations in the basis used for interpretation.

To be valid, interpretations must be based on results determined from assessment methods that are relevant and representative of the performance assessed. Administrative constraints, the presence of measurement error, and the limitations of the frames of reference used for interpretation also need to be accounted for.

V. Reporting Assessment Findings

Assessment reports should be clear, accurate, and of practical value to the audiences for whom they are intended.

1. The reporting system for a school or jurisdiction should be guided by a written policy. Elements to consider include such aspects as audiences, medium, format, content, level of detail, frequency, timing, and confidentiality.

The policy to guide the preparation of school reports (e.g., reports of separate assessments; reports for a reporting period) should be developed by teachers, school administrators, and other jurisdictional personnel in consultation with representatives of the audiences entitled to receive a report. Cooperative participation not only leads to more adequate and helpful reporting, but also increases the likelihood that the reports will be understood and used by those for whom they are intended.

2. Written and oral reports should contain a description of the goals and objectives of instruction to which the assessments are referenced.

The goals and objectives that guided instruction should serve as the basis for reporting. A report will be limited by a number of practical considerations, but the central focus should be on the instructional objectives and the types of performance that represent achievement of these objectives.

3.   Reports should be complete in their descriptions of strengths and weaknesses of students, so that strengths can be built upon and problem areas addressed.

Reports can be incorrectly slanted towards "faults" in a student or toward giving unqualified praise. Both biases reduce the validity and utility of assessment. Accuracy in reporting strengths and weaknesses helps to reduce systematic error and is essential for stimulating and reinforcing improved performance. Reports should contain the information that will assist and guide students, their parents/guardians, and teachers to take relevant follow-up actions.

4.   The reporting system should provide for conferences between teachers and parents/guardians. Whenever it is appropriate, students should participate in these conferences.

Conferences scheduled at regular intervals and, if necessary, upon request provide parents/guardians and, when appropriate, students with an opportunity to discuss assessment procedures, clarify and elaborate their understanding of the assessment results, summary comments and grades, and reports, and, where warranted, to work with teachers to develop relevant follow-up activities or action plans.

5.   An appeal process should be described to students and their parents/guardians at the beginning of each school year or course of instruction that they may use to appeal a report.

Situations may arise where a student and his/her parents/guardian believe the summary comments and grades inaccurately reflect the level of performance of the student. A procedure by which they can appeal such a situation should be developed and made known to them (for example, in a school handbook or newsletter provided to students and their parents/guardians at the beginning of the school year).

6.   Access to assessment information should be governed by a written policy that is consistent with applicable laws and with basic principles of fairness and human rights.

A written policy, developed by teachers, administrators, and other jurisdictional personnel, should be used to guide decisions regarding the release of student assessment information. Assessment information should be available to those people to whom it applies—students and their parents/guardians, and to teachers and other educational personnel obligated by profession to use the information constructively on behalf of students. In addition, assessment information might be made available to others who justify their need for the information (e.g., post-secondary institutions, potential employers, researchers). Issues of informed consent should also be addressed in this policy.

7.   Transfer of assessment information from one school to another should be guided by a written policy with stringent provisions to ensure the maintenance of confidentiality.

To make a student's transition from one school to another as smooth as possible, a clear policy should be prepared indicating the type of information to go with the student and the form in which it will be reported. Such a policy, developed by jurisdictional and ministry personnel, should ensure that the information transferred will be sent by and received by the appropriate person within the "sending" and "receiving" schools respectively.

B-2

Guidelines for Student Reporting for The Kindergarten to Grade 12 Education Plan

September 1994

Introduction

The policy for reporting student progress is based on ministerial orders and regulations authorized under the School Act. It outlines reporting requirements for formal and informal reporting, as well as the roles and responsibilities of the ministry, school administrators and teachers for the implementation of this policy. The policy outlined in this document is effective September 1994. The use of the symbol IP (In Progress) is optional in the 1994–95 school year but is required for the 1995–96 school year.

This document provides teachers and administrators with guidelines for reporting student progress for the primary, intermediate and graduation years.

During the 1994–95 school year, if IP is not used, D and E may be used as letter grades and F (Failed) may be assigned without the previous use of an IP.

The Reporting Process

The information in this resource is based on a reporting process that involves the setting of criteria and the using of a wide range of assessment techniques.

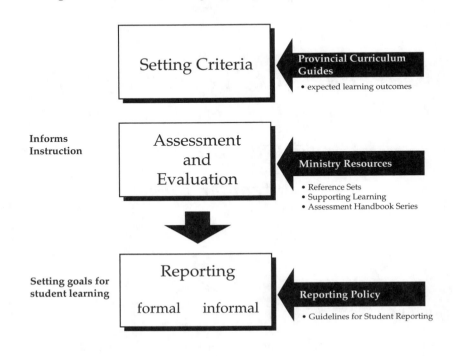

Policy for Reporting Student Progress in British Columbia

Provincial regulations for the reporting of student progress require that parents be provided with a minimum of:

- *three formal written report cards.* The formal written report must be on a form approved by the Minister or school board and must follow the requirements for the specific grade and program as stated in legislation and this policy document. One of the formal reports shall be made at the end of the school year. Formal reports provide documentation of student progress and are placed in the Permanent Student Record file.
- *two informal reports each school year.* At least two informal reports must be provided to parents or guardians each school year. Teachers determine how they will communicate informally with parents.

Formal reports (structured written reports and letter grades) and informal reports communicate to parents significant aspects of students' progress in learning. They describe, in relation to the curriculum, student progress in intellectual, social, human and career development.

Structured Written Reports

Structured written reports are most effective when they use direct, plain language. These reports must follow the specific requirements in the Student Progress Report Order for each grade level.

Comments in a student progress report describe, in relation to curriculum:

- what the student is able to do
- areas of learning that require further attention or development
- ways the teacher is supporting the student's learning needs (and, where appropriate, ways the student or the parents might support the learning).

Letter Grades

Criterion-referenced letter grades in Grades 4 to 12 indicate students' levels of performance as they relate to the expected learning outcomes set out in provincial curriculum guides for each subject or course and grade. No letter grades are required for Kindergarten to Grade 3. Letter grades will appear on report cards in Grades 4 to 7 unless the district chooses an alternative way of communicating them to parents. Letter grades must be on report cards in Grades 8 to 12.

Informal Reports

Each school year, teachers must provide parents with a minimum of two informal reports. In relation to curriculum, informal reports may describe:

- what the student is able to do
- the areas of learning that require further attention or development
- ways the teacher is supporting the student's learning needs (and, where appropriate, ways the student or the parents might support the learning).

Informal reports provide an important link between home and school and can be accomplished in a variety of ways, such as:

- telephone calls
- interim reports (written or oral)
- conferences (parent-teacher, three-way, student-led, etc.).

It is recommended that schools ensure that parents have the opportunity to meet with teachers for a conference at least once each school year. A record of each informal report noting the date of report, type of report and topic(s) of discussion should be kept.

Specific Guidelines for Primary, Intermediate and Graduation Years

Primary Reports (Kindergarten to Grade 3)

Formal reports for each student in Kindergarten to Grade 3 must:

- include a structured written report that clearly describes, in relation to the expected learning outcomes set out in curriculum
  a) what the student is able to do
  b) areas in which the student requires further attention or development
  c) ways of supporting the student in his or her learning
- provide comments (written on the report card or communicated orally to the parents) about student progress with reference to the expected development for students in a similar age range
- include written comments to describe student behaviour, including information on attitudes, work habits, and effort.

At the end of the school year, the following information must be placed in each student's Permanent Student Record file:

- a copy of the final formal report
- documentation of the oral or written statements provided to parents regarding the student's progress with reference to the expected development for students in a similar age range.

Intermediate Reports (Grades 4 to 7)

Formal reports for each student in Grades 4 to 7 must:

- include a structured written report that clearly describes, in relation to the expected learning outcomes set out in curriculum
  a) what the student is able to do
  b) areas in which the student requires further attention or development
  c) ways of supporting the student in his or her learning
- include written comments to describe student behaviour, including information on attitudes, work habits and effort
- follow district policy for communicating letter grades to parents

- use Ministry-approved letter grades as set out in the Provincial Letter Grades Order to indicate the student's level of performance as it relates to the expected learning outcomes for each subject or course and grade.

At the end of the school year, the following information must be placed in each student's Permanent Student Record file:

- a copy of the final formal report
- documentation of the student's progress as indicated by letter grades.

Intermediate Reports (Grades 8 to 10)

Formal reports for each student in Grades 8 to 10 must:

- provide Ministry-approved letter grades as set out in the Provincial Letter Grades Order to indicate the student's level of performance as it relates to the expected learning outcomes for each course or subject and grade
- include written comments, where appropriate, that describe, in relation to the expected learning outcomes set out in curriculum
    a) what the student is able to do
    b) areas in which the student requires further attention or development
    c) ways of supporting the student in his or her learning
- include written comments to describe student behaviour, including information on attitudes, work habits and effort.

Graduation Reports (Grades 11 and 12)

Formal reports for each student in Grades 11 and 12 must:

- provide Ministry-approved letter grades as set out in the Provincial Letter Grades Order to indicate the student's level of performance as it relates to the expected learning outcomes for each course or subject and grade
- include percentages for all courses numbered 11 and 12
- include written comments, where appropriate, that describe, in relation to expected learning outcomes set out in curriculum
    a) what the student is able to do
    b) areas in which the student requires further attention or development
    c) ways of supporting the student in his or her learning
- include written comments to describe student behaviour, including information on attitudes, work habits and effort.

Reports for Students with Special Needs

Where a student with special needs is expected to achieve or surpass the learning outcomes set out in the provincial curriculum, regular letter-grading and reporting procedures will be followed. However, instructional and assessment methods for some students with special needs may differ, and this will be reflected in their Individual Education Plans (IEP's).

Where it is determined that a student with special needs is not capable of achieving the learning outcomes set out in the provincial curriculum and substantial course or program modification is necessary, specific individual goals and objectives will be established for the student in his or her IEP. The use of letter grades and percentages for reporting the progress of these students is not appropriate. Structured written comments will be used to report the level of the student's success in achieving these modified goals and objectives. In these circumstances the efforts of these students will be recognized by providing them with a Provincial School Completion Certificate.

Where a professional support person other than the classroom teacher is responsible for providing some portion of the student's educational program (e.g., speech pathologist, orientation and mobility instructors), those persons should provide written reports on the student's progress for inclusion with the report of the classroom teacher.

Ministry-Approved Letter Grades and Descriptions

On student progress reports in Grades 4 to 12, teachers must use the approved letter grades as set out in the Provincial Letter Grade Order. In Grades 11 and 12, percentages must accompany letter grades.

Letter Grades for Grades 4 to 12

Teachers use the following letter grades in student progress reports to Grades 4 to 12.

A   The student demonstrates excellent or outstanding performance in relation to the expected learning outcomes for the course or subject and grade.

B   The student demonstrates very good performance in relation to the expected learning outcomes for the course or subject and grade.

C+ The student demonstrates good performance in relation to the expected learning outcomes for the course or subject and grade.

C   The student demonstrates satisfactory performance in relation to the expected learning outcomes for the course or subject and grade.

C- The student demonstrates minimally acceptable performance in relation to the expected learning outcomes for the course or subject and grade.

IP In Progress. The student is making progress, but it has been determined that additional time is required to meet the expected learning outcomes for the course or subject and grade. Guidelines for assigning an IP must be followed. Expectations and timelines must be attached for each assigned IP. *(Optional year 1994–1995; required 1995–1996)*

F   Failed or Failing. The student has not demonstrated, or is not demonstrating, minimally acceptable performance in relation to the expected learning outcomes for the course or subject and grade. F (Failed) may only be assigned if an IP (In Progress) has been previously assigned.

Administrative officers may assign the following on student progress reports:

W   Withdrawal. According to board policy, the administrative officer in charge of a school may grant permission to a student to withdraw from a course or subject. This may be done on the request of the parents or, when appropriate, the student.

The following may be used only on final reports in Grades 4 to 12:

SG   Standing Granted. Although completion of normal requirements is not possible, a sufficient level of performance has been attained to warrant, consistent with the best interests of the student, the granting of standing for the course or subject and grade. This symbol can be used in such cases as serious illness, hospitalization, late entry or early leaving, but may only be granted as the result of an adjudication process authorized by the administrative officer in charge of the school.

TS   Transfer Standing. Transfer Standing may be granted by the administrative officer in charge of a school on the basis of an examination of records from an institution other than a school, as defined in the *School Act*. Alternatively, the administrative officer in charge of a school may assign a letter grade on the basis of an examination of those records.

Percentages Associated with Letter Grades

A	86–100
B	73–85
C+	67–72
C	60–66
C-	50–59
F	0–49

The successful completion of a course numbered 11 or 12 requires a minimum of a C-.

The use of IP is optional in the 1994–95 school year but is required for the 1995–96 school year.

During the 1994–95 school year, the following letter grades may be used.

D   The student demonstrates unsatisfactory performance in relation to the expected learning outcomes for the course or subject and grade

E   Probable failure

F   Failed

Requirements for Assigning a Student an IP

The IP symbol replaces the I and D designations and is based on the following principles.

- If a student is failing to meet expectations, she or he needs to be made aware of what must be done in order to succeed.
- A student may need additional opportunities to work to meet expectations before a failing grade is given.
- The home must be informed when a student fails to meet expectations and should be offered the opportunity to become a partner in remediating difficulties.
- Early intervention can prevent the cumulative effects of not meeting expectations over a prolonged period of time.

An IP (In Progress) is used when a student is making progress, but requires additional time to meet the expected learning outcomes. When teachers assign an IP, they must:

- accompany it with comments to indicate areas that need further attention or development and specific requirements that need to be fulfilled in relation to the expected learning outcomes
- define a time period for completion of the requirements and the review and evaluation of the student's performance
- convert the IP to another letter grade before the student's records are forwarded when a student transfers or moves to another school, unless an agreement exists between the two schools
- consult with parents if an IP is used on two consecutive reports for a specific subject or course
- accompany an IP on a final report with information for the next year's teacher about the student's progress toward meeting the expected learning outcomes and ways the teacher, student or parents can support the student's learning
- convert an IP to another letter grade by the end of the first reporting period of the next school year (or semester), if an IP is carried into a new school year

> In the 1994–95 school year, F (Failed) may be awarded without the previous use of an IP but in 1995–96, F may only be used as a grade if an IP (In Progress) has been previously assigned.
>
> IP may be used on an optional basis for the 1994–95 school year. Schools should be planning and implementing effective strategies to assist students who need more time to achieve minimally acceptable performance. These "best practice" strategies will be shared widely throughout the province during the 1994–95 school year.

- courses awarded an IP or an F will not appear on the official transcript of grades.

Roles and Responsibilities

The Ministry, school boards, school administrators and teachers have different, yet complementary, roles and responsibilities in reporting to parents.

It is the responsibility of the Ministry of Education to:
- provide legislation and policy regarding reporting student progress and make this information available to parents
- provide relevant provincial curriculum guides that define the expected learning outcomes for each subject or course
- provide descriptions of student performance through provincial learning assessment activities
- provide resources to assist school districts and educators in their work to implement provincial policies
- provide provincial report-card forms
- evaluate the effectiveness of reporting requirements
- provide parents with information about what they can expect their children to be learning and how this learning will be reported to them.

It is the responsibility of school boards to:
- ensure that provincial legislation and policy is followed in schools
- offer each school assistance in following reporting policy and procedures
- establish local policy for the communication of letter grades to parents of students in Grades 4 to 7
- approve the use of local report-card forms that satisfy Ministry content requirements, if the provincial report-card form is not used
- monitor the effectiveness of new reporting practices and address deficiencies.

It is the responsibility of school administrators to:
- ensure that teachers follow provincial legislation and policy
- use approved report-card forms
- follow the procedures established by the school board for the communication of letter grades to parents of students in Grades 4 to 7
- assist teachers with reporting procedures and monitor parental satisfaction with reporting practices
- establish a school policy for withdrawal and transfer of students in Grades 8 to 12
- maintain complete and accurate records of reports as required by the *School Act*, regulations made under it, and ministerial orders

- determine the most appropriate way of ensuring that schools respond to parents' requests for information on the curriculum taught in schools.

It is the responsibility of teachers to:
- follow provincial legislation and policy for reporting on student progress
- provide parents with complete, easily understood and accurate evaluations of their children's performance based on the provincial curriculum
- provide written reports to parents of students with special needs that follow the legislation and the guidelines and procedures established in the policy related to students with special needs

> The use of IP is optional in the 1994–95 school year, but is required for the 1995–96 school year.

- indicate, in relation to expected learning outcomes as set out in the curriculum, what each student is able to do, the areas in which the student requires further attention or development, and ways of supporting the student in his or her learning
- provide a description of each student's behaviour, including information on attitudes, work habits and effort that are not included in grade
- indicate, where appropriate, how parents and students can support classroom learning
- follow the guidelines when assigning a student an IP (In Progress).

Evaluating Student Performance

Evaluation of student performance is based on standards. Standards are realistic expectations of what students *need to know* and *be able to do* as a result of their education. In British Columbia, provincially mandated curriculum guides express these standards as expected "learning outcomes." They outline what schools are expected to teach and what students are expected to learn.

Teachers use professional judgment along with the goals, objectives and expected learning outcomes (knowledge, skills, and attitudes) from the provincial curriculum to determine what they expect students to learn and be able to do for the subject, course or area of learning. Using the expected learning outcomes and the expected levels of performance, teachers set specific criteria to evaluate students' learning. These criteria form the basis of evaluating and reporting on student progress.

In the primary years, children's progress is reported in relation to the expected development for students in a similar age range.

In Grades 4 to 12, letter grades are used to indicate students' level of performance in relation to the expected learning outcomes set out for each subject or course and grade.

The reference sets *Evaluating Writing Across Curriculum* and *Evaluating Reading Across Curriculum* provide descriptions of the range of performance that students demonstrate as they acquire skills. Additional reference sets are currently being developed for oral communication, numeracy and problem solving. *Supporting Learning: Understanding and Assessing the Progress of Children in the Primary Program,* provincial curriculum guides and the publication: *Parents' Guide to Standards* also contain information about students' development in specific grade ranges.

Assessment and Evaluation

Assessment is the systematic gathering of information about what students know, are able to do and are working toward. Assessment methods and tools include: observation; student self-assessments; daily practice assignments; quizzes; samples of student work, pencil-and-paper tests; holistic rating scales; projects; oral and written reports; reviews of performance; and portfolio assessments.

> The Assessment Handbook Series— *Performance Assessment, Portfolio Assessment, Student Self-Assessment, Student-Centred Conferences*—provide information and suggestions for teachers.

From the information collected through assessment activities, teachers evaluate student performance. They use their insight, knowledge about learning and experience with students, along with the specific criteria they establish, to make judgments about student performance in relation to expected learning outcomes.

Students benefit most when evaluation is provided on a regular, ongoing basis. When evaluation is seen as an opportunity to promote learning rather than as a final judgment, it shows learners their strengths and suggests how they can develop further. Students can use this information to redirect efforts, make plans to practise the learning, and establish future learning goals.

Evaluation may take different forms depending on the purpose.

- Criterion-referenced evaluation is best used to evaluate student performance in classrooms. It is referenced to criteria based on expected learning outcomes described in the provincial curriculum. When a student's program is substantially modified, evaluation may be referenced to individual goals. These modifications are recorded in an IEP.
- Norm-referenced evaluation is used for large-scale system assessments.

Criterion-Referenced Evaluation

In criterion-referenced evaluation student performance is compared to established criteria rather than to the performance of other students.

EVALUATION REFERENCED TO CURRICULUM

Evaluation referenced to curriculum requires that criteria are established based on the expected learning outcomes listed in curriculum guides for a particular subject and grade or course.

Criterion-referenced evaluation involves the following steps.

1. Identify the expected learning outcomes (as stated in curriculum guides).
2. Identify the key learning objectives for students.
3. Establish and set criteria.
4. Involve students, when appropriate, in establishing criteria.
5. Plan learning activities that will help students gain the knowledge or skills outlined in the criteria.

> When teachers evaluate student performance, they consider:
>
> - the expected learning outcomes
> - the expected level or quality of the student performance in achieving these outcomes.

6. Inform students about the criteria their work will be evaluated against prior to the learning activity.
7. Provide examples of the desired levels of performance.
8. Implement the learning activities.
9. Use various assessment methods based on the particular assignment and students.
10. Review assessment data and evaluate each student's level of performance or quality of work in relation to the criteria.
11. Report the results of evaluation to students and parents.

EVALUATION REFERENCED TO INDIVIDUAL GOALS

Students whose programs are substantially modified must have an Individual Education Plan (IEP) that outlines the goals they are working toward. Because these students are not expected to achieve the learning outcomes outlined in the provincial curriculum, an evaluation system referenced to individual goals is used. To evaluate their learning, their performance is then compared to these established individual goals. Such evaluation has the following characteristics.

- Specific individual standards or expectations are set for the students based on their ability and past accomplishments.
- The learning goals and expectations are set by teachers, parents and students and are recorded in the student's IEP.
- Student performance is evaluated with reference to the goals, expectations and criteria recorded in the IEP.

- Structured written reports are provided to parents for reporting purposes.

Students with special needs who can achieve the expected learning outcomes stated in the provincial curriculum with only modifications to the instruction or assessment methods (e.g., having a teacher write for them, tape-recording their answers) will use an evaluation system referenced to the provincial curriculum.

Setting criteria with students and communicating it to parents:

- improves instruction and clarifies expectations for student performance
- makes evaluating and reporting on students' work more objective and better understood
- provides important information about students to better meet their learning needs
- involves students in setting the criteria with the teacher, which increases student motivation, provides structure and clarity for students, and helps them understand the marking and gracing of their work
- informs students about what is expected of them and the standard for success before they begin the learning activity and, as a result, makes success accessible to all students
- provides students with opportunities for self-evaluation against criteria that facilitate the setting of specific and achievable goals
- informs students of what letter grades are based on
- enhances parents' understanding of the expectations for their children's learning
- allows parents to better assist their children
- builds a sense of appropriate expectations in the minds of parents and an increased understanding of how their children are progressing in relation to the subject, course and grade.

Norm-Referenced Evaluation

A norm-referenced evaluation system is not meant for classroom assessment because a classroom does not provide a large enough reference group.

Norm-referenced evaluation compares one student's achievement to that of others. It is based on a "normal distribution." A normal distribution shows how achievement in a particular area is distributed over an entire population. To use norm-referenced evaluation appropriately, a student's achievement must be compared with a reference group large enough to represent the population. Norm-referenced evaluation is used to:

- gather information for large-scale system analysis, such as components of the Provincial Learning Assessment Program
- determine ranking for scholarship competitions
- diagnose students with learning difficulties using tests such as the WISC-R.

Placing student achievement on a curve does not accurately describe a student's individual progress; it compares student achievement to that of others rather than comparing how well a student meets the criteria of a specified set of learning outcomes.

Computer programs that generate percentiles, stanines and student ranking are based on a norm-referenced system and are not appropriate for classroom assessment and evaluation.

Formal and Informal Reporting

Legislation requires that teachers provide parents with three formal reports each year. Specific requirements for formal reports are outlined in the policy section of this document. The following provides guidelines and suggestions for assigning letter grades, writing structured written reports, reporting on student behaviour and techniques for informal reporting.

Assigning Letter Grades (Grades 4–12)

Letter grades are used to indicate a student's level of performance in relation to expected learning outcomes. Letter grades may be assigned for an activity, a unit of study, a term or as a final grade at the end of the year or at the completion of a course or subject.

The following examples show the steps generally followed for assigning letter grades for an activity, assigning letter grades on a formal report and assigning a final letter grade.

Assigning Letter Grades for an Activity or Unit

1. Learning outcomes for the activity and unit are identified to make clear what the student is expected to know and be able to do.

   The provincial curriculum outlines broad learning outcomes. From these, specific learning outcomes for the unit and learning activities are established by the teacher.

2. Specific criteria for the unit and activity are established.

   It is helpful for students to be involved in the establishing of criteria. In this way they understand what is expected of them.

3. Different levels of performance or models are developed.

   Students are more likely to be successful when they clearly understand the criteria and the level of performance expected.

4. Students participate in learning activities to allow them to practice the skills and acquire the required knowledge.

   Feedback is provided to help the students continue their learning. Practice exercises help students meet the criteria and achieve the expected level of performance. Results from practice exercises support the student's learning but should not contribute to the term or final letter grade.

5. Students are given opportunities to demonstrate their learning.

   Teachers may have students represent their learning in a variety of ways. Assessment data is collected from tests, teacher observations, student self-assessment, written assignments, portfolios and performance tasks.

6. Students' levels of performance are evaluated in relation to the criteria.

   Evaluation of each student's performance is based on the assessment data collected and is compared to the established criteria.

7. The teacher assigns a letter grade for the activity.

   The letter grade indicates how well the criteria were met. Teachers often include written feedback to students along with a letter grade. In this way students gain the information necessary to continue their learning.

The Ministry of Education provides a full range of authorized letter grades for use. Teachers choose the appropriate letter grade for each student and for each grade level, subject or course.

EXAMPLE #1

A Grade 5 teacher planned a social studies unit on immigration. One of the learning outcomes selected from the provincial curriculum guide was the skill of interviewing. The students interviewed their families to find out immigration patterns within their class. The teacher and students established criteria for an effective interview.

The teacher provided examples of interview techniques, had the students practice the techniques and gave them feedback on their performance. The students worked in pairs to conduct an interview to demonstrate these skills. The students understood the criteria their performance would be judged against.

The evaluation of students' work for this activity was based on self, peer and teacher evaluations. The letter grades assigned for this activity were based on the teacher's judgment of the students' levels of performance demonstrated in relation to the criteria. The teacher recorded the students' letter grades so that they could be included in their term marks. Samples of the students' work were placed in their portfolios.

Criteria for an interview

The student will:

- open and close the interview
- make eye contact
- ask questions in an open-ended manner
- paraphrase responses
- ask probing questions
- show appreciation to the person being interviewed.

EXAMPLE #2

In a secondary English course, the teacher selected learning outcomes from the provincial curriculum related to writing for different purposes and audiences. The students were to apply their skills by writing instructions such as those found in "how-to" manuals. The students were to demonstrate the ability to write clear, concise instructions that allow for accurate completion of a task. The teacher and students developed a set of criteria for evaluating their written instructions.

The teacher and students established the following performance scale:

One: (IP) These are not really directions. It is impossible to do the activity using the directions. Only one or two steps are given. There is no introductory or concluding sentence. A maximum of two of the criteria are met.

Two: (C) Three or four steps are given in sequence. Of the eight criteria, up to four are present.

Three: (B) There are five to seven criteria of good instructions present including numbers seven and eight. The rough copy shows evidence of revision.

Four: (A) Six to eight criteria of good instructions are present inclucing numbers six and seven. The rough copy shows evidence of revision.

The students' written assignments were evaluated in relation to the criteria and to the performance scale. The teacher incorporated the results into the letter grade for the term.

Criteria for Good Written Directions

1. The title includes the word "directions", "instructions" or a synonym.
2. The first sentence indicates the purpose of the directions.
3. The instructions list the materials needed to carry out the task.
4. The instructions are numbered (1,2) or lettered (A,B) or done as Step 1, Step 2 or an alternate sequence is used.
5. Each instruction is written in sentences directed to a single reader but without "you". For example, use "Turn the handle to the right", not "You turn the handle to the right".
6. The instructions are worded simply.
7. Concrete physical descriptions (directions of movement materials) are given where needed.
8. The concluding sentence indicates that the directions are finished.

EXAMPLE #3

A Grade 4 class was studying the life cycle of the salmon and the factors that influence the cycle. One of the specific learning outcomes established by the teacher was for the students "to know and be able to represent the life cycle of the salmon".

The students were to use the criteria to develop their representation of the life cycle from the learning centre materials by answering the question: "What will you need to include in your life cycle of the salmon to show its whole life?"

The students' representations of the life cycle were evaluated in relation to the stated criteria and recorded to contribute to their term marks.

Criteria for the Representation

1. All main stages of the cycle must be present.
2. The stages must be represented in the correct order.
3. The beginning and end of the cycle are in the same place.
4. All stages of the cycle are clearly labelled.

Assigning Letter Grades on a Formal Report

Throughout the term, teachers record assessment and evaluation data regarding students' levels of performance in relation to criteria established for the activities. The records may be in the form of teacher observations, work samples, tests, assignments and performance tasks. Prior to issuing report cards, the teacher reviews the evaluation data and judges each student's overall performance for that term.

Generally, these steps are followed when assigning letter grades for a term.

1. The teacher determines the relative importance of each learning activity in relation to the expected learning outcomes for the term.
2. The assessment and evaluation of the student's performance demonstrated through the learning activities is collected and recorded.
3. When these evaluations for the unit or term are reviewed, the teacher assesses the importance (weighting) of each activity to decide the relative worth of each. Some activities may be of more worth than others; for example, the marks from a short test may be of less worth than the mark for a large project. Furthermore, because learning is cumulative, students may not demonstrate the same high level of performance at the beginning of the unit as they do near the end. The letter grade should represent the student's abilities in relation to the outcomes for the term, which implies that the averaging of marks may not provide a true picture of the student's abilities.
4. The teacher judges the student's overall performance in relation to the outcomes for the unit or term and decides whether the overall performance is outstanding, very good, good, satisfactory, minimally acceptable, progressing but needs more time to complete requirements or not demonstrating minimally acceptable performance.
5. The Ministry-approved letter grades that correspond to the level of performance demonstrated by the student are assigned.

EXAMPLE #1

A Grade 5 teacher developed a unit on immigration using the following learning outcomes from the provincial curriculum. Students need to acquire:

- knowledge of the different areas of the world from which people emigrated in the past
- knowledge of recent immigration patterns
- understanding of the various challenges people encountered settling in Canada.

The teacher designed and implemented various learning activities with specific criteria attached.

To assign letter grades for the term, each student's performance was reviewed.

For example, a particular student:

- demonstrated outstanding performance in her interviewing skills (The student was observed while conducting an interview and demonstrated all criteria at a high level of performance. The written assignment that accompanied the interview met all the required criteria at an exceptional level. It showed she was able to gather facts from an interview and use them effectively in written work.)
- demonstrated in her essay the ability to critically analyze and understand the concepts presented in the unit
- accurately completed a map to show immigration patterns.

The teacher judged the student's performance for the term to be at an outstanding level. The Ministry letter grade descriptions were reviewed and the A most matched the student's overall performance.

EXAMPLE #2

A secondary English teacher developed a unit that required students to write for different purposes and audiences. The activities included the writing of a set of instructions (as found in a manual), a letter to the editor and a résumé. The teacher worked with the students to develop specific criteria for each writing assignment.

The teacher designed various learning activities with the specific criteria attached so that the students understood the relationships between the purpose, audience and the form of the writing.

To assign a letter grade for the term, each student's performance was reviewed.

For example, a particular student:

- completed the writing of instructions, meeting six of the criteria for writing good instructions and demonstrated a B performance on the scale
- completed the letter to an editor, meeting five of the eight criteria for the activity and demonstrated a C performance on the scale
- completed the résumé, meeting six of the nine criteria, but missed an important component and therefore demonstrated a C performance on the scale. (This activity was determined to be the most complex and required the student to develop a creative format for the résumé.)

The teacher reviewed the evaluations of the student's performance on the assignments and determined that, in his professional judgment, the student's performance was meeting all the criteria at a reasonably high level. The teacher reviewed the Ministry letter grade descriptions and assigned a C+, the letter grade with the corresponding description that best matched the student's performance.

Assigning a Letter Grade as a Final Mark

At the end of the school year or at the completion of a course, teachers assign a letter grade to indicate each student's overall performance in the subject and grade or course. The teacher may give the final term work greater importance, as it indicates more accurately the performance of the student in relation to the outcomes; i.e., the final letter grade is not necessarily derived by averaging the term marks.

Reporting on Student Behaviour

The School Act requires that teachers provide parents with information regarding their children's behaviour, and policy for student reporting in British Columbia requires that in formal reports teachers do this using written comments, including information about attitudes, work habits and effort.

Parents are interested in how their children get along with their peers, in their work habits and efforts toward learning, and in their attitudes toward, level of interest in and motivation toward their studies. Assessing behaviour, effort, motivation and interest and including them in a grading system is problematic. Such traits are difficult to define and assess objectively. As much as possible, teachers should use systematic, dependable methods when assessing student attitudes and behaviour.

Often a student's achievement is affected by behaviour and, as an indirect result, the letter grade will be affected. However, reducing grades as a deterrent is unfair and self-defeating. Behaviours and personal traits are best reported to parents through written comments and in conferences.

Structured Written Reports

Writing Clear, Concise Reports

Written reports provide parents with information and documentation about their children's growth and progress in school and should do so clearly and concisely. The following are some guidelines for writing clear reports.

- Anticipate the questions parents may ask about their children's growth and progress.
- Recognize that parents may vary widely in their educational experiences and familiarity with educational terms.
- Write directly to parents about what their children are able to do and areas they need to develop. For example, instead of "When writing, Jason often needs to be reminded to use correct punctuation," write "Jason needs to work on using punctuation correctly."

Plain Language	
Instead of	*Try using*
a majority of	most
a number of	many, several
as a means to	for, to
assist, facilitate	help
communicate	talk, write, call
constitutes	is, forms, makes up
due to the fact	because, since
endeavour	try
exhibit a tendency	tend
factor	reason, cause
for the purpose of	for
in the course of	during
in the near future	soon
it will be necessary	I/we/you must

- Use only as many words as necessary to make the message clear.
- Use simple, direct words and short, clear sentences.
- Use plain language (see the suggestions provided).
- Consider using point form to help parents move from one idea to the next.
- Avoid expressions that may be unfamiliar to parents. For example, instead of using ". . . able to decode words and use context clues" use ". . . able to figure out unfamiliar words by using clues from the letters and surrounding words."
- Provide an explanation in parentheses if a word may be unfamiliar to parents. For example, if you use "high-frequency spelling words," add (common words used often in writing).

SUGGESTED WORDS AND PHRASES

The following are some suggestions, words, and phrases to use in reports to respond to each of the questions that must be addressed.

To describe what students are able to do, use words like the following:

- shows
- can
- continues to
- works well
- is practising

- demonstrates
- is able
- is increasing
- has completed

To describe areas that require further attention, use phrases like the following.

- needs an adult to help with
- needs guidance from an adult
- requires more time and practice

- needs reminders to
- avoids work that requires
- finds _____ challenging
- is working at
- needs practice with
- is a concern
- requires ongoing support
- is receiving help from the learning-assistance teacher in

To describe areas that require further development, use expressions like the following:

- is working towards
- is developing
- is beginning to
- is continuing to
- is increasing
- is practising
- is given opportunities to
- is becoming
- provide experiences that interest him or her by
- provide experiences that challenge him or her by
- challenge and expand his or her
- the success he or she experiences in _____ will be strengthened further by

To write about ways that learning is being supported, use expressions like the following:

- to continue to support
- to develop a variety of strategies
- to provide opportunities
- the plan for _____ is
- will continue to
- his or her goals for continued growth in this area
- my goals for _____ are
- it would support _____'s _____ if he or she

To report on student progress at the primary level, with reference to the expected development for students in a similar age range, use expressions like the following:

- is typical in this age range
- like many children of his or her age

- development is characteristic of many children in his or her age group
- easily meets the widely held expectations
- not comfortable working independently with the mathematics materials and ideas that one would expect of children in his or her age range
- fulfills the expectation for learning within his or her age range
- will take longer to reach
- is not meeting the expectation
- at this time his or her achievement in ＿＿＿＿ is not yet within the widely held expectations of his or her age range. I am confident that with ongoing support and encouragement from home and school, he or she will meet the expectations in ＿＿＿＿.

To report on student progress at the intermediate level, in terms of the student's level of performance as it relates to the expected learning outcomes for each subject or course and grade, use expressions like the following:

- easily meets the expectations of his or her grade
- met the expected learning outcomes
- meeting the outcomes expected
- below expectations for his or her grade level and requires assistance
- completed ＿＿＿＿ in a manner beyond what is typical of a Grade ＿＿＿＿.

Writing About What Students are Able to Do

Comments about what a student is able to do should note significant events in the student's growth, development, progress, and learning. The following are excerpts of this kind of comment from actual written reports.

KINDERGARTEN TO GRADE 3

Emily
Emily is now able to:
- write simple sentences in her stories and in her journal
- use capitals and punctuation marks correctly (I have included a sample of her writing, as she has improved in this area.)
- read her own stories and selected passages to the class with more confidence
- recognize many words and self-correct while reading orally
- add and subtract numbers to 20.

Jon
Jon's skill in mathematics has improved steadily since the last reporting period. For example, he now understands the value of numbers to

10. He can use objects to show numbers up to 10 and count up to 29. He is very proud of his learning.

GRADES 4 TO 7

Mike

Mike's cheerful, positive, and enthusiastic attitude toward school and his strong academic skills have helped him make many friends and adjust quickly to a new school. In the short time Mike has been here, he has shown that he can:

- read aloud fluently and with expression (others enjoy listening to him read)
- understand what he reads (his summary of *Gentle Ben* was excellent)
- follow directions (he carefully read the written directions and made a model of a fur-trading fort)
- read maps, charts and graphs to locate information.

Nikki

In science, Nikki developed a three-dimensional display and wrote a report to tell about her concerns for the environment. Her work showed that she can:

- identify and explain issues
- locate and use information from many sources
- use graphs and charts accurately to display information
- express her opinions strongly in writing
- use a word processor to present her work in published form
- present her ideas artistically.

GRADES 8 TO 12

Peter

Peter's analytical abilities have improved since the beginning of the year. His essays and projects this term show that he can analyze a contemporary Canadian political issue from several points of view and support his position on the issue. In a class debate, he stated his position, supported it with evidence and articulated it clearly to others.

Courtney

Courtney has demonstrated that she understands the science concepts covered this term. In her lab reports she clearly detailed the process of cellular regeneration and explained how the various components of the V-rebs cycle function.

Writing About Areas That Require Further Attention or Development

Parents need to know about areas in which their children may require further attention or development. Teachers should tell parents about areas of concern in a meeting or a phone call *before* sending them a written report. The written report should state concerns clearly, provide specific examples whenever possible, and describe methods to support further development or improvement in these areas. Parents also need to know areas in which their children excel and those that require further challenges to promote development. The following are excerpts from reports of this kind.

KINDERGARTEN TO GRADE 3

Heather

As we have discussed, I am concerned about Heather's reading. Most children in her age range are reading books with lots of print and only a few pictures. Heather is reading mainly picture books with four or five words on a page. Her understanding continues to be based largely on the illustrations.

Each day, I listen to Heather read orally for five to ten minutes, and since September I have regularly tape-recorded Heather's reading. I have noticed that she can recognize a greater number of words by sight. I will send the tape home so that you can hear how her reading has developed over the past few months.

At home, you could support Heather's reading development by reading to her each night and by encouraging her to read a passage of her choice to you.

Parents are reassured when the written comments relate to what their child needs to learn, further learning goals and ways to support their child's learning.

Carlos

As discussed during our telephone conversations:

• I am concerned about Carlos's writing. I believe he has the ability to accomplish much more.

• Carlos writes in simple sentences. He is being encouraged to expand his thoughts by including more detail in his stories.

• It appears easier for him to focus on the writing task if he selects his own topic.

• Having him write for an audience that he knows is one way to encourage him to put more effort into his writing. We are currently setting up pen pals with a neighbouring school, which will give him a real audience for his writing.

- He and I will keep you informed of his progress through his learning log, which he takes home once a week.

Parents like to know what areas need attention and what actions should be taken.

Katerin
Katerin has shown natural leadership qualities. I am challenging her to build on this strength and to take a leadership role in various school projects, such as introducing guest speakers and organizing the puppet show. She is very excited about playing the lead role in our spring drama production.

Parents want to know about their children's successes, accomplishments, and growth in learning.

GRADES 4 TO 7

Lyla
I am sending Lyla's writing portfolio along with this report. For this term her portfolio includes a mystery story, a report on a novel (*Amish Adventure*), a letter to the prime minister, and several paragraphs on topics covered in social studies and science. When Lyla and I reviewed her work, we noted the following:
- Her ability to write effectively for different purposes has improved (to tell a story, to explain, to summarize ideas).
- She needs to add more specific details and examples in her writing.
- She is now using a greater variety of sentences. (This was a goal that was set for Lyla last term.)
- She knows the correct format for business letters and how to write a paragraph that has one central idea.
- She needs to edit (check her work) more carefully for spelling, punctuation, and grammar. Her goal for next term is to edit more carefully. She will meet with her peer editor before she hands in her work.

All parents want to know that their children are being challenged, even when the children are meeting or exceeding expectations. It is helpful for parents to see what their children will be learning next.

Kim

Kim is working to improve his spelling skills. In his daily work he misspells many high-frequency words (common words that people use a lot in writing, such as *beautiful, because,* and *remembered*). He is trying hard to overcome problems in this area by keeping a small dictionary in his desk and learning to use the spell-checker on the word processor. We also do work with spelling patterns each week.

It is important to let parents know when their child recognizes an area requiring further attention and is determined to do something about it.

Laura

Laura can read and understand stories and articles that are short and simple and have few new words. To help Laura read more advanced material, she is:
- provided with extra practice in figuring out unfamiliar words by strategies such as using context clues (using surrounding words to figure out the unfamiliar words), picture clues, and phonics
- reading for different purposes, adjusting her speed when she reads to follow directions compared to when she scans (looks over rapidly) to locate specific information
- being challenged to infer (figure out what the author means)
- locating and using information from several different sources to complete research projects.

It is helpful to parents if they know about the next step in their child's learning or development.

GRADES 8 TO 12

John

When writing historical essays, John needs to support his ideas with accurate historical facts and details. When researching a topic, John needs to use more sources and to cite them in his work.

Yari

Yari effectively completed the planning and design phases of her technology projects, but must ensure that she completes all of the required parts of the product. I will have her develop checklists to help her keep track of what needs to be done.

Writing About Ways to Support Students' Learning

Setting goals is important for all students. While some of these goals are set by teachers, students should select other goals as important for themselves. Parents are often included in this goal-setting process so that they can offer support at home for continued success at school.

Learning about their child's future learning goals lets parents know what their child will be working on next. Linking those goals to areas that need further work or development lets parents see the natural progression that learning takes, from what the child knows to begin with to new learning. This area of the report should be developed with the child and parent when appropriate.

KINDERGARTEN TO GRADE 3

Jay
Jay is easily distracted. Through discussion, one of the goals Jay and I have set together is for Jay to move to a space where he can work on his own when he finds it difficult to concentrate.

Jane
Here is a goal that Jane set for herself for next term: "I want to start to learn how to write instead of printing." I will support her interest in learning handwriting by setting time aside for handwriting practice. In addition to handwriting with the whole class, there is a handwriting centre in our classroom where Jane often works. Jane wants you to notice her handwriting in her journal, so I have included two samples with this report. One is from a month ago, and one is dated last week. We would like you to notice her growth in this short time.

Teachers provide examples of student work that illustrate how the student has met the goals.

GRADES 4 TO 7

Jeremy
In a conference, Jeremy and I discussed ways to help him improve the organization of his work. He will now keep a daily assignment book to record his homework assignments. This will help him remember deadlines, especially for assignments such as long-term research projects. Before he leaves class each day, I will check to see that he has his assignment book and has recorded homework assignments. You could support Jeremy's learning by making sure that he completes his homework and that he returns the assignment book each day.

Jessica

Jessica needs to memorize her addition and multiplication facts. To support this goal:

- I will give Jessica practice drills each day to improve her accuracy and speed
- Jessica will take a drill sheet home each night to practise
- you could assist her learning of the basic facts by using flash cards with her each night.

Mark

In our three-way conference, we agreed to the following goals for Mark for next term in science:

- independently, Mark will use science materials to investigate science questions
- Mark will generate more than one hypothesis (a theory based on some evidence) when he does experiments.

These goals will be supported by:

- my encouraging his independence during his experiments
- Mark asking his partner for help before asking the teacher
- Mark handing in his experiments with at least two hypotheses listed.

GRADES 8 TO 12

Inder

Inder needs to improve the clarity and expression of his oral presentations. In order to help him achieve this goal, I have shown him ways to practice speaking clearly and with expression. Inder has agreed to use a tape recorder so that he can monitor his clarity and expression. I will listen to him practice his speech and provide suggestions for him to use in his next presentation.

Tara

When writing instructions for her electronics project, Tara's goal is to fully analyse the task and make sure that she has included all the important steps. Tara plans to research technical manuals to identify models she can adapt to her purpose. Tara will meet with me prior to her next project to review the model she has chosen.

Teachers explain ways in which students will be supported in reaching their goals.

Communicating About Standards

Teachers make judgments about student performance relative to expected learning outcomes outlined in provincial curriculum guides. Teachers indicate the student's level of performance in relation to these outcomes. They then communicate their evaluation to parents through the reporting process.

Teachers organize conferences (parent-teacher, teacher-student, student-led, three-way) as one way of establishing learning goals.

KINDERGARTEN TO GRADE 3

Jason

Jason has made some progress in developing his reading skills. He can identify all the letters of the alphabet, which is characteristic of a child his age. But overall, he has not yet reached the level of reading development that is typical for this age range (five to seven). I will continue to support Jason so that he becomes aware that all the print around him and in books has meaning. You might help Jason by printing notes to him.

Jasminder

Jasminder has made gains in her learning this year. However, at this time she is not comfortable working independently with the reading material that most children in her age range (five to seven) are able to read. She:
- enjoys looking at books
- understands that print is read from left to right
- can recall the story that has been read to her
- realizes that printed words have meaning.

In order to further her progress in this area, I will support her by having her practise listening to part of a story and trying to complete it on her own.

Evelyn

Evelyn has experienced success in all aspects of the Primary Program and has easily met the expectations for development for children in her age range. Discussing goals with her has two purposes: continuing to develop and extend her skills in all areas of the Primary Program and supporting her wide range of interests. A personal goal that Evelyn has set for herself is to write a story on horses. She intends to use the computer for this project.

Supporting Learning: Understanding and Assessing the Progress of Children in the Primary Program contains the standards of development ("widely held expectations") for student growth and development and should be used when providing this information to parents. It includes:
- standards of development (widely held expectations) of children's learning from birth to thirteen years of age
- responses to specific questions by parents
- many suggestions for ways in which parents can help their children learn. (For example, page 39 can be copied for use with the home reading program. It goes back and forth with the child in a Ziploc bag. Copies of pages 52 and 53 can be pasted into the covers of journals to highlight developmental skills in writing.)

GRADES 4 TO 7

Joey

Joey understands place value in whole numbers and decimals. He is able to estimate and calculate the answers to multiplication and division questions. He has learned how to divide and multiply decimals by a one-digit whole number (e.g., $32.76 \div 6$). Math is a particularly strong area for Joey. He has easily met the expectations in mathematics for a student in his grade.

Joey is a willing writer. He enjoys recording his thoughts in writing. However, spelling continues to be a problem. His written work has many spelling errors that do not seem to concern him. I do not want to dampen his enthusiasm for writing, but at the same time I want to see improvement in his spelling. In this area, he is not reaching the expectations for a student in his grade.

Teachers describe students' levels of performance and indicate the goals for continued development.

David

David's progress in writing is below expectations for his grade level. He is able to write about his immediate personal experiences and interests but has difficulty expanding ideas and including details. David's writing lacks a flow (the ideas are not organized or joined together smoothly). The sentences he uses tend to be short and simple. David still spells most words phonetically and often misspells simple, common words. David will need support in writing in order to make progress toward the standards for his grade.

Krista

Krista's achievement and performance in social studies and science easily meets the expectations for her grade. Krista has:

- completed the introductory unit of geography, including the summary of world-map terms
- demonstrated an understanding of the daily assignments and quizzes
- completed the Peru project in a manner beyond that typically expected of a Grade 7 student
- shown deep understanding of environmental influences in her essay
- completed all the task cards for the Birds of Prey unit
- demonstrated that she can read for information and facts through her data collection in science and her paragraph writing in social studies
- presented high-quality work on daily assignments and projects
- learned to study and prepare for tests so that she has consistently high test results.

Teachers provide information to parents about areas where a student requires further challenges and support.

GRADES 8 TO 12

Minh Yen

Minh Yen's class work and test results indicate that she has obtained the course objectives. Her achievement and performance meet the expectations for this subject. Her portfolio and projects are complete and of high quality.

Jeffrey

Jeffrey has not yet attained the objectives for this course. I have attached a plan outlining the additional assistance he will receive, the requirements he must fulfill and the timelines for completion.

Informal Reporting

Informal reporting is the ongoing communication between parents and teachers that occurs throughout the school year. Informal reports may include such things as telephone conferences, interim reports, written communication, portfolio reviews and face-to-face conferences.

The School Act requires that teachers provide parents with two informal reports each school year. Teachers should keep a record of such communication, noting the date, the topic or focus of the informal report, a summary of the discussion and any follow-up action decided on.

Conferences

Conferences provide an important exchange of information between home and school. It is recommended that teachers meet with parents at least once each school year to discuss their children's progress.

Teachers schedule the type of conference that is best suited to the needs of parents, students, and themselves. They may schedule a parent-teacher conference in which they meet alone to discuss student progress and/or a student-centred conference such as a student-led or a three-way conference in which the student is actively involved. Conferences may be held before or after one of the formal reports. *Student-Centred Conferences* in the Assessment Handbook Series, published by the Ministry of Education (February 1994), provides additional information on student-led and three-way conferences.

PREPARING FOR THE CONFERENCE

Teachers send letters home inviting parents to attend the conference. The letters outline and explain the type of conference and establish conference times. Teachers often ask parents to fill in preliminary surveys and forms regarding specific areas they would like information about or topics they would like to discuss. Teachers often ask parents to provide additional information regarding their own observations of their children and their learning.

SUGGESTIONS FOR A SUCCESSFUL CONFERENCE

Before the conference teachers should:
- set up the conference area in a way that promotes communication
- familiarize themselves with the child's history by reviewing background information and the student's permanent files
- determine the area or areas for discussion. It is not a good idea to try to discuss everything; time will not permit it, and parents may feel overwhelmed. Teachers should pick key areas to highlight in the conference
- prepare a conference form for record keeping, to focus the discussion, and to record any further action or follow-up that is decided on.

The conference can help teachers:
- understand parents' impressions and expectations of the school and the educational program
- obtain additional information about the children in their class
- encourage parents' understanding and support of the program
- communicate children's development and progress and suggest ways in which parents can support their children's learning
- strengthen the communication between home and school.

During the conference teachers should:

- make parents feel welcome and at ease (casual conversation at the beginning of the conference can help build good rapport)
- establish the conference parameters and briefly explain the role of each of the participants
- ask open-ended questions, listen closely, take notes and paraphrase parents' concerns to be sure everyone is understood
- avoid educational jargon, as this terminology may cause confusion or exclude parents from the conversation
- be specific when illustrating what the child does or does not do, giving specific examples of learning and behaviour rather than generalities
- keep the focus of the conference on the student, gently refocusing the conference if necessary
- conclude the meeting by briefly summarizing its highlights, planning follow-up actions and, if necessary, setting a date for another conference.

The conference can help parents:
- gain better understanding of the school program
- increase their understanding of learning and assessment
- heighten their awareness of their children's abilities
- learn about ways in which they can support their children's growth, progress and learning
- participate in the reporting process

After the conference teachers should:

- send a note home thanking parents for attending and asking them for feedback on the conference
- record specific information, concerns, and actions discussed on a conference form
- file the conference form
- begin to implement any follow-up action required
- continue to communicate with parents in follow-up notes, conferences, or telephone calls.

The conference can help students:
- join with their parents and teachers in examining and reflecting on their learning
- demonstrate their skills and abilities
- be active participants in the setting of personal goals for future learning
- be involved in their own evaluation, helping them take responsibility for their learning
- gain knowledge of themselves and enhance their self-esteem.

Promotion and Retention

In the primary years, students should not repeat a year. In Grades 4 to 12, the decision to advance or repeat a grade or course will be made in the best interest of that student by the teachers, parents, and the school principal.

Retention

Students generally take 13 years to graduate from secondary school. In most cases during their school years, students will meet the expectations of the subject and grade or course and have acquired the confidence they need to move on to the next grade or course. However, there may be special circumstances where, in the judgment of both the parents and the teacher, retention or some other course of action is in the student's best interest.

In cases where consideration is given to have a student repeat a grade or course, teachers and parents must realize the educational, emotional and social effects of retention on the student. Teachers must also consider what alternative materials and instructional strategies should be used to overcome previous areas of difficulty.

Promoting with Intervention

As soon as a student begins to show signs of not meeting expectations, intervention should begin by clearly identifying the problem and setting out a plan of action to remedy it. When a student does not achieve expected learning outcomes in one or more areas by the end of a school year, but is promoted to the next grade, it is in the best interest of the student to develop a concrete intervention strategy. Where possible, the intervention plan should involve both the promoting teacher and the receiving teacher, in order to determine the best course of action to address the student's learning problem.

In cases where a student is identified as a special needs student, policy and procedures are in place to provide him or her with an IEP (Individualized Education Plan). In other cases, a plan for intervention is developed based on a diagnosis of the problem, including information about what has been done previously to assist the student.

Intervention strategies are as varied as the students who require them. Assigning an IP and developing an individualized plan for assistance indicate that an intervention strategy is in place; however, not all interventions are associated with an IP. Intervention strategies may include provisions for one or more of the following.

- the classroom teacher, learning-assistance teachers, or support personnel provide individualized instruction
- parents give extra help at home

Research on Promotion and Retention

The research on retention generally supports promotion *with intervention* over retention. The following is a synopsis of research on promotion and retention.

- The achievement and adjustment of students who are retained tends to be no better than those of comparable children who are promoted.
- Repeating a grade does not ensure that children will overcome the areas of deficiency.
- Students who repeat the same material without new instructional strategies tend not to attain the same levels of competence as students who are promoted.
- Retained students tend to have a more negative attitude toward school.
- Students who are retained often develop problems in the areas of personal adjustment and socialization.
- Students who have been retained are more likely to drop out of school.
- Where students have been retained and show significant increases in achievement there have been marked changes in instructional strategies.

- computer-managed/assisted learning
- summer school programs
- distance learning
- before- and after-school programs
- adult, student, or teacher mentors
- peer or cross-age tutoring.

It is the responsibility of schools to structure learning environments that help students achieve expected learning outcomes. However, intervention may also include programs offered in the community or workplace.

Assigning an IP (In Progress)

The IP designation allows students to continue working toward the expected learning outcomes without failing or repeating an entire year or course. An IP is assigned when a student is making progress, but requires additional time and assistance to meet the expected learning outcomes.

When teachers assign an IP they outline a plan of assistance that includes the time frame for completion and learning expectations for the student. These expectations include areas that require further attention or development or specific requirements that must be fulfilled to meet the expected learning outcomes. When they develop the assistance plan, teachers follow the requirements for assigning a student an IP. (See pages B 2-8 and B 2-9.)

When an IP is assigned during the school year, it is a signal to the student and parents that the student's work is not meeting expected standards.

The plan of assistance informs them about what the problem is and identifies clearly what needs to be done in order to address the problem.

When an IP is assigned at the end of the school year, the student may be able to address the problem during the summer. If not, the plan should assist the receiving teacher to decide the best course of action to take in order to help the student overcome the problem and meet the expectations of the subject of course.

In secondary schools, the teacher who assigns the IP is responsible for assessing the student's progress to the completion of the subject or course and converting the IP to another letter grade. Since a student may not be able to register in a subsequent course until the IP has been converted, teachers should establish timelines for IP completion that consider the school's timetable and course registration requirements.

There may be situations where the teacher who assigned the IP is not available, such as when the teacher has moved or retired. In these situations the school administrator, with the assistance of other staff members, will review the documentation accompanying the IP, make a decision as to whether the requirements have been met, and use this as a basis to convert the IP to a letter grade.

Although an IP can be used in courses numbered 11 and 12, it will not appear on the final transcript of grades. A student may receive an F as a result of failing a provincial examination without having received an IP in his or her school marks.

The following are examples of interventions used to assist students in achieving expected learning outcomes.

Naomi

Naomi is a I 10-year-old Grade 4 student.

Naomi's Grade 4 teacher was concerned about her reading abilities. Naomi was able to read picture books independently, and with much individual support from the teacher she could read simple chapter books. Although, through the year she progressed, she was still below the expected level for her age and grade. Naomi's parents were concerned that she might fall behind and be unable to catch up. They believed that repeating a grade might be the only answer.

Naomi's teacher referred her to the learning-assistance teacher for a formal assessment of her reading abilities. This assessment provided a profile of her strengths and weaknesses, which was used in developing an intervention plan.

In consultation with Naomi's parents, the teacher outlined a program for summer reading activities and suggested possible summer school programs. He consulted with the receiving teacher regarding the information he had gathered, and they discussed the possibility of referring Naomi for individual learning assistance for the following year. He and the receiving teacher developed a detailed summary of Naomi's strengths and weaknesses and used this to develop a plan to address Naomi's reading development in the Grade 5 classroom.

Eric

Eric is a 13 year-old student entering Grade 8.

Eric's Grade 7 teacher was concerned because he was working below the expectations for the course and grade in mathematics, except in geometry. Eric had limited knowledge of basic facts and operations with whole numbers and was unable to add, subtract and multiply decimals and fractions. Prior to the December reporting period, the teacher set up a conference with Eric's mother to alert her to his difficulties and to inform her that Eric would receive an IP on his report card.

In the December report card, she outlined the goals for Eric over the coming term. She provided an outline of activities so that Eric's mother could help him at home (this was used for only a short time because the mother had to take on an additional job to support the family). Eric was referred to the school's computer learning centre, where he worked with a computer program at his own pace to correct areas of deficiency. He was also assigned a peer tutor to help him practice his basic facts.

The combination of intervention strategies was only partly successful in correcting the areas in which Eric was having difficulty. By the end of the year his teacher felt confident promoting him to Grade 8 as long as he continued to receive intervention. In consultation with the teachers at the junior high school, Eric received an IP in mathematics along with the requirement to attend summer school or complete appropriate units of distance education.

Jennifer

Jennifer is a 16-year-old, Grade 11 student

In the first few weeks of the course, Jennifer's chemistry teacher recognized that she was having serious difficulties. Jennifer did not hand in her labs, her in-class assignments showed that she had limited understanding of the course work, and she was absent for the unit test. In discussion with Jennifer and her parents, the teacher decided to give her an IP on the first report rather than an F, since Jennifer agreed to complete her labs and do a make-up test within a designated time. Jennifer met this obligation.

During the second term, the timeliness of Jennifer's work was still a problem. The teacher outlined all assignments and expectations and gave the list to Jennifer and her parents. Jennifer completed her assignments slowly but more carefully.

During the last term, it became evident that Jennifer was unlikely to be successful by the end of the school year. The teacher arranged a meeting with Jennifer's parents to set out the options. Jennifer and her parents requested that she receive an IP at the end of the year and be given a list of requirements for completion before September 1. The parents agreed to monitor her work and employ a tutor as required to help her.

During the first week of September, the teacher reviewed Jennifer's work and found it incomplete. Jennifer's IP was converted to an F and she repeated the course.

Resources

British Columbia, Ministry of Education. *Assessment and Education Resource Package (Primary).*Victoria: Ministry of Education, B.C., 1992.

British Columbia, Ministry of Education. *Parents' Guide to Standards.* Victoria: Ministry of Education, B.C., 1994.

British Columbia, Ministry of Education. *The Primary Program Resource Document.* Victoria: Ministry of Education, B.C., 1992. See the assessment and evaluation blackline masters in the appendix on page 345.

British Columbia, Ministry of Education. *Evaluating Writing Across Curriculum: Using the Writing Reference Set to Support Learning.* Victoria: Ministry of Education, B.C., 1992.

British Columbia, Ministry of Education. *Evaluating Reading Across Curriculum: Using the Reading Reference set to support Learning and Enhance Communication.* Victoria: Ministry of Education, B.C., 1994.

British Columbia, Ministry of Education. Assessment Handbook Series: *Student-Centred Conferences, Portfolio Assessment, Student Self-Assessment, Performance Assessment.* Victoria: Ministry of Education, B.C., 1994.

British Columbia Primary Teachers' Association. *Evaluation Techniques and Resources, Book II.* Vancouver: BCPTA, 1992. See especially sections 10.1 to 10.72.

Appendix C

Smerging Data: Grading . . .
More Than Just Number Crunching

APPENDIX

C

Smerging Data: Grading . . . More Than Just Number Crunching

Alberta Assessment Consortium
AAC . . . everyday assessment tools for teachers

#500, 11010 – 142 Street, Edmonton, AB Canada T5N 2R1
Phone: (780) 447-9420 Fax: (780) 447-2531
www.aac.ab.ca E-mail: aac@compusmart.ab.ca

The Alberta Assessment Consortium would like to thank the members of the writing, review and editing teams for this handbook written for teachers and administrators and, especially, school staffs.

Alberta Assessment Consortium
Robert Hogg

Edmonton Public Schools
Tanis Marshall and Sandra Carl-Townsend

Calgary Board of Education
Susan Brims

Living Waters Catholic Schools
Dwain Tymchyshyn

Edmonton Catholic Schools
Monique Gibeau

Parkland School Division
Marnie Beaudoin

Special thanks to reviewers and editors: Dale Armstrong (University of Alberta), Carole Beaton (Canadian Rockies), Delores Dante (Holy Spirit), Barb Eklund and Catherine Moir (Chinook's Edge), Fred Kirby (Fort Vermilion), Carol Anne Inglis, Mary Michilaides and Anne Mulgrew (Edmonton Public), Jo-Ann Reil (St. Albert Protestant), Jacqueline Skytt (ATA) and Chris Zarski (Living Waters)

AAC recognizes that Anne Mulgrew first coined the phrase *smerging data*.

October 2001
For additional copies, please contact AAC.

Smerging Data: Grading . . . More Than **Just** *Number Crunching*

Contents

Smerging Data: **Grading . . . More Than *Just* Number Crunching** is the fourth in a series of resources produced by the Alberta Assessment Consortium (AAC). The intent of these resources is to provide teachers with practical approaches for assessing, evaluating and communicating student learning. As a companion to *A Framework for Communicating Student Learning, Smerging Data:* **Grading . . . More Than *Just* Number Crunching** promotes thinking and discussion about classroom grading practices and encourages the adoption of fair, reliable and valid grading and reporting practices in a school and district.

The first three AAC resources are as follows:

- *A Framework for Student Assessment* (1997) and
- *A Framework for Communicating Student Learning* (1999). Both of these provide a foundation for implementing an effective classroom assessment program.
- The third resource, ***How to Develop and Use Performance Assessments in the Classroom*** (2000), enables teachers to build on the foundation and to develop and use performance assessments for improving student achievement in the classroom.

SMERGING DATA: GRADING . . . MORE THAN JUST NUMBER CRUNCHING

is a handbook for professional development that

- promotes further thinking and discussion about grading practices and encourages the use of fair, reliable and valid grading and reporting practices;
- encourages teachers to explore the difficult task of reducing a term's work to a single phrase, letter or number that goes beyond simple number crunching;
- enables teachers to reflect on their current grading practices, examine issues using real-life vignettes, consider possible solutions, and make the decision either to continue with current grading practice or initiate changes. By the way, ***there is no 'answer key'!*** ; and
- provides a model for how teachers, schools and jurisdictions can review and revise grading and reporting practices. Marzano (2000) advises that proposed changes be communicated to all interested parties—students, parents, district leaders—and that changes need to be well thought out and tested on a wide scale prior to implementation.

✏ *Initiating and Communicating Change,* **R&R**, C71.

The handbook is most effective when used by an entire school staff and implemented in a manner appropriate to the school. A planned approach and schedule will produce best results.

There are many ways to use *Smerging Data* in a school. For example, a school could

- complete, tabulate and discuss the results of the Self-Reflection survey on pages C12-13 and then dedicate portions of several staff meetings to a vignette or a cluster of vignettes pertaining to one of the issue questions, or
- dedicate a professional development day to an in-depth exploration of the school's grading practices.

O'Connor's *The Mindful School: How to Grade for Learning* (Skylight, 1999) is recommended as a companion resource to *Smerging Data*.

> The most crucial part of communicating student progress is to ensure a shared understanding between the person providing the information and the person receiving the information. Letter grades, percentages or comments from an activity, test, or assignment must be clear and comprehensive.
>
> Effective communication informs the student, parent, and others about what has been accomplished and what the next steps are in the learning process. The communication process involves all the key players. However, the greater the role students are given in this process, the richer the information that is shared and the greater the impact on future student learning.
>
> —*Adapted from A Framework for Student Assessment,*
> *Alberta Assessment Consortium, 1997*

"Not everything that counts can be counted, and not everything that can be counted counts."

—*Sign hanging in Einstein's office at Princeton*

GRADING AND COMMUNICATING STUDENT LEARNING

Grading—A Short History

Time	Grading Systems
In the late 1800s, modern grading practices began with teachers determining whether a student was ready to move from one grade to another.	Simple lists of skills mastered and those requiring additional practice
By 1910, larger, more diverse student populations and more complex curricula resulted in a mathematical approach to determine a grade.	Percentages used to measure student achievement in high schools
Widely fluctuating marks on English and geometry papers raised serious concerns (subjective grading, and spelling and neatness policies) about the grading system, resulting in a system to reduce teacher/grade variations.	Percentages replaced by rating scales such as • Excellent, Good, Average, Poor and Failing; • A through F
By the 1930s, there was an attempt to distribute achievement grades more fairly using methods common to intelligence testing.	Grading on the curve: • Rank student performance in relation to others • Assign student grades in tiers
By the 1980s, school reform and restructuring responded to a world requiring children to demonstrate complex and subtle forms of thinking. Today most schools maintain vestiges of traditional grading systems, but also implement alternative systems to communicate the scope of student learning and achievement.	Variations from traditional systems may include • demonstrations of competency (e.g., performance assessments, conferences and the use of portfolios) • anecdotal reporting • elimination of grades altogether • combination of traditional and alternative grading systems

Based on Pardini (1997)

✏ *New Tools*, **R&R**, C49

Purpose of Grading

"Communicating student achievement is the primary purpose of grading. ... Communication is most effective when it is clear and concise; grades are certainly concise, and they can be clear communication vehicles if there is a shared understanding of how they are determined and, thus, what they mean" (O'Connor, 1999, 11-12).

Parents ask us, **"So, how's my kid doing?"** and we respond with a mark, a letter grade or a comment. Sometimes we even provide them with some form of comparison, such as the class average, their child's performance relative to provincial standards or the extent of the progress their child has made since the last formal evaluation.

But what do we mean by the term *grading*? Grading can mean the number or letter we assign to a student at a given moment to represent how well he or she has performed on a specific task or series of tasks, tests, projects or other activities according to predetermined criteria. Alternatively, grading can be an average of the marks derived from a number of performances.

Whatever the method, the information that is condensed in this symbolic representation called a grade is open to interpretation.

In addition to grades that reflect performance in subject areas, teachers also continually evaluate the social and emotional progress and behaviour of their students. This information, which comprises a teacher's evaluation of effort, attitude, behaviour, participation and attendance, should be reported separately from a student's achievement of curriculum goals.

"... [T]he key question is, 'What information provides the most accurate description of students' learning at this time?'" (Guskey, 1996, 21).

Obstacles to Communicating Student Learning

Have you ever wrestled with how to communicate the achievement and progress of your students? Teachers have been reporting on student achievement and progress for years, but continue to struggle with important issues that have no easy answers:

- What is an A? What is a B? Although receiving an A is considered a measure of success in school, there is often no agreement on what an A actually means or what a student needs to do to get one.
- What kind of feedback is most helpful to students in order to improve learning?
- How do students determine how well they are doing?
- Students learn a great deal in school. Should all of this be reported?

- Should all that is assessed and evaluated be reported as an achievement grade?
- How often should students receive feedback, formal or informal, on how well they are doing?
- How important is consistency in the way student learning is reported or communicated?
- What kinds of information (letter grades, marks, anecdotal comments, observations) best communicate what and how well a student is learning?
- What do marks and letter grades really mean? Is there a more meaningful way to communicate student learning?
- What if a student neglects to complete assignments and assessment tasks? What are the consequences of non-performance? Does the teacher assign a zero for each incomplete task and, in the end, say that the student failed to meet the standard?
- How should effort and attitude be assessed and evaluated? Where does participation fit in?
- How does a teacher know if the student is achieving at grade level in language arts, mathematics, science and social studies?

Roles of the Principal, Teacher, Student and Parent

The **role of the principal** is to

- "ensure that students in the school have the opportunity to meet the standards of education" (*School Act*, 1988 cS-3.1 s15); and to
- "supervise the evaluation and advancement of students" (*School Act*, 1988 cS-3.1 s15).

The **role of the teacher** is to

- "regularly evaluate students and periodically report the results of the evaluation to the students, the students' parents and the board" (*School Act*, 1988 cS-3.1 s13);
- "promote goals and standards applicable to the provision of education" (*School Act*, 1988 cS-3.1 s13);
- ensure that students know what is expected of them; and
- establish clear and fair criteria and standards (with student involvement when appropriate).

The **role of the student** is to

- "be diligent in pursuing his/her studies" (*School Act*, 1988 cS-3.1 s7);
- know what is expected;
- participate in developing criteria and standards where appropriate;
- self-evaluate based on established criteria and standards;
- learn from the feedback obtained from self-evaluation, peer evaluation, teacher evaluation and possibly that of others, if provided; and
- communicate this information in a manner that indicates his or her responsibility for learning.

The **role of the parent(s)** is to

- ensure that students "have access to an education program" (*School Act*, 1988 cS-3.1 s1);
- support learning at home with time, study space and support;
- join the student in the discussion about learning during formal conferences;
- ask teachers and students about the goals set for the student;
- ask the teacher what to look for in the student's portfolio (materials collected representative of the student's work);
- spend time assisting with student work, portfolio management, personal learning plans and student self-evaluation;
- look for and acknowledge progress rather than demand perfection so that the student is encouraged to take risks in his or her learning; and
- advise the school which method of reporting they find most meaningful.

Parent role adapted from *Partners in Learning*
(Alberta Teachers' Association, 1996)

✏ *Assessment as the Basis for Communicating Individual Student Achievement*, **R&R,** C51.

CLASSROOM GRADING PRACTICES

Introduction

Letter grades and percentage scores have been used to indicate student achievement for more than a hundred years. According to Marzano (2000) literature and research suggest that the current grading system faces criticism in one or more of three problem areas. Teachers may

- consider many factors other than academic achievement when determining grades,
- use inappropriate weightings for assessments, or
- misinterpret single scores on classroom assessment.

Self-Reflection on Classroom Grading Practices Survey

How to use the survey

The self-reflection statements and rating scale promote thinking, self-reflection and discussion about classroom grading and reporting issues. As a first step in looking at your perspectives on grading, *circle* your response to each item from the standpoint of **what you do**, <u>not</u> **what you wish you did or should do**.

- Use the glossary on page C14 to help clarify language used in the survey.
- Compile data for the school staff using the Grading Practices Tally on page C13.
- Discuss results before proceeding.

Hint: Revisit the survey for a quick refresher and to help you keep on track as you use this handbook.

☞ *Personal Grading Practices* (for further reflection and discussion) **R&R**, C53.

Self-Reflection on Classroom Grading Practices Survey

Classroom Grading Practices	To a Great Extent			Very Little
1. I grade and communicate student **achievement** based on the Alberta Program of Studies.	4	3	2	1
2. I grade and communicate student **achievement** based on the Alberta Program of Studies.	4	3	2	1
3. I inform students about grading criteria and methods used for determining a grade at the beginning of and throughout the unit, term/year.	4	3	2	1
4. I assess student achievement and assign a grade based on predetermined and consistent criteria.	4	3	2	1
5. I use formative assessments to provide information about student progress and direction for improvement, but not for determining an achievement grade.	4	3	2	1
6. I use summative assessments to make judgments about student achievement at the end of a period of instruction and for determining a grade.	4	3	2	1
7. I emphasize the most recent achievement data when determining a grade.	4	3	2	1
8. I gather achievement data to inform my professional judgment in determining a grade.	4	3	2	1
9. I use a reliable recording system to track student achievement.	4	3	2	1
10. I "crunch" numbers fairly to determine a grade.*	4	3	2	1
11. I use a variety of assessments to determine a grade.	4	3	2	1
12. I determine a grade based on achievement of learner outcomes, rather than on motivation and control.	4	3	2	1
13. I report on work habits (effort, participation, behaviour, and attendance) separately from achievement grades.	4	3	2	1
14. I establish procedures to address work habit issues so that consequences do not distort a grade.	4	3	2	1

* crunch: to manipulate or process numerical data

Adapted from O'Connor (Florida 2001)

Grading Practices Tally

Item	4	3	2
1			
2			
3			
4			
5			
6			
7			
8			
9			
10			
11			
12			
13			
14			

Glossary

achievement a student's demonstration of knowledge, skills and attitudes relative to grade level curriculum standards

assessment process of collecting information on student achievement and performance. A balanced assessment includes a variety of assessment tasks.

criteria indicators by which student responses, products or performances are judged

criterion-referenced grading relative to grade level curriculum standards

curriculum standards what students are expected to know and be able to demonstrate based on the Program of Studies

data information collected about an individual student or a group of students

evaluation a judgment regarding the quality of overall student performance based on the curriculum

formative assessment provides information about student progress and direction for improvement and/or adjustment to a program for individual students or for a whole class, but is not part of an achievement grade (adapted from O'Connor, 1999)

grade (mark) a summary statement of student achievement relative to curriculum standards

grading a process to determine a student's level of achievement within a subject area or course

norm-referenced grading in relation to other students within a group

progress a positive change in the student's demonstration of outcomes measured against the graded curriculum

score the number or letter given to a student on any single assessment

summative assessment provides information to make judgments about student achievement at the end of a period of instruction and for determining an achievement grade (adapted from O'Connor, 1999)

GRADING—ISSUES AND POSSIBILITIES

Introduction

This section of *Smerging Data* explores grading issues using classroom-based vignettes and provides a framework to consider further development and refinement of grading and reporting practices in consideration of the law, literature and research. As you explore the issues, consider how grading practice is communicated to parents so they understand it.

Issues

- What are the foundations of grading practices?
- What factors should be considered in determining a grade?
- How are fair and accurate grades determined for a student?
- How is data used in determining a grade?

Study and Discussion Dimensions

The four issues are accompanied by several vignettes presented in this format:

- Vignette
- Think and Discuss
- Literature and Research Say . . .
- Self-Reflection

Grading and Reporting Practices

What fair, reliable, and valid grading and reporting practices will be used in our school?

Reflections

Issue . . . What are the foundations of grading practices?

Vignette 1: What's the right mark?

Sally Brown, a beginning teacher, has come into the staff room for some advice from Natasha Shamji, a veteran teacher whom she respects a great deal.

"Natasha, I have been working on my report card marks, and I need some advice about arriving at Dale's mark. When we started the year he was really struggling. He wasn't even ready to tackle work at grade level. He has worked so hard and is at grade level now, doing work in the C range. In my heart I want to reward him for the tremendous progress he has made and am thinking about bumping the mark up to a B. What do you think?"

"Sally, as someone who may be Dale's teacher next year, I think you should be honest about his achievement mark and have it reflect how well Dale is performing against the learner outcomes of the Program of Studies. Then next year I can mark against the expectations for the next grade, and we will be able to celebrate that progress. If you inflate a grade, for whatever noble reasons, that may set Dale up for a future disappointment. You can comment on his progress through the comment section."

"I am going to have a lot of comments!"

"Not necessarily. Remember the report card is not your only way to communicate to parents. You can use student agendas, personal notes, phone calls and student-led open houses. In this case I would call Dale's parents before the report card goes home and let them know how proud you are of his progress. That way they can be ready to compliment him when they get his report card. You may also want to have a short interview with him before he takes the report home."

Think and Discuss

- What is your reaction to Natasha's advice?
- What other solutions may there be to Sally's problem?

Literature and Research Say . . .

Bailey and McTighe (1996, 121) state that "grades often reflect a combination of achievement, progress and other factors ... this tendency to collapse several independent elements into a single grade may blur their meaning." The theme in the literature on this topic is that the clearest grade will be arrived at when only an individual's achievement is considered. O'Connor (1999, 40) defines achievement as the "[demonstration of] knowledge, skills and behaviors that are stated as learning outcomes for a course or unit of instruction."

According to the University of Alberta's Joint Advisory Committee (1993, 9) *Principles of Fair Student Assessment for Education in Canada*, "combining disparate kinds of results into a single summary should be done cautiously. To the extent possible, achievement, effort, participation, and other behaviors should be graded separately."

Self-Reflection

- What processes do I use to come up with a report card mark?

☞ O'Connor, *Grading Individual Achievement*, C37–C52.

Issue . . . What are the foundations of good grading practices?

Vignette 2: Let the Kids Know What's Coming!

Mr. Scullion and Ms. Emerson were sitting in the staff room at the beginning of the school year. Mr. Scullion was watching Ms. Emerson assemble booklets of what appeared to be extensive course outlines. "What are those booklets you are stapling together?" asked Mr. Scullion.

"They are my course introductory packages which tell my students all about my courses," responded Ms. Emerson. "You know, evaluation and weighting issues, learner outcomes in each unit, a complete overview of what is expected of them, and how they will be evaluated this year. I want my students to know exactly where they are going and what I will expect of them."

"Looks like an awful lot of work," said Mr. Scullion.

"Well, how else am I to ensure their success? They need to know what target they have to hit and what they need to do to be successful in my class. Don't you prepare similar packets?" asked Ms. Emerson.

"No," replied Mr. Scullion, "I just prepare a simple outline for my students."

"I know what I do looks like a lot of work but it helps me in so many ways. It helps with planning and assists me with deciding where I want my students to go," stated Ms. Emerson. "I feel that I am an effective teacher when I do this."

Think and Discuss

- Why does Ms. Emerson inform her students about course expectations and evaluation beforehand?
- How does pre-planning of classroom instruction help grading practices?
- How can students benefit from knowing grading practices at the beginning of a course? In what ways can this information affect student success?

Literature and Research Say . . .

Current research tells us that students are most successful when they have a complete understanding of the evaluation and expectations of a course at the beginning of the school year. Prior knowledge about a teacher's grading practices helps students hit the achievement target and thus be more successful at completing the learner outcomes in the course. O'Connor (1999,

139) suggests that teachers involve students in a discussion of grading during the first week of a course.

Students need to know what is expected of them. By establishing a fixed target of expectations at the beginning of a course, a teacher gives students a sense of how they will be graded and how they can best achieve at the highest level. In order to achieve success "a student needs to have a clear performance goal and to keep that goal in constant view as different points of view emerge" (Wiggins and McTighe, 1998, 54). A set of hazy expectations confuses students and prevents them from achieving at an optimum level because they are never sure what the course expectations are. Consistent, established, and clearly communicated grading practices are optimal practices.

Self-Reflection

- How and when do I share the learning outcomes and evaluation criteria with students?
- How do my students know how to succeed in my class?
- How can I improve the way I establish fixed achievement targets for my students?

"Students can hit any target they can see and holds still for them."
—*attributed to R. Stiggins*

"Assessment is not something that is done to students separate and apart from instruction; assessment must be—and must be seen to be—something that is done with students, an integral part of the learning process."
—*O'Connor, 1999, 144*

". . . good design and good teaching are dependent on clear purposes."
—*Wiggins and McTighe, 1998, 159*

Issue . . . What are the foundations of grading practices?

Vignette 3: Get with the Program!

Mr. Fisher, a new Grade 8 Social Studies teacher, found himself scrambling near the end of the school term. He thought that he had banked enough time to cover all three remaining topics and would have time to review before the final test. But he was concerned that the lengthy and fairly comprehensive multiple choice tests, used as final exams, and given to him by last year's social studies teacher, had dragged down his students' grades considerably. When asked by a parent how marks were determined ("the exam lowered the mark" comment appeared on his son's final report card), what content was supposed to be covered and why students had spent so much time on project work, Mr. Fisher had difficulty defending his choices with respect to curriculum expectations and his grading practices.

In his initial planning, he had found the Program of Studies difficult to understand. He, therefore, trusted that what needed to be taught was likely in the teacher's manuals and textbooks. Then, during the course of the year, Mr. Fisher opted to develop interesting activities that arose from the texts; for example, tracing family trees in Canada and mapping. Unfortunately, these activities had taken more time executing and presenting than he had anticipated. His students, however, had greatly enjoyed them and liked how their term grades reflected the time spent on these tasks.

Think and Discuss

- What are the grading issues for Mr. Fisher?
- How might he resolve them?

Literature and Research Say . . .

Aligning planning, teaching, and assessment with the Program of Studies presents an enormous challenge to teachers. Mr. Fisher would have greatly benefited from a mentor who had experience using the Program of Studies, accessing relevant resources, integrating meaningful activities, and connecting assessment and grading to provincially mandated learner outcomes. His use of the teacher's manual and the textbooks as curriculum planners was inadequate because these resources are meant to be used as tools to *support* the Program of Studies, not to serve *as* the Program of Studies.

There should be no surprises for students or parents at reporting periods. It is important to identify the big ideas or principles within the Program of Studies and to use these as a basis for measuring student achievement.

Equally important is connecting all classroom activities to specific outcomes, and clearly communicating assessment and grading information at the beginning of the learning.

Self-Reflection

- How do my grading practices reflect instruction and curriculum?
- What standards do I use to come up with a mark?
- How can a grade book be set up to assist me in aligning my teaching with the Program of Studies?

"When important problems and questions anchor the curriculum, a clear overarching purpose for student learning and performance is established.

"As with an encyclopedia or almanac, it doesn't follow that we should teach the textbook from page to page."

—Wiggins and McTighe,
1998, 134, 150

". . . grading should be directly linked to an explicitly defined set of instructional goals."

—Marzano, 2000, 22
citing Terwilliger

✏ *Teaching Quality Standard,* **R&R,** C56.

Issue . . . What factors should be considered in determining a grade?

Vignette 4: What Counts?

During parent-teacher interview week in November, Principal Svoboda receives a visit from Mr. Sanchez, the parent of one of her students. Mr. Sanchez is unhappy about one aspect of the interview that just occurred with his child's teacher. He is concerned about his child's language arts grade. In previous years, his son, Juan, had always received very high grades (80+) in language arts. This term Juan received a mark of 68. Mr. Sanchez and Juan were confused by the report card mark, since the work that Juan had brought home had been judged as very good. Mr. Sanchez had asked Juan's teacher to clarify how the mark was determined. The teacher explained that, while Juan had been producing very good work, he had deducted marks because Juan "just doesn't listen during instruction." Mr. Sanchez felt that the mark of 68 didn't reflect how Juan had been performing against the expectations of the Program of Studies and was in fact misleading, so he had come to the Principal to seek clarification on the school's grading policy.

Think and Discusss

- What should count for achievement grades (marks)?
- What should not count?

Literature and Research Say . . .

The literature consistently asserts that the only factors to consider in determining an achievement grade are indicators of individual performance against the expectations of the Program of Studies. Work habits, effort, and other non-achievement factors do contribute to students' achieving learner outcomes and usually have a positive impact on the quality of student performance. However, including these factors in the calculation of the student's achievement grade blurs the meaning and should not be done according to grading and reporting writers including O'Connor, Guskey, Stiggins, McTighe, and Wiggins.

Some teachers argue that giving marks for non-achievement factors helps motivate and control students. Studies show that most students view high grades as positive recognition of their success, and some students work hard to avoid the consequences of low grades. However, there are no studies that support the use of low grades as punishment for low academic performance. Instead of promoting greater effort, low grades more often cause students to withdraw from learning (Guskey and Bailey, 2001, 34–35).

J. McTighe (as cited in AAC, 1999, 21) observed that clearly defined reporting standards are necessary to increase the communication value of a reporting document. According to McTighe, reporting documents should distinguish between the following factors:

- **achievement**—performance relative to identified learning outcomes based on collected evidence and judged against established criteria (based on summative data)
- **progress**—degree of growth toward mastery of the learning outcomes, based on a performance continuum (based on formative data)
- **work habits**—includes effort, completion of assignments, behaviour and attendance

McTighe also noted that each of these factors should be reported separately.

Self-Reflection

What role do achievement and non-achievement factors play in how I determine a grade?

Issue . . . What factors should be considered in determining a grade?

Vignette 5: Getting What They Deserve?

"So, let's wrap this up quickly," Helene said to her three colleagues as they settled down around the table. "As members of this department," she addressed Joan, the newest teacher on staff, "we need to be consistent in how we deal with lates, homework completion, attitude, etc. I hate it when parents and students accuse me of being unfair, especially if other teachers aren't following the same rules!"

"Why don't we keep last year's policy," suggested Mary, "which was 10% off every day for lates, up to three days, zeroes for kids who are suspended or have unexcused absences, and a 5% bonus for participation and effort at each reporting period?"

"That sounds right to me," stated Helene, "and I had this great idea over the summer on how to prevent lates—let's give a short quiz at the beginning of each class—you miss, you get a zero! That would work." Mary looked admiringly at her colleague; Helene always thought of such interesting and motivating ideas!

Joan squirmed in her chair, certain that her forthcoming question would **not** be met with enthusiasm. "It doesn't sound like students get a grade that truly represents their academic achievement," she ventured. "Why don't you keep non-academic factors separate?"

Helene responded quickly, "Well, it *does* reflect achievement; teachers will know that students aren't good workers if their marks are low. They don't deserve a high grade if they don't work for it all year long."

"But if I'm looking at a grade," Joan continued, "shouldn't I expect it to tell me only what the student is capable of achieving, as opposed to guessing what behaviour he or she is exhibiting? There's no doubt that work habits influence the mark, but you end up with a fairly meaningless mark if the two areas are not separated. I think that we might talk about a different approach to reporting student progress, don't you?"

Think and Discuss

- What is the position Joan has taken and how can it be supported?

Literature and Research Say . . .

Marzano (2000) suggests categorizing work habits into three major topics: effort, behaviour and attendance. He further defines each of these to encompass the major attributes valued in the world of business and human resource development, as well as by parents.

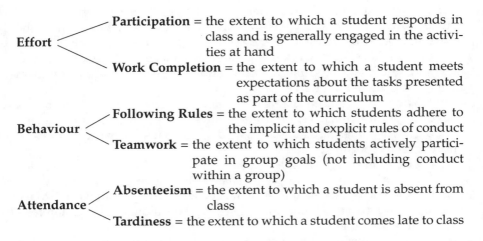

Effort

Participation = the extent to which a student responds in class and is generally engaged in the activities at hand

Work Completion = the extent to which a student meets expectations about the tasks presented as part of the curriculum

Behaviour

Following Rules = the extent to which students adhere to the implicit and explicit rules of conduct

Teamwork = the extent to which students actively participate in group goals (not including conduct within a group)

Attendance

Absenteeism = the extent to which a student is absent from class

Tardiness = the extent to which a student comes late to class

"Employability skills are developed in school and through a variety of life experiences outside school. The student, the family and the education system, supported and enhanced by the rest of society, share this responsibility."
            —*Adapted from the* Employability Skills Profile: the
            Critical Skills Required of the Canadian Workforce, 1996

"Factoring effort into the grade may send the wrong message to students. In real life just trying hard to do a good job is virtually never enough. If we don't deliver relevant practical results, we will not be deemed successful, no matter how hard we try."
                                                —*Stiggins*, 1997

According to Marzano (2000), when non-achievement factors have been clearly identified and defined, it is possible to measure student performance with a rubric scale such as the one illustrated in **R&R,** C68–69. These non-achievement factors may be calculated over the course of weeks, months, or a school term and communicated to relevant stakeholders informally or on a report card. Marzano suggests that these scores form a major part of reporting.

Self-Reflection

What work habits do I value in my classroom?

☞ *Rubrics for Non-achievement Factors,* **R&R,** C68.

> "Comments such as 'a pleasure to teach' and 'try for honours next term' do little to provide understanding of student achievement or directions for the future."
>
> —*O'Connor,* 1999

Reflections

Issue . . . What factors should be considered in determining a grade?

Vignette 6: Don't Borrow Trouble!

After a staff meeting, two teachers discuss a change in school grading policy to exclude non-achievement factors when determining report card grades.

"Jill, I wanted to chat with you about the staff meeting. I understand why I need to exclude non-achievement factors when I am arriving at a grade. It is very punitive to my struggling students. But I am trying to figure out how to deal with things like late or missing work. In the discussion it seemed that you have really wrestled with this and have come up with a solution that works for you."

"Jack, I did in fact wrestle with the idea until I found a solution that works for me. First, make sure you don't borrow trouble! I found that when I set a deadline most assignments came in on time. I spoke with individually with the students who didn't hand in the work at the deadline. As it turns out the reasons for not handing in the work were as different as the students themselves, so the solutions were individual too. I found that it has led to a positive change in my classroom atmosphere. All of my kids feel like their learning is the most important thing in our classroom. It's a system that works for me. You will need to figure out one that works for you."

Think and Discuss

- What are some difficulties Jack would need to overcome to no longer use marks to control his students?
- What other strategies could be employed to deal with late or missing assignments?

Literature and Research Say . . .

Often late, missing or poorly done work is symptomatic of a larger problem or issue in the student's life. Jill's procedure of speaking with the students is part of her child-centered classroom, where she listens to and values the voice of her students. In her classroom the focus is on helping every child succeed. Classrooms where the teachers' needs are the focus tend to be more focused on rules and control issues.

The teacher's responsibility is to ensure that he/she has made every effort to help that child be successful. The student's responsibility is to achieve to the best of his or her ability or desire.

Teachers who establish procedures to deal with work-habit issues avoid a litany of penalties. Some effective approaches include

- meeting with the student to develop a plan,
- early contact with parents to work collaboratively to help the student, and
- on-going review of assignments to allow for completion or second chances.

Schools may want to consider a change in grading policy. For example, teachers at a middle school record students' grades as A, B, C or I (Incomplete). Students who receive an I are required to do additional work in order to bring their performance up to an acceptable level. (Guskey and Bailey, 2001, 35).

Self-Reflection

- How do I control and motivate my students if I don't use marks as an incentive?
- What fair consequences could I establish regarding late/missing/poor quality work so that grades only communicate what students know and **can** do?

"Effective classroom management will increase the chances of an effective classroom and school-wide discipline policy.

"Classroom management is a critical and complex component in the creation of effective learning environments.

"The ability of the teacher to prevent and respond to student misbehavior will determine whether or not meaningful classroom learning will effectively occur."

—*Bennett and Smilanich, 1994*

Issue . . . How are fair and accurate grades determined?

Vignette 7: The Mighty Bell Curve!

Dakota's teacher, Mrs. Vandekamp, was presenting final marks to her English 20 class. Hoping to receive at least 80% as an overall mark, Dakota had worked hard on all her papers and assignments and had received grades of over 80% for most of them. She needed at least an 80% in English 20 to maintain her honours standing for a Rutherford Scholarship. When Mrs. Vandekamp handed out the marks, Dakota was shocked to see a 79% on the grade sheet. Because Dakota was so upset, she went after school to see Mrs. Vandekamp to discuss the grade. When asked about the possibilities of raising the grade to 80, Mrs. Vandekamp replied, "I've already given out six 80s, therefore your 79 remains. The normal distribution of grades in this class does not allow for more than six marks over 80%. I am sorry, but I cannot raise your mark." As a result, Dakota did not qualify for the Grade 11 portion of the Rutherford Scholarship.

Think and Discuss

- How did Mrs. Vandekamp's decision affect Dakota's grade and life?
- What is the basis for Mrs. Vandekamp's grading practice?
- How does Dakota's mark reflect her actual achievement?

Literature and Research Say . . .

Mrs. Vandekamp used a norm-referenced approach to grading, which bases overall grades on the bell curve. Criterion-referenced grading, on the other hand, would have judged student achievement based on the graded curriculum.

The literature indicates that norm-referenced grading makes learning highly competitive. Students compete against one another for scarce rewards (high grades) distributed by the teacher. Under these conditions, students see the success of others as a threat to their own chances for success. Learning becomes a game of winners and losers and because the number of rewards is kept arbitrarily small, most students are forced to be losers. In Dakota's case, Mrs. Vandekamp had predetermined the number of As that she would award in the subject. In order for Dakota to get an A she would have to do better than someone else. (Guskey, 1996)

O'Connor (1999, 116) states that even for technical reasons the use of a normative approach to classroom grading is inappropriate. In order to establish a normal distribution, the sample size must be large—at least several hundred, preferably thousands.

In reporting student results on Diploma Examinations Alberta Learning does the following: if a student's final blended mark results in a score of 47.5 to 49.5 (based on the 50/50 blend), the final mark is raised to 50%. Previously, the examination mark was adjusted to achieve this; it is now accomplished using a footnote, without adjusting the component scores. Thus, what is now reported is a 48% exam mark, a 50% school awarded mark, and a 50% final blended mark, with a footnote. The student would then receive credits for the course.

Self-Reflection

- What role does the Program of Studies play in my determination of students' grades?
- How does knowing each student as a person make a difference in my grading practices?
- Why is criterion-referenced grading a better grading practice than the mighty bell curve?
- How can I be sure that my assessments are so reliable and valid that there is no room for error?

"The best referencing system for grading is content-specific learning goals: a criterion-referenced approach."
—Marzano, 2000, 23

"No student grade should ever depend on what other students do."
—Glasser, 1990, 108

"There should be no artificial rationing of high grades. The number of good grades should not be artificially limited so that one student's success makes another's unlikely."
—AAC, 1999, 16

✎ *Assessment as the Basis for Communicating Individual Student Achievement,* **R&R,** C51.

✎ *Curves, Criteria and Reporting Systems,* **R&R,** C66.

Issue . . . How are fair and accurate grades determined?

Vignette 8: Decisions, Decisions

When Mr. Brit completed his marking for the year, he smiled as he thought of his Grade 6 students. What a long way they had come together! As he read over their final science projects, he knew that all of the hard work had been worth it—all the homework, editing of writing drafts, self-assessment, and late nights writing feedback to students using formative assessment. Sure, some students didn't always finish their homework, mistakes were made, and perhaps the fourth draft of Jason's story was tedious. But, as Mr. Brit began to calculate the achievement grades, he needed to decide what to include. What fairly and accurately represented achievement?

Think and Discuss

- What should Mr. Brit include to calculate each student's grade?
- What should not be included?

Literature and Research Say . . .

Research indicates that both formative and summative assessments are useful. However, each plays separate roles in helping students learn and providing them with opportunities to perform at their best.

According to Davies (2000, 11), formative assessment is a valuable tool because learning involves taking risks and making mistakes, and then doing things differently as a result. Mistakes provide assessment evidence—they give learners feedback about what is not working and help them figure out what will work. Unless students understand that mistakes are essential for learning, they may not take necessary risks.

> "It is essential that teachers distinguish between formative and summative assessment."
>
> *—O'Connor, 1999, 56–57*

✏ O'Connor, *Formative and Summative*, C56–C64.

Continual formative assessment allows for this process. If formative assessment counts towards an achievement grade as much as summative assessment does, students may be unwilling to take risks for fear of making mistakes that will affect their grade. As Mr. Brit reflects on his year, these issues come to mind. Formative assessment provides the learner with valuable feedback that, when properly used, makes for greater success at later stages of learning. Formative assessment provides students with on-going feedback, coaching, motivation, and encouragement to take risks.

All scores count, but all scores should not count for achievement grades. According to O'Connor (1999, 64), formative assessment is essential during the course of the learning to help students improve and to inform the teaching. Formative assessment scores should not be included when grades are calculated. Summative scores should be the only scores used for the report card. A teacher's professional judgment determines which scores are formative and which are summative.

The table following illustrates the relationship between the two forms of assessment (O'Connor, 1999, 57).

Comparison of Formative and Summative Assessments

	Formative	*Summative*
Purpose	To monitor and guide an on-going process/product while it is still in progress	To judge the success of a completed process/product at the end
Time of assessment	During the process or development of the product	At the end of the process or when the product is complete
Types of assessment techniques	Informal observation, quizzes, homework, teacher questions, worksheets	Formal observation, tests, projects, term papers, exhibitions
Use of assessment information	To improve and change a process/product while it is still going on/being developed	Judge the quality of a process or product, then grade, rank, promote

Self-Reflection

- How do I deal with formative and summative scores when determining a grade?
- How can my students benefit from formative assessment? To whom should formative results be communicated?

Issue . . . How are fair and accurate grades determined?

Vignette 9: Ryan's Impending Doom!

Ryan began the semester nervous about his prospects for success in English 10. He had never been a successful English Language Arts student. His teacher, Ms. Wong, was an excellent mentor and she made every attempt to help Ryan cope with his insecurities. During the first four weeks of the semester Ryan did not do very well but eventually his achievement began to improve. As his skills and confidence improved so did his test and assignment results, and by the last six weeks of the semester Ryan's grades had risen from between 30% and 40% to between 50% and 60%. School policy required Ms. Wong to use all grades for the whole semester to calculate Ryan's final grade, and so Ryan's final mark in English was 45%. Even though Ryan's most recent performance during the last third of the semester showed much improved achievement compared to his work during the first part of the semester, his final grade did not reflect this improvement. Ryan felt completely defeated even though he had worked diligently all semester in English Language Arts, and he went into his diploma exam feeling that he could not possibly pass the course.

Think and Discuss

- How accurately did Ryan's final grade reflect his achievement?
- How does the final grade affect Ryan's self-perception as a learner?
- What data best reflect student achievement?

Literature and Research Say . . .

The use of all evaluation data is relevant in determining a student's grade. As Davies (2000, 68) states, "[t]o evaluate well, we should look at all the evidence—observations, products, and conversations. We can then use this evidence to determine whether the student has met the widely held expectations for his or her age." However, while all the evaluation data should be considered, is it practical to use all the data to calculate a student's achievement grade? O'Connor (1999, 71) believes that only the most recent data gathered from a student should be used to calculate a grade, because ". . . students then get full credit for their improvement rather than a score based on artificial manipulation of numbers."

Student improvement is best considered as a reporting variable and not primarily as a grading variable. Grades based on a student's highest, most consistent level of performance will usually be his or her most recent performance. These grades will demonstrate what the student has actually achieved in relation to the learner outcomes in the Program of Studies. In Ryan's case this would have meant that only the best marks at the end of the semester would have counted, and he would have gone into the diploma exam with a grade more reflective of his achievement in English.

Guskey (1996) affirms O'Connor's position on the issue of what information provides the most accurate description of student's learning. If students demonstrate that past assessment information no longer accurately reflects their learning, that past information must be de-emphasized or dropped and replaced by the new information. Continuing to rely on past assessment data miscommunicates students' learning. Thus using the most recent data to determine a student grade appears to be an optimal practice.

The same principle can be applied to the teacher's decision to eliminate specific pieces of data when calculating students' grades. If a specific assignment grade or test score is an aberration from the rest of a student's marks, should it be counted in the final grade calculation? If Ms. Wong had been able, on the basis of professional judgment, to eliminate specific assignment marks or test scores from Ryan's final grade calculation, the results would have better reflected Ryan's achievement in English Language Arts and certainly would have given him some hope of success in the diploma exam.

> "In middle school, high school, and college, basing grades on recent performance applies to some extent in most subjects, but is probably most obvious in modern languages, mathematics, writing, drama, and other courses that emphasize skill development and/or performance."
>
> —*O'Connor, 1999, 71*

✏ *Grading Formulae: What Grades Do Students Deserve?* **R&R**, C57.

Self-Reflection

- How can I ensure that what I report includes only data reflective of the student's true achievement level?
- How might the nature of a subject determine the fair and accurate grading practice used?

Issue . . . How is data used in determining a grade?

Vignette 10: Mme. Wagner's Dilemma

Pierre had been consistently achieving honours marks all year in Mme. Wagner's Grade 8 French Language Arts class. In June, Pierre started working several hours at his father's landscaping business, and Mme. Wagner observed that he was frequently tired and unfocused in class. Before writing his final exam, Pierre admitted to Mme. Wagner that he had spent so much time working that he was unable to study for the exam. Pierre's exam mark of 50% reflected his lack of study time. When Mme. Wagner calculated his final term mark, which was lower than all of his marks during the term, she found that Pierre's French Language Arts average came out to 70%. Mme. Wagner did not feel that this mark accurately reflected Pierre's true abilities in Language Arts and was inclined to adjust his grade.

Think and Discuss

- What should Mme. Wagner do?
- What factors might influence Mme. Wagner's decision?
- What difference would it have made if Pierre had been sick or had participated on a school team?

Literature and Research Say . . .

Current research tells us that assessment scores should reflect a student's consistent performance as it relates to the Program of Studies and that professional judgment plays an essential role in grading practices. Teachers must also consider extenuating circumstances in students' lives.

Guskey and Bailey (2001, 33) state that "subjectivity in the process of grading and recording isn't always bad. Being subjective doesn't mean that grades lack credibility or are indefensible. Because teachers know their students, understand various dimensions of student work, and have clear notions of the progress made, their subjective perceptions can yield very accurate descriptions of what the students have learned."

> "Teachers should strive . . . to have grades with meaning and to have grades that support learning, grading must be an exercise in professional judgment, rather than simply a mechanical, numerical exercise."
>
> —O'Connor, 1999, 71

Self-Reflection

- To what extent should I accommodate extenuating circumstances in students' lives when determining a grade?
- To what extent do I rely on numbers, and to what extent do I make a professional judgment about the performance of each student?

Issue . . . How is data used in determining a grade?

Vignette 11: Mean or Median?

Joy Chang was a very strong student in Mr. Reid's Math class. She received perfect or near perfect scores on all of the work and tests she completed. Every Tuesday, Joy was pulled from class to receive ESL support and instruction during the Math period. Because of this, Joy often missed in-class assignments and quizzes.

During winter break, Joy's family travelled back to China to attend to family matters, causing Joy to be absent for an additional two weeks of school. During this time, she missed a major assignment. As a result, the teacher gave Joy several zeroes for the in-class assignments and quizzes missed, as well as for the major assignment. If Mr. Reid calculated Joy's grade based on the mean score—adding scores of all tests written and dividing by the number of all tests given—her grade would be 63%. If Mr. Reid calculated the final mark using the median to the midpoint of all the scores— Joy's final grade would be 97%.

Think and Discuss

- How should Mr. Reid calculate Joy's final grade?

Literature and Research Say . . .

Research tells us that teachers need to consider using the median to calculate grades. Even strong students may perform differently on various assessment tasks. Rather than viewing these variations as failures, we must consider them as opportunities for learning.

When deciding on grades, teachers should consider the following (Guskey, 1996):

Assigning a score of zero to work that is late or missed or neglected does not accurately depict student's learning. Is the teacher certain the student has learned absolutely nothing, or is the zero assigned to punish students for not displaying appropriate responsibility?

> "Use care when crunching numbers: The arithmetic mean may not be the best way to calculate the score."
>
> —*AAC, 1999, 16*

A zero has a profound effect when combined with the practice of averaging. Students who receive a single zero have little chance of success because such an extreme score skews the average.

Averaging may fall far short of providing an accurate description of what students have learned. If the purpose of grading and reporting is to provide an accurate description of what students have learned, then *averaging as the only way to crunch numbers must be considered inadequate and inappropriate.*

Definitions

Mean (average)
To find the mean (or arithmetic mean) add all the scores together and then divide by the number of assignments (tests) given.

Median
To find the median, place numbers in value order and find the middle number.

Mode
To find the mode (or modal value), put the numbers you are given in order and identify the number that appears most frequently.

Self-Reflection

- What factors should be considered when using mathematics to determine a final grade?
- How would you explain the method you use to students and parents?

"There is no single right way to do it; however whatever is done needs to reflect evidence of students' level of mastery of the targets of instruction."

—*Regional Education Laboratory 1998, Handout A46, H3, p. 5 cited in O'Connor, 1999, 107*

✏ *Grading Formulae: What Grades Do Students Deserve?* **R&R,** C57 and O'Connor, 1999, 99–101.

Issue . . . How is data used in determining a grade?

Vignette 12: A Cautionary Tale . . .

Mr. Wood, a Grade 3 teacher, was conducting parent-teacher conferences after the first report card of the year. When Susan Ellis's parents sat down across from him, he could tell they were not pleased. After listening politely to Mr. Wood's general explanation about Susan's grade in science, they asked Mr. Wood how their daughter's mark was calculated. Mr. and Mrs. Ellis felt that the marks on assignments and tests that Susan had brought home didn't match the grade on the report card. Mr. Wood explained that the grade was calculated from activities such as quizzes, tests, reports, presentations and journal writing, and he did not necessarily record them all in his automated marks program.

Then Susan's parents asked what specific criteria Mr. Wood used to assess Susan's achievement and how those criteria were connected with the Program of Studies. Mr. Wood was not able to produce specific criteria.

Think and Discuss

- What advice would you have for Mr. Wood?
- What does a reliable and accurate recording system look like?
- What are the pros and cons of automated marks programs?

Literature and Research Say . . .

It is important for teachers to create and maintain a reliable and accurate system for recording student data on achievement factors. Teachers should be able to easily and precisely communicate how they determined a student's grade to the student, parent or administrator.

Research tells us that teachers must "keep careful and timely records of student achievement. The key point here is that records must be recorded somewhere—on paper or on a computer—not just held in the teacher's head." (O'Connor, 1999, 131)

Effective marks systems (paper and automated) should comply with the requirements of the Freedom of Information and Protection of Privacy (FOIP) Act, Statutes of Alberta, 1994, Chapter F-18.5, with amendments in force as of April 25, 2001. Issues such as security, privacy, record maintenance, permanency and access are referred to in the legislation (see **R&R**, C59). Automated marks programs are commonly incorporated into comprehensive information systems by school jurisdictions. Stand-alone record systems are also available. There are advantages and disadvantages of these record systems, which are essentially sophisticated spreadsheets.

Advantages of Stand-Alone Record Systems

- fingertip, at-a-glance access to student data to help provide better programs/learning experiences for students
- easy, user-friendly maintenance of student records
- easy and convenient to use data and information at home
- quick tracking of individual achievement
- easy weighted number crunching and preparation of interim and term reports
- handy anecdotal comment-builder library

Disadvantages of Stand-Alone Record Systems

- possible privacy and security considerations when using data and information at home
- automated number crunching based primarily on averaging
- summative in nature
- false sense of accuracy
- based on a narrow view of assessment, evaluation, grading and communication of student learning
- some programs have standardized and impersonal anecdotal comment builder library

Self-Reflection

- How clearly does my system of recording student data reveal how well students are achieving?
- How well does my system help me communicate to students, parents or administrators?
- How completely do my records reflect the learner outcomes in the Program of Studies?

"Grades are meaningful only if they are based on quality assessment instruments that are both valid and reliable. Record and date results; do not rely on your memory."

—AAC, 1999, 16

☞ *Legislation Affecting Student Records,* **R&R,** C59.

Issue . . . How is data used in determining a grade?

Vignette 13: Apples and Oranges

Mr. McIntyre, a Grade 10 Social Studies teacher, felt comfortable with the way he had taught the Program of Studies during the term. He had a variety of achievement data from various sources. When he looked in his mark book, he saw scores on performance assessments, short answer tests, matching quizzes, multiple choice exams, student self-evaluations and presentations. Because the class had participated in many group projects, Mr. McIntyre had many group scores that he could include in determining grades. However, in spite of all the information available, he found the task of number crunching the disparate* data into a report card grade frustrating.

* disparate: fundamentally distinct or different, such as rubric scores and percentages

Think and Discuss

- What part should group scores have in determining a grade?
- How are rubric scores used with other types of scores to determine a grade?
- How are weightings determined?
- How can Mr. McIntyre arrive at a single grade?

> "In Mathematics we teach that you cannot average apples, oranges and bananas, but we do it in our grade books!"
>
> —*O'Connor, 95, citing Canady*

Literature and Research Say . . .

Teachers have the difficult task of translating disparate data into a single grade using a method that is fair and defensible. Using a mean may not reflect how well students have met the learner outcomes in the Program of Studies.

Grading individuals based on their group's achievement is indefensible according to Kagan (1995). O'Connor (1999, 41–42) notes that even with the increasing emphasis on the ability to work effectively with others at school and at work, "students' grades appear on their report cards and therefore should not be contaminated by the achievement (or lack of achievement) of other students."

The literature suggests that weighting be used to reflect the teacher's intent to determine a final grade, recognizing that certain summative assessments will have greater importance than others. For instance, a complex performance assessment may have twice the weight of a simple paper and pencil test.

> "Even when two teachers base grades on exactly the same information, they frequently assign different grades to students simply because they consider different homework assignments, quizzes, and tests as important." (Marzano, 2000, 6)

Performance assessment rubric scores can be included with other types of assessment data using a consistent method of crunching the data as illustrated in **R&R**, C61.

Self-Reflection

- How will I merge a variety of data recorded in different formats into a single grade?

> "Combining disparate kinds of results into a single summary should be done cautiously."
>
> *—AAC, 1999, 39*

> "In fact, a strong case will be made that there is no truly meaningful way to combine scores on various topics into an overall grade."
>
> *—Marzano, 2000, 79*

☞ *Group Grades*—O'Connor, 41–47.

☞ *How to Convert Rubric Scores to Grades,* **R&R,** C61, and O'Connor, 1999, 105–107.

☞ *Curves, Criteria and Reporting Systems,* **R&R,** C66.

Guidelines for Communicating Student Learning

The preceding vignettes illustrate many of the issues that teachers face on a day-to-day basis. When a school has effectively dealt with these issues and established fair, equitable, and transparent processes to deal with them, then the communication link between teachers, students and parents is enhanced.

The following excerpt from *A Framework for Communicating Student Learning* (AAC, 1999, 15–16) summarizes and provides advice about many of the issues addressed by the vignettes.

Communicating student learning should be carried out so that it supports continuous learning and development. O'Connor (1999) has put forth the following guidelines to help ensure that the meaning of grades is clear and that grades support learning and encourage student success.

1.8 Make achievement the only factor in assessments.

- Achievement of the curriculum outcomes should be the only basis for grades.
- Effort, participation, attitudes, and other personal and social characteristics should be reported separately.

A low grade for effort is more likely to be read as "You're a failure even at trying." On the other hand, a high grade for effort combined with a low grade for achievement says "You're just too dumb to succeed."

2.8 Sample student performance—don't mark everything.

- Provide feedback on formative assessment to help students know what to do to improve their knowledge and skills.
- Include only summative assessment results in report card grades.

A wide variety of assessment approaches should be used to take account of different learning styles and multiple intelligences.

3.8 Grade in pencil and use up-to-date information

- Brightly coloured pen marks on paper can look aggressive and judgmental—always use pencil. Also, be sure to use the most recent information. Be prepared to replace old information with more recent information that better demonstrates each student's real achievement.
- Provide second (or more) assessment opportunities. Students may need multiple opportunities to perform at their best, but there should also be some evidence of their using feedback about past mistakes to enhance future success.

4.8 Relate grading procedures to intended learning.

Teachers must have a clear understanding of what learning results are expected—grading must be related to these results. It is also critical that teachers evaluate learning on clear, pre-established standards. Therefore, the use of detailed rubrics or scoring guides is essential.

5. Use care when crunching numbers.

The arithmetic mean may not be the best way to calculate a score. Consider using medians—they provide more opportunities for success by diminishing the impact of a few high or low marks.

6. Use absolute or preset standards to distribute marks.

There should be no artificial rationing of high grades. "The number of good grades should not be artificially limited so that one student's success makes another's unlikely" (Kohn, 1994). Do not mark on a curve.

7. Properly record evidence from quality assessment instruments.

Grades are meaningful only if they are based on quality assessment instruments that are both valid and reliable. Record and date results; do not rely on your memory.

8. Describe assessment and evaluation practices to students at the beginning of the course.

Students must receive clear, concise information on how grades for each course will be determined. Whenever possible, students should be involved in the development of criteria by which their work will be judged.

Articulating Our School's Grading Practices

What fair, reliable and valid grading and reporting practices will be used in our school?

Our grading practice foundations will include . . .

Factors we will not use to determine an achievement grade include . . .

We will determine fair and accurate grades for a student by . . .

When we collect and crunch data, we will ensure that . . .

In determining a final grade, factors we will take into consideration include . . .

We will report academic achievement and progress by . . .

We will report work habits and behaviour by . . .

We will inform students about how we grade by . . .

We will inform parents about how we grade by . . .

REFERENCES AND RESOURCES (R&R)

New Tools

Eisner, 1999, 658–659

PERFORMANCE assessment is one of the "hot topics" on the agenda of education reform—and for good reason. **Performance assessment is a closer measure of our children's ability to achieve the aspirations we hold for them than are conventional forms of standardized testing.** Indeed, our educational aspirations have been influenced by the fact that our children will inhabit a world requiring far more complex and subtle forms of thinking than children needed three or four decades ago. For example, our children will need to know how to frame problems for themselves, how to formulate plans to address them, how to assess multiple outcomes, how to consider relationships, how to deal with ambiguity, and how to shift purposes in light of new information.

These modes of thought will be critical in a society in which citizens are apt to change vocations several times during the course of a work life, in which mobility has increased and new forms of adaptability are required, and in which choosing a course of action requires the consideration of diverse and sometimes conflicting information. No longer will most jobs, particularly those that are the most desirable, require the use of routine skills and rote memory . . . these changing expectations for the outcomes of education reflect a non-behaviorist view of human nature. When learning was conceived of as the acquisition and aggregation of reinforced units of information, "practice makes perfect" could serve as a guiding principle for teaching. The kind of thinking that students are now being encouraged to engage in requires much more than what Edward Thorndike, the father of American psychological connectionism, dreamed of. Context matters, judgment counts, and the opportunity to act in order to try out one's speculations is of critical importance.

The demise of behaviorism and the emergence of constructivism in our view of human nature are not the only sources of our changing conception of children and education. We have come to realize that meaning matters and that it is not something that can be imparted from teacher to student. In a sense, all teachers can do is to "make noises in the environment." By this I mean that we have in education no main line into the brains of our students. We are shapers of the environment, stimulators, motivators, guides, consultants, resources. But in the end, what children make of what we provide is a function of what they construe from what we offer. **Meanings are not given, they are made. And we are interested in enabling students to make their activities in school meaningful, not merely because of the grades they**

receive but, more important, because of the satisfactions and insights their efforts make possible.

We have also come to realize that the kinds of meanings that our students can make are related to the forms of representation they can employ themselves or can decode when others have used them. Each of the forms of representation that exist in our culture—visual forms in art, auditory forms in music, quantitative forms in mathematics, propositional forms in science, choreographic forms in dance, poetic forms in language—are vehicles through which meaning is conceptualized and expressed. A life driven by the pursuit of meaning is enriched when the meanings sought and secured are multiple.

In addition to these considerations, we have also begun to recognize that the aim of schooling is not merely to enable our children to do well in school. The stakes are considerably higher. What we are after is to enable our children to do well in life outside of school; the scores generated by the kinds of tests we have been using are proxies, but, alas, we have found that as proxies they are most useful for making inferences about the scores students are likely to receive on other tests. We want more. **What we want is an approach to assessment that possesses what psychometricians call concurrent *or* predictive validity. That is, we want test scores to tell us about how students address tasks beyond the classroom.**

These factors—the virtual demise of behaviorism, the emergence of constructivism, the importance of meaning, the desire for concurrent and predictive validity—have provided the ground for interest in performance assessment. Despite the lack of a single definition, performance assessment is aimed at moving away from testing practices that require students to select the single correct answer from an array of four or five distractors to a practice that requires students to create evidence through performance that will enable assessors to make valid judgments about "what they know and can do" in situations that matter. **Performance assessment is the most important development in evaluation since the invention of the short-answer test and its extensive use during World War I.**

Assessment as the Basis for Communicating Individual Student Achievement

Source: *Guide to Education: ECS to Grade 12, Student Achievement ECS to Grade 9.* Alberta Learning, 2001.

When students are placed in age-appropriate groups for instruction, parents can become confused about the distinction between the grade in which their child is placed (the instructional group) and the grade level of the various subject areas at which their child is actually working; e.g., the child is placed in a Grade 4 class but is working at approximately the Grade 3 level in language arts. Where such confusion exists, parents can misinterpret information regarding their child's progress. They may think that indications of satisfactory progress are made with reference to the instructional group the child is in rather than to the actual grade level at which the child is working. The provision for Assessment as the Basis for Communicating Individual Student Achievement is intended to reduce this type of confusion and to support the professional responsibilities of teachers to provide clear communication in describing student progress.

Teachers shall ensure that information is effectively communicated to parents about:

- **what their child knows and can do in the courses being studied**
- **how well their child is doing in those courses**
- **the grade level(s) the child has achieved in relation to the grade levels of the provincial programs of study for language arts, mathematics, science and social studies.**

The provision does not restrict the communicating of achievement to written reports, nor does it require schools to use a particular type of instructional grouping or placement policy.

Teachers should communicate the grade levels at which they judge a student to be working, in at least the four specified subject areas of the curriculum. The basis for their professional judgement in these matters also needs to be clear so that parents can readily understand how student learning has been assessed.

Principals determine how to implement this provision, in consultation with teachers, parents and school councils and in a manner consistent with any related school jurisdiction policies. The communication can take place in a wide variety of ways, including parent–teacher conferences, assessment portfolios, report cards or student work samples. An individual program plan (IPP) is a method often used by teachers when there is a gap between a student's level of achievement and that student's grade placement. Whatever methods are chosen for implementing this provision, often face-to-face methods are the most successful for achieving clear and open communication.

All of the assessment information should be shared, not only with parents, but also with students when it is in the students' best interest to do so. Communicating with students about their levels of achievement is particularly important when students are planning their future courses and making program choices.

To assist teachers in assessing student achievement in relation to provincial standards, Alberta Learning has developed classroom assessment materials, in English and in French, for teachers' discretionary use in language arts, mathematics, science and social studies in Grades 1, 2, 4, 5, 7 and 8. There also are science materials for Grade 3. These materials were supplied to all schools. Additional materials are available for purchase from the Learning Resources Centre.

Personal Grading Practices

Adapted from Guskey, "Using Assessments to Improve Student Learning," *National Conference on Standards and Assessment*, National School Conference Institute, Phoenix, AR., April 1999

Directions: Please read each question carefully, think about your response and answer each as honestly as you can.

1. What do you believe are the major reasons we use report cards and assign grades to students' work?

2. Ideally, what purposes do you believe report cards or grades should serve?

3. Although classes differ, on average, what percent of students in your classes receive the following grades:

    A ____   B ____   C ____   F ____

4. What would you consider an ideal distribution of grades (in percent) in your classes?

    A ____   B ____   C ____   F ____

5. The current grading system in many schools uses a combination of letter grades, percentages, and/or (assumed) categories:

    A   80%–100%   Work meets the standard of excellence
    B   65%–79%   Work exceeds the acceptable standard
    C   50%–64%   Work meets the acceptable standard
    F   0%–49%   Work does not meet the acceptable standard

O'Connor, 1999, 24.

6. If you could make any changes in this system, what would they be?

7. Grades and other reporting systems are developed to serve a variety of purposes. Based on your beliefs, rank the following purposes from 1 (most important) to 6 (least important) independent of the method of grading and reporting.

___ Communicate achievement status

___ Provide self-evaluation opportunities to students

___ Group students for certain educational programs

___ Provide incentives for students to learn

___ Evaluate the effectiveness of certain instructional programs

___ Provide evidence of students' lack of effort or inappropriate responsibility

8. Teachers use a variety of factors in determining students' grades (achievement based on the graded curriculum). Among those listed below, please indicate which ones you use and estimate the percentage by which each contributes to the grade.

Factors	Use	%
Major tests or compositions		
Reports or projects (performance assessments)		
Classroom quizzes		
Classroom participation		
Homework completion		
Homework quality		
Work habits and neatness		
Effort put forth		
Attendance		
Classroom behavior		
Progress made		
Other (describe)		
Other (describe)		

9. What are the most positive characteristics of report cards and the process of assigning grades?

10. What do you like least about report cards and the process of assigning grades?

Policy 4.2.1 Teaching Quality Standard Applicable to the Provision of Basic Education in Alberta

Approved: May 14, 1997

Pursuant to Section 25(1)(f) of the School Act,

The Minister may do the following:

By order adopt or approve goals and standards applicable to the provision of education in Alberta

Teachers gather and use information about students' learning needs and progress.

Teachers

1. monitor students' actions on an ongoing basis to determine and respond to their learning needs.
2. use a variety of diagnostic methods that include observing students' activities, analyzing students' learning difficulties and strengths, and interpreting the results of assessments and information provided by students, their parents, colleagues and other professionals.
3. select and develop a variety of classroom assessment strategies and instruments to assess the full range of learning objectives.
4. differentiate between classroom and large-scale instruments, such as provincial achievement tests, administer both and use the results for the ultimate benefit of students.
5. record, interpret and use the results of their assessments to modify their teaching practices and students' learning activities.
6. help students, parents and other educators interpret and understand the results of diagnoses and assessments, and the implications for students.
7. help students develop the ability to diagnose their own learning needs and to assess their progress toward learning goals.
8. use their interpretations of diagnoses and assessments as well as students' work and results to guide their own professional growth.
9. assist school councils and members of the community to understand the purposes, meanings, outcomes and implications of assessments.

Grading Formulae: What Grades Do Students Deserve?

(Adapted with permission, Guskey, 2000)

The table shows the performance of seven students over five instructional units. The summary scores and grades for these students are calculated using three different methods:

   A. Simple arithmetic average of unit scores
   B. Median (or middle) score from the five units
   C. Arithmetic average, deleting the lowest score from the group

Consider the following information about each student's performance over the five units.

Student 1 struggled in the early part of the term (marking period), but continued to work hard, improved in each unit and did excellent work in unit 5.

Student 2 began with excellent performance in unit 1, but then lost motivation, declined steadily during the term and received a failing mark for unit 5.

Student 3 performed steadily throughout the term, receiving three As and two Bs, all near the A–B cut-score.

Student 4 began the term poorly, failing the first two units, but with new-found interest performed excellently in units 3, 4 and 5.

Student 5 began the term excellently, but then seemed to lose interest and failed the last two units.

Student 6 skipped school (unexcused absences) during the first unit, but performed excellently in every other unit.

Student 7 performed excellently in the first four units, but was caught cheating on the assignment for unit 5, resulting in a score of zero for that unit.

Student	Unit 1	Unit 2	Unit 3	Unit 4	Unit 5	Average Score	Grade	Median Score	Grade	Deleting Lowest	Grade
1	49	59	75	89	99	74.2	B	75.0	B	80.5	A
2	99	89	75	59	49	74.2	B	75.0	B	80.5	A
3	77	80	80	78	80	79.0	B	80.0	A	79.5	B
4	39	49	98	99	100	75.0	B	98.0	A	86.5	A
5	100	99	98	49	39	75.0	B	98.0	A	86.5	A
6	0	88	88	89	90	71.0	B	88.0	A	88.8	A
7	90	89	88	88	0	71.0	B	88.0	A	88.8	A

Grading standards: 80%–100% = A
65%–79% = B
50%–64% = C
0%–49% = F

Questions: Which grading method is fairest?

What difference would weighting make?

What grade does each student deserve?

"Grades based on averaging have meaning only when averaging repeated measures of similar content. Teachers [calculate] marks on fractions, word problems, geometry and addition with marks for attendance, homework and notebooks—and call it mathematics. In mathematics we teach that you cannot average apples, oranges and bananas, but we do it in our grade books!"

—*R. L. Canady, workshop ASCD Annual Meeting, April 1993*

Legislation Affecting Student Records

Freedom of Information and Protection of Privacy (FOIP) Act. Statutes of Alberta, 1994, Chapter F-18.5 with amendments in force as of April 25, 2001.

How long should a school keep its paper/electronic records?

- Under section 51(1)(a), the Commissioner has the power to conduct an investigation into how a school is managing its records. Specifically, the Commissioner can check to make sure that a school is following any by-law it has regarding the destruction of records.
- Schools are required by section 34 to keep personal information about an individual for at least one year if that personal information has been used by the school to make a decision about the individual.

Section 34—Accuracy and Retention

34. If an individual's personal information will be used by a public body to make a decision that directly affects the individual, the public body must

(a) make every reasonable effort to ensure that the information is accurate and complete, and

(b) retain the personal information for at least one year after using it so that the individual has a reasonable opportunity to obtain access to it, or for any shorter period of time as agreed to in writing by

(i) the individual,

(ii) the public body, and

(iii) if the body that approves the records and retention and disposition schedule for the public body is different from the public body, that body.

1994 cF-18.5 s34;1999 c23 s21

Can teachers write comments on student assignments or tests as well as the student's grade?

- There is no barrier in the *FOIP Act* to prevent teachers from commenting on students' work.

Can students' grades and detentions be posted in the hallway or classroom?

- Posting students' grades or detentions may be a breach of privacy. The educational benefits need to be taken into consideration. In a Grade 1 class, a poster with student names and stickers for each book read by a student is entirely appropriate. By contrast, posting Math 30 exam results with the students' names in the hallway has no educational benefit, and so would be an unauthorized disclosure of personal information.

Can parents find out how their children's marks compare to those of other students in the class?

- Class averages may be provided. If required, parents may receive a list of other students' marks that excludes the names of other students and [that is] organized in such a way as to ensure anonymity and privacy of other students.

Can parents receive information on the performance of a school?

- Yes. This is not a privacy issue [because] the performance of individual students would not be released.

Can students mark each other's tests?

- Personal information of students is disclosed when students mark each other's tests.
- This disclosure is permitted when it is done for an educational purpose. Group learning activities may be used in the classroom, and students can learn from critiquing the work of other students.
- Schools should consider the merits of this practice in the classroom and use it at the discretion of teachers.
- If this method of marking is convenient, but not educational, it should not be used.

Can students read their essays aloud in class?

- If the school decides that this activity is part of an educational program, there is no barrier to this in the *FOIP Act*.

How to Convert Rubric Scores to Grades

Adapted from *Toolkit98* with the permission of Jerry Kirkpatrick, Director of Development and Communications, Northwest Regional Educational Laboratory (NWREL) 101 SW Main, Suite 500, Portland, OR. 97204

Introduction

There is no simple or single way to manipulate rubric scores so that they can be incorporated into end-of-term letter grades. Whatever approach you choose to use, it is important that you inform your students and parents about your system. How grades are calculated should be open to students rather than a mystery. In addition, you must be certain that the process you use is reasonable and defensible in terms of what is expected of students based on the graded curriculum.

It may not be appropriate to use the marks from all tests and assessment tasks students have completed as the basis for your end-of-term grades—you might choose certain pieces of student work, choose to emphasize certain traits for certain pieces, let students choose their seven best pieces, etc. You might only want to score certain traits on certain tasks.

You might consider placing most emphasis on work completed late in the grading period if it fairly represents a student's level of achievement. This ensures that students who are demonstrating strong achievement at the end of a term are not penalized for their early failure. It also encourages students to take risks during the course of their learning. Whatever you choose to do, it is important to have a clear idea about how you will communicate student performance. Representative samples of student work are needed so that you can be confident in the grades you assign to each student.

Methods

The methods described here can be used with any assessment tasks that are scored using rubrics or rating scales. The example used is from writing assessment, but the methods identified here are not restricted to writing.

In **Table 1** we have Johnny's scores on the five pieces of writing we agreed to evaluate this term on all six traits and a 4-point rubric.

Table 1: *Johnny's Writing Scores on Five Papers*

Johnny's Scores	Ideas and Content	Organization	Word Choice	Sentence Fluency	Voice	Conventions	Total
Paper 1	2	1	1	2	1	3	10
Paper 2	3	1	2	3	2	3	14
Paper 3	4	3	4	4	1	2	18
Paper 4	3	3	3	3	1	3	18
Paper 5	4	4	4	4	3	3	22
Totals	16	12	14	16	8	14	82

METHOD 1: Frequency of Scores Method. Develop a logical rule for assigning grades. The following are just four of many possible ways you could go about setting up a rule for assigning grades in writing.

- To get an A in writing at least 50% of the marks need to be 4; no scores in Ideas and Content, Conventions, or Organization can be below 3.
- To get a B at least 50% of the marks have to be 3 or higher; no scores in Ideas and Content, Conventions or Organization can be below 2; in other areas, scores below 2 can be counterbalanced by scores of 3 or higher.

OR

In this class, in writing,

- Mostly 3s and 4s translates to an A
- Mostly 2s and 3s translates to a B
- Mostly 2s translates to a C

OR

To get an 80%-100% in writing, at least 50% of your scores must be 4; no scores in Ideas and Content, Conventions, or Organization can be below 3.

To get 65%-79% in writing, at least 50% of your scores must be 3 or higher; no scores in Ideas and Content, Convention, or Organization can be below 2, in other areas, scores below 2 can be counterbalanced by scores of 3 or higher.

OR

To get a C in writing, all scores must be 2 or higher. To get an A or a B, students need to complete 5 papers, describe the grade they should get on those papers, and justify the grade using the language of the six-trait model and specific examples from the written work.

Depending on how the rule finally plays out, Johnny might either get an A (mostly 3s or 4s) or a B (lots of 3s or 4s, but there are more 3s than 4s) or 65%-79% (there is one 2 in Conventions) for the writing part of his grade. Or you might assign an A by citing specific examples from the written work and the six-trait rubric that show he really understands what constitutes good writing and is ready to be a critical reviewer of his own work.

METHOD 2: Total Points. Add the total of possible points students can get on rubric scored papers.

First figure out the number of points possible. To do this, multiply the number of papers being evaluated by the number of traits assessed. Then, multiply that by 4 (or the highest score possible on the rubric). In this case, with 5 papers we would multiply 5 (papers) times 6 (traits) times 4 (highest score on the rubric) and get 120 total points possible.

Then we factor in a student's scores (Johnny has 80 points) and divide by the total possible score: $80 \div 120 = 0.67$. Johnny has 67% of possible points, so his writing grade will be 67%. This will be combined with other scores to determine a single letter grade or percentage for the subject.

METHOD 3: Total Weighted Points. Add the total of possible points students can get on rubric scored papers weighting those traits deemed most important.

First, figure how many points are possible. A weight needs to be assigned to each trait. In **Table 2**, assume that we decided to weight Ideas and Content and Organization three times as important as the other four traits. First, you add all of the scores for each trait (adding the numbers in the column), and then multiply the total in each column by its weight. Finally you add up the total in each column to come up with the grand total number of points.

Table 2: Total Possible Weighted Points

Johnny's Scores	Ideas and Content	Organization	Word Choice	Sentence Fluency	Voice	Conventions	
Paper 1	4	4	4	4	4	4	
Paper 2	4	4	4	4	4	4	
Paper 3	4	4	4	4	4	4	
Paper 4	4	4	4	4	4	4	
Paper 5	4	4	4	4	4	4	
Totals	20	20	20	20	20	20	
Weights	3	3	1	1	1	1	
Weighted Total	60	60	20	20	20	20	200

Table 3 shows Johnny's scores again and the total using the weighted formula. Johnny has 135 out of 200 weighted points or 68% of total points in writing.

Table 3: Johnny's Writing Scores on Five Papers with Weighted Totals

Johnny's Scores	Ideas and Content	Organization	Word Choice	Sentence Fluency	Voice	Conventions	
Paper 1	2	1	1	2	1	3	
Paper 2	3	1	2	3	2	3	
Paper 3	4	3	4	4	1	2	
Paper 4	3	3	3	3	1	3	
Paper 5	4	4	4	4	3	3	
Totals	16	12	14	16	8	14	
Weights	3	3	1	1	1	1	
Weighted Total	48	36	14	16	8	14	136

Depending on your focus, you might want to include only the traits you have been working on, weighting others as 0.

Using **Table 4** consider how you would record four pieces of writing completed and one paper that was not submitted, blank or not completed due to absence.

Would it have made any difference if the 5th incomplete paper had not been submitted?

Table 4: Johnny's Writing Scores on Five Papers with Weighted Totals

Johnny's Scores	Ideas and Content	Organization	Word Choice	Sentence Fluency	Voice	Conventions
Paper 1	2	1	1	2	1	3
Paper 2	Blank	Blank	Blank	Blank	Blank	Blank
Paper 3	4	3	4	4	1	2
Paper 4	3	3	3	3	1	3
Paper 5	4	4	4	4	3	3
Totals						
Weights	3	3	1	1	1	1
Weighted Total						

METHOD 4: Linear Conversion. Come up with a direct connection between scores on the rubric and percentages.

We might find that the assigning of 2 on the six-trait scales comes close to our definition of what a C is in district policy, then turn the rubric score into a percent score based on the definition.

Applying the standards of Alberta Learning, the conversion would look like this:

$$1 = 0\%–49\%$$
$$2 = 50\%–64\%$$
$$3 = 65\%–79\%$$
$$4 = 80\%–100\%$$

You can then treat the rubric scores the same way you treat other grades in your grade book.

Conclusion

It is important to decide upon a method for converting rubric scores to a scale comparable to one used with other forms of assessment for grading and reporting purposes. The methods that have been outlined suggest possibilities for your consideration. It is recommended that there be consistency in the school with respect to how data is used for communicating student learning based on the graded curriculum.

Curves, Criteria and Reporting Systems

Grant Wiggins is a supporter of criterion-referenced assessment and a critic of normative comparisons. He explains why it is beneficial to enhance conventional reporting systems that require the use of aggregated scores. To complement the report card, more detailed and rich information that profile student accomplishments can be conveyed through the use of portfolios, conferences, and other reporting systems as described in *A Framework for Communicating Student Learning* (AAC, 1999).

Source: Excerpt from Wiggins (1994, *Educational Leadership* 52, 2: 34–35)

> The use of the standard curve for giving grades exacerbates [an] already bad situation [that teachers are not required to agree on the criteria by which similar products are judged]. The single grade is an artifact that bears no obvious relation to performance, criteria and standards [learner outcomes]. That the use of the curve in the classroom is statistically unwarranted doesn't stop many teachers from using some form of it. It allows them to bypass the harder, but more fruitful, work of setting and teaching performance criteria from which better feedback, learning and performance would follow. And, it precludes a concern with fairness that would lead us to factor in expectations in a separate grade . . .
>
> What is needed is a reporting system that yields a more accurate and rich profile of the student's accomplishments.
>
> Why, then, do we arbitrarily average grades and scores in school—where the dimensions of performance are even more complex and diverse—to arrive at a single grade per subject? Problem solving is not research, is not writing, is not discussing, is not accuracy, is not thoroughness, is not mastery of the facts. And, why do we compute averages over the course of a year? One is either achieving at a certain level, or one is not. Why would we use your earlier grades and scores, for example, if you are now performing at a higher level?
>
> Why not encourage all math teachers to disaggregate their letter grades into separate grades based on data from tests where rubrics are used for each standard? Why not make sure that English teachers report each student's performance on different genres of writing, because performance across genres is not constant, as many writing assignments have shown?

More disaggregated scoring—where achievements and progress are separated, and where performance is separated into its many sub-scores—would increase the incentives of the report for students as well as the clarity of the report for parents. Particular strengths would more likely be revealed; particular weaknesses would more reliably be identified.

The complaint that grades lead to invidious ranking is also misconceived. The aim is to better evaluate performance and efficiently, but effectively, communicate results. Ranking is a different urge, one *hampered* through the use of multiple grades and scores . . . The urge to rank is based on a failure to compare performance to *criteria* and, instead, to compare performers to one another. Our urge to reduce things to one number and our over-use of norm-referenced testing and grading are the culprits, not the letter grades themselves.

Rubrics for Non-achievement Factors

Adapted from Marzano (2000, 131–132)

Effort Rubric

Criteria Level	4 Excellent	3 Proficient	2 Adequate	1 Limited *	Insufficient / Blank *
Participation	Eagerly engages in activities and discussion, and encourages peers to get involved	Participates in classroom activities and discussions willingly and consistently	Participates in classroom activities and discussions according to the structure provided by the teacher	Requires continual prompting to engage in activities or discussions	No score is awarded because there is insufficient evidence of student performance based on the requirements of the assessment task.
Assignments	Consistently turns in assignments on time and fulfills the requirements stated in teacher directions in a unique and creative manner	Usually turns in assignments on time and thoroughly fulfills requirements stated in teacher directions	Turns in assignments on time with some prompting and fulfills sufficient requirements stated in teacher directions	Rarely turns in assignments on time even with prompting and minimal evidence of meeting requirements stated in teacher directions	No score is awarded because there is insufficient evidence of student performance based on the requirements of the assessment task.

* When work is judged limited or insufficient, the teacher makes decisions about appropriate intervention to help the student improve.

Behavior Rubric

Criteria Level	4 Excellent	3 Proficient	2 Adequate	1 Limited *	Insufficient / Blank *
Working in Groups	Works cooperatively towards group goals and provides encouragement and support for peers	Works cooperatively toward group goals	Works toward group goals with some prompting	Requires frequent supervision and prompting to participate as a group member	No score is awarded because there is insufficient evidence of student performance based on the requirements of the assessment task.
Following Rules	Takes ownership for classroom rules and procedures and encourages peers to abide by them	Consistently adheres to classroom rules and procedures	Follows classroom rules and procedures when occasionally reminded or prompted	Requires frequent prompting to follow classroom rules and procedures	

* When work is judged limited or insufficient, the teacher makes decisions about appropriate intervention to help the student improve.

Attendance Rating Scale

Criteria	Consistently	Frequently	Occasionally	Rarely, if ever
1. is present and provides a valid explanation when absent				
2. is on time and provides a valid explanation when late				

Comments

Initiating and Communicating Change

Einstein once said, "We can't solve problems by using the same kind of thinking we used when we created them."

A different kind of thinking is required if grading and reporting practices are going to be changed. Change will not come easily. According to Marzano (2000, 2), "Without doubt, changing the way students are graded alters what people associate with 'real school.' Consequently, one can expect opposition to new grading techniques." Effective methods of initiating and communicating change are necessary to effect change.

The Alberta Teachers' Association resource "Module Five: Professional Development and Change," *Leadership in Professional Development* (1998), provides practical change strategies and a transition model of change.

Selected Bibliography

Alberta Assessment Consortium. *A Framework for Communicating Student Learning.* Author: Edmonton, AB. 1999.

Alberta Learning. *Guide to Education: ECS to Grade 12.* Author: Edmonton, AB. September 2001.

Alberta Teachers' Association. "Module Five: Professional Development and Change" *Leadership in Professional Development,* Author: Edmonton, AB. November 1998.

Bailey, J. and McTighe, J. "Reporting achievement at the secondary level: what and how?" *Communicating Student Learning: ASCD Yearbook 1996,* edited by T.R. Guskey, ASCD: Alexandria, VA. 1996.

Bennett, B. and Smilanich, P. *Classroom Management: A Thinking and Caring Approach.* Bookation: Toronto, ON. and Perceptions: Edmonton, AB. 1994.

Davies, A. *Making Classroom Assessment Work.* Connections Publishing: Merville, BC. 2000.

Eisner, E. "The Uses and Limits of Performance Assessment," Phi Delta Kappan, Phi Delta Kappa International: Bloomington, IN. May 1999.

Glasser, W. *The Quality School,* Harper Perennial: New York, NY. 1990.

Gregory, K., Cameron, C., and Davies, A. *Knowing What Counts Book One: Setting and Using Criteria.* Connections Publishing: Merville, BC. 2000.

Gregory, K., Cameron, C., and Davies, A. *Conferencing and Reporting.* Connections Publishing: Merville, BC. 2000.

Guskey, T. "Reporting on student learning: lessons from the past—prescriptions for the future," *Communicating Student Learning: ASCD Yearbook 1996,* edited by T.R. Guskey, ASCD: Alexandria, VA. 1996.

Guskey, T. and Bailey, J. Developing Grading and Reporting Systems for Student Learning. Corwin Press: Thousand Oaks, CA. 2001.

Guskey, T. *How's My Kid Doing?: A Parent's Guide to Grading and Reporting,* John Wiley & Sons: New York, NY. in press.

Joint Advisory Committee of Professional Organizations. *Principles for Fair Student Assessment Practices for Education in Canada.* University of Alberta, Centre for Research in Applied Measurement and Evaluation, Edmonton, AB. 1993.

Kagan, S. "Group Grades Miss the Mark," *Educational Leadership,* ASCD: Alexandria, VA. May 1995.

Kohn, A. "Grading: The issue is not how but why." *Educational Leadership,* ASCD: Alexandria, VA. October 1994.

Marzano, R. *Transforming Classroom Grading,* ASCD: Alexandria, VA. December 2000.

McTighe, J. "What happens between assessments?" *Educational Leadership,* ASCD: Alexandria, VA. December 1997.

O'Connor, K. *The Mindful School: How to Grade for Learning.* Skylight: Arlington Heights, IL. 1999.

Pardini, P. "Report Card Reform," *The School Administrator,* American Association of School Administrators: Arlington, VA. December 1997.

Rolheiser, C. *Self-Evaluation . . . Helping Students Get Better at It!* VISUTroniX: Ajax, ON. 1997.

Stiggins, R.J. *Student-centered Classroom Assessment.* 2d ed. Merrill/Prentice Hall: Upper Saddle River, NJ. 1997.

Terwilliger, J.S. (summer workshop, 1989) *Classroom standard setting and practice,* Educational Measurement: Issues and Practice.

Wiggins, G. "Toward Better Report Cards," *Educational Leadership,* ASCD: Alexandria, VA. December 1994.

Wiggins, G. and McTighe, J. *Understanding by Design.* ASCD: Alexandria, VA. 1998.

Web Sites

Directive 4.2.1—Teaching Quality Standard Applicable to the Provision of Basic Education in Alberta

http://www.learning.gov.ab.ca/educationguide/pol-plan/polreg

Employability Skills Profile—The Critical Skills Required of the Canadian Workforce— Human Resources Development Canada

http://www.on.hrdc.gc.ca/thunder-bay/rpts/empskill.htm

Toolkit98, Northwest Regional Education Laboratory

http://www.nwrel.org/assessment/toolkit98.asp